DATE		

Adult Development and Aging

Adult Development and Aging

F. Philip Rice

University of Maine

Allyn and Bacon, Inc.
Boston   London   Sydney   Toronto

Series Editor: Jeffery Johnston
Production Coordinator: Susan Freese
Editorial/Production Services: Grace Sheldrick, Wordsworth Associates
Text Designer: Judith Ashkenaz
Cover Coordinator: Linda K. Dickinson
Cover Designer: Christy Rosso

514 50004

Library of Congress Cataloging in Publication Data

Rice, F. Philip.
  Adult development and aging.

  Bibliography: p.
  Includes index.
  1. Adulthood. 2. Aging. 3. Developmental
psychology. I. Title.
BF724.5.R5 1986   155.6   85–19962
ISBN 0–205–08613–6

Contents

Preface

Adult Development and Aging is a general college textbook on the psychology of adulthood and aging. The book is eclectic in its orientation, presenting most major theories of adult development and aging, contributions of various theorists, the emphasis in different approaches and philosophies, and their applications in everyday life.

Three common themes run throughout the discussion. The first is that development continues throughout each person's life span; it does not suddenly stop at adolescence. Human potential thus becomes almost unlimited, and the knowledge gained up to the time of high school or college graduation is only a small fraction of what will be learned subsequently.

A second theme is that life demands change and adaptation. Some changes come from within the human organism; others occur in relationships; others in the external environment. Successful living requires understanding these changes.

Adult Development and Aging discusses various models that have contributed toward understanding life's changes. Some models focus on biological changes, others on cognitive changes, others on moral changes, others on psychological or sociological factors.

In a third theme, this book reflects a life-cycle point of view. Different writers delineate various phases or stages of life. Some outline developmental tasks; others describe life events, such as marriage, parenthood, or retirement. A more general concept is life periods.

Adult Development and Aging divides the adult life cycle into three major periods: early adulthood (the twenties and thirties), middle adulthood (the forties and fifties), and late adulthood (the sixties and over). These somewhat arbitrary divisions make sense when considering the developmental tasks of each age group. The book highlights the tasks during each phase, while reflecting that life is continuous.

The book is divided into seven major parts. Of the seven, only Part I, on the adult years, is chronological. Parts II through VII, on biological, emotional, intellectual, personal, social, and vocational dimensions of adulthood, are topical, since these emphases are more important than chronology in understanding the development process.

The first chapter introduces the importance and scope of the subject of adult development and aging and the life cycle, developmental theme. Some of the major research issues in obtaining and interpreting data are also outlined. The other three chapters in Part I present an overview of the three major periods in the adult life cycle.

Part II focuses on physical development through the life cycle, including theories of biological aging, changes in bodily systems and sensory perception, and important factors in maintaining physical attractiveness, fitness, and health. Changes in sexual functioning, behavior, and reproductive capacities are also described, as are some problems of drug abuse, alcohol abuse, and smoking. Chapter 9 on death and dying discusses mortality rates, prolongevity, and attitudes toward death in our culture.

Part III outlines factors important in maintaining good mental health. The discussion focuses on handling stress, on mental illnesses, and on suicide.

Part IV focuses on intellectual and cognitive development: on intelligence—its meaning, measurement, and change over the adult years—and on memory, learning, thinking, problem finding, problem solving, comprehension, and creativity. The primary emphasis is positive—on maintaining and developing these abilities.

The focus of part V shifts to various personal living situations: never-married adults, marriage over the family life cycle, parenthood, postparental years, widowhood, divorce, and the reconstituted family.

Part VI discusses vocational and career development: career establishment, mid-life careers, the older worker, retirement, and financial planning and management for and during late adulthood.

Part VII concludes by looking to the future. As the population ages, the shift will be away from a youth-oriented culture to a more adult-centered society, with political power and opportunities for older adults increasing. As older adults assume important roles, prejudices against them will decline and society will become less age-segregated; the lives of older adults will become meaningful and fruitful.

This change presents a special challenge to psychologists of adulthood to direct more research toward the study of adults.

Adult Development and Aging is as comprehensive as possible within the confines of one textbook, emphasizing all periods of adulthood. The presentation is well grounded in research, including findings from hundreds of studies. Many charts and graphs clarify the discussion and add general interest to the material. Real-life examples also illustrate important points. The complete bibliography, glossary, and indexes will prove valuable aids in researching special topics for additional study.

The general purpose of *Adult Aging and Development* is to enable students to understand the changes and challenges of different phases of life so as adults they can live their own lives to the fullest and can work effectively with others seeking this fulfillment.

Special thanks go to the professors who made invaluable suggestions and offered guidance in the development of this book: Eleanor Simon, Department of Psychology, California State University, Dominguez Hills, California; Chad Karr, Department of Psychology, Portland State University, Portland, Oregon; Barbara Lemme, Social and Behavioral Science Department, College of DuPage, Glen Ellyn, Illinois; Thomas Ludwig, Department of Psychology, Hope College, Holland, Michigan; and Robert Bornstein, Department of Psychology, Miami University, Oxford, Ohio.

My heartfelt thanks also go to the editorial staff of Allyn and Bacon:

Steve Mathews, Bill Barke, Jeff Johnston, and Lauren Whittaker; and also to Grace Sheldrick, managing editor of Wordsworth Associates, for their valuable editorial services. Lastly, a special thanks to Irma Rice for her hours of proofreading, valuable suggestions, and moral support.

F.P.R.

Adult Development and Aging

Part 1

The Adult Years

1

The Study of Adulthood and Aging

ADULT DEVELOPMENTAL PSYCHOLOGY

Importance

Two-thirds of the people in the United States are adults. Given this fact, it seems unbelievable that for years the major focus of psychological studies was children and adolescents. Yet this is true. Only since World War II has much attention been paid to the study of adult development. Even now, many of the textbooks on human development end with the study of adolescence. Similarly, dozens of textbooks examine child and adolescent psychology, but only a handful address adult psychology. The average college psychology department still offers many more courses of study on children and youth than on adults.

Undoubtedly, the emphasis on early childhood experiences as determinants of later life adjustments is one reason for this imbalance. Freud's concern with early influences led subsequent scholars to focus on childhood development. However, contemporary research is revealing the difficulties of predicting adult success or failure, or adult adjustment, simply on the basis of earlier experiences (Brim and Kagan 1980; Vaillant 1977b). This does not mean the early years are unimportant; however, it does suggest that many factors once thought important to later success and adjustment are actually inconsequential.

A second reason for the psychological concern with the early years is the incredible notion that development starts prenatally and stops with adolescence. In the past it was assumed that most aspects of development (physical, cognitive, emotional, social, and moral) reach their zenith in late adolescence and somehow magically stop after that point. Nothing is further from the truth. True, some aspects of physical growth stop, but development in terms of change and adaptation continues throughout life. Even in the physical sense, persons who were sickly and ill during childhood and adolescence can become healthy and robust adults. Emotional maturation continues, as does the socialization process. Some measures of intelligence indicate that cognitive development continues past the sixties.

Moreover, the latest findings suggest that even octogenarians suffering from organic brain syndrome can learn and improve their intellectual functioning.

Previous generations stressed the education of young people; today's adults are more concerned about their own schooling. Learning is now considered a lifelong endeavor. The more we study adult development, the more we realize that human potential is almost unlimited. The knowledge possessed at twenty is only a small fraction of what will subsequently be learned, especially the practical knowledge necessary for day-to-day living.

A third reason for the lack of emphasis on adult development is that most psychological studies of adults have focused on the maladjusted, the abnormal, the neurotic, or the psychotic. This was a practical necessity. Those people least able to function independently required the most attention and care. As a result, little time, attention, money, or personnel was directed to those normal adults who had to make their own way through the many difficult phases of the life cycle. These individuals could falter and stumble through early adulthood, middle age, and into late adulthood, but unless they truly failed, no one paid much attention.

This lack of attention is now regarded as a mistake. Young and middle-aged adults need help to accomplish their many developmental tasks, as do late adults to restructure their lives, as do the abnormal to function as individuals. Most adults who seek counseling are normal people, but they are confused or distraught about their lives. No wonder books such as Sheehy's *Passages* (1976) and Levinson's *The Seasons of a Man's Life* (1978) have been best-sellers.

Scope

The subject matter of adult developmental psychology and aging is as broad as the range of psychology itself. In fact, it borrows from other such disciplines as the biological sciences, medicine, and sociology and must encompass most other branches of psychology to present the total picture. Therefore, information from these many disciplines must be used in any comprehensive presentation.

Perceptions of the Life Span

At present, few accepted conceptual frameworks encompass adult development and aging. No one paradigm for describing changes over the life span commands consensus. Some writers delineate the various phases or stages of life, from early adulthood to old age (Gould 1972). Others outline developmental tasks, each of which must be mastered before moving on to the next (Havighurst 1972). Still others describe life events (such as marriage, parenthood, or retirement) as possible markers of personality changes and adaptation. A more general concept is that of life periods, such as early adulthood, middle adulthood, or late adulthood. Neugarten (1976) makes further distinctions (the "young-old" and "old-old"). Each of these approaches has made important contributions to the total understanding of adult development.

This book treats the adult life cycle from many viewpoints and theories, believing that an eclectic approach presents more truths about human adult development and aging than any one theory.

ADULT DEVELOPMENT FROM A LIFE-CYCLE VIEWPOINT

The Human Life Cycle

In discussing adult development, we will use the phrase *human life cycle*. In some ways, it is similar to the expression *human life span*. However, *life cycle* is richer in meaning. *Life span* implies a straight-line time interval from birth to death, reflecting the length of life, not the content. *Life cycle* is described by such expressions as "a round of years," "a recurring period of time," "a series of occurrences that is repeated," "a succession of periodically recurring events," "a complete alteration," and "to pass through cycles" (*The Random House Dictionary* 1973; Stein 1973). Accordingly, life is composed of cycles, phases, or stages, each with its own distinctive characteristics, each different from those preceding it or following it. The emphasis is on *alteration and change* from one phase of the cycle to another. Living is not a simple, continuous, unchanging flow of years. Life changes as one moves from early to middle to late adulthood.

Levinson likens the phases or stages of the life cycle to the seasons:

> Every season is different from those that precede and follow it, though it also has much in common with them. . . . Spring is a time of blossoming, winter a time of death but also of rebirth and the start of a new cycle. . . . Change goes on within each, and a transition is required for a shift from one season to the next. . . . Every season has its own time; it is important in its own right and needs to be understood in its own terms. . . . Each has its necessary place and contributes its special character to the whole. It is an organic part of the total cycle, linking past and future and containing both within itself. (Levinson 1978, 6, 7)

The term *cycle* also implies repetition. There is, for example, some repetition of adjustment phases during anyone's life. Entering the thirties may involve reappraising and reevaluating one's life, but so does entering the forties (Levinson 1978). Likewise, vocational adjustments are necessary when one enters or retires from employment.

In addition to the repetition in an individual life, there is repetition from one life to another. Different persons may experience similar phases or stages of life, although at different times and with infinite individual and cultural differences. Different influences shape different lives, producing alternate routes (for example, one marries, another remains single). A variety of factors speed up or slow down the timetable, or even stop the developmental process altogether. But where similarities in developmental phases do exist, one can learn from the experiences of others. This fact makes a life-cycle approach meaningful.

If there is change with each phase of life, there is also continuity among them. Life is continuous, one phase flowing gradually into the next, allowing for periods of transition. And what happens in one phase does influence the next. For example, how thoroughly one prepares for a vocation during adolescence and early adulthood partially influences later success. The extent of fulfillment during middle age partially determines the ability during late adulthood to be at peace with oneself and with growing older. In studying developmental phases, therefore, we must link the present with the past and the future to obtain a complete picture.

Cautions Concerning Life-Cycle Theories

Before examining several developmental theories, the careful student must acknowledge certain cautions.

Child psychologists were the first to use *stage theories* describing successive phases children pass through, each phase qualitatively different from the others. Efforts to apply stage theories to the adult life span have been only partially successful. Critics argue that the stages of adult life cannot be sharply defined, and that progression from one stage to another varies in inevitability, desirability, reversibility, and repeatability. Development in adults takes place not only because of inner changes (which vary tremendously among different persons) but also because of changing environments, institutions, relationships, societal expectations, cultural influences, and political, economic, and social events. Part of an individual's change is his or her reaction to a changing society, such as the onset of a major depression. Thus, life stages do not unfold inevitably nor is life predestined by some inborn psychological design.

In addition, do not unduly emphasize the age divisions established by different theorists. Although it is helpful to divide the human life cycle into broad phases, the emphasis should be on events occurring during various phases, not on exact chronological age divisions. These divisions vary as much as plus or minus ten years, or more. For example, it is important to focus on the process of vocational or marriage establishment, which ordinarily takes place during the early adult years. However, some people complete vocational establishment early or late during these years. Similarly, some people marry in their twenties, others in their thirties or later. It is more important to understand what happens during the developmental phases than to memorize age divisions.

Age divisions are partly arbitrary and vary with different ethnic, socioeconomic, or cultural groups. Each society has its own specific age norms when particular status is granted or sex roles are required. For example, in societies where people ordinarily live only to their mid-forties, adult status and responsibilities are granted much earlier than in our society, where most people live into their seventies. However, these persons still experience periods of preparation for adult living, periods of marital and vocational adjustment, and so forth. So, although the ages vary, the developmental tasks are similar.

Another consideration is that much research on adult development has been conducted by white, middle-class researchers on their peers. Even assuming this research still applies to individuals in different socioeconomic or ethnic groups, it would apply at different age periods. We know, for example, that lower-class persons who do not go on to higher education look for permanent jobs and marry at younger ages than do middle-class persons. The whole process accelerates so that age norms established with middle-class samples cannot be applied to lower-class samples. Consider the research sample when interpreting the results.

Finally, research findings established by studying groups of people are not valid predictions of future events in individual lives, nor are they descriptions of what individuals should experience. If the findings show that many adults experience a mid-life crisis, these results will be valuable in understanding the adjustments of other adults experiencing the same thing. However, if adults are having marital or work-related problems, it would be false and misleading to attribute them to a mid-life crisis, anymore than a physician can blame all health problems in middle-aged females on menopause. The problem with predictions is that they can become self-fulfilling prophecies. Those conditioned to expect certain experiences at each age may have those experiences only because they think they should.

PSYCHOLOGICAL THEORIES OF DEVELOPMENT OVER THE HUMAN LIFE CYCLE

Different Approaches

With these cautions in mind, let us examine some representative psychological theories of development over the human life cycle. These psychological theories represent only one approach among many. Two additional approaches, biological and sociological theories of development and the aging process, are discussed in subsequent chapters (primarily chapters 4 and 5). Cognitive theories are discussed in Part IV (chapters 11, 12, and 13). Moreover, the contributions of numerous other psychologists are touched on throughout this book.

The major psychological theories of Buhler (1935, 1968), Erikson (1959), and Havighurst (1972) are discussed here. Their personality theories of development were selected because they apply to the whole life cycle and present a fairly complete picture of the continuity of life and the necessity of change and adaptation as one moves from phase to phase.

Buhler

Charlotte Buhler (1935), a Viennese psychologist, and her students were among the first to divide the entire life span into developmental phases or stages. Buhler's theory was based on an analysis of about four hundred biographies of individuals from various nations, social classes, and vocations, plus additional data from clinical interviews. Three types of data were collected: the external events surrounding a person's life, the internal reactions to these events, and the accomplishments and production of each person. From these data, Buhler outlined five phases of the life span and showed the parallels between biological and psychological development during each phase (Buhler and Massarik 1968). Table 1.1 illustrates the phases outlined by Buhler (1935).

The age divisions are averages based on data from Austrian culture of the 1930s. The divisions might be somewhat different today. Nevertheless, these studies are rich in hypotheses relating to the psychological trends and problems during life phases.

Buhler rejected the contention of psychoanalysts that restoring *homeostasis* (equilibrium) through release of tensions is the goal of human beings. "I myself expressed the opinion that homeostasis is no goal at all, only a comfortable basis of functioning, and that human beings' real goal of life is what I called a fulfillment, which they hoped to attain by various things they accomplished in themselves and in the world outside" (Buhler 1977, 21). She emphasized that the human basic tendency is toward fulfillment through *self-actualization* or self-realization, which is accomplished through creativity. She agreed with Maslow (1962) that the peak experiences of self-actualizing persons come through creativity. In the last phase of life,

TABLE 1.1   Buhler's Developmental Phases of Life

Phase	*Development*
Phase One: 0 to 15 Years	Progressive biological growth; child at home; life centers around narrow interest, school, family
Phase Two: 16 to 27 Years	Continued biological growth, sexual maturity; expansion of activities, self-determination; leaves family, enters into independent activities and personal relations
Phase Three: 28 to 47 Years	Biological stability; culmination period; most fruitful period of professional and creative work; most personal and social relationships
Phase Four: 48 to 62 Years	Loss of reproductive functions, decline in abilities; decrease in activities; personal, family, economic losses; transition to this phase marked by psychological crises; period of introspection
Phase Five: 63 Years and over	Biological decline, increased sickness; retirement from profession; decrease in socialization, but increase in hobbies, individual pursuits; period of retrospection; feeling of fulfillment or failure

Adapted from: C. Buhler, "The Curve of Life as Studied in Biographies," *Journal of Applied Psychology* 19 (1935): 405–409.

most human beings evaluate their total existence in terms of fulfillment or failure.

Erikson

Erik Erikson (1959) outlined eight stages of development over the human life span, based on his own clinical impressions and a revision of Freud's views. In each of the eight stages, the individual is confronted with a psychosocial task, crisis, or conflict to be overcome before moving to the next stage. If the conflict is successfully resolved, a positive quality is built into the personality and further development takes place. An unsatisfactory resolution damages the ego by incorporating a negative quality. The individual is challenged to resolve the conflict and develop a positive ego identity at each stage.

The eight stages of development are each shown with the positive resolution to the psychosocial task and the negative result of an unsuccessful resolution.

Infancy: Developing *trust* versus mistrust
Toddler: Developing *autonomy* versus shame and doubt
Preschool age: Developing *initiative* versus guilt
School age: Developing *industry* versus inferiority
Adolescence: Developing ego *identity* versus identity diffusion
Young adulthood: Developing *intimacy* versus isolation
Middle adulthood: Developing *generativity* versus stagnation
Late adulthood: Developing *ego integrity* versus disgust and despair

Only the last three stages are discussed here. In young adulthood, the key issue is to achieve *intimacy;* the alternative is isolation.

Sexual intimacy is only part of what I have in mind, for it is obvious that sexual intimacies often precede the capacity to develop a true and mutual psychosocial intimacy with another person, be it in friendship, in erotic encounter, or in joint inspiration. The youth who is not sure of his identity shies away from interpersonal intimacy or throws himself into acts of intimacy which are "promiscuous" without true fusion or real self-abandon.

Where a youth does not accomplish such intimate relationships with others—and, I would add, with his own inner resources—in late adolescence or early adulthood, he may settle for highly stereotyped interpersonal relations and come to retain a deep sense of isolation. (Erikson 1968, 135–136)

During middle adulthood, the chief psychosocial task is to achieve *generativity;* the negative alternative is stagnation. Generativity includes not only productivity in one's work, but also establishing and guiding the next generation, losing oneself in developing the growing bodies and minds of others. When this fails, the individual becomes personally impoverished, stagnating in self-indulgence and self-love. Even those who reject the right to procreate, such as those in monastic orders, strive to care for the creatures of this world and perform acts of charity on their behalf (Erikson

1963). The outcome of this stage is care, "the widening concern for what has been generated by love, necessity, or accident" (Erikson 1976, 24).

The development of *ego integrity* is the goal of the final stage of life. This entails evaluating one's life and accepting it for what it is, without regret or wishing to start anew. Erikson feels that the individual with integrity is aware of various life-styles that give meaning to human striving, but at the same time is ready to defend the dignity of his own life-style against all threats (Erikson 1963). The alternative is to reject the value and worth of one's own life. Recognition of impending death gives rise to despair, "the feeling that time is now short, too short for the attempt to start another life and to try out alternate roads to integrity" (Erikson 1963). Remorse and despair over one's life signify incomplete ego integration. The development of ego integrity brings one full circle through Erikson's life cycle.

Havighurst

In his book *Developmental Tasks and Education* (1972), Robert J. Havighurst outlined the major *developmental tasks* from infancy to later maturity. Havighurst sought to establish a psychosocial theory of development by combining the consideration of individual needs with societal demands. Developmental tasks require an active learner interacting with an active social environment. They are tasks individuals must learn in order to judge themselves and be judged reasonably happy and successful (Havighurst 1972). Some developmental tasks arise from biological changes, others from cultural pressures of society, and others from personal values and individual aspirations. Developmental tasks differ among different classes and ethnic groups, and from culture to culture, depending on the relative influence of biological, psychological, and cultural elements.

Havighurst (1972) divided the life span into six age periods:

Birth to 6 years of age: Infancy and early childhood
6 to 12 years of age: Middle childhood
12 to 18 years of age: Adolescence
18 to 30 years of age: Early adulthood
30 to 60 years of age: Middle age
Over 60 years of age: Later maturity

We are concerned with the last three age periods. Table 1.2 shows the developmental tasks of early adulthood, middle adulthood, and later maturity, as outlined by Havighurst.

Havighurst described early adulthood as a time of unusual readiness to learn and a time of special sensitivity. It is an individualistic and lonely period of life because young adults receive minimal social attention and assistance in tackling the most important tasks of life. It is a period with many challenges, especially in middle-class society.

According to Havighurst (1972), in the middle years of thirty to sixty, men and women reach their influential peak in society, and society makes the greatest demands on them. These years are also marked by physiological changes.

TABLE 1.2   Havighurst's Developmental Tasks of Adulthood

Early Adulthood	Middle Adulthood	Later Maturity
1. Selecting a mate 2. Learning to live with a marriage partner 3. Starting a family 4. Rearing children 5. Managing a home 6. Getting started in an occupation 7. Taking on civic responsibility 8. Finding a congenial social group	1. Helping teenage children become responsible and happy adults 2. Achieving adult social and civic responsibility 3. Reaching and maintaining satisfactory performance in one's occupation 4. Developing adult leisure-time activities 5. Relating oneself to one's spouse as a person 6. Accepting and adjusting to the physiological changes of middle age 7. Adjusting to aging parents	1. Adjusting to decreasing physical strength and health 2. Adjusting to retirement and reduced income 3. Adjusting to death of spouse 4. Establishing an explicit affiliation with one's age group 5. Adopting and adapting social roles in a flexible way 6. Establishing satisfactory physical living arrangements

Adapted from: R. J. Havighurst, *Developmental Tasks and Education* (New York: D. McKay, 1972).

Havighurst (1972) described later maturity (over age sixty) as a time of adjustment and possibly disengagement from some of the more active roles of middle age. Physical, mental, and economic changes impose limitations, requiring considerable adjustments.

Havighurst emphasized that every period of life has its teachable moments, when the body is ripe and the self is ready, and when society requires that we learn new tasks. Thus, development and learning are a lifelong process, not a process that stops with adolescence.

PSYCHOLOGICAL STUDIES OF DEVELOPMENTAL PHASES DURING EARLY AND MIDDLE ADULTHOOD

In addition to the psychological theorists who have dealt with all the phases of the life cycle, some researchers have focused only on the early and middle adulthood periods. We will discuss Gould (1972, 1978), Levinson et al. (1976, 1977, 1978), and Vaillant (1977a, b). Theories of development during late adulthood are discussed in chapters 4 and 5.

Gould

Psychiatrist Roger Gould (1972, 1978) reported on two studies. One was a descriptive report of cross-sectional observations of psychiatric outpatients divided into seven age-homogeneous groups. (Cross-sectional studies are discussed in the Research Issues section of this chapter.) At the end of six months, a second set of seven groups was constituted. Each of the fourteen groups was observed continuously over a period of months. The second study was based on questionnaire answers of 524 middle-class adults not in psychotherapy.

Gould's seven arbitrary age groupings were:

Ages 16 to 18: Desire for autonomy, to get away from parents, for deep, close relationships with peers.

Ages 18 to 22: Desire not to be reclaimed by family, for intimacy with peers, to recreate with peers the family they are leaving; real living is just around the corner.

Ages 22 to 29: Engaged in work of being adults, in proving competence as adults; now is the time for living as well as growing and building for future; on guard against extreme emotions.

Ages 29 to 35: Role confusion; question self, marriage, career; begin to question what they are doing; weary of devoting themselves to the task of doing what they are supposed to; desire to be what they are, to accept their children for what they are becoming.

Ages 35 to 43: Increasing awareness of time squeeze; realignment of goals, increasing urgency to attain goals; realization that control over children is waning.

Ages 43 to 50: Acceptance of finite time as reality, settling-down stage, acceptance of one's fate in life; desire for social activities and friends, need for sympathy and affection from spouse; watchful of young adult children's progress.

Ages 50 to 60: Mellowing, warming, more accepting of parents, children, friends, past failures; also renewed questioning about meaningfulness of life; hunger for personal relationships.

Gould admitted the dangers in reporting cross-sectional data since changing cultural values, rather than age, could influence results. Gould's reported fluctuations are not necessarily age specific for one individual. That is, changes occurring over certain periods of time do not necessarily occur at the same ages in all individuals. He acknowledged that his studies were designed to cancel out individual differences in order to highlight sameness existing in an age group. But he defended his findings on the basis that many of them were supported by other studies using different methodologies and populations.

In particular, our curves on marital happiness, contentment to remain the same age, anxiety in the 40s in relation to performance, a sense of finiteness of time in the mid-30s, reconciliation in the 40s, health concerns, decreased interest in social activities in the 30s, and increased interest in friends and organizations in the 40s all conform to the results of previous studies. (Gould 1972, 531)

Some findings from his second study are illustrated in Figure 1.1. In this study, the subjects were asked to respond to a series of statements in

FIGURE 1.1 Sample Curves Associated with the Time Boundaries of the Adult Life Span

Age in Years

Age in Years

Extent of Agreement with Statement

1. My personality is pretty well set

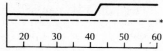

2. I wish that people would accept me for what I am as a person

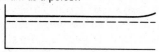

3. I wish my mate would accept me for what I am

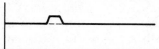

4. I would be quite content to remain as old as I am now

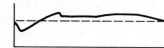

5. There's still plenty of time to do most of the things I want to do

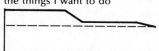

6. I try to be satisfied with what I have and not to think so much about the things I probably won't be able to get

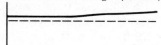

7. Life doesn't change much from year to year

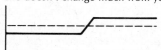

8. Too late to make any major change in my career

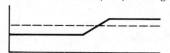

9. I don't make enough money to do what I want

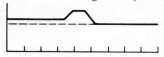

10. My greatest concern is my health

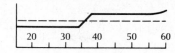

11. I can't do things as well as I used to

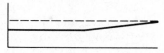

12. I like a very active social life

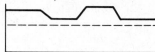

13. For me marriage has been a good thing

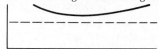

14. How important are these people to you overall?

children
parent

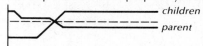

15. My parents are the cause of many of my problems

16. I regret my mistakes in raising my children

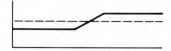

17. How important are these people to you overall?

spouse
self

18. I would feel lost without my friends

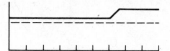

*The horizontal dashed line is placed arbitrarily to help show the trends of the graph lines.

Reprinted from: R. J. Gould, "The Phases of Adult Life: A Study in Developmental Psychology," *The American Journal of Psychiatry* 129 (November 1972): 521–531. Copyright, 1972, the American Psychiatric Association. Reprinted by permission.

a questionnaire. Gould concluded his discussion by stating that strong evidence indicated that a series of distinct stages could be demarcated.

Levinson

Daniel Levinson (1978), a social psychology professor from Yale, and his associates made a cross-sectional study of forty men between thirty-five and forty-five years of age over a period of several years. The subjects were divided into four groups: ten hourly workers, ten Ph.D. biologists, ten novelists, and ten executives from two companies. Seventy percent had completed college, all had married at least once, 20 percent were divorced, 80 percent had children, and 50 percent were Protestants. Subjects were interviewed weekly for several months, with a follow-up interview after two years. The interviews were taped and interpretations made from the data. The interviews included much retrospective data from childhood on, as well as information about the present. Thematic Apperception Test (TAT) pictures were used to recall personal experiences. Most of their wives were interviewed once. Extensive biographical information was also used in interpreting the data.

Levinson proposed a model of adult development that included periods of relative stability (periods of structure building) interspersed with periods of transition (periods of structure changing). Figure 1.2 shows the developmental periods outlined by Levinson.

The periods can be described as follows:

Ages 17 to 22: Early adult transition: Leaving the family and adolescent groups, going to college, military service, marrying.

Ages 22 to 28: Entering the adult world: Time of choices, defining goals, establishing occupation and marriage; conflict between desire to explore and commit.

Ages 28 to 33: Age-thirty transition: Period of reworking, modifying life structure; smooth transition for some, disruptive crisis for others; growing sense of need for change before becoming locked in because of commitments.

Ages 33 to 40: Settling down: Accepting a few major goals, building the structure around central choices; establishing one's niche, working at advancement.

Ages 40 to 45: Mid-life transition: Mid-life crisis, link between early and middle adulthood, review and reappraise early adult period, modify unsatisfying aspects of life structure, adjust psychologically to final half of life; intense reexamination causes emotional upset, tumultuous struggles with self, questioning every aspect of life.

Because Levinson's (1978) original groups were younger than forty-five, his descriptions basically end with the mid-life transition. However, he does give some brief and tentative descriptions of subsequent periods, based primarily on speculation.

FIGURE 1.2 Developmental Periods in Early and Middle Adulthood

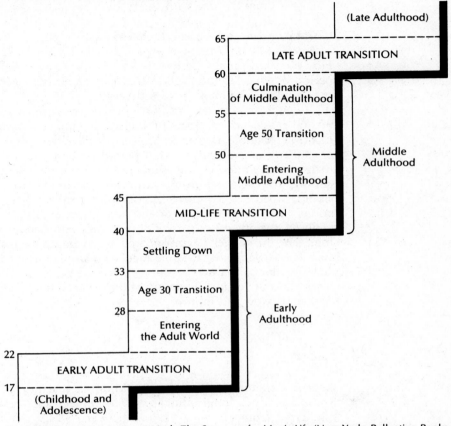

Reprinted from: D. J. Levinson et al. *The Seasons of a Man's Life* (New York: Ballantine Books, 1978). Copyright © 1978 by Daniel J. Levinson. Reprinted by permission of Alfred A. Knopf, Inc.

Ages 45 to 50: Entering middle adulthood: End of reappraisal, time of choices, forming a new life structure in relation to occupation, marriage, locale; wide variations in satisfactions and extent of fulfillment.

Ages 50 to 55: Age-fifty transition: Work further on the tasks of mid-life transition and modification of structure formed in the mid-forties; crisis if there was not enough change during mid-life transition.

Ages 55 to 60: Culmination of middle adulthood: Building a second middle adult structure; time of fulfillment for those who can rejuvenate themselves and enrich their lives.

Ages 60 to 65: Late adult transition: Conclude efforts of middle adulthood, prepare for era to come; major turning point in life cycle.

Ages 65 and over: Late adulthood: Confrontation with self, life; need to make peace with the world.

Levinson also observed that the entire period after age sixty-five is often regarded as a single era, primarily because of a lack of research data. However, with many people living to be well over eighty years, there is a period of late, late adulthood that can be either a period of further psychosocial development or of senescence.

Levinson emphasized that periods are defined in terms of developmental tasks, not in terms of such concrete events as marriage or retirement. Each stable life period has certain developmental tasks and life issues crucial to the evolution of that period. A period ends when its tasks lose their primacy and new tasks emerge, initiating a new period. Transitional periods are the times to question and reappraise, to search for new possibilities in the self and the world. Furthermore, there are ranges of variations when periods begin or end. Thus, the age-thirty transition can start between twenty-six and twenty-nine and end between thirty and thirty-four. The exact ages Levinson cited are averages for his samples. Levinson also acknowledged that some men who suffer defeats in previous periods lack the inner and outer resources to create even minimally adequate structures. Their lives lack meaning and they face future periods with feelings of constriction and failure.

Vaillant

George Vaillant (1977a, b), a psychiatrist teaching at Harvard Medical School, made a longitudinal study of ninety-four males who had been graduated from Harvard College between 1942 and 1944. These males were among 268 college sophomores who had been carefully selected for the Grant Study, begun in 1938. The average age in 1969 was forty-seven. The average income was $30,000, 95 percent had married, 15 percent were divorced, and 25 percent were doctors and lawyers. Most had served in World War II, 71 percent viewed themselves as liberals, and most were "extremely satisfied" with their professions.

A variety of research methods were used. Childhood histories were obtained by interviewing parents. Physical, physiological, and psychological examinations were conducted during the college years. After graduation, questionnaires were sent each year until 1955, and every two years after that. A social anthropologist conducted in-depth, home interviews with each subject between 1950 and 1952. Vaillant interviewed each man in 1967, usually at home, using identical interview questionnaires with each (Muson 1977).

This study provides thorough histories of the life cycles of specific men who were among the nation's best and brightest. It is a long view of maturational processes, ego development, and coping strategies and adaptation mechanisms, as these men reacted to life's challenges. Some succeeded, while others remained locked in patterns of defeat. The study also confirmed the life stages outlined by Erikson, especially the stages during adolescence (identity), young adulthood (intimacy), and middle adulthood (generativity) (Vaillant 1977b).

One of the study's most interesting aspects was the comparison of the childhoods, family backgrounds, and earlier years of the men who, in their fifties, were labeled Best Outcomes and Worst Outcomes. Table 1.3 presents the results (Vaillant 1977a). The table shows that about one-half of the men who had experienced unsatisfactory (poor) childhood environments were among the thirty Worst Outcomes. However, 17 percent with poor childhood environments were among the thirty Best Outcomes, indicating that childhood environment was not the sole determinant of adult success.

Some details were surprising. Fingernail biting, early toilet training, and mental illness failed to predict adult emotional illness. However, the comparison of twenty-three men whose childhoods were bleak and loveless with twenty-three men whose childhoods were happy and fortunate yielded four conclusions. Men with unhappy childhoods were: (1) unable to play; (2) dependent and lacking in trust; (3) more likely to become mentally ill; and (4) lacking friends.

Similarly, it was difficult to predict successful mid-life adaptation from negative traits seen during adolescence. Descriptions such as shyness, ideation, introspection, and lacking purpose and values did not predict the Worst Outcomes. Rather, these traits were merely characteristic of many adolescents. However, late adolescents labeled "well-integrated" and

TABLE 1.3　Comparison of Best and Worst Outcomes in the Grant Study

	The 30 Best Outcomes	The 30 Worst Outcomes
Poor Childhood Environment	17%	47%
Pessimism, Self-Doubt, Passivity, and Fear of Sex at 50	3%	50%
In College, Personality Integration Put in Bottom Fifth	0%	33%
Career Choice Reflected Identification with Father	60%	27%
Dominated by Mother in Adult Life	0%	40%
Failure to Marry by 30	3%	37%
Bleak Friendship Patterns at 50	0%	57%
Current Job Has Little Supervisory Responsibility	20%	93%
Children Admitted to Father's College	47%	10%
Children's Outcome Described as Good or Excellent	66%	23%
Average Yearly Charitable Contribution	$3,000	$500

Reprinted from: G. E. Vaillant, *Adaptation to Life* (Boston: Little, Brown, 1977). Copyright © 1977 by George E. Vaillant. By permission of Little, Brown and Company.

"practical and organized" were best adapted at fifty, whereas those labeled "asocial" were least likely to be Best Outcomes (Vaillant 1977b).

The study underlined the importance of achieving intimacy during young adulthood. The majority who married between twenty-three and twenty-nine were happily married. Twenty-eight of the thirty men who received the highest scores in overall adult adjustment had achieved a stable marriage before age thirty and remained married until fifty. Twenty-three of the thirty Worst Outcomes had either married after thirty or separated from their wives before fifty. Those who married before twenty-three (before developing a capacity for intimacy) and those who delayed marriage until after thirty were both likely to have the worst marriages (Vaillant 1977b).

Between twenty-five and thirty-five, the men tended to work hard, consolidate their careers, and devote themselves to the nuclear family. The most frequent psychiatric complaints of the men in their twenties reflected a retreat from intimacy, whereas the emotional complaints of those in their thirties reflected conflicts about success (occupational overachievement or neurotic defeat). Many found nonparental role models or mentors during this period of career consolidation.

At forty (plus or minus ten years), men left the compulsive, unreflective busywork of their occupational apprenticeship and once more explored the world within. The pain of this age was preparation for a new life stage. Some men who were bland and colorless during adolescence became vibrant and interesting.

> In his early 40s, one man took up underwater archaeology and deep-sea diving in the Mediterranean. Another built a dramatic, shamelessly exhibitionistic house. A third man whose projective tests at 24 suggested an inner life like "some Brazilian jungle spilling out onto a North Dakota plain" was at 50 finally able to let the Brazilian jungle emerge into his conscious life; yet, he was the last man that the study ever expected to have an exciting love affair. (Vaillant 1977b, 41)

The enrichment of these years also extended into the lives of the most successful businessmen. Their career patterns suddenly broadened in middle life; they assumed tasks for which they were untrained. The men who enjoyed the best marriages and richest friendships became the company presidents.

Vaillant continued to study these men in their fifties. The men reported having attained a certain tranquility, perhaps suffused with a mild undercurrent of regret.

Comparison and Critique of Studies

Table 1.4 compares the results of the Gould, Levinson, and Vaillant studies. It must be emphasized that Gould purposely used arbitrary age group-

TABLE 1.4   Stages or Phases of the Life Cycle

Age in Years	Gould	Levinson	Vaillant
60	Mellowing, warming; acceptance of parents, friends, past failures; but renewed questions about life's meaning; hunger for personal relationships		Middle adulthood: mild mid-life crisis around 40, inner exploration, reassessment, reawakening of instinctual urges including sex, throwing off some overrestraint of 30s, intergenerational conflict, establishing generativity versus stagnation
50	Settling down stage; acceptance of one's life, finite time; desire for social activity, friends; need for spousal affection; watch children		
40	Time squeeze, realignment of goals, urgency to attain goals; realization that control over children is waning	Mid-life transition: crisis, review, reappraisal, modify life, emotion turmoil, upset	
		Settling down: acceptance of a few major goals, central choices, establish niche, work at advancement	Young adulthood: achieve intimacy, career consolidation
30	Role confusion, question self, marriage, career; waning of duty, desire to be self; accept children as are	Age 30 transition: reworking, modifying life structure, need for change now	
	Working, proving competence as adults; living, growing for future; control of emotions	Entering adult world: choices, defining goals, occupation, marriage, explore versus commit	
20	Getting away from parents; desire for intimacy with peers	Early adult transition: leaving family, adolescent groups, college, service, marriage	Adolescence: search for identity
16	Desire for autonomy		

Adapted from: R. L. Gould, "The Phases of Adult Life: A Study in Developmental Psychology," *American Journal of Psychiatry* 129 (November 1972): 33–43; D. J. Levinson et al., *The Seasons of a Man's Life* (New York: Knopf, 1978); G. E. Vaillant, *Adaptation to Life* (Boston: Little, Brown, 1977).

ings to organize the outpatients into age-homogeneous groups. Although he divided them into seven groups with particular age ranges, he could have used fewer or more groups, changing the age range of each. The age ranges, therefore, are themselves not important.

Levinson used five time periods (five to six years each) between the ages of seventeen and forty-five. Each major time period, which is a period of settling down and becoming established, was interspersed with an unsettling, restless period of transition and change. The beginning and end of the age periods were averages for Levinson's samples; he acknowledged that for individuals the beginning and end of each period may differ. Levinson also projected five-year age periods to sixty-five and over, interspersing main periods with transition periods.

Vaillant used much broader life periods in seeking to confirm Erikson's descriptions of the psychosocial tasks of each life stage. Young adulthood is a period of intimacy achievement and career consolidation. But although Vaillant related restlessness and desire for change with the age of forty, he said that some individuals experience this as much as ten years earlier or later. Again, the exact age is not as important as the actual step in development.

All three researchers described a period of transition between adolescence and early adulthood, a period according to Levinson in which "The Dream" is formed. The Dream is a concept of what one wishes to accomplish. Some envision riches and fame, others a home and children.

These researchers also described a period of struggle, achievement, and growth as individuals in their twenties enter the adult world, striving to succeed in their occupations and in marriage.

One question that arises when comparing these studies is whether there are dual crisis periods during early and middle adulthood: one during the age-thirty transition, followed by a period of settling down, and a mid-life crisis as one enters the forties. For Gould, there was one period (from twenty-nine to forty-three) of role confusion and realignment, and questioning of oneself, marriage, and career plans. Gould gave the impression that this entire period was devoted to reworking and adjusting one's life. Levinson (1978) made the clearest distinction between an age-thirty transition period, about seven years of settling down, and another transition period in the early forties. But he also found that only 62 percent of the men experienced a moderate or severe crisis during the age-thirty transition period. The rest did not report a crisis at age thirty. Vaillant described no age-thirty transition period; for him, the period from twenty to forty was one of intimacy and career consolidation.

All three described a *mid-life crisis*. For Gould, it occurred between thirty-five and forty-three, for Levinson between forty and forty-five, and for Vaillant at forty (give or take a decade). Gould and Levinson reported a time of marked crisis. According to Vaillant, severe crises were rare. Mild upsets occurred that created some anxiety, which often resulted in new challenges and vigor. One man of forty-seven commented:

> I am into a whole new life, a personal renaissance, which has got me excited most of the time. If I can make it pay adequate to my family responsibility, I will "really be livin'," man. (Vaillant 1977a, 221)

Psychologically healthy adults were able to reorganize their life patterns during their forties and emerge with a new sense of personal happiness and fulfillment.

Causes of Change and Transition

These studies also raise the question of the causes of change and transition throughout life. The causes can be grouped into two broad categories:

external and internal forces that shape individual lives. External forces are influences or events that affect behavior. Socialization is part of this process. People are taught social norms and to strive for particular goals at specific ages. In effect, they are given a social age clock. Thus, during late adolescence, they are expected to get a job, or enter college; during early adulthood, to pursue a career and get married. Likewise, different behaviors are expected at middle age. Societal expectations and the ways people are socialized exert a strong influence on development during various phases of the life cycle.

Social and historical changes also influence behavior. The women's movement, for example, has encouraged numerous changes in womens' lives that may influence their expectations and adjustments during various life stages.

Specific events, such as the draft, divorce, loss of employment, a death in the family, a job transfer, economic depression, and pregnancy, force changes and usher in periods of transition. Levinson (1978) told of a black novelist who was divorced at twenty-eight. He spent the following years trying to overcome his guilt over "abandoning" his wife and children, moving frequently, working at numerous jobs with little income, attempting suicide, getting therapy, and falling in love again. Finally, at thirty-four, his life was again in balance. Transition periods do not just happen; they are usually triggered by specific events that force a review of certain aspects of one's life. A man who walked through the streets of Hiroshima weeks after the atomic bomb was dropped decided to leave engineering and become a minister. After her husband divorced her, a woman decided to return to college. Another resumed her career after her children left home. A new boss who was impossible to work for was enough to stimulate another man to go into business for himself.

Internal forces—for example, the biological time clock—also shape people's lives. Adults who see physical signs of aging may change their behavior and goals. Menopause forces a woman to think about her life after her child-bearing years are over. A drastic change in health may necessitate complete restructuring of one's activities. Emotional factors also stimulate changes and events in one's life. Anxiety, boredom, and depression—any one of a number of feelings—can cause a behavior change.

Some types of transitions are normative; that is, they are expected according to the social norms at particular times of life. These transitions include such events as graduation from high school or college, marriage, parenthood, grandparenthood, and retirement. These normative transitions are part of an internalized social clock and partially regulate the timing of events in one's life.

Other transitions are idiosyncratic. Because they are unusual and unexpected, they usually have a more disturbing influence than normative transitions. Divorce is one example. It is not normative and is sometimes very sudden and unexpected, causing a major period of upset and reorientation (Chiriboga 1978). The death of a spouse or a child and major health problems are other examples of idiosyncratic transitions.

RESEARCH ISSUES

Types of Research Designs

Students of adult psychology must understand the basic research designs used to study adults, so they can better evaluate the information obtained. The following four developmental designs are used in studying adults: (1) *cross-sectional studies,* (2) *longitudinal studies,* (3) *time lag studies,* and (4) *sequential studies* (Schaie and Baltes 1975). Each design has its own characteristics.

A cross-sectional study is when one age group, or *cohort,* is compared with another age group at one time of testing. A cohort is comprised of persons who were born at the same time or within a short time interval. Thus, it might include all individuals born in 1950 or between 1949 and 1951. To try to discover differences in adults due to age, a cross-sectional study would compare one age group or cohort with another. For example, a cross-sectional study conducted in 1990 might compare four groups or cohorts: those born in 1930 with those born in 1935, 1940, and 1945. As illustrated in Figure 1.3, group D (forty-five-year-olds born in 1945) would be compared with group G (fifty-year-olds born in 1940) with group I (fifty-five-year-olds born in 1935) with group J (sixty-year-olds born in 1930). This method measures the different age groups during one testing period and compares these groups to determine differences. As shown, comparisons of groups C, F, and H during 1985, or groups B and E during 1980, also represent cross-sectional studies.

Longitudinal research studies one group of people repeatedly over a period of years. For example, a select group might be studied at ages forty-five, fifty, fifty-five, and sixty. Referring to Figure 1.3, if the group of adults born in 1930 were studied during 1975, 1980, 1985, and 1990 (those groups labeled A, E, H, J), the study would be longitudinal. Similarly, a study of the 1935 cohort during 1980, 1985, and 1990 (groups B, F, I), at ages forty-five, fifty, and fifty-five, or the 1940 cohort during 1985 and 1990 (labeled C, G), would be longitudinal as well.

Cross-sectional studies confound age and cohort effects; that is, they fail to differentiate whether age differences versus cultural influences or compositional differences are responsible for change. Longitudinal studies confound age and time of testing; that is, they fail to differentiate whether age differences or differences due to time of testing are responsible for change.

A third type of design, the time lag study, uses an interval in the time measurements during which people of different cohorts are examined. This design eliminates age effects (all the subjects are the same age), but it confounds cohort and time measurements. Thus, in Figure 1.3, groups A, B, C, and D constitute a time lag comparison. Similarly, groups E, F, and G or H and I are time lag studies.

Ideally, time lag, cross-sectional, and longitudinal studies should all be conducted. Although each design is confounded by two sources of vari-

FIGURE 1.3   Research Designs

Age

	45	50	55	60
1930	1975 data A	1980 data E	1985 data H	1990 data J
1935	1980 data B	1985 data F	1990 data I	
1940	1985 data C	1990 data G		
1945	1990 data D			

Year of Birth (cohort)

Cross-Sectional Studies

> 1990 Study: DGIJ
> 1985 Study: CFH
> 1980 Study: BE

Longitudinal Studies

> Groups AEHJ in 1975, 1980, 1985, and 1990
> Groups BFI   in 1980, 1985, and 1990
> Groups CG   in 1985, and 1990

Time-Lag Studies

> Compare ABCD
> Compare EFG
> Compare HI

ation, examining the results of the three approaches can yield a more accurate picture.

A fourth pattern of research, the sequential study, offers three types of designs: *cross-sequential, time-sequential,* and *cohort-sequential* (Schaie and Baltes 1975).

The cross-sequential study is a combination of cross-sectional and longitudinal designs. Referring to Figure 1.4, four age-cohort groups are tested at two different times: 1985 and 1990. The study asks three questions of these groups (Schaie and Labouvie-Vief 1974).

First, are the four age-cohort groups different in test scores? This is answered by comparing groups A + F with B + G with C + H with D + I. In this instance, age and cohort effects are confounded. Time measurements are the same.

FIGURE 1.4   Sequential Designs

Testing Year

	1985 data	1990 data
1945	Age 40 A	Age 45 F
1940	Age 45 B	Age 50 G
1935	Age 50 C	Age 55 H
1930	Age 55 D	Age 60 I
1925	Age 60 E	

Year of Birth (cohort)

Cross-Sequential Design

Are the four age-cohort groups different in test scores? Compare A + F with B + G with C + H with D + I.

Are the average scores of test time 1985 different from those of 1990? Compare the average scores of A + B + C + D with F + G + H + I.

Do the scores change from 1985 to 1990 in a greater way for one age-cohort group than for another? Compare A–F with B–G with C–H with D–I.

Time-Sequential Design

Are the age-cohort groups different in test scores? Compare B + F with C + G with D + H with E + I.

Are the scores of 1985 different from those of 1990? Compare the average scores of B + C + D + E with F + G + H + I.

Do the scores change from 1985 to 1990 in a greater way for one age-cohort group than for another? Compare B–F with C–G with D–H with E–I.

Second, are the average scores of test time 1985 different from those of 1990? Thus, the average score of A B C and D is compared with the average of F G H and I. In this example, age and time measurements are confounded. The cohorts are the same.

Third, do the scores change from 1985 to 1990 in a greater way for one age-cohort group than for another? The answer is found by comparing

A − F with B − G with C − H with D − I. In this example, age and cohort effects are confounded. The time measurements are the same.

The time-sequential study is a time lag analysis. The same questions are asked as in the cross-sequential design, but the answers refer to different effects.

Are the age-cohort groups different in test scores? Referring to Figure 1.4, the answer is found by comparing B + F with C + G with D + H with E + I. Here, age and cohort effects are confounded; the time measurements are the same.

Are the scores of 1985 different from those of 1990? The answer is found by comparing the average of B C D and E with F G H and I. In this instance, cohort and time measurements are confounded; the ages are the same.

Do the scores change from 1985 to 1990 in a greater way for one age-cohort group than for another? The answer is found by comparing B − F with C − G with D − H with E − I. Here, age and cohort effects are confounded; the time measurements are the same.

The cohort-sequential study is probably the best sequential design for separating the effects of different ages and cohorts. The simplest cohort-sequential study is illustrated by Figure 1.5. Two age groups (forty-five and fifty) and two cohort groups (born in 1945 and 1940) are measured three different times (1985, 1990, and 1995). By comparing A + B with C + D, age and time measurements are confounded, but cohort effect is eliminated. By comparing A + C with B + D, cohort and time measurements are confounded, but age effect is eliminated. Of all the assumptions that can be made in aging research, the assumption that time of testing is unimportant may be the most tenable. If so, the effects of age and cohort are sorted out, and they can be meaningfully compared with this research design. Of course, the longer the total time span of the study, the more effect time measurement will have.

FIGURE 1.5   Cohort-Sequential Design

Age

	45	50
1945	1990 Data A	1995 Data C
1940	1985 Data B	1990 Data D

Year of Birth (cohort)

Cohort effect eliminated, age and time of measurement confounded:
    Compare A + B with C + D.

Age effect eliminated, cohort and time of measurement confounded:
    Compare A + C with B + D.

Each type of study design has advantages and disadvantages that need to be discussed.

Advantages and Disadvantages of Research Designs

The primary purpose of a cross-sectional study is to compare age groups. But this method makes it difficult to determine the exact cause of any detected age differences. For example, if intellectual decline is found, is it due to physical and mental deterioration with age, or to the life situations of the older groups? Older adults are generally less educated than younger adults and perform less effectively on intellectual tests. As a result, cross-sectional studies exaggerate intellectual decline with age. What cross-sectinal studies often attribute to age may in fact be due to cohort effects. Furthermore, comparing a sampling of twenty-year-olds with a sampling of persons over forty fails to show changes occurring in the intervening years. Are those changes gradual, sudden, or concentrated at specific ages?

The chief advantage of the cross-sectional approach is that data for different age groups can be obtained over the same time period, usually a brief one. Therefore, it is easier to obtain information and conclude the study fairly quickly.

A longitudinal study periodically compares the same group of people over a period of years, for example, from age forty-five to sixty. Obvious difficulties are the amount of time and money necessary to complete the study. In addition, researchers might die or lose interest. And subjects might move, leaving no address, or otherwise become unavailable. Some might even die before the study was completed. Consequently, the study results would be influenced by selective subject dropout and availability. Those who tended to perform poorly would become less available over time than those who performed well. As time passed, the most competent would remain, tending to minimize any effect of age on intellectual decline. If only the superior subjects remain, invalid conclusions could result.

The primary advantage of a longitudinal study is that it eliminates cohort effects. Because the same people are studied, changes with age and time really are due to these factors.

Time lag studies eliminate age effects but confound cohort and time measurements. Assuming time measurements have no effect (a reasonable assumption if the time between testing periods is short), then cohort effect may be partially determined. This method will not yield age differences (the subjects studied are the same age), but it does help differentiate other effects.

Cross-sequential studies tend to combine the advantages and disadvantages of both cross-sectional and longitudinal studies. They do not completely eliminate age-cohort-time effects. At best, only time or cohort effect can be eliminated at one time, leaving either age-cohort or age-time confounded. Sometimes one factor is assumed to have no effect in order to see what changes occur in the other factor. By analyzing the data in various ways, much more information can be obtained. For instance when analyzing the effect of age in an age-cohort analysis, assume that cohort has no effect.

Time-sequential studies are time lag analyses. Time or age effects can be eliminated separately, but not at the same time. Thus, when time is held constant, age and cohort are still confounded; when age is held constant, cohort and time are still confounded. However, by assuming one of the two has no effect, the changes in the other can be noted. Different methods of analysis can produce more meaningful data than only one method.

Cohort-sequential studies come closest to sorting out differences due to age versus cohort effects, but only if you assume that the time of testing has no effect.

Data-Gathering Methods

Some studies use various means of gathering information: psychological tests, observations, interviews, questionnaires, and case histories. The findings obtained by one method can be compared with those obtained by others to ensure consistent results. Data collected from written questionnaires or psychological tests are especially prone to erroneous conclusions, particularly with older adult subjects who have not been properly oriented and instructed in test taking. Data from observations, interviews, or case histories are vulnerable to researchers' subjective interpretations unless objective evaluation standards are established.

Experimental Research

Experimental research studies are usually conducted in laboratory settings in order to sort out and control variables, allowing only the desired factors to influence results. Certain studies lend themselves to experimental methods. For example, measuring physiological changes with age is accomplished best in a laboratory setting. Measuring changes in pulse rate, metabolism, respiratory volume, reaction time, and peripheral vision requires special laboratory equipment. Other changes, such as personality changes, are not easily assessed by experimental research methods.

Sampling

Random samples are often taken from groups intended for study. A truly representative sample of a population includes the same percentages of people from the different cultural, ethnic, socioeconomic, and educational backgrounds contained in the population. In addition, sufficient numbers are necessary to represent the much larger group. Unfortunately, practical considerations often prohibit such sampling.

These factors do not invalidate all studies. However, they do suggest that a study is more valid for the population studied, and that it would be unscientific to generalize and apply the findings to whole populations.

Test-Retest Intervals

Test-retest intervals also affect results. Long intervals between test and retest may not show important intervening changes. However, short intervals may not show important eventual changes. Or the results may be contradictory. An interval of two years or less may show an age-increase effect, whereas an interval of six to eight years may show a significant age-decrease effect. Therefore, care is needed when interpreting results based on excessively short or long test-retest intervals. Also recognize that those people retested at frequent intervals may show improvement, due not to any age changes but to the effect of test practice.

Terminal Drop

Studies of older adults are influenced by *terminal drop,* a decline in performance before death. Those who perform poorly or have declined from former levels tend to die sooner, reflecting their poorer health. A comparison of the decline scores of those who later die with the scores of survivors shows that the decline scores (terminal drop) are greater for those who soon succumb (Botwinick 1984).

Cautions

The careful student should consider these influential factors when evaluating the results of research studies. Research is a valuable tool in obtaining information, but careless evaluation can distort the truth.

SUMMARY

For years, psychologists focused their major attention on the study of children, adolescents, and abnormal adults. This focus was due to the emphasis on the importance of early childhood experiences, the individual notion that development stops with adolescence, and the fact that emotionally disturbed adults needed help. Now we recognize that early childhood experiences are not the only factors in predicting adult performance, that development continues for a lifetime, and that normal adults also need help. Therefore, adult developmental psychology has taken on new meaning and importance. It borrows from many disciplines and encompasses other branches of psychology to present a complete picture.

Adult development from a life-cycle viewpoint implies that life is composed of cycles, phases, or stages, each with its own distinctive characteristics, changes, and challenges. Life is not one continuous, unchanging flow of years. It is constantly changing, requiring transition and adaptation from one phase to the next. There is, however, some repetition of tasks from one phase to another, and some repetition among lives. Where similarities exist, people can learn from the repetition in their own lives and from the experiences of others.

We cannot assume that the stages of adult life are always clearly defined and inevitable. Adult development occurs not only because of inner changes (which are variable), but also because of changing environments, institutions, relationships, societal expectations, cultural influences, and political, economic, and social events. Life stages are not predestined according to some inborn psychological design. Developmental trajectories are modified by the effects of race, class, generation, sex, social changes, and many other factors.

In studying various life-cycle theories, remember that the exact age divisions assigned to the different phases are largely arbitrary and vary with different individuals and theories. Events that might happen during each phase should not become self-fulfilling prophecy, since infinite individual variations still exist. Research findings apply to groups, not to individuals, and are best used to interpret the present, not to predict the future.

This first chapter discusses the psychological life cycle theories of Buhler, Erikson, and Havighurst. In her research, Buhler emphasized the external events of life, internal reactions to these events, and the accomplishments of individuals during their life phases. She outlined five phases of the life span and demonstrated the parallels between biological and psychological development during each phase. She emphasized the human tendency toward fulfillment through self-actualization and self-realization.

Erikson outlined eight stages of lifetime development. In each stage, the individual is confronted with a psychosocial task that must be overcome before moving to the next stage. We examined the last three stages: young adulthood, middle adulthood, and late adulthood. The chief psychosocial tasks of these phases are to develop intimacy (young adulthood), generativity (middle adulthood), and ego integrity (late adulthood).

Havighurst divided the life span into six periods. Again, we examined the last three: early adulthood, middle age, and later maturity. The chief psychosocial tasks during early adulthood include marriage, starting a family, managing a home, starting a career, assuming civic responsibility, and finding social groups. Middle adulthood tasks are guiding teenagers, maintaining career performance, developing leisure activities, accepting the changes of middle life, relating to a spouse as a person, and adjusting to aging parents. In later maturity, one must adjust to physical changes, retirement, reduced income, and the death of a spouse. One must adapt social roles and establish satisfactory living arrangements.

This chapter also discusses the psychological studies of developmental phases during early and middle adulthood, as reported by Gould,

Levinson, and Vaillant. Only Vaillant's study was longitudinal; the others were cross-sectional views of life's phases. The age divisions are arbitrary, but there is some similarity of findings among the three researchers. All noted a period of transition between adolescence and early adulthood, during which people form "The Dream" of what they want to do and become. Only Levinson found a crisis period of transition, adjustment, and change as one enters the thirties. However, about 40 percent of Levinson's sample did not experience this crisis. For Gould and Vaillant, the entire period of the twenties and thirties was one of building and settling down.

All three researchers found a mid-life crisis associated with the forties, although the exact ages differ with each researcher. This crisis involves a reexamining of oneself, goals, and values to determine a direction for the next stage of life.

Periods of change and transition in human life are stimulated by many external forces: the socialization process that instills a social age clock, social and historical events, and specific (sometimes traumatic) happenings. Changes are also caused by internal forces: some biological (e.g., menopause), others emotional (e.g., anxiety). Normative transitions (usual and expected) usually are not as upsetting as idiosyncratic transitions (unusual and unexpected).

Psychology students must consider some important research issues when interpreting research results. Those issues include types of research designs, data-gathering methods, experimental research and its use, sampling methods, test-retest intervals, and other factors that influence results, such as terminal drop. Types of research designs include cross-sectional studies, longitudinal studies, time lag studies, and sequential studies. Each type has advantages and disadvantages. Some studies use several means of data gathering in order to compare the results of each method. Sampling definitely influences results. Samples of a particular group may be selected randomly, or a truly representative sample may be carefully chosen. Practical considerations often prevent the study of large numbers of subjects. However, it is unwise to generalize the findings from studies of limited samples and apply them to whole populations. Experimental research methods sort out and control variables so only the desired factors influence results. Such factors as test-retest intervals and terminal drop influence research results.

2

Early Adulthood

THE EARLY ADULT GROUP

Demographics

Adults now between twenty and thirty-nine constitute the *"baby boom" generation*. This generation began immediately after World War II, when the birthrate skyrocketed. It reached its peak in 1947 and remained high for the next fifteen years. Following are the ages in 1985 of people born during the postwar baby boom.

Birthdate	Age in 1985
1945	40
1947	38
1950	35
1955	30
1960	25

As a result of this high birthrate, this age group has shown the largest population gain of any cohort. This group now constitutes almost one-third (33 percent) of the total population of the United States (see Figure 2.1). Of this group, 12 percent are black, and females outnumber males by a small margin (37,673,000 females to 37,269,000 males).

The Happiest Years

One survey of 216 men and women, ages sixteen to sixty-seven, showed that approximately 40 percent of the respondents regarded the twenties as the best age of life. Eighteen percent chose the thirties. The middle years of life (the forties and fifties) were considered best by 19 percent. Only 2 percent chose the sixties (Chiriboga 1978). This finding agrees with other studies showing the young adult years to be the happiest.

When broken down into age groups, however, this same study indicated that each group reported the present a satisfying time of life. Most young adults felt that their age was the best age; but among those of

FIGURE 2.1   **Distribution of Resident Population, by Age, 1981**

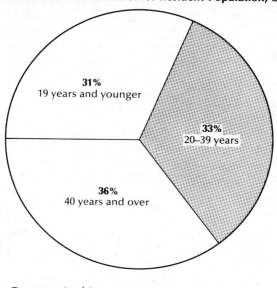

The median age of the population is 30 yrs. (1981 census data)

Adapted from: U.S. Department of Commerce, Bureau of the Census, *Statistical Abstract of the United States: 1982–83,* 103d ed. (Washington, D.C.: U.S. Government Printing Office, 1983).

preretirement age, **44** percent of the men and **61** percent of the women felt that the forties and after were the best periods of life (Chiriboga 1978). Since life expectancy at forty is still over thirty-six years, these individuals have nearly half a lifetime ahead. It is encouraging that most looked forward to those years with expectation and optimism.

THE MEANING OF ADULTHOOD

Adulthood means different things to different people. To a child, it means special privileges like staying up late or not having to go to school. To the child's parents, being an adult means acting grown up and assuming responsibility. To the adolescent, adulthood means being on one's own, having an apartment, and freedom from parental control.

Social Dimensions

Whatever else it is, the primary meaning of adulthood is social. One cannot declare oneself an adult; one is perceived as such. Inevitably, this perception reflects a mature, rational, and responsible person. It is unthinkable to call an undisciplined, irrational, undependable, socially irresponsible person an adult.

Biological Dimensions

Dictionaries define an adult as one who has attained full size and strength, a fully grown person. This definition implies biological maturity, reaching the limits of physical development and attaining reproductive capacity. Yet, this definition alone is inadequate. Adolescents in our culture may attain their full height and strength and become sexually mature but still behave childishly and dependently, their identities nebulous and their stations in life undetermined.

Emotional Dimensions

Being an adult also includes emotional maturity. It implies a high degree of emotional stability, including good impulse control, a high frustration tolerance, and freedom from violent mood swings. Another requirement of adulthood is to break childish dependency ties with parents and to function autonomously.

Legal Dimensions

Laws attempt to differentiate who should and should not be accorded adult rights and responsibilities. They designate chronological ages at which privileges are granted and duties required. Thus, the Twenty-sixth Amendment to the United States Constitution established the legal voting age as eighteen. Child labor laws partially define whether one is entitled to gainful employment and the type of work permitted at ages sixteen, eighteen, or twenty-one. Federal law restricts the age for military service and for obtaining contraceptives. Constitutional law limits membership in the United States House of Representatives to people twenty-five and over, in the Senate to age thirty and over, and election to the presidency of the United States to those thirty-five and over.

The states retain the privilege of deciding at what age to grant some other rights, for example, the age a person may purchase alcoholic beverages, obtain a driver's license, or marry without parental consent. States also decide the legal age for making binding contracts, obtaining credit, disposing of property, or being tried in court as an adult. Whatever age legislatures select, the decision also affects when adolescents may make decisions without parental consent and when they no longer are legally entitled to financial support from parents.

One problem of deciding adult status by law is that chronological age is not always the best determinant of capability. An eighteen-year-old may be eligible to vote but completely unqualified. The only positive value of automatic entitlement at eighteen is that all persons are treated equally. While the law can bestow adult status in one way, the person may not be an adult in other ways.

TRANSITION TO ADULTHOOD

Difficulties

Becoming an adult is a complicated process, especially in a pluralistic and highly industrialized society in which different segments seek to protect their own interests by erecting barriers to admission. Trade unions may require long periods of apprenticeship; businesses require years of formal education. Until the preparatory requirements of a group are fulfilled, one is denied adult membership in that society. As these requirements become more stringent, the age of admission to the adult labor force is delayed and the period between childhood and adulthood lengthens (Modell et al. 1976).

Passages and Rites

Primitive societies have definite *rites of passage* through which children become adults. When boys become sexually mature they may have to endure harsh, sometimes cruel, initiation ceremonies to test their courage, endurance, strength, and worthiness to be men. Circumcision rites are common to these ceremonies.

Among girls, initiation ceremonies are likely to center around the onset of menstruation, an obvious signal of approaching sexual maturity. Some societies require seclusion; most require ritual purification before the girl can assume the status of a woman.

In our culture, numerous rites of passage take place before adulthood can be reached. They include religious confirmations, Bar Mitzvahs, drivers' license tests, and school graduation ceremonies. Unlike primitive cultures, however, each rite in our culture is only one small part of the process of reaching adulthood. Even if various tests are passed, there may still be some question whether an individual is an adult in other ways (Rice 1984). This makes the passage more ambiguous and lengthy than in primitive societies.

Socialization

An important part of becoming an adult is the accompanying *socialization*. Socialization involves learning and adopting the norms, values, expectations, and social roles required by a particular group. It is the process that grooms a person for life in companionship with others.

Part of socialization is anticipatory: preparation for certain tasks. Education for a specific profession is one example. At other times, resocialization is required. An adult must relearn something or learn something new in anticipation of a new task or role. Thus, a college graduate may have to return to school before taking a job requiring additional knowledge. Resocialization may be necessitated by role changes, occupational transfers, changes in family structure, relocation, retirement or other reasons. Socialization does not happen only to children and adolescents in preparation for adulthood; it occurs throughout adulthood, particularly during periods of transition and preparation for new experiences.

Developmental Tasks

Becoming an adult also involves the successful completion of a number of developmental tasks. A developmental task is a "task which arises at or about a certain period of life of the individual, successful achievement of which leads to his happiness and to success with later tasks, while failure leads to unhappiness in the individual, disapproval by society, and difficulty with later tasks" (Havighurst 1972, 2). Each society defines what tasks must be accomplished and at what ages. Once these tasks are completed, the individual can enter another period or phase of life.

DEVELOPMENTAL TASKS OF THE TWENTIES

Developmental tasks of the twenties have been grouped in different ways. One arrangement is to group them into nine categories.

1. Achieving autonomy
2. Molding an identity
3. Developing emotional stability
4. Establishing and consolidating a career
5. Finding intimacy
6. Becoming part of congenial social groups and of a community
7. Selecting a mate and adjusting to marriage
8. Establishing residence and learning to manage a home
9. Becoming a parent and rearing children

Achieving Autonomy

Detaching oneself from parents is one important step in becoming an adult. During their teens, adolescents turn to their peers for companionship, emotional fulfillment, and guidance. This step helps break the close parental ties. However, adolescents generally still live at home, under the partial direction of parents. They are financially dependent on parents, and turn to them for assistance in countless ways.

At the same time, adolescents are anxious to separate from parents.

> They feel themselves to be halfway out of the family and are worried that they will be reclaimed by the family pull and not make it out completely. (Gould 1972, 37)

Establishing a separate residence helps in achieving autonomy, whether the residence is a dormitory room at school or an apartment in the community. Most adolescents say they look forward to getting their own apartment, but most have to wait a number of years before they can afford one. In the meantime, they have ambivalent feelings about parental separation: they wonder if they can make it on their own. One girl, away at college for the first time, remarked: "It's a lot easier living at home; you have your mother to do your laundry." She was learning that being on her own required assuming responsibility for dozens of small but necessary tasks.

Achieving emotional autonomy is even more important than physical separation. The task is to break the close, dependent emotional ties that have been formed, realigning those ties on the basis of equality—one adult to another. Becoming an adult does not mean ceasing to love one's parents; it means turning away from an emotional dependence on them and finding other love objects for emotional satisfaction and companionship. It is learning to make personal decisions and manage one's own life.

Molding an Identity

In detaching themselves from their families, adolescents gain an opportunity to form their personal identities. Individuals whose lives are inextricably wrapped up in those of their parents have more difficulty discovering who they are, what they think and feel, and what they want out of life. Separation at least provides the opportunity to become a unique person. Erikson (1968) suggests that identity formation neither begins nor ends with adolescence. It is a lifelong process of selection and assimilation of parental, peer, social, and self-perceptions and expectations. Establishing identity requires an individual to evaluate personal assets and liabilities and learn how to use them. Becoming an adult involves integrating various aspects of identity, resolving conflicts among them, and developing a complete personality.

Some aspects of identity take shape more easily than others. Generally, physical and sexual identities are established earliest; the onset of puberty forces people to come to terms with their physical and sexual selves. People who learn to accept their body images, their physical and sexual selves, and their sex roles develop positive identities in these areas. Social identity comes as they establish broadened social relationships, seek membership in a variety of social groups, and become part of a community.

Vocational, ideological, and moral identities evolve more slowly. Individuals must reach an advanced stage of cognitive growth and development that enables them to explore alternative ideas and courses of action. The exploration of and preparation for occupational alternatives is the most immediate task of college students. Religious and political ideologies are examined during late adolescence and early adulthood and may be in a state of flux for years. One author suggests that identity formation is the process of gaining authenticity; that is, arriving at a state of inner expansion in which we know our potentialities and possess the ego strength to direct their full reach (Sheehy 1976).

Developing *Emotional Stability*

A major task in becoming a mature adult is developing the capacity to tolerate tensions and frustrations without undue upset or anxiety. Frustrations are recognized as a part of life and are either overcome or accepted without undue hostility and aggression. During their twenties, young adults strive to avoid extreme emotions and to modulate their emotional tone, because they discover that emotional highs are followed by lows and sometimes by disappointments (Gould 1972). The ability to control emotions is one measure of the degree of maturity achieved (Douglas and Arenberg 1978). Various defense mechanisms are used to help control anxiety, but mature persons do not use them excessively or in ways that distort their perception of difficulties that must be faced and managed.

Mature individuals have positive self-concepts; inner doubts and conflicts about their worth and abilities have been resolved. With dependency conflicts resolved and the boundaries of self secure, a person no longer fears the loss of personal identity when seeking intimacy with others. If the person's gender identity is secure enough, there is no need to prove femininity or masculinity by compulsive sexual expression, through feminine passivity or seductiveness, or through masculine aggression. Adult men and women are secure in their sexual identities and roles. Free from inner doubt and tension, the individual can be as creative and productive as possible and can relate to others in mature relationships.

Establishing and Consolidating a Career

This task involves making an occupational commitment, completing one's education, entering the work world, gaining proficiency in one's work, and becoming economically independent. Most young adults have an emotional as well as a social and economic need to achieve (Shimonaka and Nakazato 1980). Career success provides a sense of fulfillment and worth. Enjoyable work contributes to personal happiness and adds meaning to life.

Finding Intimacy

"Intimacy includes the ability to experience an open, supportive, tender relationship with another person, without fear of losing one's own identity in the process of growing close" (Newman and Newman 1984, 384). Intimacy suggests the capacity to give of oneself, to share feelings and thoughts, and to establish mutual empathy. It may involve expressing sexual feelings; it does involve giving up isolation and complete independence and developing some dependent emotional ties.

This may be more difficult for males who, in our culture, have been conditioned to be independent and to hide tender emotions. Some individuals are ill at ease with tender feelings, intimate expressions of affection, and gentle caresses, so they erect barriers to protect their fragile egos from exposure (Waterman and Whitbourne 1982).

Becoming a Part of Congenial Social Groups and of a Community

Participation in congenial social groups is a psychosocial need of young adults. This process, begun in childhood and continued during adolescence, is consolidated during young adulthood.

Selecting a Mate and Adjusting to Marriage

In the 1800s, the median age of marriage was twenty-five for females and twenty-seven for males (Modell et al. 1976). Now, half of all persons who marry do so in their early twenties (twenty-one for females and twenty-three for males), often finding themselves unprepared for the responsibilities (U.S. Dept. of Commerce 1983). The earliest years of marriage are the most difficult, requiring extensive adjustments and readjustments as couples learn to live together harmoniously. Most young adults, however, are seriously committed to making their marriages work (Stein et al. 1978). Some disillusionment sets in when couples encounter difficulties, but most overcome these feelings and remain together (Gould 1972). For the one-third who divorce, the median duration of their marriages is 6.8 years (U.S. Dept. of Commerce 1983). Divorce is a traumatic experience, requiring numerous readjustments.

Establishing Residence and Learning to Manage a Home

Young adults must decide where and in what type of housing to live. More young adults are moving to the West and South than to other sections of the United States. First, they must choose between urban, suburban, or rural areas. Like the rest of the population, about 60 percent live in urban areas, but not necessarily in the inner city. Then, they must select an apartment or other rented unit, a mobile home, condominium, single-family home, or multiple-family dwelling. Typically, young adults rent an apartment and try to save money toward the purchase of their own home after marriage. As the price of single-family homes skyrockets, more couples are being forced to rent or buy into multiple-family dwellings. Learning to manage and maintain their own residence is a new experience for most young adults. It often requires years of experience before they can do so efficiently.

Becoming a Parent and Rearing Children

The numbers of persons remaining voluntarily childless are increasing, but they include only about 4 percent of married couples (Rice 1983). The others turn their attention to becoming parents and raising a family. This task requires major economic, social, and emotional adjustments as family responsibilities increase and marital roles are realigned. Due to the increasing pressures, marital satisfaction declines, usually reaching its lowest ebb when the children reach school age (Spanier, Lewis, and Cole 1975). The majority of couples are in their late twenties or early thirties during this period. Once these years pass, family responsibilities decline and pressures ease.

THE THIRTIES: REFLECTION, CRISES, ROOTING, AND EXTENDING

Adults in Their Thirties

Most adults in their thirties have been married for eight to ten years. For the most part, they report being happy in their marriages. However, some report maximum role strain as they strive to fulfill both vocational and family responsibilities. They have heavy financial obligations (a house, one or two cars, and a family). Most have one or two children of late preschool or early school age who require much of their time and attention. About half the wives work outside the home and thus are pressed for time to do everything expected of them. Some husbands are working harder and assuming more responsibility than ever before in their lives.

Many people whose marriages failed are divorced by their late twenties or early thirties. The wives usually have custody of the children, and for a while they struggle hard to survive on inadequate salaries and child support payments. Husbands contributing to the support of their children and ex-wives are burdened more than before. About half of the men and women who divorce are remarried within three years. The majority of the others remarry some time after. Most divorced fathers live apart from their own children in reconstituted families, usually as stepfathers.

It is a mistake, however, to put all adults in the same category when they reach their thirties. Levinson et al. (1976) found that about 40 percent do not experience any crisis at all. They continue to build their careers without interruption and are happy with their jobs. Having worked through the early adjustments of marriage and parenthood, they are reasonably happy with their situation. They generally enjoy life and all it offers. As one couple expressed it:

> We're happier than we have ever been. We now have most of the things we need, and more money than when we were younger. The children get along fine at school and in the neighborhood. We have a good marriage and a lot going for us. We really are fortunate.

These adults find their life pleasant and interesting and are happy.

Reflection

Others, however, become discontented. Up to this point, these adults were so intent on establishing their careers and setting up a home and family that they had no time to pause and reflect. With these goals accomplished, pressures ease and the opportunity for reflection presents itself (Gould 1975). After spending most of their twenties building their lives, they now begin to think about how they can tear them apart and change and reconstruct the pattern they have built up (Sheehy 1976). They begin to question the meaning of life and their own self and values (Stein et al. 1978). They ask, Am I really doing what I want to do? Isn't there more to life than just working at the same old job? They may desire a career change. If marriage has become routine, they consider divorce. As one thirty-year-old husband, who had married at nineteen, expressed it: "I've been married all of my life. I'd like to see what life is like out there." A more adequate income level provides more flexibility when considering options.

These adults thrive on challenges, hate day-to-day routine, and need new goals for which to strive. Once they accomplish certain goals, they become restless and search for new ones, enriching their lives by continued growth.

Crises

Other young adults become discontented because they are tired of struggling and solving problems. They weary of devoting themselves to doing what they are supposed to do, and want to be just what they are (Gould 1972). They listen to inner voices that they used to ignore. This is especially true of women who denied their own identities while devoting themselves to being wives and mothers. Women who gave up their jobs to marry and raise children now consider returning to work because the children are in school. Women who for years felt the urge to expand now grasp the opportunity. If their husbands and children cooperate, the transition is easier. But if family members see this as competition for the time and attention they want, these women may encounter massive struggles before gaining their independence (Sheehy 1976). Both men and women continue looking within, questioning their self, their values, and life itself. For the first time, they become aware of a time squeeze. They see that there is little time left to influence their children or to succeed in their chosen vocation. The crisis of the thirties involves sorting out conflicting desires and finding renewed integration and motivation to move ahead.

Rooting and Extending

The late thirties also can be a time of rooting and extending. After a period of reappraisal, working men and women focus on making their careers successful. Couples who have worked through their marital problems or remarried find renewed love and pleasure in each other's company. Satisfaction with children grows as parental responsibilities for their daily care diminish and as the children show evidence of more maturity and responsibility. Increasing personal and social maturity make interpersonal relationships more satisfying and harmonious. Finite time and its passage are accepted as realities, but a growing feeling exists that there is still time to make dreams come true if one hurries (Gould 1972).

SUMMARY

Adults now in their twenties and thirties have shown the largest population gain of any cohort, primarily because of the high birthrate during the fifteen years following World War II. These adults are highly educated and fairly happy with their jobs. Most are married and have children. Despite the high divorce rate, most of them remarry.

Being an adult has social, biological, emotional, and legal dimensions. Society considers one who assumes expected social responsibilities an adult. Biologically, an adult is a fully grown, physically mature person. Emotionally, an adult is one who evidences emotional maturity. Legally, adult rights and responsibilities are granted at fixed ages.

The transition to adulthood is long and involved in highly industrialized societies, where different segments of society formulate their own requirements for adulthood and erect barriers to admission until certain qualifications are met. Primitive societies have definite rites of passage. Our society has numerous rites, including religious confirmation, licenses, and graduations.

Becoming an adult also involves successfully completing a number of developmental tasks: achieving autonomy, molding an identity, developing emotional stability, establishing and consolidating a career, finding intimacy, becoming part of congenial social groups and of a community, selecting a mate and adjusting to marriage, establishing residence and learning to manage a home, and becoming a parent and rearing children.

Adults in their thirties can be divided into at least three groups. Those in the first group, about 40 percent of the total, are happy and contented. Passage into their thirties involved no crisis. They continue to build their careers without interruption, are fairly happy in their marriages and as parents, and generally find life pleasant and interesting.

Members of the second group, who are generally successful in their developmental tasks, find entrance into the thirties a time of crisis. They begin to feel restless and bored. Most of their goals have been accomplished and pressures have eased. Now they need new challenges. They question themselves, their values, their lives, their jobs, and their marital situations, and they rethink their course in life. Some consider job changes or divorce to escape day-to-day routine and boredom.

Adults in the third group also find entrance into the thirties a crisis. They have grown tired of struggling and solving problems, and weary of doing what they are expected to do. They want to be themselves and do what they want for their own satisfaction and happiness. Like the second group, they look within, questioning their vaues, their goals, and life itself in an attempt to find fulfillment. They also recognize a time squeeze in which there is less time to do what they want.

Overall, the thirties is a time of reflection, crisis, rooting, and extending.

3

Middle Adulthood

WHO IS MIDDLE-AGED?

When does *middle age* begin and end? There are no generally accepted ages. Chronologically, the mid-thirties is the midpoint of life for those in Western culture. But in underdeveloped societies with poor health care, the midpoint of life is the mid-twenties. Many government census reports define middle age as the ages forty-five through sixty-four. But most people would not accept the forty-four-year-old as a young adult nor the sixty-four-year-old as middle-aged. Biologically, some consider middle age begins when reproductive potential ends, but this occurs twenty to thirty years earlier in women than men. Are the forty-nine-year-old woman and the seventy-nine-year-old man middle-aged? It seems very discriminatory. Other people consider themselves middle-aged when children leave home, but this varies from thirty-five to seventy or so years of age. Still others say, "You are as young as you feel." Obviously, there is little agreement on when middle age begins and ends.

The age divisions by Levinson et al. (1978) seem the most sensible. He describes middle adulthood as forty to fifty-nine years of age, and *late adulthood* as age sixty on. These age divisions are adopted in this book. Forty to forty-five is a period of mid-life transition; sixty to sixty-five is a period of transition during late adulthood (Levinson 1977). Each transitional period links the previous period with the following period and brings a new set of developmental tasks. Transitional periods are necessary to reexamine priorities, make new choices, and commit oneself to a revised life structure.

DEMOGRAPHICS

Adult men and women ages forty through fifty-nine represent 20.1 percent of the population (a little over one out of every five persons) in the United States (U.S. Dept. of Commerce 1983). The middle-aged population is increasing, however, as the babies born after World War II grow older. The cohort born in 1947 will be forty in 1987, ushering in the largest group of middle-aged adults in the history of the country. By the year 2000, middle-aged adults (forty to fifty-nine) will represent more than one-fourth (26.9 percent) of the United States population (U.S. Dept. of Commerce February 1980b). Figure 3.1 shows the trends.

THE PARADOX OF MIDDLE AGE

Middle age has been described both as a wonderful time of life and as a period of crisis (Borland 1978). Both of these views, however contradictory, need to be examined.

The Positive, No Crisis View

Middle age has been described as the prime of life (Borges and Dutton 1976), partly because it is a period of maximum capacity and ability to handle a highly complex environment and a highly differentiated self (Neugarten 1968). Middle-aged adults control most of the social and economic resources in the country. They are the nation's decision makers. They form the bulk of the employed generation and enjoy the privileges and responsibilities associated with productivity (Bader 1980). The middle-aged individual is more mature, grasps reality better, exercises better judgment, and possesses strategies for coping with life. As one woman expressed it:

> I know what will work in most situations and what will not. I am well beyond the trial and error stage of youth. I now have a set of guidelines. . . . I am practiced. (Neugarten 1968, 97)

Middle-aged men also sense a heightened capacity to manage the environment, an increased sense of autonomy and authority, and a feeling of expertise. Upper middle-class men particularly take great pride in their objectivity, polish, ease of operation, and incisiveness (Clausen 1976).

Middle age is a time of new personal freedom. The children are launched, allowing couples more time for their own activities. Personal income is at a maximum, and people can afford leisure-time activities, luxuries, and a life-style once prohibitive. Work life is characterized by an increased intellectual ability to make decisions, high-status jobs, and relatively good physical and mental health allowing one to work regularly (Jackson 1974). Middle age has been described as a time of expanding family networks and social roles, such as grandparenthood, and a period of marital life that is equally or more satisfying than the parental years (Glenn 1975).

Some studies of life satisfaction, fun, or happiness substantiate this positive view of middle age. Cameron (1972, 1975) conducted 7,000 interviews of males and females between the ages of 4 and 103 and found very few relationships between mood and age, or the amount of fun and happiness reported and age. Nor was there any evidence of depressed or

FIGURE 3.1   Population Estimates, 1978 and 2000, United States

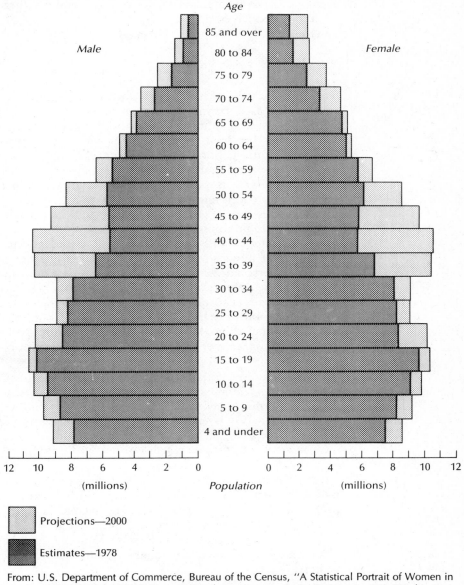

Projections—2000

Estimates—1978

From: U.S. Department of Commerce, Bureau of the Census, "A Statistical Portrait of Women in the United States: 1978," *Current Population Reports,* Series P–23, No. 100 (Washington, D.C.: U.S. Government Printing Office, February 1980), p. 5.

negative moods among middle-aged males or females. Longitudinal data from the Duke University studies confirmed the finding that life satisfaction neither rose nor declined as the subjects passed through the middle years of life (Palmore and Luikart 1972). But the degree of satisfaction varied with individuals. It was strongly related to health, sexual enjoyment, and involvement in social organizations, rather than to age itself (Palmore and Kivett 1977).

The Negative, Crisis View

The opposite view of middle age portrays it in negative terms. It describes middle age as a period of decline in physical stamina, general health, youthfulness, and glamour (Jackson 1974; Rosenberg and Farrell 1975). One reaches the final career plateau, with its accompanying disappointment, frustration, boredom, and fear of youthful colleagues (Bardwick 1975). There are financial responsibilities for adolescent and young adult children, as well as parents. Intergenerational conflict increases. It is a period of boredom and complacency with a tired marriage, and there are increasing feelings of emotional loss as children leave home, or as friends, a spouse, or aging parents die.

More importantly, middle age is described as a period of crisis, with a number of dimensions. Middle age represents a crisis of time, a realization of personal mortality. Time is running out, and one must act in some definite, important, and dangerous way.

This leads also to a crisis of goals and roles. A person asks, What have I done with my life? Where is it going (Gould 1979, 3)? Goals once ardently pursued no longer seem as important. A forty-seven-year-old computer programmer reflected on the monotony of his life.

> As I was driving to work, a big truck had a flat tire. Cars were backed up for miles and miles. I sat in a stalled car, staring at smelly cars all around me, inhaling monoxide from exhausts. I said to myself, "What the hell am I doing? This is my life?" For more than twenty years, since I finished graduate school, I've been making this same trip—it's crazy. I hate it. Locked in a hot car, stuck on a highway. (adapted from Davitz and Davitz 1979)

Women who have devoted themselves primarily to home and family may be especially upset when the last child is launched if they have not prepared for a life of their own. The second half of life may require a complete reorientation of their life roles and goals.

Middle age represents a crisis of values. Adults become more aware of current value changes that conflict with their traditional values. LeShan writes:

> We are caught in the middle between the idealism of what we have tried to do all our lives, and the feelings of despair that we failed. A lot of us believed that strong unions, social security, and unemployment insurance would wipe out poverty; there are more poor and their plight is more terrible today. We believed that science would work for the betterment of man's life on earth— all we had to do was learn, discover, invent, and so we have the atomic bomb, the pollution of our air and water. . . . (LeShan 1973)

LeShan continues:

> We are caught in the middle of a sexual revolution as well. When I was a growing and impressionable girl, I could not conceive of anything more romantic or passionate than seeing Leslie Howard kiss the palm of a girl's hand. Today I feel a vague sense of guilt because I'm not dying to try fifty-seven new varieties of sexual activities and positions. . . . I have had to adjust in my middle age to attitudes about sexual relations that have made me embarrassed and ashamed of the "prehistoric romanticism" of my youth. (LeShan 1973, 17)

It doesn't take middle-aged adults long to discover they are also involved in a crisis of authority, especially with their children. For years, their children needed guidance and advice. Now, as adolescents or young adults, they seek independence, the right to govern their own lives and make their own decisions. Some parents have difficulty letting go and relating to their children as growing adults. It is difficult for parents to accept that their advice, however wise, is no longer sought. One of their most important roles as guide and teacher is lost.

Overall, these crises represent a crisis of identity. Adults have to rethink who they are, what they want from life, what they value, and what their roles are. This involves some personality restructuring and adapting to changing situations. This task is never easy.

Which View?

Actually, both views are correct. Mid-life can be a happy, satisfying time and a period of crisis. The word *crisis* has a negative connotation. It implies doomsday, or an emergency, when it should emphasize a turning point, the need for change and adaptation (Robertson 1978). Change of any kind can cause stress, but it can also be a positive, motivating force to change one's values, goals, and roles in ways that achieve more meaning and satisfaction. For example, the departure of the last child from home is considered problematic, and researchers speak of the empty nest syndrome. But a child's departure does not typically have an enduring negative effect. It can be a great relief. Adjustments are required, but most couples are subsequently happier during this period of their married lives (Palmore et al. 1979). The changes accompanying middle age do not have to be crises (Lawrence 1980).

DEVELOPMENTAL TASKS OF MIDDLE ADULTHOOD

Middle age presents a number of challenges or developmental tasks. If these challenges are met and the conflicts resolved, middle age can be a time of continued growth, much personal satisfaction, and happiness. If these psychosocial tasks are not accomplished, however, the period can be one of stagnation and increasing disillusionment (Erikson 1959). Here, the tasks are divided into nine categories, representing a slight alteration and expansion of those delineated by Havighurst (1972).

1. Adjusting to the physical changes of middle age
2. Finding satisfaction and success in one's occupational career
3. Assuming adult social and civic responsibility
4. Launching children into responsible, happy adulthood
5. Revitalizing marriage
6. Reorienting oneself to aging parents
7. Realigning sex roles
8. Developing social networks and leisure-time activities
9. Finding new meaning in life

Adjusting to the Physical Changes of Middle Age

The day comes when some adults realize they are paunchy and out of shape; they cannot run as fast, lift as much, or perform as much physical work without tiring. Some women equate their loss of reproductive capacity at menopause with a loss of sexuality and youthfulness. These physical changes of aging require psychological adjustments. Those who have always emphasized youthfulness must learn to value maturity and wisdom over physical attractiveness. Physical changes also require adjustments in life-style and health habits to keep as fit and healthy as possible.

Finding Satisfaction and Success in One's Occupational Career

Ordinarily, middle age is the most fruitful period of professional and creative work. Middle-agers become the senior persons at the office, due a certain amount of respect and deference because of experience and seniority.

But several things can happen. Their superiors may take them for granted and pass them over for promotions. Or, they may become bored or disillusioned with their work. An assistant sales manager of a large corporation told his story at forty-three.

> I was brought up in the old school. Work hard and you got it made. You can't miss. So what does it get you? I've found out. . . .
>
> I was at the office. . . . Out comes one of the vice-presidents with a young guy next to him. He greets me and we talk and he turns and tells this kid, "Want you to meet Bob Henning, one of our steady hands in sales." He grabs my shoulder and says, "People like Bob are rocks around here. Firm couldn't get along without our old steadies."
>
> That afternoon our division gets an announcement about a new manager. That kid. You know, I sat there with that memo, and I kept hearing

"old steady" pounding in my head. . . . Passed over for a kid—maybe thirty. Takes the wind out of you. Twenty-two years, and all you got to show for it is a slap on the back and "old steady." (Davitz and Davitz 1979, 12)

Middle age may be a time of unfulfilled expectations. The realization that the dreams of earlier years are not going to come true comes as quite a shock.

A more positive awareness may also develop. Realizing they no longer find their work interesting and challenging, adults begin to rethink what they want to do for the second half of their lives. They modify the dream in terms of new directions or locations in their present occupation, or in terms of a completely different career. They look for new careers, offering challenge and fun. Charles Darrow at forty-five lost his job as a stove salesman; he invented the game Monopoly, which earned him more than a million dollars. Jane Pfeiffer, who turned down an offer to join President Carter's cabinet, was elected chairman of the National Broadcasting Company at forty-seven. Many middle-aged women enter the job market during this period of time.

Assuming Adult Social and Civic Responsibility

Adults forty to sixty years old have been called "the ruling class" or "the command generation" (Stevenson 1977). Although they make up only one-fifth of the population, they control our society and social institutions. They are the norm bearers, the decision makers, the office holders. Their participation in community life is essential for society's progress. Ordinarily, community concerns and participation increase during these years.

Launching Children into Responsible, Happy Adulthood

When men marry at the median age of twenty-three and women at the median age of twenty-one, the average father is fifty-three and the average mother fifty-one when the last child leaves home (Rice 1983). But before this day occurs, there are long years preparing dependent children for independent adult living. Ordinarily, children's dependency on parents gradually lessens and parental control slowly wanes, until the children are capable of managing their own lives. Occasionally, the children are dependent because the parents will not let go. They continue to support their twenty-five-year-old, unemployed son living on a commune in Pennsylvania when they should have stopped long ago (Spingarn 1977). Some parents go to the other extreme, pushing their teenagers out of the house before they are ready for independence.

Once the children are launched, some parents are miserable because their children do not fulfill their expectations.

> We were the first parents in the era of the child-centered family; when we became parents our children tended to come first. . . . We were the first crop of parents to take our children's failures and limitations as an indication of *our* inadequacy, not theirs; the first to believe even briefly, that one could aspire to being a perfect parent. (LeShan 1973, 16)

Part of the developmental task at this point is to let go of the responsibility, as well as the control, and not feel guilty when the children make mistakes.

Revitalizing Marriage

Marital needs depend on what the marriage has experienced over the years. It is common for marital satisfaction to decline during the early and middle years of the life cycle (Schram 1979; Spanier et al. 1975). If partners have been busy with personal career advancements, raising children, or separate community affairs and social activities and have neglected one another, the marriage may be in trouble. Lack of communication, infrequent demonstration of affection, and failure to work out differences result in misunderstanding, frustration, resentment, and increased alienation. A couple whose children are independent now have only one another. They face the task of working out problems, eliminating resentments, getting reacquainted, and being close all over again. Goldstine (1977) suggests that there are three cycles in most marriages—falling in love, falling out of love, and falling back in love—and that the last cycle is the most difficult and rewarding. People whose marriages failed during early adulthood have since remarried. The challenge is to revitalize troubled, intact marriages. Some cannot be revitalized, and the couple may divorce in mid-life, often remarrying and starting over. Only a small percentage are widowed during middle adulthood and have to adjust to living without a spouse.

Reorienting Oneself to Aging Parents

By the time adults reach forty, their parents are anywhere from fifty-eight to eighty years of age, with sixty-five to seventy most common. Therefore, during middle adulthood children watch their parents grow old, retire, perhaps become ill, and die.

This presents several challenges to middle-aged adults. Watching parents grow old is a sad and often upsetting experience. Adjusting to their death is even more difficult. Middle-agers become more responsible for providing assistance to aging parents: economic support, personal care, transportation, food, companionship, medical help, housekeeping or yard help, or a place to live. Only 10 percent of married elderly couples and 17 percent of widows and widowers actually live with a married child; but more than three-fourths of aged parents live within a thirty-minute drive from at least one of their children (Rice 1983).

Middle-agers have been called the "sandwich generation," the generation between aging parents and young adult offspring. Young adult children may still make demands and aging parents may need them. Middle-agers are the ones expected to give and to help out, which puts added pressure on them.

Realigning Sex Roles

Once children are independent, there are more opportunities to develop those personal aspects that were neglected during the years of parental responsibility. Crossing of sex roles is more apparent. Women become more assertive and men become more affiliative (Robertson 1978). One reason is that women become less dependent on their husbands when they start working outside the home. This increasing economic independence gives them more authority, and the husband is called on to perform more services formerly provided by the wife. Some husbands object to their wives' independence and to their own revised roles. Realigning masculine-feminine roles is quite common during middle adulthood.

Developing Social Networks and Leisure-time Activities

Middle age brings a shift in the focus of social activities. Parents previously involved in family-centered social activities find an increasing need for couple-centered activities. Teenagers go out with friends. Grown children move out of the house, leaving the couple to their own resources. As a result, adult friendships assume greater importance.

Mid-life may bring increased interest in having fun, in pursuing one's own interests and hobbies, or in developing entirely new leisure-time pursuits. It is not unusual for middle-agers to explore interests that they ignored during their child-rearing years. Some travel to places they always longed to visit.

Pfeiffer and Davis (1971) found that many middle-aged persons were unprepared to use their leisure time. Vacations were institutionalized events involving a trip of two to four weeks. Otherwise, these adults spent twelve to fourteen hours per week watching television and about eight and one-half hours per week reading. Sports, hobbies, and volunteer work took up minimal time. They reported spending about three hours per week just sitting. The challenge is to use leisure time in creative and personally satisfying ways (Stevenson 1977).

Finding New Meaning in Life

The overall goal of the middle years is to find new meaning in life. This should be a period of introspection, in which to examine oneself in terms of feelings, attitudes, values, and goals. There is a need to redefine one's identity and to answer the questions: Who am I? Where do I go from here? According to Levinson et al. (1978), these are years of transition ending in the culmination of adulthood, a time of rejuvenation of the self and enrichment of one's life. According to Erikson (1959), it is a period of generativity or stagnation.

SUMMARY

There is little agreement on when middle age begins and ends. It depends in part on one's subjective point of view. For purposes of discussion, this book includes the ages forty through fifty-nine, which coincides with Levinson's stage. According to this age division, middle-aged men and women represent a little more than one out of every five persons in the United States.

There are conflicting views of middle age. One is that middle age is the prime of life because it is a period of maximum capacity and ability to handle complex problems and the self. Middle-agers are more mature, have a better grasp of reality, and exercise better judgment than when they were younger. Their sense of autonomy increases as the responsibilities of parenthood wane.

The other point of view is negative, describing a period of physical decline, a leveling off in one's career, increased financial responsibilities both for children and parents, a time of boredom and complacency, and a time of loss as children leave home and parents die. Most importantly, this view describes a period of crisis: a crisis of time, as one senses personal mortality, a crisis of goals and roles, and a crisis of values, as one's value system becomes outdated. In addition, there is a crisis of authority, the loss of control over one's children, and a crisis of identity, as adults rethink who they are and what they want from life.

Actually, both views are correct. Mid-life can be both a happy, satisfying time of life and a period of crisis. So much depends on how one adjusts and grows.

Middle-agers are also faced with a number of developmental tasks: adjusting to physical changes of middle age, finding satisfaction and success in one's career, assuming social and civic responsibility, launching children into responsible, happy adulthood, reorienting oneself to aging parents, revitalizing marriage, realigning sex roles, developing social networks and leisure-time activities, and finding new meaning in life. The overall goal of middle age is to find new meaning in life, through introspection and a redefinition of one's identity in answer to the questions: Who am I? Where do I go from here? Middle age can be the culmination of adulthood, a time of rejuvenation and enrichment of life.

4

Late Adulthood

DEMOGRAPHICS

Proportions of Elderly

The population of the world is growing older. Figure 4.1 shows the increase in the proportion of elderly (aged sixty and above) in England and

FIGURE 4.1   Proportion of Elderly Persons (Aged 60 and Above) in England (including Wales) and in France Since the Eighteenth Century

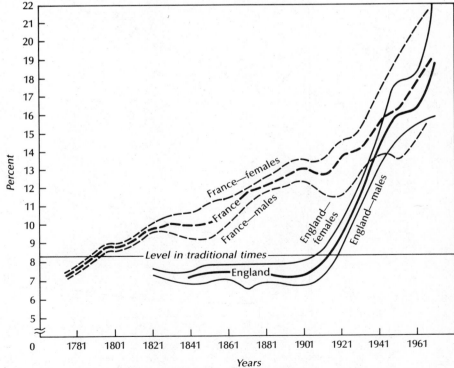

From: P. Laslett, "Societal Development and Aging," *Handbook of Aging and the Social Sciences,* R. H. Binstock and E. Shanas, eds. (New York: Van Nostrand Reinhold, 1976), 104.

France since the eighteenth century. The increase since 1911 is particularly pronounced.

The percentage of elderly in the United States is less than in France and England, although the percentages are increasing. Figure 4.2 shows the increases in the elderly population in the United States since 1950 and the projection to the year 2000. The general rise in the birthrate, partic-

FIGURE 4.2   Proportion of Elderly People in the Total United States Population, 1950–2000

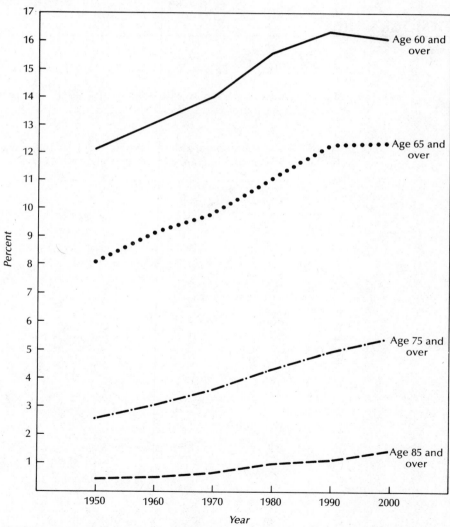

Adapted from: J. C. Siegel, "Prospective Trends in the Size and Structure of the Elderly Population, Impact of Mortality Trends, and Some Implications," *Current Population Reports*, Series P–23 No. 78 (Washington, D.C.: U.S. Department of Commerce, Bureau of the Census, January 1979), 8.

ularly up to the early 1920s, is the principal factor accounting for these increases. Declining death rates, plus the heavy volume of immigration before World War I, have also augmented the number of elderly persons. The drop in the rate of increase commencing in 1990 reflects the lower birthrate during the depression years. Between 2005 and 2010, the large cohort born during the postwar baby boom after 1945 will reach sixty and the percentage of elderly persons will increase very rapidly. By the year 2020, approximately 22 percent of the United States population will be sixty or over (Siegel 1979). Between 1970 and 1990, the group sixty and over will increase about two and one-half times faster than the total population.

There are a number of important implications to the increase in the proportion of elderly. As the elderly increase in number, they wield more political power and receive more and more national attention (Peterson et al. 1976; Randall 1977). Related social problems also increase. One such problem is the increase in dependency ratios: the ratio of Americans sixty-five and over to Americans eighteen to sixty-four who might be expected to support the elderly through public transfer programs. In 1981, the dependency ratio was nineteen Americans aged sixty-five or over to every one hundred who were eighteen to sixty-four years old. In the year 2030, the ratio probably will increase to more than thirty to one hundred (Treas 1981). This means there would be slightly more than three working Americans for each person over sixty-five. Eventually, the costs of meeting the elderly's needs may outstrip society's capacity to provide for them. Medical services, housing facilities, social resources, and various public and private support systems will be severely strained. Liberal retirement benefits, financed by a younger generation, may be feasible for a small cohort of the aged but not for the aging baby boom cohort.

Where Do the Elderly Live?

Older persons comprise a far bigger part of the population in some states than in others (see Table 4.1). Florida has the largest percentage of persons sixty-five and over; Alaska has the smallest ("65 and Over—Where They Are" 1982). Surprisingly, it is not only warm weather states that have the greatest percentage of elderly. Northern states, including South Dakota, Pennsylvania, Maine, North Dakota, Wisconsin, and Minnesota, have a large percentage, whereas Hawaii, which has the warmest year-round temperature, has a small percentage. The two states with the largest total populations, New York and California, have only an average percentage of elderly.

The changes in elderly population concentrations have not been uniform across regions or within metropolitan or nonmetropolitan areas. Some states or regions, including Florida, the North Central states, and New England, have comparatively high numerical concentrations due to differential growth in the aged population within the last few decades. In addition, central cities and some rural areas tend to have disproportionally large concentrations of elderly, whereas suburban areas generally have a small percentage of aged. These concentrations reflect growth in place as

TABLE 4.1   Percent of Population of Each State in the United States Age 65 or Over, 1981

	Residents 65 or Over	Share of Population
Florida	1,759,000	17.3%
Arkansas	320,000	13.9%
Iowa	394,000	13.6%
Rhode Island	130,000	13.6%
South Dakota	92,000	13.4%
Missouri	658,000	13.3%
Pennsylvania	1,571,000	13.2%
Nebraska	208,000	13.2%
Kansas	311,000	13.1%
Massachusetts	739,000	12.8%
Maine	144,000	12.7%
North Dakota	82,000	12.5%
New York	2,187,000	12.4%
West Virginia	243,000	12.4%
Oklahoma	382,000	12.3%
Wisconsin	578,000	12.2%
Minnesota	490,000	12.0%
Connecticut	376,000	12.0%
New Jersey	883,000	11.9%
Oregon	315,000	11.9%
Arizona	326,000	11.7%
Mississippi	295,000	11.7%
District of Columbia	74,000	11.7%
Tennessee	533,000	11.6%
Alabama	452,000	11.5%
Kentucky	418,000	11.4%
Vermont	59,000	11.4%
New Hampshire	106,000	11.3%
Illinois	1,288,000	11.2%
Ohio	1,199,000	11.1%
Indiana	599,000	11.0%
Montana	87,000	11.0%
Washington	448,000	10.6%
North Carolina	628,000	10.5%
Delaware	62,000	10.4%
California	2,493,000	10.3%
Michigan	940,000	10.2%
Idaho	98,000	10.2%
Texas	1,412,000	9.6%
Georgia	535,000	9.6%
Virginia	523,000	9.6%
Louisiana	414,000	9.6%
Maryland	409,000	9.6%
South Carolina	300,000	9.5%
New Mexico	121,000	9.1%
Colorado	255,000	8.6%
Nevada	72,000	8.5%
Hawaii	81,000	8.3%
Wyoming	38,000	7.7%
Utah	114,000	7.5%
Alaska	12,000	2.9%

From: "65 and Over—Where They Are," *U.S. News and World Report* (July 5, 1982): 66.

well as movements of young people from the country and city to suburbia, leaving concentrations of elderly behind (Golant 1975; Graff and Wiseman 1978; Lichter et al. 1981).

Sex Ratios and Life Expectancy

The number of men in the older population is considerably less than the number of women. In 1981, there were sixty-seven males to every one hundred females age sixty-five and over. The ratio drops to fifty-five to one hundred at age seventy-five and over, and to forty-four to one hundred at age eighty-five and over (Siegel 1979). The discrepancy is due to the longer life expectancy of women. In 1979, life expectancy at birth was 69.9 years for men and 77.6 years for women (U.S. Dept. of Commerce 1983). Table 4.2 shows the life expectancy of males and females age fifty-five and over. At age sixty, females are expected to live an average of five years longer than males. Note that by age eighty-five, part of this gap in life expectancy has been closed. Rural farm areas continue to show the largest proportion of males to females, reflecting more husband and wife families and a lower male mortality rate.

ATTITUDES TOWARD AGING AND THE AGED

Ageism

The term *ageism* was coined in 1968 by Robert Butler, a physician and former director of the National Institute of Aging. He used the word to

TABLE 4.2   Life Expectancy, by Sex and Race, at Each Age 55 and Over, United States, 1979

Age in 1979	White		Black		Total
	Male	Female	Male	Female	
55	21.2	26.7	18.8	24.0	23.9
56	20.4	25.9	18.2	23.2	23.1
57	19.6	25.0	17.6	22.5	22.3
58	18.9	24.2	17.0	21.8	21.5
59	18.2	23.4	16.5	21.1	20.8
60	17.5	22.6	15.9	20.4	20.0
61	16.8	21.8	15.4	19.8	19.3
62	16.1	21.0	14.9	19.1	18.6
63	15.5	20.2	14.4	18.5	17.9
64	14.8	19.5	13.9	17.9	17.3
65	14.2	18.7	13.3	17.2	16.6
70	11.3	15.0	10.7	13.9	13.4
75	8.8	11.7	8.6	11.5	10.6
80	6.9	9.0	7.8	10.7	8.4
85 and Over	5.5	7.0	6.8	9.2	6.7

From: U.S. Department of Commerce, Bureau of the Census, *Statistical Abstract of the United States, 1982, 83* (Washington, D.C.: U.S. Government Printing Office, 1983), Table 107, 72.

describe deep and profound prejudice against the elderly. Like *sexism* and *racism,* ageism represents discrimination of one group against another, in this case based on age. Ageism can also apply to prejudice against the young, but when applied to the elderly it reflects negative attitudes and feelings toward them, unfair and false stereotyping, differential medical or employment treatment, and emotional rejection. It may involve disdain and dislike, efforts to avoid contact, and discriminatory practices in housing or other services. It may make them the subjects of thoughtless epithets, cartoons, or jokes. Or it may result in the denial of proper medical care or employment for which they are qualified, geographical isolation, complete neglect, or institutionalization.

Ageism assumes many forms in our society. An examination of prescription drug advertising in two journals *(Medical Economics* and *Geriatrics)* generally showed the elderly as active people, but the written descriptions of them were negative. They were described as aimless, apathetic, debilitated, disruptive, hypochondriacal, insecure, needing insatiable reassurance, low in self-esteem, out of control, sluggish, seclusive, and temperamental (Smith 1976). Of course, these ads were written to persuade people to buy certain products that would help them avoid these characteristics. However, more and more positive ads are being written showing older people who look young and vigorous, who take good care of themselves, and who stay younger than their years.

Ageism is evident in various professions. One study, which examined the attitudes of the clergy toward work with the elderly, revealed that the clergy preferred youth and younger adults to the aged (Longino and Kitson 1976). One study of sixty-nine graduate students in the fields of social work, law, and medicine showed that not one student registered a first choice preference for working with the elderly (Geiger 1978). An examination of the curriculum of the University of Michigan, where these same students were studying, revealed no required courses dealing specifically with gerontological content. On the other hand, the number of courses in aging has skyrocketed in recent years, and they are well attended, especially by professionals in the field who seek the training they missed previously. The author has also found considerable interest in courses in aging among young undergraduate students.

Television

Television perpetuates a negative image of the elderly. Commercials portray nice eighty-year-old grandmothers (today many are forty) in old-fashioned clothes, all agog over a laundry detergent. Most often they are shown buying laxatives or denture cleansers. Researchers at the University of Pennsylvania indicated that the elderly represented less than 3 percent of the major characters on prime-time, dramatic programming, and most of them were shown as ugly, toothless, sexless, incontinent, senile, confused, and helpless (Tennenbaum 1979). The elderly are often pictured living in nursing homes, when actually only 6 percent of people over sixty-five are institutionalized (U.S. Dept. of Commerce 1979c).

There have been a few exceptions to these negative images. Problems of the aged have become a more viable subject for television; they are now being shown as misunderstood by the young and perfectly capable of getting along without their children's help. In fact, the capabilities of the aged, especially as represented by national leaders and entertainment figures, are gaining recognition.

Humor

A number of studies have analyzed the humorous portrayal of the elderly in jokes, birthday cards, and cartoons (Richman 1977). Sheppard (1981) analyzed sixty cartoons dealing with older people and identified four thematic categories: disparagement of the aged, ineffectuality, obsolescence, and isolation. Smith (1976) analyzed the content of ninety-five magazine cartoons depicting the elderly and found a generally negative portrayal. The most frequent negative themes were unsightly physical appearance, sexual dysfunction, and ultraconservatism. A typical example is "Granny" who appears occasionally in *Playboy*. She is generally shown as an active, resourceful, sexually oriented woman. But she is pictured with grossly sagging breasts, a distended stomach, and disproportionally thin legs. Consequently, male characters are repulsed by her appearance and amorous attempts. In one cartoon, she was standing nude before a group of stagecoach robbers, one of whom was saying, "Honest, lady, we don't *want* to rape anyone" (Smith 1976, 410).

Birthday cards deal most often with the subject of age itself: the associated physical and mental characteristics, the inevitability of growing older, the concealment of age, aging as a state of mind, the aging of others but not oneself, and concern about age (Demos and Jache 1981). The emphasis on decline in physical appearance is illustrated by the following card:

> Another birthday? You're not old until you go to the beauty parlor on Tuesday, come home on Thursday . . . And still look like you did on Monday. (Demos and Jache 1981, 212)

Demos and Jache conclude their study by suggesting that birthday messages appear to reflect stereotypes about aging and consequently may reinforce ageist ideas.

Literature

The views of older people presented in contemporary poetry and works of fiction present a contradictory picture of the aged. An analysis of old age in eighty-seven contemporary novels revealed that the majority of characters were middle-class WASPs, depicted by authors of the WASP middle-class (Sohngen 1977). Institutionalization of the old, retirement, individual isolation, and segregated living were favorite themes. Generational conflicts depicting power struggles between older and younger generations were frequent. Some novels, however, were fairy godmother stories, in which the elderly used their wealth and power to bring happiness to young people, or in which they performed admirable feats of bravery or ingenuity. A significant plot element was life review, a reminiscence over the past, sometimes in preparation for death.

An analysis of contemporary American poetry showed that a number of poems equated growing old with diminishment, whereas others expressed a striving for continued change, growth, and self-realization in old age (Clark 1980). The elderly are sometimes portrayed as having a "vigor beyond their youth"; even though bones may creak, eyes grow bleary, and breasts wither, the aged are endowed with strength arising from their individuality. Age is referred to as "the hour for praise . . . praise that is joy." There is also a keen sense of the passage of years, and the desire in the time left, with the strength given, to do "that which is worthy of heaven." There is a realization too that age offers opportunities for love that are not available to the young.

> Ours is the late, last wisdom of the afternoon.
> We know that love, like light, grows dearer
>   toward the dark. (Clark 1980, 190)

The aged are described negatively as having "no faces," "no voices," with "riches gone." The old are diminished in value "as merchandise marked down." They are "sitters by the wall," and the poet asks: "Is there a song left then for aged voices?" (Clark 1980)

An analysis of poetry by Sohngen and Smith (1978) also emphasizes loss with age: loss of beauty and strength, speed and endurance, sexual ability and interest, mental functioning, companionship, employment, usefulness, and hope. The elderly are poor and "weary of pain." The metaphors of old age reportedly emphasize decline: sunset, evening, twilight, dying fires, winter, snow, and frost. In old age, you "take in sail" and "run on the same old rails too long." The aged are like leaves "all green and wildly fresh without, but worn and gray beneath" and they are "dying inward like an aging tree" (Sohngen and Smith 1978, 183).

But despite the emphasis on loss, the retention of pleasant memories is often mentioned. The older person learns to become patient, placid, tranquil, content, and quiet. Some older people still weave "nets of dreams," laugh, and appreciate the beauty of nature; the fortunate even retain the poet's ability to "sing" (Sohngen and Smith 1978, 183).

Attitudes of Children and Youth

Many views of the aged as portrayed by the mass media and literature have influenced children and youth. An analysis of the responses of 180 children (ages 3 to 11) on the Children's Attitudes toward the Elderly Test revealed that children reacted negatively to the aged. However, only 22 percent of the children reported knowing elderly persons outside the family (Jantz et al. 1977). When shown four pictures of adult males of different ages (see Figure 4.3), 58 percent of the children said they would prefer to be with the youngest man; 20 percent preferred to be with the oldest man (Seefeldt et al. 1977). The majority of the children identified the oldest man on the basis of physical features: "he has the most wrinkles," "his lips are pulled in," and "he hasn't much hair." When asked how they felt about being old, the majority responded by: "I would feel awful," "I'll be nearly dead," "It will be terrible," "I'll be sick and tired and ready to be buried." Positive responses were: "I'll feel good," "I'll have a house," and "I'll be rich." When asked what activities they could do with the oldest man pictured, the children implied that he was helpless, passive, and generally incapable of caring for himself. They suggested, "get his glasses," "help him clean, cook, shop," "bury him," "carry things for him," and "push him in his wheelchair." When asked what the oldest man would do with them, the children's answers reflected passive, stereotypic views: "go to church," "play cards," "watch TV," and "help me with my homework." Or, they reported that the oldest man was rich and "he could give me a car" or "money" or "things." The researchers found that until the third or fourth grades the children were unable to assign correct ages to the pictures; but children as young as three were generally able to identify the oldest man. Even young children can be introduced to the concept of age and become acquainted with active, attractive, and healthy elderly persons. In this way, children can develop more positive attitudes toward the elderly (Seefeldt et al. 1977).

A number of studies reflected the attitudes of adolescents and college students toward older people. Generally speaking, older people whom adolescents know personally, such as grandparents, are perceived much more favorably than those who are relative strangers (Bader 1980). Weinberger and Millham (1970) compared the attitudes of undergraduates toward representative seventy-year-olds with their attitudes toward a particular seventy-year-old stranger, whose picture was given to them and whom they were permitted to meet, if they wished. The latter, personalized older person was rated more positively than the former, generalized older person.

Ivester and King (1977) found that ninth- and twelfth-grade adolescents living in a rural area had fairly positive attitudes toward the aged. These adolescents associated more frequently with grandparents in the extended family than did adolescents who were growing up in the city away from grandparents. Adolescents of higher social classes had more positive views of the aged than did lower-class adolescents. This may be a result of the nature of family life among the poor. Grandparents may be seen by lower-class adolescents and their parents as financial burdens, thus fostering more negative attitudes toward them (Ivester and King 1977).

O'Connell and Rotter (1979) measured college students' ratings of aging persons on three dimensions: effectiveness, autonomy, and personal acceptability. The students viewed aging as a negative process; but ratings

FIGURE 4.3   Pictures of Adult Males Used to Explore Children's Attitudes toward the Elderly

Ages 20-35, 35-50, 50-65, 65-80.

C. Seefeldt et al., "Using Pictures to Explore Children's Attitudes toward the Elderly." Reprinted by permission of *The Gerontologist* 17 (December 1977): 507.

in absolute terms became negative on only one dimension, effectiveness. On the dimensions of autonomy and personal acceptability, scale ratings remained positive but decreased with age. Males were perceived as more effective and autonomous than females until age seventy-five. By that age, both sexes were considered equally ineffective and dependent. At all ages, females were perceived as more personally acceptable than males. Another study of college students' attitudes toward older workers showed that overall evaluations were not negative, but depended on worker competence: the highly competent elderly person was viewed quite positively (Perry and Varney 1978).

Self-Concepts

How do the aged feel about themselves and about aging? Many older people deny their own aging and cling tenaciously to *self-concepts* of middle-aged or even young (Peters 1971). A ten-year, longitudinal study of the age-identities of persons seventy and older revealed that many rejected the possibility that they were, in fact, old (Bultena and Powers 1978). They acknowledged getting older after the ten-year period had elapsed, but a majority continued to define themselves in other ways (e.g., as middle-aged). Those who acknowledged changes in their expressed age-identities did so because of altered life situations: particularly declines in physical independence and health. Role losses, especially those involving health and physical independence, constituted critical turning points at which the self-concept of middle-aged had to be relinquished (Bultena and Powers 1978).

How individuals compared themselves with age peers was important in the formulation of their age-identities. Those who felt that they were healthier, needed less help, were physically more independent, and had favorable relationships with siblings most often considered themselves middle-aged rather than old. Good physical health and independence were among the most prized attributes of elderly persons (Bultena and Powers 1978).

There may be actual psychological advantages in middle-age identification by older persons. Middle-age identifiers tend to be better adjusted and to have more positive self-images because they identify with the rights, privileges, and power associated with middle age. Middle-age identifiers see themselves as they were in earlier, perhaps better years. Unwavering optimism is a clearly established characteristic of American elders (Bader 1980), and older people try to recognize the rewards that accompany old age.

In an article entitled "Advantages of Aging," Palmore (1979) lists fourteen advantages. Some benefit society: older people are more law abiding; they vote more frequently (62 percent over age sixty-five vote); they participate more in voluntary organizations; they are better workers; and they are more vigilant. Other advantages benefit the individual. Contrary to popular opinion, they suffer less criminal victimization. They have fewer accidents, and receive economic advantages, such as social security, pensions, supplemental security income, lower taxes, medicare, free services, and reduced rates. Freedom from child rearing and freedom from work (for those who want it) are two important personal advantages. Palmore concludes, "It is time to 'accentuate the positive' in order to compensate for unwarranted fears and prejudices against old age" (223). Borges and Dutton emphasize:

> Happy productive adulthood is not a state of existence on limited hold; rather it is a dynamic process in which problems are attacked and pleasures sought. . . . Lust for life is available to all ages. (Borges and Dutton 1976, 223)

GROWING OLD IN AMERICA

Growing old in America would be considerably easier were it not for several trends that profoundly influence the lives of the elderly.

Industrialization

One important trend has been the change from an agricultural to a modern industrial society (Achenbaum and Stearns 1978). In agricultural America, every family member was needed to produce the essential goods of life. Parents, children, grandparents, and aunts and uncles worked together farming, weaving, cooking, and preserving food. The elderly not only helped on the farm, but, in most cases, they owned the property. They were the overseers and respected heads of the economic unit. They lived out their lives contributing to and being cared for by their families.

Relocation

The industrial revolution brought profound changes. Most noticeable was the migration of families from farms to the cities. Young people moved to the cities to obtain good jobs, leaving the elderly behind. As the number of family members decreased, and the costs of land, equipment, and farm management increased, the elderly found it more difficult to make a living on the family farm. Many sold their land to investors or corporations and moved to the inner city closer to their children. Three out of four, however, continued to own their own homes (U.S. Dept. of Commerce 1979c).

Changing Family Roles

Increasing geographic mobility and the separation of home from the work place gradually broke up the *extended family*—at least in terms of residence. Young couples moved into single-family houses that had no room for aged parents. Most parents were not neglected; many children visited regularly and provided assistance of many kinds. But parents generally were expected to live independently and to be as economically self-sufficient as possible.

As extended families split into smaller units, older people lost their roles as family heads. Although most remained independent, some were unable to live alone because of failing health, immobility, and poverty. They became dependent on their children, some of whom refused or were unable to care for their parents. Consequently, old-age assistance and other public programs had to be developed to care for people who were formerly cared for by family members. Even so, only 6 percent of the population had to be institutionalized. Most of these had no family to help them.

Declining Employment

The numbers of gainfully employed older people declined with industrialization. The growing specialization of work and the demand for industrial efficiency resulted in age-related standards of usefulness. Most industrial workers were twenty to forty-five years of age. After years of exhausting labor, the older workers were considered useless in many jobs. "The age decline is creeping down on these men. I'd say that by forty-five they are through," was a recurrent verdict of superintendents of major factories in Middletown in the 1920s (Lynd and Lynd 1929). "I started out as a janitor again," said a sixty-four-year-old factory worker. Consigning older workers to the industrial scrap heap was a nightmare of modern society.

Labor unions tried to solve the problem of older workers by establishing the seniority principle, but they were only partly successful. During the depression, social security programs were set up, not to benefit the older worker but to force retirement and make jobs available for younger people. The elderly were pensioned off, often at a poverty level. If they earned more than a specific amount, they were penalized by reductions in their social security.

Figure 4.4 shows the decline in the labor force of those sixty-five and over. In 1900, about two-thirds of all males over sixty-five were in the labor force. By 1981, fewer than one out of six men and one out of thirteen women over sixty-five were employed. As a result, about 15 percent of persons sixty-five and over live below the poverty level. This figure is 39 percent for blacks and 26 percent for Hispanics (U.S. Dept. of Commerce 1983).

In 1977, the Supreme Court ruled that mandatory retirement at sixty-five was unconstitutional, and Congress raised the mandatory retirement age to seventy in 1978. Elimination of forced retirement at sixty-five may have little effect on the employment situation. Some elderly cannot work because of their health; those who do work are employed primarily in agriculture or in unskilled, low-paying jobs. Despite laws against age dis-

FIGURE 4.4   Percentage of Persons over 65 Years of Age in the Labor Force, 1840–1981

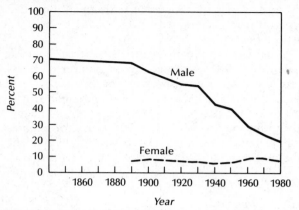

Adapted from: U.S. Department of Commerce, Bureau of the Census, *Statistical Abstract of the United States, 1980, 82, 83* (Washington, D.C.: U.S. Government Printing Office, 1980, 1983), and other census data.

crimination, employers still are prejudiced against hiring older workers. The majority of employers encourage early retirement to reduce the labor force, particularly in hard-pressed, dying industries.

Loss of Status, Self-Esteem

The aged have high status and prestige in primitive societies because they possess the greatest knowledge of traditions and ceremonies considered essential for group survival. The elderly also have high status in agricultural societies because they control the property, have the greatest knowledge of farming skills, are able to perform useful tasks, and are the leaders of the extended family. But as our society becomes more industrialized and modern, the elderly lose their economic advantages and their leadership roles in industry and in the extended family. Consequently, they lose their status and prestige (Balkwell and Balswick 1981). Figure 4.5 shows many factors that have resulted in the decreased status of the elderly (Cowgill 1979).

Religious Ideology

Religious ideology relative to the elderly has also changed. Traditional religious ideology emphasized respect and obedience toward one's parents, grandparents, and other older people. They were to be treated with deference and honor. As religious influence has waned, so has the emphasis on respect for the elderly.

FIGURE 4.5   Modernization and the Decreased Status of the Elderly

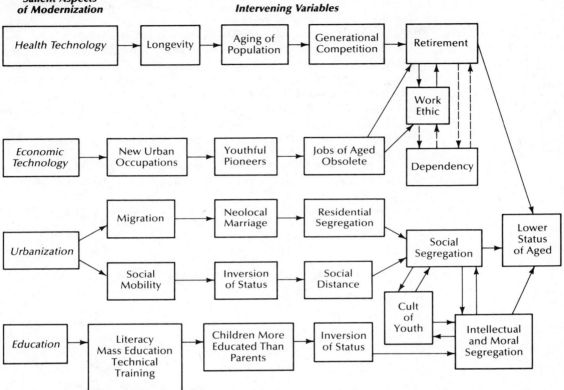

From: D. O. Cowgill, "Aging and Modernization: A Revision of the Theory," *Late Life: Communities and Environmental Policy*, Jaber F. Gubrium, ed. 1981. Courtesy of Charles C. Thomas, Publisher, Springfield, Illinois.

Age Grading, Stratification, and Segregation

Increasing industrialization and the development of the nuclear family have resulted in a degree of *age grading, stratification,* and segregation. People are assigned to age groups chronologically, regardless of their ability to function and to contribute to society. This works to their disadvantage. The aged prefer to live among young people (not with them), but the young prefer to live among their age peers. This results in geographical isolation.

Older Women

It is difficult to be old. For a number of reasons, it is even harder to be old and female (Posner 1977). Because women outlive men, there are far greater numbers of elderly females than elderly males. Women are also more likely to be widowed in old age than are men. Figure 4.6 shows the marital status of persons sixty-five and over. In 1981, 83 percent of men sixty-five and older, who were outside of institutions, lived in families; only 57 percent of women did so (U.S. Dept. of Commerce 1983).

Far fewer women sixty-five and over work than do men (8 percent of women versus 18 percent of men). Those who do receive lower pay than men. As a result, more women than men at this age have incomes below the poverty level (U.S. Dept. of Commerce 1983). (See Figure 4.7.) Consequently, working women hesitate to retire. Work is important to them, and many experience psychological stress when forced to stop. Women who have only a retirement pension, who live alone in unsuitable

FIGURE 4.6   Percent of Persons 65 Years and Over, by Marital Status and Sex: 1981

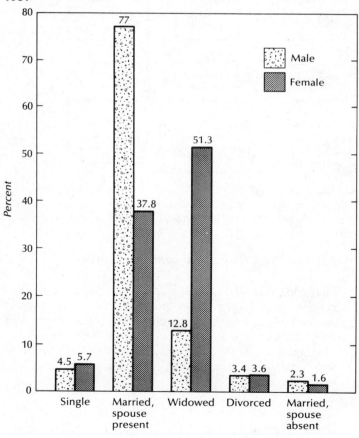

From: U.S. Department of Commerce, Bureau of the Census, *Statistical Abstract of the United States, 1982, 83* (Washington, D.C.: U.S. Government Printing Office, 1983), 31.

FIGURE 4.7   Percent of Persons 65 Years and Over Below Poverty Level in 1980, by Family Status, Race, and Sex

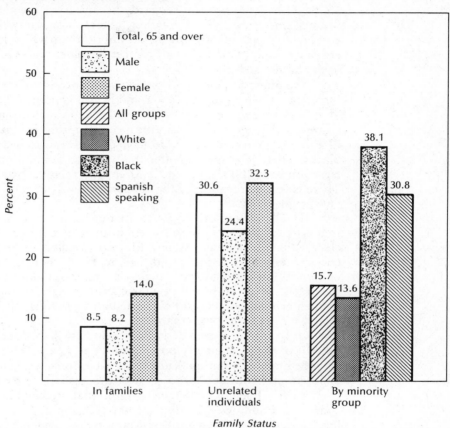

From: U.S. Department of Commerce, Bureau of the Census, *Statistical Abstract of the United States, 1982, 83* (Washington, D.C.: U.S. Government Printing Office, 1983), 442.

housing with no relative nearby, and who suffer from multiple illnesses fare the worst (Green 1977).

Minority Aged

The aged in minority groups have a particularly difficult time. Studies of aged blacks indicate that more than one-third live below the poverty level (see Figure 4.7). Most are ineligible for social security. Although they worked all of their lives, their jobs usually were not covered by the program. They have less education than whites, poorer health, and fewer contacts with social service workers. Their old age is a bitter culmination of the discrimination suffered all their lives. They live in double jeopardy:

they are disadvantaged because of minority group status and they suffer from the status devaluation associated with old age (Dowd and Bengtson 1978). Others are in triple jeopardy because they are also poor (National Council on Aging 1972). However, blacks under sixty-five have more favorable attitudes toward the aged than do their white counterparts. They are more likely than whites to respect the elderly and to include the aged in the family structure (Wylie 1971).

The plight of elderly Hispanics is somewhat similar to that of blacks. Income and education are lower and health is poorer than among whites. They report lower life satisfaction than do whites, as measured by such scores as the degree of tranquility or of optimism with advancing age. Elderly Hispanics, however, do have one advantage over both whites and blacks. There is a much greater frequency of familial interaction (i.e., interaction with children, grandchildren, and relatives) among these people. There is less segregation of the elderly from other family members (Dowd and Bengtson 1978).

Of all the minority groups in the United States, native American Indians probably are the most traditional in their life-style. A study of elderly Pueblo Indians in New Mexico revealed some significant differences from whites (Rogers and Gallion 1978). For instance, the sex ratio of elderly Pueblo males to females is nearly 1:1. Life expectancy among the Indians is lower, but the men live as long as the women. Elderly Pueblo women are more likely to be married and less likely to be widowed than their white female counterparts.

Only 9 percent of elderly Pueblo Indians live alone, compared to 27 percent of the total elderly population of all races. The majority live in an extended family situation. They share their home with children and grandchildren, and continue to do so after the husband (or wife) dies.

Elderly Pueblos prefer their traditional attached and terraced adobe apartment buildings even though they lack running water, indoor plumbing, electricity, and telephones. Many of the young build new, modern, ranch-style adobe homes with modern conveniences, but the elderly are generally reluctant to accept the new housing. This creates a conflict for the elderly between their family and their home.

The elderly are fairly isolated from the larger, white community. In rural areas, transportation costs are prohibitively high. Round trips for medical or shopping services often exceed one hundred miles. More than half the elderly rarely or never go into town; more than one-third rarely or never travel to the store.

There is generally no proscribed age for retirement among the Pueblos. Women move from mothering to grandmothering, retaining the caretaking role. Men continue to work the farms, reducing their activities as physical limitations increase. Gardening and crafts are also important parts of their lives.

The elders are regarded as "keepers of the culture," and many of them are active in storytelling and relaying the legends, traditions, and native language to the children. Few older Indians can read or write English. They speak their tribal language, and many speak Spanish as a second language.

Since there are few birth certificates or records of baptism, no clear-cut evidence of age exists. Age is sometimes exaggerated, with individuals claiming to be *older* than they actually are. In a country that places a premium on youth, the Pueblos place the greatest premium on old age.

SOCIAL-PSYCHOLOGICAL THEORIES OF AGING

One task of social scientists is to develop theories explaining social phenomena. Theories of aging attempt to explain the process of aging in its many dimensions. The biological process and the explanatory theories of aging are described in chapter 5. This chapter discusses five social-psychological aspects of aging.

Disengagement Theory

The *disengagement theory* of aging was originally formulated by Cumming and Henry (1961). The theory states that as people approach and enter old age, there is a natural tendency to withdraw socially and psychologically from the environment. Older people tend to detach themselves voluntarily from outside social activities and to become less involved with other people. At the same time, they withdraw emotionally, turning inward to their own thoughts and feelings. This disengagement frees older people from the stress that arises from numerous role obligations and family and community responsibilities. It also allows them more time and opportunity to pursue those activities, values, and ideas they consider important. Thus, disengagement enhances their life satisfaction as they grow older.

While the individual voluntarily withdraws from others, society promotes disengagement through mandatory retirement or by requiring adults to relinquish their roles as parents or community leaders. This transfer of power from the old to the young gives younger people a chance to occupy the slots previously occupied by their elders.

Since its conception, disengagement theory has been criticized severely. Critics argue that disengagement is not universal, inevitable, or inherent in the aging process. Some older people never disengage; they remain active and productive all their lives. Benjamin Franklin was seventy when he helped draft the Declaration of Independence. Guiseppi Verdi, the distinguished Italian opera composer, was seventy-three when he composed *Otello* and eighty when *Falstaff* was first performed in Milan. Karl Menninger, the outstanding psychiatrist who received countless awards, wrote *The Crime of Punishment* at seventy-five. In his eighties, Arthur Fiedler was directing the Boston Pops Orchestra. Oliver Wendell Holmes,

Jr., served on the Supreme Court until he was ninety-one. Michelangelo continued his great work as an octogenarian. At ninety-two, Sebastian Kresge was still active as board chairman of the Kresge store chain. One can cite countless individual examples to cast doubt on the inevitability and universality of disengagement.

Critics also insist that the theory does not consider those individual differences in health and personality that influence activity. Furthermore, it is continued activity, not disengagement, that produces the most life satisfaction for older people.

Longitudinal studies suggest that aging has little impact on activities, and that the elderly who are disengaged have probably been that way all their lives (Palmore 1968). Also, disengagement may represent the failure of society to provide opportunities for older people, not personal preference.

The real question is, Who disengages from whom? Does the older person withdraw from society or society from the older person? Brown (1974) interviewed a group of people fifty-five and older. From the data gathered, he presented three important implications regarding disengagement: (1) much disengagement is voluntarily entered into by the elderly but not preferred; (2) disengagement is not chosen by the elderly even when the choice is between almost no social contacts and nonsatisfying contacts; and (3) the elderly seem to enter into fewer formal relationships and into more personal and individual relationships. These individual relationships may be more intense and satisfying than larger group participation.

Activity Theory

Activity theory suggests that continuance of an active life-style will have a positive effect on the sense of well-being and satisfaction of older people (Maddox 1970). This personal satisfaction depends on a positive self-image, which is validated through continued participation in middle-aged roles. When these roles end, they must be replaced to avoid feelings of decline and uselessness.

Finding substitute activities for roles that have ended is one key to successful adjustment. Old age offers "role exits," such as loss of work, income, health, and family roles. Loss of these roles can be devastating if no substitutes are found. But old age can offer opportunities for the individual to use leisure time constructively and to achieve positive, well-integrated roles in the family and community.

Psychologists and social gerontologists give only partial support to this oversimplified theory. Simply engaging in activities does not automatically maintain one's feeling of self-worth, especially if those activities are less meaningful than the roles one has given up. Will a retired corporation president have as adequate a self-concept playing Bingo as he did when working? It is unlikely. Busywork alone is not the answer.

Another difficulty is that the activity theory neglects persons who cannot maintain middle-age standards physically, mentally, or emotionally. Some people are forced to shift roles for health or other reasons yet still find great satisfaction. Not everyone must maintain a high level of activity to be happy. Overall, there is an association among morale, personality adjustment, and activity levels, but different persons may prefer different types of activities and different degrees of participation to be satisfied (Turner and Helms 1979).

Personality and Life-Style Theory

Because of individual differences in activity and disengagement, many gerontologists seek a theory that relates personality to successful aging. Neugarten (1968) investigated older people between the ages of seventy and seventy-nine, identified four major personality types, and categorized the role activities of those comprising the major types. Table 4.3 shows the four major personality types: *integrated, armored-defended, passive-dependent,* and *unintegrated.* The integrated include the *reorganizers,* who substitute new activities for lost ones and engage in a wide variety of activities. The *focused* have integrated personalities with high life satisfaction. They are selective in their activities and derive major satisfaction from one or two role areas. The *disengaged* are integrated personalities with high life satisfaction but with low activity. They have voluntarily moved away from role commitments because of preference.

The armored-defended include two types: the *holding on* and the *constricted.* Aging is a threat to the holding-on group, so they maintain middle-age patterns as long as possible. They are successful in their attempts and maintain high life satisfaction at medium or high activity levels.

TABLE 4.3   Personality and Theories of Aging

Personality type	Role activity	Life satisfaction	Number
1. Integrated			
—Reorganizers	High	High	9
—Focused	Medium	High	5
—Disengaged	Low	High	3
2. Armored-defended			
—Holding on	High or medium	High	11
—Constricted	Low or medium	High or medium	4
3. Passive-dependent			
—Succorance-seeking	High or medium	High or medium	6
—Apathetic	Low	Medium or low	5
4. Unintegrated			
—Disorganized	Low	Medium or low	7

Based on statistical material from: B. L. Neugarten, R. J. Havighurst, and S. S. Tobin, "Personality and Patterns of Aging," *Middle Age and Aging,* B. L. Neugarten, ed. (Chicago: University of Chicago Press, 1968), 173–177.

They say, "I'll work until I drop" or "So long as you keep busy, you will get along all right" (Neugarten 1968, 176). Those people in the constricted group deal with losses by constricting their social interactions and energies and by closing themselves off from experiences. This tactic works fairly well, giving them high or medium life satisfaction.

Those in the passive-dependent group are either *succorance-seeking* or *apathetic*. The succorance-seeking have high dependency needs and are fairly satisfied, as long as they have others to lean on who can meet their emotional needs. The *apathetic* are the rocking-chair types who have disengaged, who have low role activity, and only medium or low life satisfaction.

The unintegrated or *disorganized* exhibit gross defects in psychological functions, loss of emotional control, and deterioration of thought processes.

Neugarten and associates concluded from their research that the activity and disengaged theories did not adequately explain what happened as people grow older. People are not at the mercy of their social environment or intrinsic processes. They continue to make choices, selecting in accordance with their long-established needs. Personality is "the pivotal dimension in describing patterns of aging and in predicting relationships between level of social role activity and life satisfaction" (Neugarten et al. 1968, 177). Other personality theorists group individuals into different categories.

The relationship between aging, personality, and predominant life-style was outlined in a longitudinal study by Maas and Kuypers (1974), who interviewed young parents in 1930 and again forty years later. The 142 surviving subjects were grouped into ten different life-styles.

1. *Family-centered fathers:* their way of life was centered around the spouse-parent-grandparent roles.
2. *Hobbyist fathers:* their home-based lives revolved around instrumental leisure-time activities.
3. *Remotely sociable fathers:* they were socially active but minimally involved.
4. *Unwell-disengaged fathers:* they had poor health, which resulted in withdrawal from the world.
5. *Husband-centered wives:* their marriage was the center of their activity.
6. *Uncentered mothers:* they were not involved in work or clubs but visited family and friends informally and often.
7. *Visiting mothers:* they were highly involved in both informal visiting and group activities.
8. *Employed (work-centered) mothers:* their lives revolved around their work.
9. *Disabled-disengaged mothers:* they showed the same basic pattern as the unwell-disengaged fathers.
10. *Group-centered mothers:* they had many recreational interests outside the family.

The researchers found considerable stability of life-style among all the men except the family-centered fathers, whose roles changed considerably as spouses, children, and grandchildren got older. The women were affected more than the men by circumstances. The husband-centered wife, for example, was dependent on the health, income, and residence of her husband. Employed mothers showed considerable change compared to earlier life-styles. Employment often brought economic independence and gratifying new life-styles, especially after an unsatisfactory marriage. Maas and Kuypers (1974) emphasized that there is no one pattern of aging.

Exchange Theory

The *exchange theory* rests on four basic assumptions:

1. Individuals and groups act to maximize rewards and minimize costs.
2. The individual uses past experience to predict the outcome of similar exchanges in the present.
3. An individual will maintain an interaction if it continues to be more rewarding than costly.
4. When one individual is dependent on another, the latter accrues power.

According to this theory, social exchanges involve not only financial transactions but also psychological satisfaction and need gratification. The person having the greater needs loses power; the other person gains power. Power is thus derived from unequal needs or imbalances in social exchange.

Exchange theory was not formulated originally as a theory of aging. The first person to apply the theory to the aged was Martin (1971). He used the theory to describe visiting patterns among family members. The aged who have financial resources that younger persons need or who can offer valuable services such as baby-sitting hold positions of power and put their children in dependent positions. Those who have little to offer—who, for example, have to beg others to visit—are forced to pay a high price. Their relatives visit reluctantly and begrudgingly, demonstrating to the elderly that it is a chore or a burden.

Dowd (1975) offers four alternatives to the existing power balance:

1. *Withdrawal:* voluntary disengagement
2. *Extension of the power network:* development of alternative relationships that are more rewarding
3. *Emergence of status:* recognition of a critical skill possessed only by the less powerful
4. *Coalition formation:* banding together of the less powerful to exert sufficient power to achieve rewards.

When the elderly band together in groups, they wield more political and social power. For example, efforts to alter social security benefits have been resisted by powerful senior citizens' organizations. The Supreme Court's decision declaring retirement at sixty-five unconstitutional has also increased the power of older workers in exchange relationships involving their work.

Social Reconstruction Theory

Kuypers and Bengtson (1973) have used the social breakdown syndrome as developed by Zusman (1966) to show how our society causes negative changes in the self-concept of the aged. Four steps are involved (see Figure 4.8):

1. Our society brings about role loss, offers only sparse normative information and guidance, and deprives the elderly of reference groups, so that they lose the sense of who they are and what their roles are.
2. Society then labels them negatively as incompetent and deficient.
3. Society deprives them of opportunities to use their skills, which atrophy in the process.
4. The aged accept the external labeling, identify themselves as inadequate, and begin to act as they are expected to act, setting the stage for another spiral. (Kuypers and Bengtson 1973)

Kuypers and Bengtson also believe that a person can change the system and break the cycle through three types of action. One, we must eliminate the idea that work is the primary source of worth. The Protestant work ethic is inappropriate to old age. People need to be judged by their

FIGURE 4.8   Social Breakdown and the Aged

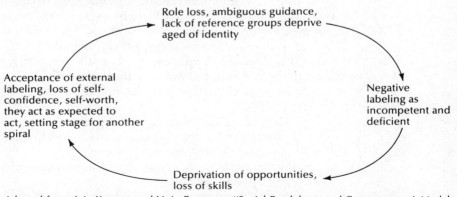

Role loss, ambiguous guidance, lack of reference groups deprive aged of identity

Negative labeling as incompetent and deficient

Deprivation of opportunities, loss of skills

Acceptance of external labeling, loss of self-confidence, self-worth, they act as expected to act, setting stage for another spiral

Adapted from: J.A. Kuypers and V. L. Bengtson, "Social Breakdown and Competence: A Model of Normal Aging," *Human Development* 16 (1973): 181–201.

character, personality, and humanitarianism. Two, the social services, housing, health care, and financial status of the aged need to be improved. Finally, we must give the elderly greater powers of self-rule, to determine the political and social policies and the programs that affect them. This will develop greater self-confidence and feelings of self-worth and help maintain their personal competency and social power.

Which Theory?

Each of these theories contributes something to the total understanding of the aging process. No one theory can explain the process in every individual. People are different; they live in different environments, their personalities and needs are different, and they act and react in different ways to social pressures. The more thoroughly these different determinants are analyzed, the more clearly we will understand the developmental tasks of aging in our culture.

DEVELOPMENTAL TASKS OF LATE ADULTHOOD

Many books on aging say little about developmental tasks during late adulthood. One explanation is that ideas of development or growth are inappropriate as applied to older people. Older people have already developed and grown, so the emphasis is on decline not on improvement. The author disagrees. Certainly, changes take place that require adjustments. But not all change is decline; some is growth. This section emphasizes change that requires adjustments and continued growth.

The developmental tasks of late adulthood include:

1. Staying physically healthy and adjusting to limitations.
2. Planning finances to ensure adequate means of support.
3. Learning and adjusting to revised work roles.
4. Learning to use leisure time pleasurably.
5. Finding companionship and friendship.
6. Establishing new roles in the family.
7. Achieving integrity through acceptance of one's life.

Staying Physically Healthy and Adjusting to Limitations

The task of staying healthy becomes more difficult as people age. Yet this is one of the important challenges of late adulthood. It involves good health habits and preventive medicine, that is, getting regular medical and dental checkups and paying close attention to such potential health problems as high blood pressure. Many illnesses in later years develop into chronic problems because of neglect, not because of aging. Older adults should also attend to their physical appearance. If they feel they look nice, they generally have a better mental attitude toward themselves and the world.

Physical health depends partially on mental attitude. Some elderly people move in a decreasing spiral, centered around a growing preoccupation with their physical state. Others practice body transcendence; they may suffer physical discomfort, but they learn to find happiness in satisfying human relationships or creative mental activities.

Planning Finances to Ensure Adequate Means of Support

Most older adults prefer financial independence. But this requires careful long-term planning. Some adults have the means and desire to retire early; others discover they cannot afford to retire. Others find part-time work to supplement their income. The disabled who depend on others need to investigate what resources might be available from children or other relatives, public old-age assistance programs, or pension and social security benefits. Many adults have to consider revising their life-style to cut down on expenses.

Learning and Adjusting to Revised Work Roles

Retirement at sixty-five is no longer compulsory, but many workers must retire at seventy. They have to consider a major change in work roles. Some adults shift from full-time to part-time employment, gradually decreasing their work involvement. Others learn new types of work. Retirement for them means retraining, changing jobs, or going into business for themselves. Some become involved in work they always wanted but never had the chance to do. Others devote themselves to working at home, to crafts or work hobbies they enjoy. They are as busy as ever because they have substituted one type of work for another.

Certainly, retirement should be *retirement to, not from.* Retirement offers the opportunity to escape social demands. Older adults can choose their own pace, determine their own time schedule, and set their own goals. Retirement offers not only an end, but also a new beginning and opportunity.

Learning to Use Leisure Time Pleasurably

Late adulthood offers most people an opportunity to please themselves and others. As work roles decline, more leisure time is available for preferred pursuits. *The Random House Dictionary* defines pleasure as "enjoyment or satisfaction derived from what is to one's liking; gratification;

delight" (1973, 1105). Pleasure is the feeling of being pleased and happy; it is gladness and joy.

Many older adults have not learned to enjoy themselves. They are the work generation. Brought up through the depression years, they have been so involved in earning a living that they have never learned how to live. Some of these adults have no hobbies or interests apart from their jobs.

Different people derive pleasure differently: some from creative or self-expressive activities, some from serving others, some from social involvements, and some from sports or athletic activities. Others enjoy contemplative or spiritual activities, nature, sensuous experiences, educational or mental activities, or games or play activities. The important thing is pleasurable involvement.

Finding Companionship and Friendship

Loneliness is one of the most frequent complaints of older people. Their challenge is to find meaningful relationships with others. This may require joining formal organizations or groups in the community, or it may require extending oneself to others to cultivate friendships. It usually involves personal initiative in contacting others, extending invitations, or making telephone calls. Senior citizens' organizations meet the social needs of many adults. Telephone networks provide links between the infirm who cannot make personal visits.

Establishing New Roles in the Family

Several events bring about the adjustment of family roles: children marrying and moving away, grandparenthood, retirement, the death of a spouse, or becoming dependent on one's children. All of these circumstances require major adjustments and a realignment of family roles and responsibilities.

Achieving Integrity through Acceptance of One's Life

Erikson (1959) says that the development of ego integrity is the chief psychosocial task of the final stage of life. This includes life review, being able to accept the facts of one's life without regret, and being able to face death without great fear. It entails appreciating one's own individuality, accomplishments, and satisfactions, as well as accepting the hardships, failures, and disappointments one has experienced. Ultimately, it means contentment with one's life as it is and has been.

SUMMARY

The population of the world is growing older. During the seventeenth and eighteenth centuries, only a small percentage (4 to 9 percent) of the population in Europe and Japan lived to age sixty and over. By 1990, more than 16 percent of the total United States population will be sixty and over. This fact has several important implications. As the elderly increase in numbers, they will wield more political power. However, the dependency ratio (the number of aged over sixty-five in proportion to those eighteen to sixty-four) will increase, straining society's capacity to care for them.

The elderly comprise a larger percentage of the population in some states than others. Florida has the largest percentage of population sixty-five and older; Alaska has the smallest. Some regions, including Florida, the North Central states, and New England, have comparatively high concentrations of elderly, as do central cities and some rural areas. This reflects differential growth, and the movement of young people from the country and the city to suburbia. The older the age group, the higher the sex ratio of women to men, reflecting the longer life expectancy of women.

Ageism refers to negative attitudes and prejudices against the elderly, which result in differential treatment, neglect, and discrimination. Ageism is evident in medical journals; in the professional attitudes of social workers, lawyers, and physicians; in television and other mass media; in humor; in literature; in the attitudes of children and youth; and in some self-concepts of the aged. Society and the elderly need to emphasize positive attitudes toward the aged so that late adulthood can be as happy and productive as possible.

Several trends in American culture profoundly affect the lives of the elderly. Industrialization has brought about many changes: relocation of the elderly from farms to the inner city, loss of status as extended families break up, declining employment, and a sense of uselessness and loss of self-esteem. As religious influence has declined, so has respect for the elderly (which religion teaches). Increased industrialization has resulted in age grading, stratification, and segregation. In addition, there is geographical isolation of the elderly, resulting in loneliness and a need for society to provide care formerly provided by families.

The situation of older women is especially hard. They outlive men, are widowed more often, work less than their male counterparts, and receive lower wages. As a result, more older women than men have incomes below the poverty level. Minority aged have a harder time than do whites because they live in triple jeopardy: they are disadvantaged because of their minority group status, they suffer from devaluation in status associated with old age, and they are poor. Blacks fare worse than other minority groups, followed by Hispanics. Although impoverished, native American Indians live in extended family situations, give high status and important roles to their elderly as keepers of their culture, and are more likely to care for the elderly who cannot look after themselves.

Five important social-psychological theories of aging are disengagement theory, activity theory, personality and life-style theory, exchange theory, and social reconstruction theory. No one theory can explain the aging process in every individual. People are different, their personalities and needs are different, and they react differently to societal influences and social pressures.

The developmental tasks of late adulthood include staying physically healthy and adjusting to limitations, planning finances to ensure adequate means of support, learning and adjusting to revised work roles, learning to use leisure time pleasurably, finding companionship and friendship, establishing new roles in the family, and achieving integrity through acceptance of one's life.

The development of ego integrity is the chief psychosocial task of the final stage of life. After life review, one can accept the facts of one's life without regret and can face death without fear.

Part II

Physical Development

5

Biological Aging: Theories and Bodily Changes

SENESCENCE

Senescence is the term biologists, gerontologists, and others use to describe biological aging. It should not be confused with *senility,* which is a disease. Senescence describes the processes that lead to a decline in the viability of the human organism and increase its vulnerability. There is no known animal species whose individual members do not age. However, rates of senescence for most species vary from individual to individual. These individual variations increase with chronological age, making the measure a useless indicator of the degree of senescence. Some persons exhibit traits similar to those chronologically older or younger than themselves (Borkan and Norris 1980; Webster and Logie 1976). Furthermore, senescence is not one process but many, with decline occurring in different parts of the body at various rates.

Senescence has several criteria that support it as a biological process and not a disease. It must be universal, occurring in all people. One example is the decline in the body's immune system, the ability to recognize and destroy substances foreign to itself. This function declines in everyone, although at different rates, so the decline is part of senescence. Lung cancer does not occur in all individuals; therefore, it is not part of senescence.

Another criterion of senescence is that the changes come primarily from within the organism. Changes resulting from cosmic radiation, for example, would not be part of senescence.

A third criterion of senescence is that the processes occur gradually rather than suddenly. This criterion rules out any disease that appears suddenly (Fries and Crapo 1981).

A final criterion is that the process contributes to a decline in function and increasing mortality. Thus, senescence has a deleterious effect on the organism, making it more vulnerable to disease and stress.

THEORIES OF BIOLOGICAL AGING

Exactly why physical aging occurs has been the subject of much investigation and discussion. Do people have to age? Under ideal conditions, could they stay young forever? Or, does a built-in time clock control longevity, so that living much beyond an allotted time is impossible? There are no answers, but a number of different theories have attempted to explain the causes of physical aging.

Heredity Theory

The most obvious explanation is that the theoretical length of life is hereditary (*hereditary theory* of aging). The life span of a species is set by genetic characteristics that have evolved over countless years. Thus, each species has its own life expectancy. Elephants may live sixty years, the hippopotamus fifty, and primates reach or exceed thirty years. Heredity also plays an important role in human longevity, so that children whose parents and grandparents are long-lived may also live longer. Apparently, they inherit certain traits (e.g., increased resistance to disease) that contribute to a longer life.

Cellular Aging Theory

Some cells in the body, such as those in the brain and nervous system, never reproduce. Other cells reproduce, but only a finite number of times. Hayflick (1970) studied the aging of living cells maintained in cultures. He found that lung tissues, for example, multiply rapidly, at first doubling every twenty-four hours. But as the process progresses, the length of time between doublings increases; after about fifty doublings (about six months), the cells fail to double and start to die. Other cells of the body double fewer times. This fact suggests that aging is programmed by the limited capacity of cells to replace themselves.

Wear-and-Tear Theory

The *wear-and-tear theory* emphasizes that the organism simply wears out, like a machine that has run for too many years. Metabolic rate seems to be a factor. Modestly underfed animals (including humans) or cold-blooded animals living at lower than normal temperatures tend to live longer because metabolism slows down.

Metabolic Waste or Clinker Theory

The *metabolic waste* or *clinker theory* suggests that aging is caused by the accumulation of deleterious substances (by-products of cellular metabolism) within various cells of the body. The accumulation of these substances interferes with normal tissue functioning. One such substance is *collagen,* a fibrous protein associated with connective tissue. It builds up slowly in most organs, tendons, skin, and blood vessels, and is eliminated gradually, if at all. It also stiffens with age. Therefore, tissues containing collagen lose elasticity, causing deterioration in organ functions. For example, the loss of elasticity in blood vessels is partly responsible for *arteriosclerosis.* The increased stiffness is caused by change, over a period of time, in the cross-linkages between the strands of collagen molecules.

Autoimmunity Theory

The *autoimmunity theory* of aging describes the process by which the body's immune system rejects its own tissues through the production of autoimmune antibodies. When foreign substances enter the body, it produces antibodies to neutralize their effects. The response to invasion is called an *immune reaction.* When antibodies respond to mutations within the body, their response is an *autoimmune reaction.* The net result is self-destruction. For example, organs that produce antibodies show the greatest weight loss with age because the antibodies destroy part of the organ's cells. Some leading causes of death, such as cancer, *diabetes,* vascular disease, and *hypertension,* have been linked to autoimmune reactions. This promising theory may lead to the discovery of methods that retard this action and modify the aging process.

Homeostatic Imbalance Theory

The *homeostatic imbalance theory* emphasizes the gradual inability of the body to maintain vital physiologic balances. For example, the body gradually loses its ability to maintain the proper temperature during exposure to heat or cold; similarly, it loses its ability to maintain the proper blood sugar level. Older people also have difficulty adapting to emotional stress. This is why many older persons die soon after their spouses. This loss of efficiency of the physiologic response to stress is perhaps the most general theory of aging and provides the closest link between the physiological, social, and psychological aspects of aging.

Mutation Theory

The *mutation theory* describes what happens when more and more body cells develop mutations. Rates of genetic mutation increase with age. One cause is radiation, which damages the genetic material and shortens the organ's life span in direct proportion to the amount of genetic damage incurred. Cell functioning is controlled by the genetic material DNA, which is found in each cell. When mutations occur in DNA, subsequent cell divisions replicate them, and an appreciable percentage of an organ's cells become mutated. Since most mutations are harmful, mutated cells function less efficiently, and the organs made up of these cells become inefficient and senescent.

Error Theory

The *error theory* is a variation of the mutation theory. The error theory includes the cumulative effects of a variety of mistakes that may occur: mistakes in RNA (ribonucleic acid) production, which affect enzymic synthesis, which affect protein synthesis, and so on. Research indicates a loss of DNA (deoxyribonucleic acid) from the cells of aging animals, which impairs the production of RNA and DNA. This, in turn, impairs cell functioning and eventually leads to cellular death (Johnson and Strehler 1972).

Which Theory?

No single theory proposed to date adequately explains the complex events that occur in aging. Aging involves a number of processes that produce time-dependent changes in an organism. In addition to hereditary factors and intrinsic changes (those occurring from within), environmental stresses, bacteria, viruses, and other influences affect the organism from without, sometimes modifying and reducing the abilities of various organs to continue functioning.

CHANGES IN BODILY SYSTEMS

Nervous Systems

The *central nervous system* consists of the *brain* and *spinal cord;* the *peripheral nervous system* includes the nerves that branch off from the brain and spinal cord to all parts of the body. The peripheral nervous system keeps the organism in contact with the outside world by receiving messages from the sense organs, and transmitting these to the central nervous system. The central nervous system interprets messages and sends them back through the peripheral system to the muscles, glands, and organs that put the messages into action. The nervous systems also coordinate all bodily activities, including those of the internal organs.

To understand what happens to various parts of the nervous systems as people grow older, let us examine the brain. The largest part of the brain, the *cerebrum,* contains about fourteen billion nerve cells *(neurons)* that are located in its outer layer *(cortex)*. The cortex is associated with three major functions. The *motor cortex* coordinates voluntary movements of the body through direct action on the skeletal muscles. The *sensory cortex* is the center of perception, where changes in the environment, which are received through the senses of vision, hearing, smell, taste, touch, and pain, are interpreted. The *associational cortex* includes areas involved in cognitive functions (reasoning, abstract thinking, memory), as well as general consciousness.

As aging progresses, the number of cells in the cortex declines, with cell loss varying in different cortical areas. Losses may range anywhere from 10 to 45 percent by the age of ninety. It must be emphasized, however, that this loss is gradual, with the average decrease varying among different persons (Yamaura et al. 1980). Nevertheless, the finding is significant because a reduction of brain cells affects all the functions that the brain controls. Several studies have related brain atrophy to senile dementia, although there are many causes of this condition (Fox et al. 1975; Morimatsu et al. 1975).

The brain's efficiency depends primarily on the amount of blood and oxygen it receives. If *arteriosclerosis* (hardening of the arteries) occurs, or damage to the heart or vascular system diminishes the blood supply, the brain cannot work properly. If, however, the blood supply is gradually lowered, the brain reacts by growing additional and larger blood vessels. Hunziker and associates (1979) studied the capillaries in the cerebral cortex of subjects in six age groups and found that subjects between ages sixty-five and seventy-four had greater capillary diameters and greater volume and total length per unit of cortex volume than did younger subjects. The researchers reasoned that these differences were adjustments the body had made to preexisting vascular disease or to moderate, long-lasting hypertension. The adjustments resulted in an increased blood supply to the cerebral cortex during old age.

Almost all bodily functions slow down with age. As a result, people talk, read, write, walk, and jump more slowly as they get older. The most widely accepted explanation for this slowing down is that nerve impulses are transmitted more slowly as people age. This is due primarily to an increase in the time required to transmit impulses across nerve connections *(synapses)* via the *neurochemical transmitters*. Whether it is due to a reduction in conduction velocities through the nerves themselves is uncertain. Some studies have shown no difference in nerve conduction velocities among age groups in both humans and laboratory animals. Other studies have shown that degenerative changes in nerve fibers and sensory axons result in lower conduction velocities (Gutmann and Hanzlikova 1976; Sabbahi and Sedgwick 1982).

Part of the reason for slower responses lies within the central nervous system. As people age, information is processed more slowly before appropriate impulses can be sent to areas of the body that must respond. Thus, older people become disproportionately slower than younger ones as tasks become more difficult and choices increase. Another reason for slower responses is that older people become more cautious when making choices—they do not want to make mistakes. It is possible, however, to increase the speed of response through practice and exercise (Murrell 1970).

Cardiovascular System

The *cardiovascular system* consists of the *heart* and *blood vessels*. The heart itself is a muscular organ that works constantly throughout life. During a seventy-year lifetime, the average human heart pumps about 900 million gallons of blood.

Several changes occur in the heart with age. Fat deposits form around the heart and at the entry points of the blood vessels. The number and size of heart muscles decline as muscle cells age and die. Collagen collects in connective tissues, valves, and artery walls, causing hardening and thickening. Arterial walls become calcified, causing the *arteries* to dilate, lengthen, and lose elasticity. The walls of the *aorta,* the largest artery, become less elastic, producing a typical increase in *systolic blood pressure* (pressure produced by the heart forcing out blood). (Systolic blood pressure is the higher of the two blood pressure readings.)

These changes cause a decline in the heart's pumping power and *stroke volume* (the amount of blood pumped out with each beat). In addition, the heartbeat rate *(pulse rate)* diminishes gradually. The net result is a decrease in cardiac output. From age twenty to age seventy-five, this output typically declines by 30 percent. It must be emphasized, however, that cardiac output is not a function of age alone in all individuals. The described changes may not occur in the most physically fit individuals. One investigation of 500 airline pilots who had no cardiovascular disease revealed no correlation between age and cardiac output or stroke volume (Proper and Wall 1972). No doubt their heredity, health habits, and exercise patterns played a part in their superior cardiac fitness.

The heart can also lose its ability to respond to stress, such as vigorous exercise. A number of studies have shown that people in their twenties exhibit a greater increase in heart rate during vigorous exercise than do older persons (DeVries and Adams 1972; Kronenberg and Drage 1973). The younger heart can also pump more blood per heartbeat, enabling it to respond better to demands for an increased blood supply.

The health of the heart depends partially on the health of the blood vessels that transport the blood. Blood is pumped out of the heart through the aorta, and on to progressively smaller arteries. These empty into tiny *capillaries* in the various organs and tissues. *Veins* then collect the blood from the capillaries. The blood enters veins of increasing diameter, terminating in the largest veins, the *caval veins,* which enter the chest.

Several types of conditions can impede the flow of blood. The arteries consist of three layers: a lining, a middle muscular layer, and an outer layer. In arteriosclerosis, progressive deposits of calcium in the middle muscular layer cause the arteries to become rigid (hardening of the arteries). Because they cannot expand as readily when blood is pumped through them, their cross-sectional volume is reduced.

As arteries stiffen and peripheral resistance increases, hypertension (an elevation of blood pressure) results as the heart works harder to force the blood through smaller openings. This puts additional strain on the heart and, in extreme cases, may cause enlargement of the heart and damage to it. This type of heart trouble is called *hypertensive heart disease.* In *atherosclerosis,* fatty deposits collect between the artery lining and the middle muscular layer. If these deposits break through into the artery, rough spots form on which blood may clot, reducing blood flow. When this happens in the coronary arteries that supply the heart muscle with blood, the oxygen supply to the heart muscle is reduced. The heart struggles to get more oxygen, resulting in chest pains known as *angina pectoris.* A complete cutoff of the blood supply to any area of the heart, as with a blood clot, is called a *coronary occlusion with myocardial infarction* (heart attack). Since there are three major coronary arteries, an occlusion of one does not ordinarily cause death (12 percent die following a first heart attack). However, each succeeding attack becomes more risky. These types of *ischemic heart disease* (that impede the flow of blood and oxygen to the heart) are the most common and serious heart diseases of the elderly. Drug therapy, dietary adjustments (salt and cholesterol reduction especially), carefully planned exercise, and life-style alterations may prevent subsequent attacks (Leon and Blackburn 1977; Mock 1977). In some cases, surgery is required to alleviate the problem (Fishman and Roe 1978).

Congestive heart failure is also common among the elderly. Diminished cardiac output accompanied by increased blood pressure results in a build-up of fluid *(edema)* in other organs, particularly the lungs, liver, and legs. Symptoms include shortness of breath, severe discomfort when lying down, and swelling of the ankles.

Cardiac *arrhythmias* are irregularities in the normal heartbeat sequence (Sato et al. 1981). They can be dangerous when they alter the heart's normal contraction cycle. Irregular contractions may result in reduced pumping capacity and inadequate nourishment of the heart muscle, which leads to conditions of *ischemia* (inadequate oxygen supply).

Heart disease is the number one killer of the elderly. Furthermore, the incidence of heart disease increases with advancing age. Figure 5.1 shows the 1979 death rates by age groups per 100,000 population. Note that the rate skyrockets for those sixty-five and over, with the rate for males greater than for females.

Rapid advances have been made in the treatment of heart and circulatory disorders, and the incidence of these diseases is declining. In most cases, high blood pressure can be controlled. New miracle drugs, such as the *dilators, beta blockers,* and *calcium blockers,* have worked wonders for patients with cardiovascular disorders. Bypass surgery is now a principal means of improving the blood flow to the heart in patients who cannot be helped by drug therapy alone. With good medical care and proper health habits, the average older person can minimize the risks of heart problems.

When the brain is the site of vascular disease *(cerebrovascular),* an accident can occur in the form of a *thrombosis* (blockage from any kind of undissolved material in the blood), an *embolism* (blockage from a blood clot), or a *hemorrhage* (a ruptured blood vessel). A *stroke* occurs, in which

FIGURE 5.1   Death Rates from Heart Disease, by Age, Sex, United States, 1979

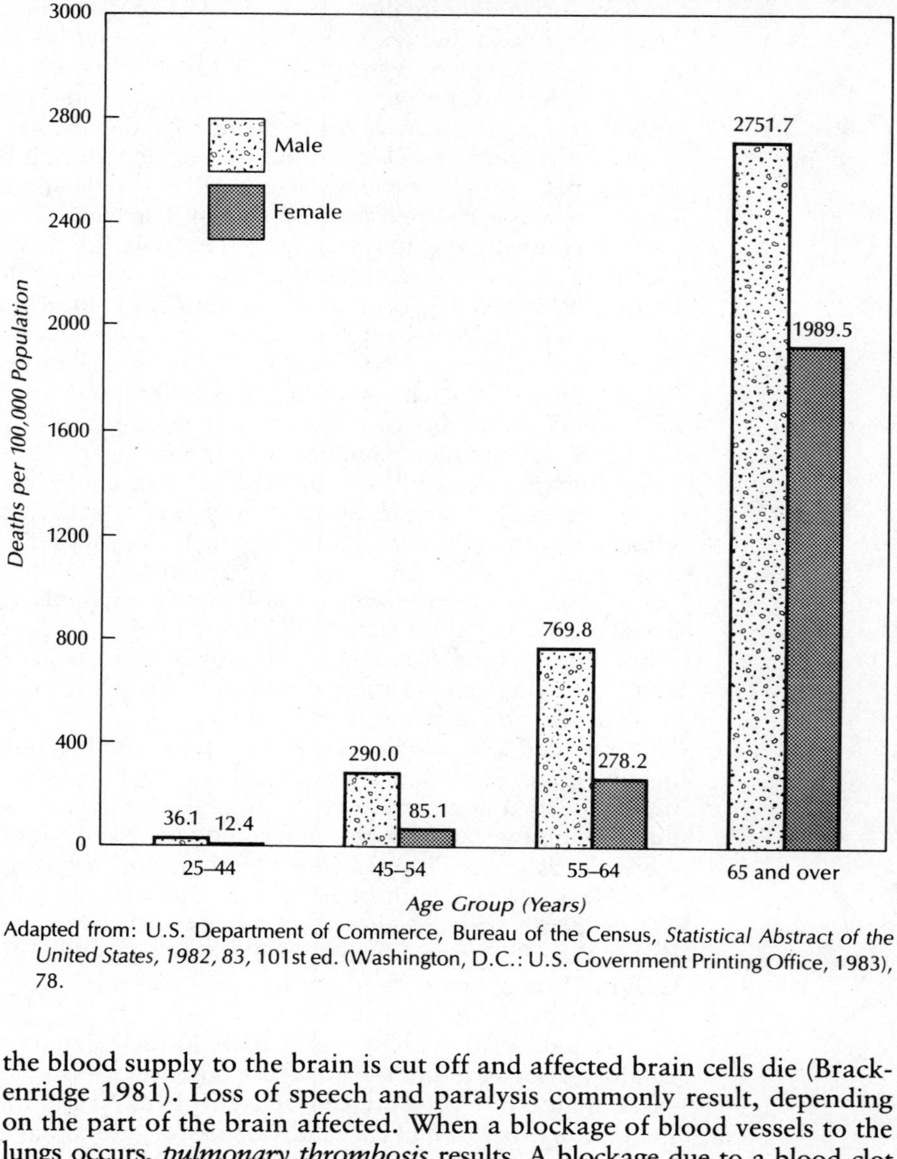

Adapted from: U.S. Department of Commerce, Bureau of the Census, *Statistical Abstract of the United States, 1982, 83,* 101st ed. (Washington, D.C.: U.S. Government Printing Office, 1983), 78.

the blood supply to the brain is cut off and affected brain cells die (Brackenridge 1981). Loss of speech and paralysis commonly result, depending on the part of the brain affected. When a blockage of blood vessels to the lungs occurs, *pulmonary thrombosis* results. A blockage due to a blood clot is called a *pulmonary embolism*.

Respiratory System

The *respiratory system* includes the *lungs* and related *air passageways*. Several significant things occur during aging to reduce lung efficiency. The rib cage and muscles become increasingly rigid, reducing the expansion and contraction capacity of the lungs. Air passageways become calcified and rigid. Together with changes in the rib cage, this results in a 55 to 60 percent reduction in maximum breathing capacity from twenty-five to eighty-five years of age (Muiesan et al. 1971). Figure 5.2 shows the trend with increasing age. Note that the actual breathing rate remains constant while breathing capacity declines. This means that the volume inhaled with each breath *(vital capacity)* declines considerably.

Several other changes occur that reduce lung efficiency. The air sacs lose elasticity, hindering their ability to expand on inhalation and contract on exhalation. Furthermore, deterioration in the capillaries and air sacs reduces the effectiveness of gas exchange between the air sacs and their blood supply.

Various studies have shown that oxygen conductance in the elderly can be increased through intensive training efforts (Adams and deVries 1973; Sidney and Shephard 1977). Part of the improvement is due to improved blood circulation, which brings more oxygen to the lungs (Niinimaa and Shephard 1978).

The changes just described commonly accompany aging. Various environmental factors can aggravate these changes. Long-term exposure to concentrations of air pollutants destroys the functional capability of the *alveoli* (lung cells) and the capillaries. Acute respiratory distress and even death may result from such conditions. Such respiratory diseases as *tu-*

FIGURE 5.2   Breathing Rate and Maximum Breathing Capacity by Age Decade Groups

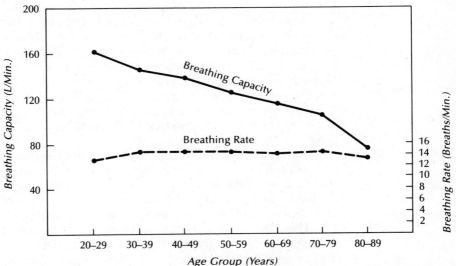

Adapted from: A. Norris, C. Mittman, and N. W. Shock, "Lung Function in Relation to Age: Changes in Ventilation with Age," *Aging of the Living,* L. Cander and J. H. Moyer, eds. (New York: Grune and Stratton, 1964), 138. Reprinted by permission.

berculosis, bronchial pneumonia, and *pulmonary infections* are most frequent in persons over sixty-five.

Smoking is one of the greatest hazards. It is a principal cause of *emphysema* and of lung cancer. The risk of lung cancer for an elderly person smoking ten to nineteen cigarettes per day is ten times greater than for an elderly nonsmoker. The risk increases linearly as exposure to tobacco increases (U.S. Dept. of HEW 1967).

Gastrointestinal System

The *gastrointestinal system* consists of the *mouth, esophagus, stomach, small intestine, large intestine, liver, pancreas,* and *gall bladder.*

The liver is the single most important organ in digestion. It is involved in the intermediate metabolism of all three nutrients: fats, proteins, and carbohydrates (which are reduced to sugars). It is also important in detoxifying drugs like morphine and steroids and in converting uric acid into urea, which then passes out of the body in urine.

The liver receives blood from the stomach and intestines and removes waste matter and poisons from it. It stores *glycogen* and emits it as sugar when the blood needs it. It stores vitamins A and D and those of the B-complex group, including vitamin B_{12}, which helps produce red blood cells and prevent *pernicious anemia.* It stores iron needed to produce *hemoglobin,* the red blood pigment. It also makes many blood proteins that prevent edema, provide resistance to disease, and ensure blood clotting to prevent extensive bleeding. The liver shrinks about 20 percent by age seventy-five; yet half of the organ can be removed and it will still function effectively. It has remarkable power to grow new cells as needed.

The liver is subject to damage, disease, and infections. *Jaundice,* in which skin tissues turn yellow, develops if the liver is not functioning properly. *Cirrhosis* is a condition in which the connective tissue thickens and then shrinks, causing the liver to become hard, lumpy, and shriveled. Alcohol, which irritates the liver, is a major cause of cirrhosis. Certain infections and poisons, an excess of fat, lack of protein in the diet, and a lack of B-complex vitamins also can cause cirrhosis, the eighth leading cause of death among diseases of the elderly (U.S. Dept. of Commerce 1983).

Gall bladder trouble is also fairly common in old age. The gall bladder stores about one and one-half ounces of *bile* at one time. It receives the bile from the liver and releases it when needed for digestion. Disease can block the bile duct and cause extreme pain. If the bile becomes highly concentrated, gallstones form that must be removed.

The pancreas is also important to digestion since it secretes *enzymes* and salts that help digest proteins, sugars, and fats. It also secretes *insulin* directly into the blood stream. All body cells need insulin to help them use sugar (glucose), their main fuel. If the pancreas secretes too little insulin, as sometimes happens with advancing age, the cells cannot function properly. Sugar accumulates and is passed out of the body in urine. Sugar in urine is one of the primary symptoms of *diabetes mellitus,* the seventh leading cause of death among diseases of the elderly (U.S. Dept. of Commerce 1983). Cancer of the pancreas has only a 3 percent survival rate among those afflicted.

Older persons often complain of indigestion and gas. This may be due to a chronic inflammation of the stomach lining. This condition *(gastritis)* is also characterized by a reduced secretion of digestive juices. The incidence of stomach cancer increases with age. Although the frequency of gastric (stomach) ulcers increases in middle age, few new cases develop after age sixty.

Urinary System

The *urinary system* includes the *kidneys,* the *bladder* (which stores the urine), the *ureters* (tubes that transport the urine from the kidneys to the bladder), and *urethra* (single, excretory tube that passes urine to the outside). The overall functions of the system are to eliminate wastes from the blood, maintain a proper balance of water and salts in the body, and regulate the pH level (the measure of acidity or alkalinity) of body fluids (which should be slightly alkaline).

The kidneys filter the waste products of metabolism from the blood. They slowly lose their filtering ability and function less efficiently with advancing age. Filtration declines as much as 50 percent from twenty-five to eighty, with very little occurring before age forty (Lindeman 1975). However, the capacity is so great that if one kidney is removed, the other takes over completely. Therefore, most changes with age are not debilitating.

Diseases of the kidney can be serious, however, because poisons collect in the body if the kidneys function improperly. Various types of diseases and inflammations reduce kidney functioning, and if too many wastes accumulate in the blood, the result can be fatal.

The bladder's ability to store urine diminishes at advanced ages. Consequently, older people have to urinate more often. Almost one-third of adults over sixty-five become *incontinent,* which results in bed wetting. This is most common after strokes and in cases of organic brain syndrome. Three percent of women and 13 percent of men over sixty-five lose *all* control of urination and void involuntarily. This symptom is often associated with prostate gland problems in men (Rockstein and Sussman 1979).

Skeletal-Dental Systems

One of the most noticeable signs of advancing age is a change in stature and posture. Investigations have shown that white males lose approximately one-half inch in height every twenty years after age thirty. This loss is accelerated in blacks (McPherson et al. 1978). It is also greater in females of both races than in males.

There are several reasons for the loss in stature. There is some loss of bone mass itself and a flattening of vertebral discs. Muscles shrink; ligaments and tendons lose elasticity, shrink, and harden. The result is a posture slump or stoop, with the head, neck, and upper torso bent forward. Accordingly, height diminishes with advancing age.

Decalcification and loss of bone mass is called *osteoporosis*. It occurs in both sexes but is more extensive in females. Females show a 25 percent bone loss, as compared to a 12 percent loss in the male, over a thirty-year period. However, in the United States, black women have a lower rate of adult bone loss than do white women. In extreme cases of osteoporosis, the upper spinal vertebrae collapse, causing what is referred to in women as dowager's hump. The disease affects both men and women, but females are four times more likely to be affected with severe osteoporosis than are men (Wyshak 1981).

Most bone loss occurs on the inside of the bone. As bones get bigger on the outside, they are reduced in mass from the inside out. In tubular bones, the *medullary cavity* gets bigger, while the cortical thickness decreases, giving the appearance of less bone (Garn 1970). (See Figure 5.3.) Because bone loss takes place deep beneath the soft tissues, initially it is scarcely detectable. But as loss continues, the vertebrae become less resistant to compression and the tubular bones and neck become less resistant to stress. The bones become brittle and fracture easily. Figure 5.4 shows the cumulative probability of bone fracture as bone loss increases (Garn 1973). At present there is no certain cure and no known prevention for bone loss.

> Present approaches to prevention, including calcium supplementation and moderate doses of fluoride . . . are of doubtful and untested efficacy. . . . Massive doses of vitamin D, protein supplementation, exercise, and Premarin all have their advocates, but few proven examples. (Garn 1975, 53)

FIGURE 5.3   Age Changes at the Inner and Outer Surface of a Tubular Bone: Female Bone Remodeling, Ages Thirty to Eighty

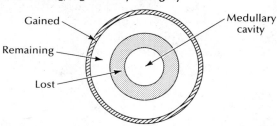

Scale: 1 mm

From: S. M. Garn, *The Earlier Gain and the Later Loss of Cortical Bone* (Springfield, Ill.: Charles C. Thomas, 1970). Courtesy of publisher.

FIGURE 5.4   Cumulative Fracture-Risk Curves (Swedish Data, Left) and Cumulative Percent Bone-Loss Curves (USA Data, Right)

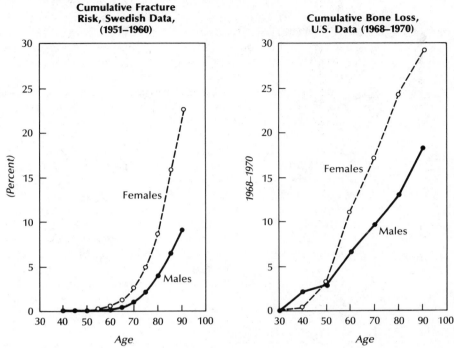

From S. M. Garn, "Bone Loss and Aging," *Nutrition Today* 27 (1973): 107. Copyright © 1973 The Williams and Wilkins Co., Baltimore.

Estrogen replacement therapy in women who experience early menopause because of surgery shows some promise in preventing bone loss at this stage of life. There is little hard evidence that estrogens reverse or delay aging in older female bones and even less evidence that testosterone slows bone loss in adult males (Davis et al. 1970).

Two other important diseases that affect the skeletal systems of the elderly are *osteoarthritis* and *rheumatoid arthritis*. Osteoarthritis is a degenerative joint disease. It occurs in different bones, including weight- and nonweight-bearing types, but it seems more common in parts of the body bearing the greatest weight. Males seem to have the disease with greater severity than females, and blacks appear more susceptible than whites. The incidence and severity of osteoarthritis increase to the age of eighty, with a striking decrease after ninety. Hereditary factors may have some influence on the probability of the disease.

Rheumatoid arthritis is less common than osteoarthritis and characteristically affects the small joints of the hands and wrists. It is marked by a swelling or disfigurement of the affected areas and is accompanied by a higher level of pain than most other types of arthritis. There is considerable evidence that the causes are partly psychosomatic, related to reactions to stress. At the present time, arthritis cannot be cured, but it can be managed, allowing people to function. Unfortunately many older people seek out all kinds of quack cures that do not help (Shuman 1980).

Years ago, women believed that they would lose at least one tooth for each child born. This often happened because nutritional demands of pregnancy and nursing depleted the mother's nutrients. Since these nutrients were not replaced through vitamin and mineral supplements, the mother's body suffered. Many older people resigned themselves to losing all their teeth by sixty-five and having to wear dentures. Even today, as many as 50 percent of people over sixty-five have lost all their teeth.

Periodontal disease (formerly called *pyorrhea*) is a major reason for tooth loss. It is a disease in which the gums become infected, swell, and shrink away from the teeth. Tooth decay is also a significant factor in tooth loss in the elderly. Yet these diseases are not inevitable results of aging. They are due primarily to neglect of the teeth and lack of proper dental care. Almost 70 percent of the elderly receive no dental care (Beck et al. 1979).

Dental health is important not only in preserving the teeth, but also in maintaining the body's health. Improperly chewed food affects digestion. People with sore gums become less interested in eating, thus receiving inadequate amounts of nutrients needed to maintain bodily health.

CHANGES IN SENSORY PERCEPTION

Seeing

Visual acuity, the ability to perceive small details, reaches a maximum around age twenty and remains relatively constant to forty. It then begins to decline. Although most older people need eyeglasses, about 70 percent have fair to adequate visual acuity to age eighty and beyond. Figure 5.5 shows the changes in visual acuity with age according to a national health survey (U.S. National Health Survey 1968). The graph shows the corrected visual acuity in the better eye. Visual acuity of 20/20 is perfect; 20/50 or worse is serious enough to make some states impose restrictions on drivers' licenses. Obviously, the percentage of persons with visual problems increases with age.

Only a small percentage (almost 2 percent) of persons sixty-five and over are legally blind, that is, they have less than 20/200 corrected vision in the better eye or a visual field subtending an angle less than 20 degrees (U.S. Dept. of Commerce 1980a). Most blindness develops late in life.

There are various kinds of visual impairments. One of the most common is *presbyopia* (farsightedness). As the lens becomes more opaque and less elastic, it begins to lose some power of *accommodation* (the power to focus so distinct vision is assured at both near and far distances). Accommodation declines from age six to sixty, after which it levels off until

FIGURE 5.5   Changes in Visual Acuity According to a National Health Survey

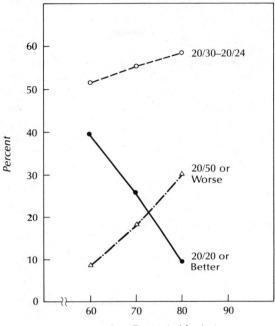

Age Group (midpoint)

Data from: U.S. National Health Survey, *Monocular-Binocular Visual Acuity of Adults,* Public Health Service Pub. No. 100—Series 11—No. 30, 1960–62 (Washington, D.C.: U.S. Department of HEW, 1968).

extreme old age. Farsighted adults must wear corrective glasses for reading, writing, knitting, or other close work.

Another common problem is a decrease in pupil size, allowing less light to reach the retina (Shore 1976). The pupil also declines in ability to open and close with changes in light intensity (loss of *adaptation*). This ability decreases linearly from age twenty to age sixty. As a result, older people have difficulty seeing at night or in dimly lit places. They actually need seven times as much light as the average twenty-year-old (*To Your Health* 1979). At the same time, glare in intense light is a problem because the eye cannot close enough to block out the excess. *Peripheral vision* also begins to show meaningful decrements when people reach their fifties and sixties. Color vision is also affected by age. The lens gradually yellows and filters out the violet, blue, and green colors toward the dark end of the spectrum (Jacobs and Krohn 1976). For this reason, older people see yellow, orange, and red colors more easily than darker colors.

A number of diseases affect vision in old age. About one-fourth of people in their seventies have *cataracts* (a gradual clouding of the lens that shuts off vision). *Glaucoma,* a condition in which the fluid pressure in the eye is too high, causes headaches, eye pain, rainbow halos to appear around light bulbs, and gradual loss of peripheral and central vision. It occurs in 2 to 4 percent of the adult population, especially in the elderly. In most cases, progression of glaucoma can be prevented (Tupper 1977).

Macular diseases account for some 45 percent of vision problems in elderly persons (Gordon 1965). The *macula* is a small part of the *retina* responsible for clearest central vision, especially vision for color and detail (Sekuler and Hutman 1980). A healthy retina is extremely important to all vision because all light rays entering the eye form the image on the retina and send an electrical impulse from there, through the *optic nerve,* to the brain. Shrinking of the *vitreous humor* (the fluid in the inner, posterior portion of the eye) seems to occur with aging. This can result in detachment of the retina if the retina remains attached to the fluid as it shrinks. A sharp blow to the eye can also dislodge the retina, so it floats into the eye fluid. Unless the retina is reattached quickly through surgery, permanent blindness can occur. Damage to the *cornea* (the clear tissue over the colored part of the eye) from injury or infection also affects vision. Surgeons use corneal transplants to replace scarred corneas.

Hearing

Hearing ability reaches its maximum around age twenty. Hearing impairment associated with advancing age is called *presbycuses.* Usually, hearing loss does not occur suddenly. There is a gradual loss from childhood on, with severe loss occurring first in the ability to hear high-pitched sounds (Potash and Jones 1977). A ten-year-old, for example, can hear high-pitched sounds with upper frequencies of almost 20,000 cycles per second (Hz). But persons aged sixty-five hear sounds only up to about 8,000 Hz. They have more difficulty hearing high-pitched voices and perceiving certain high-frequency consonants, such as *z, s, g, f,* and *t.* The elderly person may hear *ave* instead of *save, ame* instead of *game, alk* instead of *talk,* or *pa* instead of *pat.* Such words as *gaze, first, stop,* or *grass* with two or more high-frequency consonants may not be understood at all (Sataloff and Vassallo 1966).

A noticeable decline begins in the fifties, and by seventy there is a loss in hearing at all frequencies, even those below 1,000 Hz (Bergman et al. 1976). After fifty-five, men show a greater incidence of hearing loss than do women. However, when speech is clear, undistorted, and presented without competing noise, most older subjects suffer very little loss in ability to understand (Warren et al. 1978). Distorted and noise-masked speech is difficult for many older people to decipher (Bergman 1971). Shouting at them usually does not help, since this involves raising the voice to higher pitches.

Hearing losses are due to a number of different causes, including something as simple as wax build-up in the ears. Noise pollution is a frequent cause. Individuals brought up in quiet rural areas, for example, suffer less hearing loss than do those raised in noisy cities. Injury or infection may damage the ear's structure so it fails to convert sounds into neural impulses. The *auditory nerve*, which carries these impulses to the brain, can also degenerate or be damaged. Finally, damage to areas of the brain responsible for translating auditory nerve impulses to meaningful sounds is another cause of difficulty.

Hearing impairments have a variety of consequences. One is increased social isolation. In some cases, hearing loss is associated with such emotional disturbances as depression and paranoia. A decrease in hearing sensitivity limits the enjoyment of social gatherings, musical concerts, plays, radio, and television. Hearing impairment also leads to a decline in cognitive and intellectual functioning unless corrective measures are taken (Granick, Kleban, and Weiss 1976). Fortunately, some hearing problems are treatable or correctable.

Taste and Smell

Eating is such an important part of our physical and social lives that any change in the ability to taste various foods is significant. Evidence indicates that the ability to perceive all four taste qualities—sweet, salt, bitter, and sour—declines in later life, although the decrement is small (Shore 1976). Actually, taste buds continually replace themselves, and one researcher (Arvidson 1979) found no change in the number of taste buds per area as a function of age. Yet, taste sensitivity shows some decline; the number of taste buds is not as crucial as are their responsiveness and ability to transmit taste sensations through the neurons to the brain (Moore et al. 1982).

The taste for sweet and salty flavors declines faster than that for bitter and sour (Grzegorczyk et al. 1979; Moore et al. 1982). As a result, older people complain that their food tastes bitter and sour (Shore 1976). Or, they require more highly seasoned food to experience the same taste satisfactions they had when younger. This complicates the problems of those on salt-free diets. The elderly also show a decline in ability to identify foods from smell and/or taste when compared to younger subjects.

Tactile Sensitivity: Touch and Pain

Touch sensitivity is another way an individual maintains contact with the physical world. It is an important factor in the ability to locate, manipulate, and identify objects. Research reveals some decrease in tactile acuity with increasing age, but the loss is small, and a number of individuals over sixty retain high sensitivity. Loss of sensitivity may be greater in the *glabrous* (smooth and bald) skin of the palm and sole. Thornbury and Mistretta (1981) found a small but statistically significant decrease in tactile acuity on the fingertip as a function of age.

Temperature and pain sensitivity are impaired in only a small percentage of the elderly. The low frequency of occurrence suggests neuropathologies, or the involvement of spinal cord or brain lesions, rather than advancing age. One study of reactions to dentally induced pain found no age-related differences in threshold for perception of dental shocks in women (Harkins and Chapman 1976). However, a comparison of these results with those reported using similar stimulation techniques for men showed that the females exhibited a lower pain threshold (less tolerance to pain) than did the males (Harkins and Chapman 1976).

Temperature and pain sensitivity are difficult to measure, however, since they are subjective reactions. Some older people are very tolerant of pain and do not report pain that would be unbearable to other persons. Other elderly have a low pain threshold. Aging adults are more influenced by suggestion; if given a placebo with the suggestion that pain will be relieved, many report relief.

Thermoregulation

Thermoregulation is the maintenance of body temperature during exposure to heat or cold. Body temperature is usually regulated within narrow limits. Experiments have shown that young adults can regulate body heat under adverse temperature conditions, whereas older adults show significant changes in body temperature.

Sense of Balance

Hairlike projections in the inner ear act as sensory perceptors that pick up and pass on information to the brain about body positions and orientations that constitute our sense of balance. A maximum sense of balance is achieved between forty and fifty, followed by decline. One consequence is that older people tend to fall more often. We are not certain exactly why balance declines. Inner ear tissues may deteriorate with age, but not always. Possibly, a diminishing blood supply causes dizziness. Declines in nervous reflexes, psychomotor coordination, and muscular strength are undoubtedly factors. Or, failing eyesight and improper illumination may cause older adults to have more accidents.

SUMMARY

Senescence is used to describe biological aging. It should not be confused with senility, which is a disease. All animals age, but the processes are many since decline takes place in different parts of the body at different rates.

Senescence has several criteria that support it as a biological process and not a disease. It must be universal, occurring in all people. The changes come primarily from within the organism and are not a result of the external environment. It occurs gradually, not suddenly, and it contributes to a decline in function and to mortality.

Different theories have been proposed to explain why people age. The principal ones are heredity theory, cellular aging theory, wear-and-tear theory, metabolic waste or clinker theory, autoimmunity theory, homeostatic imbalance theory, mutation theory, and error theory. No single theory proposed to date explains totally the complex events that occur in aging. In addition, environmental stress plays a part in the aging process.

Various changes occur in the bodily systems as people age. The principal changes in the nervous system are atrophy of brain cells, a reduced blood supply to the brain that lowers brain efficiency, and a slowing of nerve impulses and responses so people talk, read, write, walk, and jump more slowly as they age. However, practice and exercise can alleviate some of the changes.

The changes in the cardiovascular system include a decrease in cardiac output and a reduction in the ability of the heart to respond to stress. A reduction in blood flow due to arteriosclerosis or atherosclerosis may also occur. Other specific diseases include hypertensive heart disease, angina pectoris, coronary occlusion with myocardial infarction, congestive heart failure, cardiac arrhythmias, cerebrovascular disease (in the form of a thrombosis, embolism, or hemorrhage), and pulmonary thrombosis or pulmonary embolism.

A number of factors affect cardiovascular functioning and the risk of heart attack. These include heredity, body weight, smoking, exercise, cholesterol or fat in the diet, blood pressure, gender, character or personality, stress, diabetes, vital breathing capacity, and cardiovascular abnormalities.

The most important change in the respiratory system is a reduction in the vital capacity of the lungs. Such environmental factors as exposure to air pollutants or smoking increase the risk, as do respiratory diseases, such as tuberculosis, bronchial pneumonia, pulmonary infections, pulmonary embolism, and emphysema. Smoking is the principal cause of lung cancer.

Various changes may occur in the gastrointestinal system. The liver is subject to damage, disease, and infections. Cirrhosis of the liver is the eighth leading cause of death among the elderly. Other common diseases of the gastrointestinal system are gall bladder trouble; diseases of the pancreas, such as cancer, which interfere with the secretion of insulin into the bloodstream, causing excess sugar (diabetes mellitus); chronic inflammation of the lining of the stomach (gastritis); stomach ulcers; and stomach cancer.

The most common changes in the urinary sytem include a reduction in the kidneys' ability to filter waste products from the blood and a decrease in the bladder's ability to store urine. Almost one-third of adults over sixty-five become incontinent.

The skeletal-dental systems also undergo changes. Most people experience a reduction in height due to loss of bone mass and the flattening of vertebral discs. Muscles, ligaments, and tendons deteriorate, causing an increase in posture slumping and stooping. Decalcification and loss of bone mass (osteoporosis) occur in some people, with the disease more common in females than males. The bones become brittle and fracture easily. In advanced stages, the upper spinal vertebrae collapse, resulting in dowager's hump. There is no certain cure for osteoporosis. Osteoarthritis and rheumatoid arthritis are other diseases affecting the skeletal systems of the elderly. Presently, arthritis cannot be cured, but it can be managed so people can function.

Periodontal disease, in which the gums become infected, swell, and shrink away from the teeth, is the major reason for tooth loss. Tooth decay, which is enhanced by neglect and lack of proper dental care, is also a significant factor. Dental health is important because it affects the health of the whole body.

Aging may also bring some significant changes in sensory perception. Visual acuity declines, as do the powers of accommodation and adaptation. Peripheral vision and color vision become poorer. Some of the most common eye diseases affecting sight include cataracts, glaucoma, macular diseases (including deterioration or detachment of the retina), and cornea injuries or infections.

Hearing impairment with advancing age is called presbycuses. The most common impairment is loss of ability to hear high-pitched sounds, although by age seventy there may be a loss of hearing at all frequencies. Hearing losses may result from wax build-up in the ear, noise pollution, injury or infection, damage to or degeneration of the auditory nerve, or damage to the areas of the brain controlling hearing. Hearing problems increase the possibility of social isolation, the difficulties of communication, and the possibility of misunderstanding. They limit one's enjoyment of nature, social gatherings, and entertainment and may result in a decline in cognitive and intellectual functioning. Many hearing problems are treatable or correctable.

The ability to taste, especially sweet and salty flavors, declines with age. The elderly also show a decline in ability to smell. They may complain of tasteless food or that food tastes bitter or sour.

Touch, temperature, and pain sensitivity are impaired in only a small percentage of the elderly, and the loss is not great. Since these are subjective reactions, however, they are hard to measure, and these abilities vary greatly among different persons.

Thermoregulation, the ability of the body to maintain the proper temperature when exposed to heat or cold, declines with age, as does the sense of balance.

6

Physical Attractiveness, Abilities, and Fitness

GROWTH AND AGING

Sometime during the mid-twenties, the human body is usually at the peak of its physical development. Height is at a maximum, bones and teeth are strong, muscles are powerful, the skin is supple, senses are keen, and the mind is sharp. Ironically, at the same time, aging is taking place. Every human being is born with a fantastic reserve of tissue and cells, but this reserve is gradually depleted with age. Some types of cells, such as liver and kidney cells, replace themselves over a long period of time. Other cells, such as muscle cells, have a limited replicative potential. All cells and tissue have limited lives, and the older a person gets the weaker the regenerative process becomes. Slowly, almost imperceptibly for years, the human body ages.

Each person has a different *biological time clock,* some aging faster than others. Men age more quickly than women up to the age of fifty. Cross-cultural studies indicate wide variations. Differences also exist within a particular culture. Black males age faster than do whites of the same age (Morgan 1968). Much depends on heredity, but diet, climate, exercise, and health habits are also influential. This is why *chronological age* alone is a poor measure of physical condition or aging.

The important emphasis should be on *functional age,* that is, the ability of the adult to perform regardless of age. Some forty-year-olds act, think, and behave like sixty-year-olds, and some at sixty live and perform better than those in their twenties. One study of 1,146 healthy men, ages twenty-five to eighty-three, revealed a 42 percent differential between functional age and chronological age when personality factors, abilities, and blood chemistry were considered (Fozard et al. 1972; Nuttal et al. 1971). Other extensive studies attempted to measure different aspects of functional age, such as body chemistry, anthropometric descriptions, perceptual and motor abilities, and other factors (Bell et al. 1972). These measurements, along with subjective evaluations of age (how old people say they actually look, feel, think, and act), enable researchers to make more accurate age determinations than are possible with chronological evaluations (Kastenbaum et al. 1972).

PHYSICAL ATTRACTIVENESS AND THE BODY IMAGE

Signs of Age

One characteristic of middle age is a growing awareness of personal mortality accompanying the first physical signs of aging. Most young adults are concerned about their appearance because "they want to look nice," but middle-aged adults are concerned for a different reason. For the first time, they begin to look older, with noticeable alterations in appearance.

Obvious changes occur to the hair. Graying and thinning hair, and receding hairline, particularly in men, become apparent. One of the greatest changes usually affects the contours of the body, particularly in people living sedentary lives. As Bob Hope expressed it, "Middle age is when your age starts to show around your middle." On the average, weight gain continues into the forties for men and up to age sixty for women, followed by a decline. Figure 6.1 shows the trends for men and women in the United States (U.S. Dept. of Commerce 1980a). At fifty, the average male is 5' 9" tall and weighs 177 pounds; the average female is 5' 4" tall and weighs 154 pounds. As the graph shows, women have a greater tendency to gain weight (an average of twenty-two pounds between age twenty-one and sixty) than do men (an average of fifteen pounds between age twenty-one and forty). The period of weight gain is also longer for women. It must be emphasized, however, that both men and women gain weight because of overeating and a lack of exercise, not because of aging as such.

Adults not only get heavier, but they may also get flabbier. Muscle tissue is slowly converted to fat, so the flesh loses its firmness. The breasts begin to sag. The skin becomes drier and begins to lose elasticity. It becomes coarser and darker on the face, arms, and hands. Wrinkles appear, especially if people have been exposed to the sun and weather or have had improper diets. By late adulthood, muscle flabbiness under the skin may cause bags and dark circles under the eyes. The chin may recede and the upper lip look thin because of changes in the bones, muscles, and connective tissue. Posture and movements are less graceful as the joints stiffen and muscles lose resiliency and strength. The shoulders tend to round, and the body appears to sag. The voice loses its timbre and quality (by late adulthood, most singers decide to retire). The teeth may yellow and/or decay, perhaps requiring extensive dental work or dentures. The eyes lose some of their sparkle and become increasingly opaque, with discoloration appearing at the edge of the cornea.

The extent of these changes depends on the individual. Not all older adults exhibit all these effects of aging. Superior nutrition and health care, plus close attention to exercise and physical fitness, help people look young much longer than was the case a generation ago. Everyone eventually ages

FIGURE 6.1   Average Weights, by Age, Height, and Sex, United States, 1971–1974

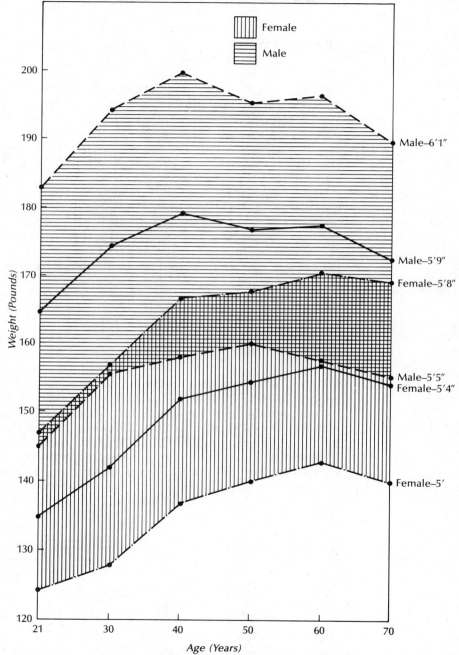

Adapted from: U.S. Department of Commerce, Bureau of the Census, *Statistical Abstract of the United States, 1980* (Washington, D.C.: U.S. Government Printing Office, 1980), 125.

physically, but some people look twenty or thirty years younger than their actual age would suggest.

Attitudes of Society

Self-consciousness about one's changing physique is accentuated by society's attitudes. In the United States, attractiveness is equated with youthfulness (Nowak 1975). To be beautiful is to be young and slender. Female models for cosmetics and clothes are thin and sinewy; male models are slender and muscular. The middle-aged adult concludes from these ads that the bodily house is crumbling. The roof is in trouble, the mortar is coming out of the joints, the floors are sagging, and the doors creak (Conway 1978).

Because it is fashionable to be slender, society rewards those who fit the ideal images. The president of a chain of employment agencies evaluated the salaries of 15,000 agency executives and found that among those who earned the highest salaries, only 9 percent were more than ten pounds overweight. Among the lowest paid, almost 40 percent were more than ten pounds overweight (Conway 1978). The president reported that his agencies received thousands of requests for thin people, but the only request they ever had for a fat person came from a company that made clothes for overweight men.

Double Standard

Generally speaking, our society accepts a double standard for men and women (Berman et al. 1981). It helps if a man is slim and youthful, but it is absolutely obligatory for a woman. Eve of Roma, a maker of cosmetics for women, emphasizes, "A man is a man—it doesn't matter if he's ugly. But a woman must look as beautiful as she can, because both are happier that way" (Weg 1977). Most modern women reject this sexist philosophy, but many are still taught that physical attractiveness is their most valuable asset. Until society views a woman's wrinkles as signs of character and experience, she will continue to react negatively to the aging process.

Reactions

Not all people react identically to the aging process. Some react with resignation, some with denial, and others with positive acceptance. Those who resign themselves to aging decide there is nothing they can or want to do; they just give up (Funk 1980). They take little interest in their physical appearance or weight. They eat what they want regardless of its effect. They put little effort into selecting appropriate clothes or making themselves attractive. Physically out of shape, they exercise less and less.

Consequently, their health may suffer. Some adopt an "I don't care" attitude and expect that others will consider them eccentric. Some do care, but not enough to take action, so the decline in attractiveness may lead to reduced self-confidence and social contacts. In extreme instances, feelings of rejection, anxiety, and depression result, accompanied by social withdrawal.

Certain people react by denying that they are getting old. They will not admit to any change. Some try to dress and act like teenagers, much to the chagrin of their grown children. Their choice of bikinis or tight pants makes them look ridiculous. They make every effort to prove they are as young and fit as ever. A clothing salesman in a menswear store commented on the tastes of his middle-aged clientele:

> I've seen it a thousand times. They start swinging when they're pushing up near fifty. . . . They come in here wearing conservative cuts, dark gray and blue, and they walk out with vests, plaids, gold buttons, hot pink shirts. I had one guy in here this morning—looked like a VP, he was in a gray flannel suit, white shirt, cuff links. You'll never believe me when I tell you he walked out of here in a turtleneck, bell trousers, a jacket that I couldn't unload on a teenager at half the price. He asks me how does he look. You make a two-hundred buck sale; the guy is standing there, with a paunch, gray hair, bags under his eyes and what do you say? You tell me. (Davitz and Davitz 1979, 93)

Another example was the fifty-year-old father who challenged his twenty-five-year-old son to a marathon race. The father dropped dead of a heart attack in the process. And one middle-aged woman reacted to menopause by developing an insatiable sexual appetite to prove to herself and her husband that she was just as desirable and sexy as ever.

Other people accept advancing age positively, not with resignation. They make realistic efforts to change their habits and life-style accordingly and take a no-panic approach to physical aging. Acceptance of the aging process motivates them to do the best they can with the assets they have.

PHYSICAL FITNESS AND HEALTH

Physical fitness and health are only partially related to chronological age. One study of middle-aged runners and joggers showed that these men compared in cardiorespiratory fitness to men who were twenty years younger and in good physical condition (Hartung and Farge 1977). Of the total group, the marathon runners were clearly superior to the non-marathoners with regard to physiological factors, body composition measures, and lower *cholesterol* and *triglyceride* levels. Another study of marathoners showed that they were immune to atherosclerosis (Boeckman 1979). Although age eventually takes its toll, good fitness and health habits certainly slow down the aging process.

Exercise

Exercise is one of the best ways to prevent ill health and maintain body fitness. Without exercise, bodies literally waste away. Muscles grow weak, bones become more porous, arteries clog up, and the heart is pressed to cope with sudden demands. A study of 16,936 men (thirty-five to seventy-four) showed that those who took part in strenuous sports had fewer heart attacks than those who were sedentary (Boeckman 1979). Exercise may be the most effective fountain of youth yet discovered. Exercise improves respiration and feeds more oxygen to the whole body, increasing circulation, nourishing the brain, improving digestion and bowel functioning, preserving the bones, toning the muscles, and relieving nervous tension, depression, and anxiety. Without exercise, the cardiovascular system's capacity to deliver oxygen to working muscles is reduced relatively early in the aging process, and the weakness and fatigability of the muscles advances rapidly (Gutmann 1977; Skinner 1973).

According to one national survey, about one-half of young adults between twenty and thirty-nine engage in some sort of regular (at least once a week) physical exercise. Walking is the most common exercise. Calisthenics, swimming, and bicycle riding are about equal in popularity. Only a small percentage jog (8 percent) or lift weights (6 percent) (U.S. Dept. of Commerce 1980a). Sports such as skiing are popular, but seasonal, and enjoyed only in certain sections of the country. Peak performance in such games as golf is usually reached in one's thirties. A national survey showed that less than half (42 percent) of this country's adults, aged forty-five to sixty-four, engaged in any form of exercise at least weekly (U.S. Dept. of Commerce 1980a).

Pulse Rate

One of the simplest measures of health and physical fitness is pulse rate. *Pulse rate* is the number of times the heart beats per minute. It can be felt in various parts of the body, but the area commonly used is the wrist artery. Count the number of pulse beats for six seconds and then add a zero; or count the beats for fifteen seconds and multiply by four. This gives the pulse rate per minute. The pulse rate is the body's most important single indicator of well-being, stress, or illness (Morehouse and Gross 1975). In the average adult male, the resting pulse rate averages seventy-two to seventy-six beats per minute. In adult females, the resting pulse rate averages seventy-seven to eighty beats per minute. In general, the lower the resting rate, the healthier the person, unless there is a major heart problem. Resting pulse rates higher than eighty beats per minute suggest poor health and fitness; the heart is working hard just to maintain the circulation in the body. For example, the mortality rate for men and women with resting pulse rates over ninety-two is four times greater than for those with pulse rates less than sixty-seven (Morehouse and Gross 1975).

The pulse rate goes up during exercise and indicates the intensity of exertion as well as one's fitness. A rate above 120 per minute borders on intensive exertion. However, the more physically fit you are, the more strenuously you can exercise without increasing your pulse rate excessively. A person whose resting pulse is racing at 100 or 110 cannot tolerate much exertion; the heart is already strained. But a person who exercises strenuously and whose pulse rate rises very little is in excellent physical condition, unless significant problems are preventing the heartbeat from increasing. The healthy person's heart is already working strongly, pumping a large volume of blood with each beat, so the pumping rate does not have to rise much even under considerable exertion. Ordinarily, the more a person exercises over a period of time, the stronger the heart becomes, and the slower the pulse rate at rest or under exertion.

There are some indexes of how much the pulse rate should increase during exercise to make certain an individual is not exerting too much or too little (Blanding 1982; Morehouse and Gross 1975). For instance, take the figure of 220 beats per minute (the theoretical maximum pulse rate), subtract your age, and multiply by a percentage. People in poor physical condition should multiply by 60 percent, those in moderate condition by 70 percent, and those in good physical condition by 80 percent. The result is a *target pulse rate.*

Suppose a person is sixty years old and in moderate physical condition.

$$\begin{array}{l} 220 \ (\text{maximum pulse rate}) \\ \underline{-60 \ (\text{age})} \\ 160 \times .70 \ (\text{for moderate condition}) = 112 \ \text{beats} \\ \qquad\qquad\qquad\qquad\qquad\qquad\qquad\qquad \text{per minute} \end{array}$$

The target rate of 112 is the rate the person should strive to achieve while exercising. If the rate is not reached, more strenuous exercise is needed. If the rate is much higher, the exertion may be too great for one's fitness level. Furthermore, the target rate should be sustained for at least fifteen to thirty minutes of continuous exercise. Some authorities advise exercise at least three or four times per week. Some recommend daily exercise to maintain cardiovascular fitness. As fitness improves, the target rate will increase, requiring one to exercise more strenuously to raise the pulse rate. Once a person is in good physical condition (using an 80 percent multiple), maintenance is achieved by raising the pulse rate to the target figure, or slightly above, during exercise.

Note that this system of monitoring physical fitness emphasized cardiovascular fitness, so important to total health as people age. Pulse rate has nothing to do with strength or with such factors as resistance to disease, but since cardiovascular fitness affects all bodily organs and functions, its importance cannot be overestimated.

Rest and Sleep

Adequate amounts of sleep and rest help to stave off physical fatigue by replenishing energy burned up while awake. Rest also helps maintain maximum intellectual functioning. A positive correlation has been found, for example, between adequate rest and high scores on the Wechsler Adult Intelligence Scale (WAIS) (Prinz 1977). Most adults regularly need seven or eight hours of sleep at night to stay healthy. But sleeping habits change as one ages, and the rest received may not be adequate.

People sleep less as they get older. Babies average about sixteen hours a day. By five, a child usually stops napping and sleeps about eleven hours daily. Starting in the late teens, most people average seven and one-half hours of sleep. On the average, people over fifty sleep an hour less, and among the elderly, deep sleep generally disappears (Feinberg 1974). Consequently, older adults sleep more fitfully and are more easily disturbed. Generally, the hours spent in bed are not as restful as they once were.

In addition, older adults usually wake earlier than when they were younger. One adult in his forties reported, "When I was younger, I used to stay in bed all morning on the weekends. Now I can't sleep past eight o'clock." If the adult goes to bed later than usual, he or she may not get adequate sleep because of the tendency to wake up early.

Numerous factors affect sleep (Freeman 1972), including one's psychological state. Insomnia may be triggered by upsetting circumstances, such as a death in the family or a job loss.

Physical factors are also important. The length of sleep depends more on body temperature at the time of sleep than on the amount of time previously spent awake. People who go to sleep when their body temperatures are high will sleep longer. Body temperature depends partially on biological rhythms; it also depends on comfortable room temperatures and adequate coverings. Health habits also affect sleep. Experts advise people to avoid alcohol and caffeine before bedtime. A small amount of liquor acts as a sedative, but overindulgence reduces sleep. It also helps to sleep on a comfortable bed in a dark room, away from noise and disturbances.

NUTRITION

Importance

Proper nutrition is another important factor in maintaining good health. It results in feelings of well-being, high energy levels to carry on daily activities, and maximum resistance to disease and fatigue. Poor nutrition may accelerate the aging process, accentuate physical handicaps, and result in generally poorer health. The saying, "You are what you eat," is certainly true.

Diet and Weight

The weight figures given earlier in this chapter indicate that the average adult in the United States is twenty or more pounds overweight. Although the average fifty-year-old woman weighs 154 pounds and the average fifty-year-old man weighs 177 pounds, these are not ideal weights. Ideal weights range from twenty to forty pounds less, depending on body frame.

Losing weight is difficult unless caloric intake is reduced. Figure 6.2 shows the daily caloric intake and expenditure in normal males. *Basal calories* are those metabolized by the body to carry on its physiological functions and maintain normal body temperature. *Activity calories* are those expended through physical activities. Because of reduced exercise, the need for activity calories falls somewhat more rapidly than for basal calories, requiring a corresponding reduction in caloric intake to avoid weight gain (Shock 1977b).

FIGURE 6.2   Daily Caloric Intake and Expenditure in Normal Males

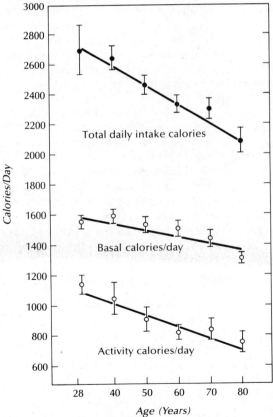

Adapted from: N. W. Shock, "Systems Integration," *Handbook of the Biology of Aging*, C. E. Finch and L. Hayflick, eds. (New York: Van Nostrand Reinhold Co., 1977), 644.

Requirements

Although energy requirements decrease with advancing age, middle-aged and older adults need as many nutrients as do younger adults. Thus, the older person's diet must provide foods of greater *nutrient density,* relative to calories (Yearick et al. 1980). Table 6.1 shows the recommended dietary allowances for persons older than fifty (National Research Council, Food and Nutrition Board 1974).

Deficiencies

Unfortunately, reduced caloric intake with age is sometimes accompanied by progressive decreases in the intake of necessary minerals, vitamins, and proteins. A number of different studies have indicated that calcium is the mineral most likely to be deficient, primarily because of a low intake of milk and dairy products (Rawson et al. 1978; Slesinger et al. 1980).

Different studies reveal a variety of other nutritional deficiencies (Loria et al. 1979). Zinc deficiency is common in the elderly because vegetable protein is often substituted for animal protein in institutional and low-income diets. Zinc deficiency is often associated with decreased taste acuity and slow wound healing (Greger 1977; Burke et al. 1981). A study of a representative sample of United States civilians over sixty showed that the most frequent deficits were those of iron, calcium, and vitamins A and C (Abraham et al. 1974). A study of one hundred noninstitutionalized elderly men and women (sixty-three to ninety-six) in Oregon revealed that calcium, vitamin A, and thiamin were the dietary nutrients most likely to be deficient, especially in women (Yearick et al. 1980). A study of rural elderly (sixty and over) in Pennsylvania showed the percentage of persons who were below two-thirds of adequacy (Recommended Daily Allowance, RDA) in each of several nutrient categories (Rawson et al. 1978). The results are given in Table 6.2. Males were more likely than females to be deficient in calories, calcium, vitamin A, thiamin, riboflavin, and niacin.

TABLE 6.1   Recommended Dietary Allowances for Persons Older Than Fifty Years

	Female	*Male*
Calories (cal.)	1,800	2,400
Protein (gm)	46	56
Vitamin A (I. U.)	4,000	5,000
Vitamin E (I. U.)	12	15
Ascorbic acid, Vit. C (mg.)	45	45
Niacin (mg.)	12	16
Riboflavin (mg.)	1.1	1.5
Thiamin (mg.)	1.0	1.2
Calcium (mg.)	800	800
Iron (mg.)	10	10

From: National Research Council, Food and Nutrition Board, *Recommended Dietary Allowances,* 8th rev. (Washington, D.C.: National Academy of Sciences, 1974).

TABLE 6.2   Percent of Respondents among Rural Elderly in Pennsylvania Who Were Below 2/3 of Adequacy, RDA

Sex	Calories	Protein	Calcium	Iron	Vit. A.	Thiamin	Riboflavin	Niacin	Vit. C
					Percentages				
Male	73%	18%	64%	18%	73%	45%	55%	45%	18%
Female	35	18	53	29	35	35	35	29	24
Total	50	18	57	25	50	39	43	36	21

Adapted from: I. G. Rawson, G. I. Weinberg, J. Herold, and J. Holtz, "Nutrition of Rural Elderly in Southwestern Pennsylvania." Reprinted by permission of *The Gerontologist* 18 (February 1978): 24–29.

Females were more likely to be deficient in iron and vitamin C. Only a small percentage (18 percent) of males and females were deficient in protein. The existence of dietary deficiencies depends primarily on the differences in eating habits of the groups studied and the circumstances under which they live.

Reasons for Deficiences in the Elderly

Dietary requirements are deficient for seven principal reasons (Cain 1977):

1. Older people lack sufficient income to buy enough proper food. Fixed incomes rule out the more expensive items, such as meat, fish, fresh fruits, and vegetables.
2. The elderly lack the knowledge and skill to select and prepare nourishing and well-balanced meals. Moreover, some elderly men have never had to cook for themselves, and they have to rely on fast foods.
3. Their limited mobility impairs capacity to shop and cook for themselves. If they have to depend on others to go shopping, they are unable to buy fresh meats and dairy products at regular intervals.
4. Older persons living alone feel rejected and lonely. They lack the incentive to prepare meals for themselves.
5. Chronic illness, loss of teeth, and/or the effect of drugs reduce their desire for food. Also, as sensitivity to taste and smell diminish, they tend to eat less or they choose foods that provide sensory stimulation (such as sweets) but little nutrition.
6. The elderly tend to follow the patterns of their ethnic and national groups (Slesinger et al. 1980). Their food habits and preferences are developed early and continued as they grow older. These habits and preferences may not provide a balanced, nutritious diet.

7. Institutionalization may contribute to poor nutrition. Some nursing homes and homes for the aged do not serve balanced meals, relying too often on starchy, inexpensive foods. Their foods may be overcooked and the use of steam tables removes many nutrients. Much depends on the practices of individual institutions.

Special Needs of Adults

Adults may require special diets, for example, diets low in *saturated fats* and *cholesterol*. Excesses of these substances in the blood stream contribute to atherosclerosis by building up fatty deposits in the arteries. The result is a higher incidence of heart disease and heart attack. Doctors have known about atherosclerosis for years, but its exact relationship to saturated fats and cholesterol in the diet has been the subject of much controversy. A definite relationship was established in the findings of a tracking study of 3,806 men (Wallis 1984), carried out over a period of ten years by The National Heart, Lung, and Blood Institute. It presents positive evidence that lowering cholesterol with diet and drugs can reduce the risk of developing heart disease or having a heart attack. The men's ages were between thirty-five and fifty-nine. None had signs of heart disease when recruited, but all had high cholesterol levels of at least 265 mg per decaliter of blood. All the subjects were put on a low-cholesterol diet limiting their intake of fatty meats, eggs, and dairy products. Half were also treated with cholestyramine, a powerful drug that lowers cholesterol; the others received a placebo.

Those on the low-fat diet alone reduced their cholesterol levels by 4 percent; levels in the men who also received the drug fell by 18 to 25 percent, with the sharpest decline coming in the first years of treatment. The greater the drop in cholesterol, the lower the incidence of heart attacks. For every 1 percent reduction in total cholesterol level, there was a 2 percent reduction in heart disease. Reducing the level of cholesterol by 25 percent reduced the risk of heart disease by 50 percent. Those on medication also had 20 percent fewer episodes of angina pectoris and 21 percent fewer coronary bypass operations to restore the free flow of blood to the heart (Wallis 1984).

The findings of this study have important implications. The average adult male in the United States ingests about 500 mg of cholesterol daily, the adult female about 350 mg: in both cases about 60 percent more than the American Heart Association recommends (American Heart Association 1979). About 40 percent of daily calories are taken in fat. A significant reduction in the amount of saturated fat and cholesterol in the diet would reduce significantly the incidence of atherosclerosis and heart disease. This means reducing primarily the intake of animal fats and whole dairy products, which are high in saturated fats and cholesterol.

Table 6.3 shows the amount of saturated fat and cholesterol in some foods in three major groups: (1) meat, poultry, and fish, (2) dairy prod-

TABLE 6.3 Cholesterol and Saturated Fat Levels in Foods

Meat, Poultry, Fish

Food	Size	Choles. mg	S. Fat gm
Beef liver	3 oz.	372	2.5
Sweetbreads	3 oz.	396	N/A
Beef frankfurters	1	49	6.6
Bacon (crisp)	2 slices	14	2.5
Lean beef	3 oz.	77	3.7
Lean pork, ham	3 oz.	76	3.4
Lean lamb	3 oz.	85	3.5
Lean veal	3 oz.	84	2.5
Chicken	3 oz.	74	1.3
Lean fish	3 oz.	43	.08
Squid	3 oz.	153	.4
Sardines (oil)	3¼ oz.	129	3.0
Salmon (can)	3 oz.	32	1.3
Tuna (oil)	3 oz.	55	1.7
Crab	½ cup	62	.5
Clams	6 lg.	36	.3
Lobster	½ cup	62	.1
Oysters	6	45	.5
Scallops	3 oz.	45	.4
Shrimp	½ cup	96	.2
Chicken egg	1 med.	274	1.7

Dairy Products

Food	Size	Choles. mg	S. Fat gm
Whole milk	1 cup	33	5.1
2% milk	1 cup	10	2.9
1% milk	1 cup	10	1.6
Skim milk	1 cup	4	.3
Buttermilk	1 cup	9	1.3
Hvy. cream	1 tbsp.	21	3.5
Lt. cream	1 tbsp.	10	1.8
Sour cream	1 tbsp.	5	1.6
Reg. ice cr.	1 cup	59	8.9
Soft ice milk	1 cup	13	2.9
Yogurt (skim)	1 cup	14	2.3
Amer. cheese	1 oz.	27	5.6
Blue cheese	1 oz.	21	5.3
Cheddar	1 oz.	30	6.0
Roquefort	1 oz.	26	.5
Swiss	1 oz.	26	5.0
Mozzarella (skim)	1 oz.	16	2.9
Muenster	1 oz.	27	5.4
Cream ch.	1 tbsp.	15	3.1
Ricotta (skim)	1 oz.	9	1.4
Cottage (4%)	1 cup	31	6.0
Cottage (1%)	1 cup	10	1.5

Fats and Oils

Food	Size	Choles. mg	S. Fat gm
Butter	1 tbsp.	31	7.1
Lard	1 tbsp.	13	5.1
Mayonnaise	1 tbsp.	8	2.0
Peanut but.	2 tbsp.	0	3.0
Veg. shorten. (hydrogenated)	1 tbsp.	0	3.2
Margarine (hydrogenated)	1 tbsp.	0	2.2
Corn oil marg.	1 tbsp.	0	2.0
Diet marg.	1 tbsp.	0	1.1
Corn oil	1 tbsp.	0	1.7
Cottonseed oil	1 tbsp.	0	3.7
Safflower oil	1 tbsp.	0	1.3
Sesame oil	1 tbsp.	0	2.1
Soybean oil	1 tbsp.	0	2.1
Sunflower oil	1 tbsp.	0	1.5
Olive oil	1 tbsp.	0	1.9
Peanut oil	1 tbsp.	0	2.3

Source: Consumer and Food Economics Institute, *Composition of Foods, Dairy and Egg Products–Raw, Processed, Prepared,* Agriculture Handbook No. 8-1, 1977. Consumer and Food Economics Institute, *Composition of Foods, Fats and Oils–Raw, Processed, Prepared,* Agriculture Handbook No. 8-4, 1978. Consumer and Food Economics Institute, *Nutritive Value of Foods,* rev., Home and Garden Bulletin No. 72, 1977. Consumer and Food Economics Institute, *Fats in Food and Diet,* rev., Agriculture Information Bulletin, No. 361, 1976. (Washington, D.C.: U.S. Department of Agriculture).

ucts, and (3) fats and oils. Note that one medium chicken egg has 274 mg of cholesterol and 1.7 g of saturated fat. Beef liver has 372 mg of cholesterol and 2.5 g, respectively. Of all the fish, squid has the highest cholesterol (152 mg) but only .4 g of saturated fat. There is not much difference in the amount of cholesterol in beef, pork, lamb, veal, and chicken, provided the meat is lean. But the total saturated fat content of red meat is considerably higher than that of poultry, and much higher than that of fish. Of all meats, lean fish, clams, oysters, and scallops have the lowest amounts of overall cholesterol and saturated fat. Crabs, lobster, and shrimp have somewhat higher levels of cholesterol but are still very low in saturated fats. Saturated fats have been included in this discussion because they tend to raise the levels of harmful cholesterol.

The harmful cholesterol discussed here is *LDL (low-density lipoprotein)*. Another type of cholesterol, known as *HDL (high-density lipoprotein)*, plays a salutary role by helping to remove LDL from circulation and reducing the risk of heart disease. The higher the HDL in relation to LDL, the less risk of heart disease.

Physicians differ on the amount of permissible LDL. Some believe that any reading over 200 mg is too high and the person should cut back on fat and cholesterol consumption. This limit would apply to more than half the United States population (the average for adults is 215 to 220). A less extreme view holds that only people with levels above 240 mg should receive serious treatment. People in this group represent 20 percent of the population, but they suffer 40 percent of the heart attacks (Wallis 1984). Whatever the maximum allowable level, a lower level of LDL is certainly healthier.

One way to reduce LDL is to increase the amount of fiber in the diet. Dr. Jon Story of Purdue University says, "LDL cholesterol can be reduced 20 percent in people with high levels just by consuming a cup of oat bran a day" (Wallis 1984). Regular, sustained aerobic exercise is a healthy way to increase protective HDL. Another beneficial way to reduce the risk of heart attack is to stop smoking.

Adults have other special nutritional needs. One of these needs is a diet low in sodium. Sodium from salt, sodium nitrates, sodium nitrites, and other sources encourages fluid retention and edema. This, in turn, may cause high blood pressure and other problems. One major treatment for hypertension is the administration of *diuretics,* which help the body eliminate excess fluids. Limiting sodium intake will minimize fluid retention.

Most adults get too much sugar in their diets. This is certainly a problem for diabetics, but everyone should be cognizant of sugar intake. Sugar has been called "empty calories" because it contains no proteins, vitamins, or minerals. More than that, it forms acids that deplete the body's source of calcium and destroy important B vitamins. Most people get enough sugar from fresh fruits and other natural foods. In addition, carbohydrates are converted into sugar during the process of digestion, so the body often gets too much sugar if the diet is rich in starches.

PHYSICAL ABILITIES

Reaction Time

One measurement of functional ability in the older adult is *reaction time,* the interval between stimulation and response. If a person is driving a car and the traffic light turns red, reaction time is the interval between the time the light changes and the time the person steps on the car brake. Numerous studies have been done to discover how this time interval changes as persons age. In general, reaction time decreases from childhood to about age twenty, remains constant until the mid-twenties, and then slowly increases. This increase has been estimated at approximately 17 percent between twenty and forty years of age (Bromley 1974). Whether this increase has any practical significance depends on the type of activity in which a person engages. Most active sports require quick reactions as well as good coordination. Consequently, most professional athletes in their thirties are considered old. However, those who play various sports for pleasure can continue to enjoy themselves and benefit from the activity.

Adults whose jobs involve physical skill, quick movements, and speed will slow down as they get older. However, they can often do as much work as younger adults because they work steadily and conscientiously. Older adults are also safer drivers than young adults, even though their reactions have slowed. Young adults respond more quickly in emergencies, but they can create problems by driving too fast.

Comparisons of athletes with nonathletes have shown the importance of regular exercise and practice in improving reaction time. Older athletes may show reaction times comparable to those of younger nonathletes. There are such wide individual differences that a researcher must be careful in making generalizations from cross-sectional studies. There are also important sex differences. In general, women react more quickly than do men, and this has to be considered when evaluating findings.

Other factors also influence performance. Older adults fatigue more easily than do young adults, slowing reaction time. However, suitable rest periods minimize fatigue and improve reaction time. Another reason older adults respond more slowly is that they are more cautious about making errors. They may show superior performance on tasks requiring accuracy without emphasizing speed.

Motor Ability, Coordination, Dexterity

Other measurements of functional ability include *motor ability, coordination,* and *dexterity.* Motor ability implies the ability to move the fingers, hands, arms, legs, or other parts of the body. This ability requires muscular strength, coordination, dexterity, and proper functioning of the central nervous system, which carries the messages from the brain to the muscles. Motor functions depend on complex sequences of action in which timing and coordination are critical factors for optimal performance. Motor skills vary from the mundane (walking, running, or dressing) to the dramatic (gymnastics or ballet). All of these abilities eventually decline with age, but the decline is minimal during early adulthood. Most of the decline occurs after the thirties. After about age thirty-three, hand and finger movements are progressively more clumsy (Fozard et al. 1972). It becomes more difficult to compete in such sports as boxing, baseball, tennis, or basketball, which require good motor ability.

Psychomotor ability affects numerous skills, including writing skill. Research on writing speed in relation to age revealed some decline with age, but this depended partially on occupation. LaRiviere and Simonson (1965) found no decline in the writing speed of clerical workers in their forties, fifties, and sixties, but considerable decline among executive, supervisory, managerial, and professional personnel, and among skilled tradesmen, machine operators, and laborers. Table 6.4 shows the results. Apparently, those who had to write the most decreased the least in speed, indicating the importance of practice.

Strength

The potential for increases in strength remains until almost age thirty. There is usually very little loss of muscular strength during the thirties. Back strength and strength of grip or pull may decline only 1 to 4 percent between thirty and thirty-nine; after this there is a steady loss of strength, usually about 10 percent between forty and sixty. Usually, weakness occurs in the back and legs before it takes place in the arm muscles. Champion weight lifters may maintain their prowess for a number of years within their age cohort, but they are eventually replaced by younger champions. Regular exercise can maintain power and even restore it to muscles that have gone unused.

TABLE 6.4   Writing Speed (Second Per Digit) in Relation to Age and Occupation

	Age Group			Percentage difference between 40–49
Occupational Group	*40–49*	*50–59*	*60–69*	*and 60–69*
Clerical without supervisory duties	.70	.68	.70	0
Executive, supervisory, managerial and professional	.55	.62	.67	22
Skilled trades, machine operation and laboring	.71	.75	.85	20

From: J. E. LaRiviere and E. Simonson, "The Effect of Age and Occupation on Speed of Writing." Reprinted by permission of *Journal of Gerontology* 20 (1965): 415–416.

One study of the effect of exercise and training on improving the muscular strength of both young male subjects (mean age twenty-two) and elderly male subjects (mean age seventy) showed significant increases in strength in both age groups in response to a progressive weight-training program over an eight-week period (Moritani and deVries 1980). The subjects were asked to flex their elbows while holding progressively heavier dumbbells. Figure 6.3 shows the maximum strengths attained by both subject groups and the percent changes in maximum strength of these subjects. The strength of the older subjects increased somewhat faster than that of the younger subjects until the seventh week of training. The maximum weight the older subjects were able to flex was 75 pounds; the younger subjects reached a maximum of 114 pounds. Considering the

FIGURE 6.3 Effect of Age and Training on Maximum Strength

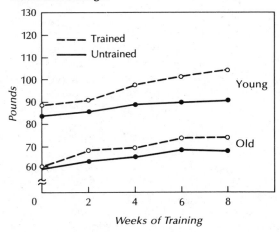

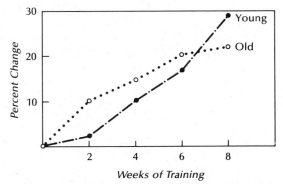

Adapted from: T. Moritani and H. A. deVries, ''Potential for Gross Muscle Hypertrophy in Older Men.'' Reprinted by permission of *Journal of Gerontology* 35 (September 1980): 672–682.

nearly fifty-year differential between the two age groups, a 52 percent differential in maximum strength does not appear considerable. The important point is that even a brief training program improved performance.

Endurance and Fatigue

The maximum work rate one can achieve without fatigue begins to decline at about thirty-five, as related to such activities as climbing stairs, using a treadmill, or cranking a wheel. The capacity for hard work at high temperatures falls off sharply before thirty. But here again, physical condition is an important factor causing abilities to overlap considerably over a broad age range.

SUMMARY

The human body's physical development usually peaks in the mid-twenties. But chronological age is not always a good measure of physical condition or aging. Some older adults are in better physical shape than are young adults. Functional age, which is the ability to perform useful tasks regardless of age, is a more appropriate evaluation of physical development and fitness.

By middle age or late adulthood, adults begin to notice physical signs of aging: changes in the hair, body contours, weight, tissues, muscles, breasts, skin, face, shoulders, voice, posture, and movements. But the extent of these changes depends on one's general health and physical condition. Everyone ages physically, but some people look twenty to thirty years younger than their actual age would suggest. Self-consciousness about one's changing physique is enhanced by social attitudes emphasizing slenderness and youthfulness. Society is generally more critical of women than of men who do not conform to these ideal images, although the ideal male physique is presented as slender and muscular.

People react to aging in three ways. Some resign themselves to their fate and do little to improve their appearance and physique. Others deny the fact that they are getting older and often dress and act in inappropriate ways to appear young. Others react with positive acceptance, changing their habits and life-style to avoid becoming overweight and physically unfit. They select appropriate clothing and carefully groom themselves to look as attractive as possible.

Proper exercise is important in preventing ill health and maintaining body fitness. Aerobic exercise, which increases respiration, blood pressure, and pulse rate, is especially important in improving cardiovascular health. Monitoring one's pulse rate and increasing it to a target rate during exercise are good ways of determining one's overall fitness and proper level of exertion.

Adequate sleep and rest help stave off physical fatigue and maintain intellectual functioning. Proper nutrition is also important in maintaining good health. Aging people need fewer calories to maintain their weight, but they still require the same amount of important nutrients. Therefore, their diets must provide foods of greater nutrient density, relative to calories.

Adults may have special dietary needs. One such need is for diets low in saturated fats and cholesterol; the higher the level of these substances in the blood, the greater the incidence of heart disease and heart attack. Other adult nutritional needs are diets low in sodium or sugar, but with reasonable quantities of fiber.

There are a number of components of functional ability, including reaction time (how quickly one reacts to a specific signal or stimulus and shows the required physical response). Motor ability, coordination, and dexterity influence a wide variety of physical skills, ranging from the everyday (walking, dressing, or writing) to the more dramatic (the ability to play various sports). All of these abilities decline, especially after the early thirties, but exercise and practice can minimize significant changes until late adulthood. Maximum strength and endurance begin a very slow decline in the thirties. However, maintaining physical condition through fitness-training programs can result in considerable overlapping of abilities over a broad age range.

7

Sexual Functioning, Behavior, and Reproduction

HUMAN SEXUAL RESPONSE

Phases and Manifestations

All normal adults are able to respond to sexual stimuli. The research of Masters and Johnson (1966), describing the physical responses of men and women under conditions of sexual excitement, has been especially noteworthy. They identified four stages of human sexual response: the *excitement phase,* the *plateau phase,* the *orgasmic phase,* and the *resolution phase.*

The excitement phase starts with the initial sexual stimulation and lasts until a high degree of sexual excitation is reached. If effective sexual stimulation continues, sexual tensions intensify until the plateau phase is reached. The third or orgasmic phase is limited to those few seconds during which sexual tension is maximized and then suddenly released, culminating in ejaculation in the male and the rhythmic release of neuromuscular tension in the female. *Orgasm* is followed by the resolution phase of the sexual cycle, during which sexual tension subsides as the body returns to the unstimulated state.

As sexual excitement increases, both men and women show similar physical responses.

Erection occurs in the penis, the clitoris, the nipples of the female breast (a majority of men also evidence nipple erection), and the labia as they become swollen and engorged with blood.

Heart and pulse rates, blood pressure, respiration, and perspiration increase. About one-third of men and women evidence perspiration during the resolution phase.

Sex flush, a noticeable reddening of the skin, usually in the form of a red splotchy rash, spreads over the body as excitement increases. About three out of four females and one out of four males show this reaction.

Tension and flexing occur in both voluntary and involuntary muscles of the arms, legs, abdomen, face, neck, pelvis, buttocks, hands, and feet *(myotonia)*. Severe involuntary muscular contractions occur during orgasm, gradually subsiding during the resolution phase.

Even though male and female sexual organs differ, they experience similar physical reactions. Regardless of the method of stimulation (masturbation, mutual love play, or intercourse), the physiological reactions are the same. The intensity and timing of orgasm may vary from person to person and in the individual: this happens in both men and women. Sexual response depends on the various physical and psychological factors governing the situation.

Male-Female Differences

In spite of similarities, important differences exist between men and women. Women are much more capable of multiple and prolonged orgasms. Some women desire multiple orgasms to be satisfied; others are satisfied with one. Only a minority of men are capable of two orgasms (rarely three), and then only if sufficient time elapses between them. Figure 7.1 shows the responses of female C (one orgasm), female A (two orgasms), and female B (no orgasms), and males who have one or two orgasms.

Some differences exist in the way men and women are stimulated sexually. Kinsey and others observed that men were aroused by erotic pictures and stories, talking about sex, looking at shapely women, observing sexual activity of humans or animals, and looking at nude photos (Kinsey 1948). These sources did not arouse women as much as reading love stories or seeing romantic movies (Kinsey et al. 1953). Thus, men were considered erotic and women romantic. More recent investigations revealed that women who viewed erotic photographs reported them to be less arousing than did men, but when examined medically, they evidenced the same degree of physiological excitement as the men (Sigusch et al. 1970). Social conditioning had taught the women that they were not supposed to be aroused, so they reported they were not, contrary to fact. Research is now emphasizing that women can be erotic and men can be romantic, provided they are not conditioned differently. Psychological factors remain an important component in the sexual stimulation and satisfaction of both men and women.

Time of arousal may also vary between men and women. If a couple copulated without prior love play, Kinsey (1953) found that the average male reached a climax in four minutes and the average female required ten to twenty minutes. But these differences were due to the fact that coitus itself, without prior love play, is not as stimulating for a woman as for a man, primarily because during intercourse the penis often does not directly rub the clitoris (the most sexually sensitive area in women). When the clitoris was stimulated manually before intromission, Kinsey found that women were able to reach orgasm in less than four minutes. Male-female differences, which are more apparent than real, can be eliminated by proper stimulation and preparation for intercourse.

The body's areas of sexual sensitivity *(erogenous zones)* differ some-

FIGURE 7.1   Human Sexual Response Cycles

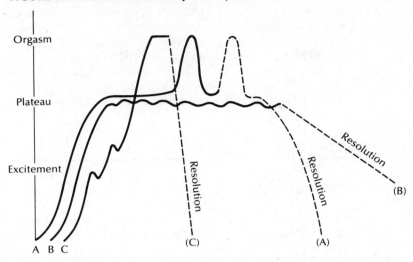

Part 1: Female.
A, B and C are three different female sexual response patterns. Female C—one orgasm, Female A—two orgasms, Female B—no orgasms.

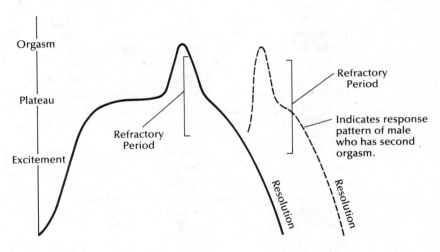

Part 2: Male.
The refractory period represents the last, irregular contractions during which sexual tension rapidly subsides.

From: W. H. Masters and V. E. Johnson, *Human Sexual Response* (Boston: Little, Brown and Company, 1966), 5. Copyright © 1966 Little, Brown and Company.

what between men and women. In women, sexual feelings are more diffuse over widespread areas of the body. In most women, the breasts and especially the nipples are highly sensitive areas. The *clitoris* itself is the most sensitive area, but most women find stimulation of the mons pubis, labia, anus, inner thighs, and buttocks quite pleasurable. Because women's feelings are diffuse, they require a period of wooing, body contact, and love play before they are physically and emotionally ready for intercourse.

The most intense sexual feelings in men are concentrated in the genital area, particularly in the penis, and especially on the end of the penis (glans). The testicles are also highly sensitive to touch. Like women, most men find that the lips and tongue are erogenous zones.

SEXUAL INTEREST AND ACTIVITY

Trends with Age

Ordinarily, there are few noticeable differences in sexual response during the twenties and thirties that can be attributed to age factors. A forty-year-old ordinarily has as much ability as does a twenty-year-old to respond sexually. Of course, there are wide individual differences due more to heredity, health, conditioning, and psychological, environmental, and circumstantial factors than to age. For example, women conditioned to inhibit sexual feelings and desires may not reach the height of physical responsiveness until their late thirties or early forties, not because of physical reasons, but because it takes years for them to overcome their culturally conditioned inhibitions. Other women raised in a liberal atmosphere, where the environment stimulates early sexual activity, may reach the height of responsiveness while in their teens. In our culture, most young men attain maximum sexual responsiveness in their teens and early twenties, partially because they are encouraged to express their sexuality. Recent research indicates a gradual elimination of the double standard of behavior for men and women, with a consequent convergence of behavior and responsiveness.

Overall, there is some gradual decline in sexual drive in both men and women after marriage (with drive measured by frequency of intercourse). According to Pearlman (1972), three out of four married men in their twenties had intercourse two to four times per week, whereas about half of married men in their thirties had intercourse that often. Among married men in their forties, 43 percent still had intercourse that often. Among men who had intercourse at least once a week, 93 percent were in their twenties, 82 percent were in their thirties, and 70 percent were in their forties (Pearlman 1972).

Age is not the only important factor in frequency of intercourse. Some men and women in their forties have more sex drive than some in their twenties. When desire wanes during early adulthood, decreases in sexual activity are usually not due to a decline in physical ability.

Interest in sex continues through middle age and well into late adulthood for the average person. A cross-sectional study of 261 men and 241 women by Pfeiffer and colleagues (1972), as part of the Duke University study, revealed the following percentages of men and women with a moderate to strong interest in sex:

Age Group	Men	Women
46–50	91%	70%
51–55	81%	56%
56–60	69%	44%
61–65	52%	12%
66–71	58%	24%

There was actually a small increase in sexual interest among those in the oldest age category, indicating that weaker persons had succumbed at an earlier age.

Unfortunately, the opportunities for sexual intercourse did not correspond to the sexual interest, especially for women. Whereas 98 percent of the men in the study were married, only 71 percent of the women were. The remainder were widowed, single, separated, or divorced. In spite of this, the following percentages of men and women had intercourse at least once per week:

Age Group	Men	Women
46–50	95%	60%
51–55	66%	39%
56–60	55%	31%
61–65	37%	10%
66–71	28%	11%

Altogether, 27 percent of the men and 42 percent of the women between fifty-six and sixty had no intercourse at all. Undoubtedly, greater percentages would be having intercourse given the opportunity. Overall, this study shows some decline in sexual activity with age.

Presently, there are no longitudinal data measuring frequency of intercourse with advancing age. Udry and Morris (1978) showed over a ten-year period that coital frequency for women increased at every age level. This indicates that women today are being socialized to be more active sexually than women in previous generations. It is thus misleading to compare coital frequency of different ages of women. The youngest cohorts have been socialized to be more sexually interested. Perhaps longitudinal studies will show less decline in sexual activity with age than the present cross-sectional studies reveal. Udry and Morris (1978) have also emphasized that actual frequency of marital intercourse never approaches physical capacity. Most adults are capable of much more intercourse than they actually have, and that physical capacity is more than adequate well into old age.

When there is a lack of opportunity for sexual intercourse with advancing age, masturbation provides physical relief for many people.

Variables

A few independent variables besides age affect the level of sexual activity. The most important is previous sexual behavior and experience. Past experience is an extremely important determinant of present behavior, not only in relation to frequency of intercourse, but also to sexual enjoyment and interest. Those who have been sexually active and who have enjoyed sex are those who are presently and will be the most active with the greatest enjoyment (Pfeiffer and Davis 1972). Persons for whom sex held little importance and enjoyment early in life are more likely to terminate their sexual activity in later life.

When the influence of previous sexual experience is eliminated, several influential socioeconomic variables emerge. The levels of income, education, and social class are positively correlated with sexual interest and enjoyment. People with high socioeconomic status usually receive more positive sex education while growing up. Kinsey and associates (1953) found that people with superior education and higher occupational status were more experimental and less rigid in sexual practice. Men and women are more likely to be considered equals and to share mutually in the responsibilities and benefits of sexual pleasures.

Being happy together is one of the most important considerations. Loving, warm relationships are conducive to satisfying sexual expression, whereas cold, hostile relationships are inhibiting. When middle-aged relationships become cold and stagnant, sexual response is affected. When hostility builds up in a relationship, sex may be used to hurt or control rather than to express love. Good sex and a happy marriage tend to go together; each enhances the other. In addition, sexual response is related to overall physical health (Pfeiffer and Davis 1972).

SEXUAL DYSFUNCTION*

Meaning

The human reproductive system, which includes the sex organs, is an amazing system. Consider, for example, the fact that thoughts can produce sexual reactions. A man can think about sex and have an erection; a woman can read a romantic story and dream about a man making love to her. A glance at a sensuous picture may produce blushing or an increase in respiratory rate or blood pressure.

Under most circumstances, the body functions quite smoothly. It reacts in predictable ways to certain stimuli. If a woman's breast is caressed, the nipple becomes engorged and firm. If a man's penis is stimulated in a

*Some material in this section is reprinted from the author's book, *Sexual Problems in Marriage*. Copyright © 1978 The Westminster Press. Reprinted and used by permission.

pleasurable way, it becomes erect. If it is stimulated enough, ejaculation occurs. These are predictable, normal reactions to sexual stimuli.

Sometimes, however, the sex organs do not respond as they should. The penis is rubbed but it remains flaccid. The breast is stimulated but the nipples do not become enlarged and erect. A couple copulate for a long period but the husband and wife fail to reach a climax. Obviously, something is wrong when a particular stimulus does not produce the expected response.

This condition is called a *sexual dysfunction,* that is, a malfunctioning of the human sexual response system. It means that a person does not react as normally expected. The particular problems of sexual dysfunction discussed here include:

> In men—Premature ejaculation, impotence, and ejaculatory incompetence.
> In women—Orgasm dysfunction, dyspareunia (painful intercourse), and vaginismus.
> In men and women—Low sexual drive.

Male Sexual Dysfunction

Premature ejaculation has been defined as the inability to delay ejaculation long enough for the woman to have orgasm 50 percent of the time (Masters and Johnson 1966). This definition assumes that the woman could ordinarily have orgasm if it were not for the man's rapid ejaculation. The definition emphasizes the man's inability to exert voluntary control over his ejaculatory reflex; once he is sexually aroused, he reaches orgasm too quickly. This is the most common sexual dysfunction in males. At best, prematurity restricts the couple's sexuality; at worst, it is highly destructive if the couple become anxious about their sexual life, or angry, or begin to reject one another. One encouraging aspect is that premature ejaculation is easily treated. Of 186 cases treated by Masters and Johnson (1970), only four were not cured.

The average man probably fears *impotence* more than anything else (Hammond and Middleton 1984). When a man is impotent, he is unable to produce an erection so that coital connection can take place, or he is unable to maintain an erection long enough to complete the sexual act. One woman told of her marital disappointment:

> From the very beginning of our marriage, I noticed Bob had trouble getting hard. Sometimes he would, and sometimes he wouldn't. I could never tell ahead of time when it would happen. Sometimes he would get hard, but only for a minute or so—long enough for him to finish, but not me. Sometimes he would wake up in the morning with an erection; we'd hurry up and begin, but as soon as he entered, he'd get soft again. It's very frustrating. I asked him if he used to have that trouble, and he said he never did until he married me. He tries to make me believe that it's my fault, that I'm doing something wrong, but I think there is something wrong with him.

Ejaculatory incompetence is an inability of the male to ejaculate while his penis is in the woman's vagina. The severity of this dysfunction varies considerably. At one extreme is the male who has never experienced an orgasm, but this form is rarely encountered in clinical practice. At the other extreme is the man who occasionally finds himself unable to ejaculate. Mild forms of the disorder may be highly prevalent, judging by the increasing number of patients applying for treatment (Maultsby 1984). In this dysfunction, the male is able to respond to sexual stimuli with erotic feelings and a firm erection. Even though he desires orgasmic release and his stimulation is more than enough to trigger a climax, he cannot ejaculate. This condition contrasts with that of the impotent man who may be able to ejaculate with a limp penis if he is sufficiently stimulated.

Female Sexual Dysfunction

Orgasm dysfunction in women is the inability to reach a sexual climax. Some women can reach an orgasm under certain circumstances or with a particular person, but not in other situations or with another person. Some women are able to reach an orgasm through masturbation, oral-genital stimulation, the use of a vibrator, or other stimulative techniques, but not through coitus. Other women may have an occasional random orgasm; otherwise they are nonorgasmic. Certain women are orgasmic in lesbian relationships but not in heterosexual encounters, whereas others have a low sexual drive and difficulty in reaching a climax, both conditions seemingly unrelated to negative conditioning or to specific traumatic experiences.

There are also women with strong sexual drive who have trouble having an orgasm. They enjoy sexual foreplay, lubricate copiously, and enjoy the sensation of phallic penetration. They show no significant inhibition of erotic feelings or of erectile response, nor are they sexually anesthetic (without feeling). But they remain at or near the plateau phase of sexual response and have great difficulty reaching a climax, even though their stimulation has been sufficiently intense to release the orgasmic discharge. Only a minority of women have never had an orgasm.

Dyspareunia is painful coitus. In this condition, penile entry into the vagina is painful and pelvic thrusts are painful (Semens and Tsai 1984). If orgasm occurs, it too is painful. Intercourse thus becomes an ordeal. Physical causes of dyspareunia are common. One cause is insufficient lubrication. The remedies for this condition are longer love play periods prior to coitus and the use of lubricating jelly or cream. Initial intercourse and the defloration of the hymen may be painful for some women. Frequent intercourse may cause pain that results from mechanical irritation of the vaginal lining and urethral opening. Dyspareunia may also have emotional causes (Scher and Rogers 1984). If medical examination fails to uncover physical problems, then tension, fear, and anxiety may be suspected.

Vaginismus is a powerful and painful contraction of the muscles surrounding the vaginal tract. Muscle spasms occur, and in severe cases any attempt to introduce the penis into the vagina produces agonizing pain and penetration becomes impossible. In less severe cases, the spasms delay intromission or make it more difficult.

Low Sexual Drive

As explained earlier in this chapter, one's sexual appetite may decline somewhat during the middle years. But if sexual drive is low or non-existent, then prompt treatment or therapy is in order. The most common cause is a gradual cooling of feelings toward one's partner. As one husband expressed it, "I just don't have any feelings left." A wife comments, "I've lost my passion." Although not unusual, such situations indicate basic disturbances in the total relationship that need to be resolved through marital therapy. In addition to physical causes, deep-seated psychological problems may need to be resolved. People who are quite depressed, for example, may lose all interest in sexual expression. Husbands or wives who become anxious about their performance may start avoiding sex altogether. One husband, fearful of impregnating his wife during menopause, avoided her completely. Stress and fatigue from overwork typically cause a loss of sexual appetite (Saunders 1984). A good vacation and/or medical treatment may be needed to restore sexual interest.

Some husbands or wives show little interest in sex from the beginning of marriage. Some wives have only a minimal interest in sexual activity or, if they participate, derive little if any erotic pleasure from the experience. On a physiological level, they show limited response: little lubrication inside the vagina and little vasocongestion. Often, they have an aversion to sex, consider it a frightening or disgusting ordeal, and try to avoid sexual contact. There are degrees of sexual interest and responsiveness, and people have dissimilar standards by which they judge. A husband who wants intercourse daily—but whose wife only desires it twice a week—may refer to her as frigid. However, a complete and permanent lack of sexual interest rarely occurs.

Strangely enough, the literature contains very few references to low sexual drive in men (Fink 1984). Perhaps it is assumed that all men have ample sexual drive. However, there are significant numbers of males who function without intercourse for days, weeks, or even months and never raise any objection. Some husbands may be interested early in marriage, but the interest declines. As one wife exclaimed, "We had a fantastic sex life on our honeymoon, but it has been going down hill ever since" (Rice 1978a, 182).

Sexual disinterest on the part of either partner is *not* normal. The couple should seek professional help to discover the cause (Cherlin 1984).

Causes of Sexual Dysfunction

In general, all sexual dysfunctions have physical or emotional causes, or both. These causes can be grouped into five categories: ignorance, inadequate stimulation, psychological blocks, negative feelings toward one's partner or a disturbance in the relationship, and physical causes.

A lack of knowledge and understanding of sexual anatomy, sexual response, and lovemaking techniques may be one reason couples have problems (Hite 1982). Sexual instincts and urges are inborn, but a knowledge of sexual anatomy, sexual response, and lovemaking is not. It must be learned.

Sexual responses may not occur because the individual has not been stimulated appropriately and long enough in the right places. One wife complained:

> I really don't enjoy sex with my husband, because I don't get anything out of it. The reason is Chuck never really tries to arouse me by kissing me or playing with me. I've tried to tell him that I need time to get worked up, but he gets worked up so quickly that he wants to hurry and enter before he comes. Afterwards, he's not interested.

Insufficient arousal through foreplay is one of the primary causes of orgasm dysfunction in women (Hite 1977). Couples have to learn where, how, and for how long to stimulate each other to achieve the desired result (Lauersen and Graves 1984).

Psychological blocks to sexual response can include any type of negative feelings: fear, anxiety, stress, depression, embarrassment, guilt, disgust, or hostility (Turner 1984). These feelings prevent individuals from participating fully in a sexual experience or prevent them from "letting themselves go" and responding fully to each other. Fear of pregnancy, of being hurt, of failure, of rejection or ridicule, or of discovery may prevail. The fear of being hurt is quite common, especially in a new bride, during pregnancy, or after childbirth (Dietz 1984). Fear of pregnancy can prevent spontaneous participation, which is one important reason that adequate contraception is a necessary prerequisite for good sexual adjustment (Eskin 1984; Kaufman 1984). Fear of failure can motivate a husband or wife to avoid intercourse entirely.

Anxiety about any number of things may be sufficient to block response (Henker 1984). A mother worried about a sick child may not be able to concentrate on making love. A husband worried about unpaid bills or about finding a job may have the same trouble. One husband described a particular problem:

> My wife and I have a fantastic sexual life except when we have company sleeping over in the next room. Our bed is old and it squeaks something awful. . . . When that happens forget it. My wife turns off like she jumped into a tub of ice cubes.

Various emotional illnesses impair sexuality. When people are emotionally depressed, sex is the farthest thing from their minds. Men or women experiencing chronic stress or fatigue may lose sexual motivation.

Embarrassment is also a strong deterrent to sexual response. Children who grow up feeling that "nice boys or girls don't think or talk about sex," may have extreme difficulty adjusting to the intimacies of married life. Guilt may be strong enough to block sexual response.

The quality and emotional tone of a couple's relationship are important to their sexual life. When relationships become hostile, angry, or resentful, couples may find it more and more difficult to respond to each other sexually. One factor that influences the wife's ability to have an orgasm is the extent to which she feels secure in her relationship to her husband. If a woman trusts her husband and knows she can depend on him, she is more likely to relax completely and give herself to the sexual experience.

Some sexual problems have physical origins. Certain drugs frequently cause dysfunction, particularly those drugs that have a sedative effect. Alcohol is probably the most common sedative. In small quantities it may have a stimulating effect, releasing inhibitions that prevent response when the couple is sober. Like alcohol, marijuana is an intoxicant. It releases inhibitions and promotes behavior that couples ordinarily avoid.

In quantity, however, alcohol acts as a sedative that dulls sensations and blocks responses, making complete participation impossible (Hammond and Middleton 1984; Wilson and Lawson 1978). Smoking large quantities of marijuana over a period of time may reduce the male hormone, testosterone, found in the bloodstream. There is some evidence that this contributes to impotence or lower sexual drive in some males. Similarly, small doses of sedatives such as barbiturates may release inhibitions temporarily, resulting in an increase in sexual appetite or response; large doses, however, act as depressants of sexual behavior and response. Chronic abuse of sedatives diminishes human sexuality, as do such narcotics as heroin or morphine, which have a depressive effect on the central nervous system and on sexual response (Dupont 1984; Greenberg 1984). Stimulants such as amphetamines, taken in small doses, may enhance the sexual interest, performance, and abandonment of some persons. Habitual use leads to physical addiction, however, and to a decrease in sexual interest and performance. Many other drugs, including many prescribed for chronic health conditions, affect sexual response (Saunders 1984). People who suspect problems should check with their physician.

Numerous physical illnesses also affect sexual life (Althof 1984; Cherlin 1984; Fletcher 1984; Silberfarb 1984). Hepatitis, diabetes, multiple sclerosis, stroke, heart disease, severe malnutrition, and vitamin deficiencies affect sexual capabilities (Bray 1984). If people suspect that sexual problems are caused by ill health, they should seek expert medical advice. With any type of sexual problem, physical factors should be examined before emotional or psychological causes are probed.

Treatment

Masters and Johnson (1970) estimated that as many as 50 percent of all couples had some sort of difficulty with sexual adjustments in marriage.

Sexual difficulties, left untreated, can wreck a marriage. This is particularly tragic because most of the difficulties might be overcome with help (O'Connor and Stern 1972).

Basically, four types of help are available: (1) medical intervention for physical problems, (2) psychoanalysis and psychotherapy when long-term counseling is needed for deep-seated emotional problems, (3) marriage counseling dealing with the total marital relationship, and (4) sex therapy emphasizing sensate-focus or symptom-focus approaches that concentrate on the immediate sexual problem (Adams 1980). This sex therapy assigns couples sexual tasks, which enable them to learn how to caress or pleasure one another in a nondemanding way until they are able to respond to one another. Whatever type of help is needed, and sometimes a combination of one or more approaches is necessary, most therapists agree that conjoint therapy (involving both the husband and wife) is desirable since sexual functioning necessarily affects both partners.

REPRODUCTION

Conception and Infertility

Approximately one couple in ten would never be able to have children without medical help (Guttmacher 1973). With help, about half of these 10 percent do have children.

Several factors influence conception rates. One is frequency of intercourse. Couples who have intercourse several times per week are more likely to achieve pregnancy in six months than couples practicing coitus once a week or less. However, if intercourse is too frequent, say several times per day, the husband's sperm count never builds up sufficiently for impregnation to occur. Another factor influencing conception is timing of intercourse. The couple may be having intercourse only during those times of the month when the wife is least likely to get pregnant. Poor nutrition, anemia, fatigue, physical illness, or emotional stress may also affect fertility.

There are four biological requirements before a husband can impregnate a fertile wife. First, he must be able to produce healthy sperm in sufficient numbers. Second, he must secrete seminal fluid in proper amounts and with the right composition to transport the sperm. Third, the sperm require an unobstructed passage from the testicles to the penis. Finally, the husband must be able to achieve and sustain an erection long enough to ejaculate within the vagina (Rice 1983).

When infertility is attributed to the wife, the first question is whether she is ovulating (providing a normal egg cell). If ovulation is normal, the next step is to determine whether the Fallopian tubes, down which the ovum must travel, are blocked. Sometimes abnormalities of the uterus prevent conception or full-term pregnancy. Occasionally, the problem is with the cervix itself, which acts as a bottleneck in preventing the sperm from reaching the ovum. In other cases, the chemical climate of the vagina is too acid, and the sperm are immobilized. The union of sperm and egg does not guarantee birth. An estimated 10 percent of pregnancies end in miscarriages (Consumer's Union 1966).

Age is an important factor that influences conception rates. The younger the husband and wife, the more likely the wife is to conceive (assuming both are sexually mature and fertile). Table 7.1 shows the relationship between the husband's age and the percentage of husbands who were able to impregnate their wives in six months or less (Guttmacher 1973, 345).

In one study regarding the length of time required for couples to achieve pregnancy, Guttmacher found that one-third of the couples achieved pregnancy the first month, more than half within three months. Fifteen percent required four to six months; 13 percent seven to twelve months, and 8 percent one to two years. More than 6 percent of those who eventually had a baby took two or more years to achieve pregnancy. The median time for conception was two and one-half months (Guttmacher 1973). Generally speaking, unsuccessful couples younger than thirty-five should wait a year before consulting a doctor. Those over thirty-five should see a doctor after six months of unsuccessful attempts (Consumer's Union 1966).

Age and Birth Defects

The mother's age is also an important influence on the birth of a healthy baby. Overall, mothers thirty-six to forty years old have twice as great a chance of bearing a defective baby as those twenty-one to twenty-five (Murphy 1954). Some defects are more likely to occur as the mother's age increases. *Mongolism,* for example, occurs with only one in one thousand mothers younger than thirty, but with one in one hundred mothers at age forty, and with one in forty-five when the maternal age is forty-five or over (Penrose and Smith 1966). Other fetal abnormalities that are not hereditary but have environmental origins increase in incidence with ma-

TABLE 7.1 Husband's Age As a Factor in Getting Wife Pregnant in Six Months or Less Time

Age	Percent Impregnation
Under 25 Years	75
25–29	48
30–35	38
35–39	26
40 and over	23

Adapted from *Pregnancy, Birth and Family Planning* by Alan F. Guttmacher, M.D., Revised and Updated by Irwin H. Kaiser, M.D. Copyright © 1937, 1947, 1950, 1956, 1962, 1965, 1973 by Alan F. Guttmacher. Copyright © 1983 by Leonore Guttmacher and Dr. Irwin H. Kaiser. Reprinted by arrangement with New American Library, New York, New York.

ternal age. These include *spina bifida* (incomplete closure of the lower spinal canal), *microcephaly* (pin head), congenital heart defects, *hydrocephalus* (water on the brain), and various types of nervous disorders (National Foundation 1977).

MENOPAUSE AND MALE CLIMACTERIC

Definitions

The "change of life" or "the change" are common expressions used to describe the time in a woman's life when she ceases to ovulate and loses her ability to conceive children. The phrases are not completely inappropriate since they do imply that changes take place. There are physical changes and sometimes dramatic emotional changes. Unfortunately, these phrases are often associated with myths and misconceptions. To some women, they suggest something sudden, calamitous, and dreadful. This period of change should not be dreaded; rather, it should be understood.

Menopause, from two Greek words meaning literally "month" and "cessation," refers to the cessation of the monthly, the end of menstruation. Common use of the term has given it a wider meaning that includes the whole period during which the periodic cyclic bleeding stops.

The word *climacteric,* from a Greek word meaning "rung of a ladder," implies the passage from one stage of life to another. Literally, the word can describe any period of life, but when applied to a woman's middle years, it includes the menopause and all the physiological and psychological changes that accompany it or occur independently at that time. When applied to a man's middle years, it refers to the many changes he experiences during this time.

The Physical Change

Menopause involves a cessation of menstruation. This gradual process usually lasts over a period of years. The ovaries gradually wither, becoming less able to fulfill their double function of egg cell production (ovulation) and hormone secretion. The follicles and ova in the ovaries slowly shrink. The pituitary gland, which triggers the monthly cycle by sending out a follicle-stimulating hormone (FSH), continues to secrete the hormone on a cyclical basis, but the ovaries are powerless to respond to this signal. The egg cells do not mature and ovulation ceases. The production of the female hormones, estrogen and progesterone, slowly declines. Because of this hormonal decrease, the uterus lining is not built up and sloughed off, and the regular, rhythmic cycle of menstrual bleeding gradually ceases.

Cyclic bleeding may continue for a while if the ovaries are still producing enough estrogen to stimulate the lining of the uterus, even though ovulation and the production of progesterone have not taken place. When estrogen reaches a certain level, the uterus lining breaks down and bleeds *(anovulatory)*, as in the young adolescent girl who begins to menstruate irregularly even before ovulation takes place. But as the amount of estrogen produced by the ovaries continues to drop, even estrogen-stimulated, anovulatory bleeding ceases. At this stage, the menopause (not the change of life) is complete.

The female body has a remarkable capacity to adjust to these changes, but apparently this capacity varies with each woman. The diminishing supply of ovarian hormones has a reciprocal action on other glands. The action of the pituitary is stepped up to stimulate other glands to respond to the decrease of ovarian hormone. The *adrenal cortex,* which also produces estrogen, may compensate somewhat for the loss of ovarian estrogen, preventing too sudden a change.

Because of the increasing stimulus of the pituitary, some women are troubled with overactive glands, such as the thyroid, which can cause irritability and tension. A condition of glandular imbalance may act on the sympathetic nerves, which in turn act on the blood vessels, causing extra spurts of blood to the head (hot flushes, sweating) and reduced blood flow to the extremities (coldness, tingling, numbness). If the ovarian hormone drops suddenly and the body has difficulty adjusting to the physical changes, marked physical (and sometimes emotional) reactions to the menopause are likely.

Artificial or Operative Menopause

Some women go through menopause suddenly as the result of an operation. The operation's effects on the body depend on what has been removed. In a partial *hysterectomy,* only the uterus is removed; the ovaries remain healthy and intact. Menstruation ceases abruptly and pregnancy is impossible. But ovulation and hormone secretion continue in the ovaries until the natural menopause, so there is no glandular change or effect on the body. Because of the body's need for ovarian hormones, surgeons try to save all or part of the ovaries. When the ovaries are removed, an *oophorectomy* is performed and both menstruation and hormone secretion stop abruptly. Even if the uterus is retained, menstruation ceases if the ovarian hormones are absent. The sudden loss of ovarian estrogen is especially disturbing and generally requires hormone therapy and other medication.

Age at Menopause

At what age does menopause occur? For women in the United States who have gone through a natural, nonsurgical menopause, the percentages are:

        1.4 percent by age 40
       15.2 percent by age 45

50.0 percent by age 49.76
59.3 percent by age 50
78.9 percent by age 52
87.5 percent by age 54
96.2 percent by age 55
100.0 percent by age 58 (Rice 1967)

Note that one half of all women having a natural menopause do so by age 49.76. It is generally agreed that there is no difference in menopausal age between married and single women. Although the age at menarche (first menstruation) has decreased with time, there is no consistent evidence of any change in age at menopause or that age of menarche and age at menopause are associated.

Signs and Symptoms

With the gradual decline of the ovarian function, menstruation usually becomes irregular. If a woman has had regular menstrual cycles, the menstrual flow may become lighter, lasting two or three days instead of the usual three to seven. Sometimes the interval between periods becomes longer. Menstruation may be missed for longer and longer periods until it ends. How long the process takes varies with different women. It may be months or several years. If a woman has had irregular menstrual periods all her life, the cycles usually become more irregular until menstruation ceases.

Other symptoms sometimes associated with menopause are hot flushes (Sherman et al. 1981), profuse perspiration, numbness or tingling of fingers or toes, headaches, dizziness, insomnia, fatigue, palpitation, weakness, gastro-intestinal upsets, pains in the joints, backaches, bladder difficulties, thickening and drying of the skin and relaxation of tissues under it, itching, dryness of vaginal tissues causing pain during intercourse, nervous tension, irritability, and depression (Rice 1967). Goodman and associates (1977) caution: ". . . these symptoms can also develop and exist independently of the hormonal imbalance characteristic of menopausal changes and that they may not be due to menopause *per se* but become manifest at the age when menopause commonly occurs and are precipitated by other life events" (292). In this study, Goodman and associates did find that 16 percent of Caucasian women and 10 percent of Japanese women—all of whom were nonmenopausal—reported these same symptoms.

Several studies also emphasize that about 75 percent of menopausal women do not exhibit these typical symptoms at all (Crawford and Hooper 1973; Goodman et al. 1977). Therefore, they are not inevitable concomitants of the change. Neither are abnormal physiological conditions associated with the menopausal state per se. Menopause is neither a disorder nor a disease, simply a normal change.

Hormone Replacement Therapy

One controversy surrounding menopause is the extent to which estrogen replacement therapy should be used to alleviate severe symptoms when they occur (Graber and Barber 1975). Many gynecologists contend that, in some women, symptoms warrant low-dosage use of estrogen over a period of years. According to the American College of Obstetricians and Gynecologists (ACOG), estrogen replacement therapy alleviates the intense hot flushes and severe night sweats that interfere with sleep (Briley 1980). But ACOG guidelines suggest short-term treatment for some women, which should be reevaluated after twelve to eighteen months. Estrogen replacement therapy also alleviates inflammation of the vaginal lining (*atrophic vaginitis*) and that of the end portions of the urinary canal (*atrophic urethritis*). These tissues depend on estrogen to retain their normal thickness. When a deficiency exists, linings may atrophy, becoming thin and possibly cracked, making intercourse painful. Urethritis can cause frequent and urgent urination. According to ACOG guidelines, these conditions may require low-dosage estrogen treatment over several years. In some cases, estrogen creams rather than pills are indicated.

One problem with estrogen is that it increases the risk of blood clots (of *thrombophlebitis* and *pulmonary embolism*). Another important problem with estrogen therapy is that women taking estrogen replacement are three times more likely than nonusers to develop cancer of the uterus (*endometrial cancer*) (Briley 1980b). However, if another female hormone, progesterone, is taken during the last few days of the cycle, estrogen users can lower their cancer risk to the level of nonusers. Hammond, at the Duke University Comprehensive Cancer Center, found that no cancer developed among long-term estrogen users who regularly added progesterone during the last part of the dose cycle ("A Way to Reduce Estrogen Risk?" 1978).

Hormones can help during and after menopause, but they should never be used indiscriminately. Their use requires good medical supervision and initial and frequent medical check-ups to make certain there are no counterindications.

Male Climacteric

The decline in reproductive function in the male is generally a gradual process. In males, in contrast to females, there is a constant replenishment of male sperm cells from puberty to old age. Consequently, reproduction is often possible into extreme old age. Men as old as ninety-four have fathered children. About half of all men between eighty and ninety have spermatozoa in their semen (Talbert 1977).

There is increasing evidence, however, that the secretion of the male hormone testosterone decreases in some elderly men. The level remains constant until about age sixty, after which it declines (Vermeulen et al.

1972). This may be partially responsible for some decline in sex drive and potency with age. There are wide individual variations, however. Testosterone levels in some eighty- and ninety-year-olds are in the high-normal range compared to levels in young adults. Also, testosterone levels fluctuate over a period of time, ranging from three to thirty days (Parlee 1978). However, the exact effect on male mood cycles is not clear. The isolation of testosterone in tests has prompted the discovery of the male climacteric, which is sometimes associated with impotence, depression, anxiety, headache, insomnia, irritability, tremors and palpitations, and digestive and urinary disturbances. These symptoms can sometimes be reduced by the implantation of crystalline testosterone supplemented with estrogen, but only when the hormone level is below normal.

Many of the reactions of men to aging are psychological. Men anxious about their virility may compensate by increasing their sexual activity. Some become involved in extramarital affairs. Others become impotent or develop other signs of anxiety. Some exhibit bizarre behavior that affects their family relationships. Others cease caring about their business responsibilities. One man wanted to sell out the family business, buy a boat, and sail around the world. Unfortunately, he had already had two heart by-passes, and his wife refused to sail across the ocean with a husband in that condition. Another man began drinking after work, bought an expensive sports car, and was arrested frequently for reckless driving. Up to this time, he had been an ultraconservative. Middle age can be a restless period during which personality changes occur (see chapter 3).

SEX AND THE ELDERLY

Myths

It is unfortunate that a young male interested in sex is considered normal, whereas an elderly male with the same interest is looked on as a dirty old man. It is equally unfortunate that a young woman can enjoy intercourse, and an elderly woman is supposed to lose interest. Such attitudes reflect a widespread belief that people who were passionately interested in sex when they were young suddenly cease being sexual beings when they are old. How many married children are shocked when they discover that their aging parents still have sex? Young people who feel that sex is perfectly normal for them may have difficulty accepting it as perfectly normal and appropriate for their own parents. If grandfather starts courting a younger woman, "He's making a fool of himself." If grandmother finds romance, she is told to "act her age."

When children feel ashamed or jealous of an elderly person's satisfying sexual relationship, the children have a problem, not the parents. Nevertheless, their children's negative attitudes affect parents. One recently remarried, seventy-eight-year-old man revealed that his daughter greeted him every morning with a derisive, "How did it go last night?"

(Lobsenz 1974). Because of such attitudes, many elderly feel guilty about their sexual feelings and fear the ridicule of others regarding their continued interest. One couple in their early seventies continued to make love every day, yet both believed they were doing something unnatural (Lobsenz 1974). One study of 300 subjects divided into three age groups (young [eighteen to twenty-five], middle-aged [forty to fifty-five], and old-aged [sixty-five to seventy-nine]) revealed considerable differences in beliefs about sexual behavior of the three age groups. Young adults were believed to have more sex, to attempt and desire more sex, to have higher virility, and be more physically capable. Middle-aged adults were considered to know more about sex and be better skilled in the sex act. The old were seen as sexless—desiring little, knowing little, attempting little, and getting less (Cameron and Biber 1973).

The denial of sex in the elderly and to the elderly is dramatized by the segregated practices of most nursing and old age homes. Even married couples may be separated. Few institutions provide an area where a couple can be alone together to talk, much less to court. If only one spouse is in a home, the other seldom has the right to privacy during a visit. One administrator said her staff respected the patient's privacy but added, "We run a bed-check every two hours to make sure they are all right" (Lobsenz 1974). A director of a home for the aged explained:

> Because of their cultural background, older people tend to separate what's "right" in public from what's "right" in private. So a woman rebuffs a man's overtures, or a man turns a blind eye to a little flirting—but I think they would act differently if there weren't so many witnesses. They are caught in a bind. Either they behave "acceptably" and miss out on emotional satisfactions, or feel they must run the risk of disapproval and embarrassment. (Lobsenz 1974, 96)

Importance

Sexual expression can be very important in the lives of older people. Even though people age, they still need love and affection. Touching, holding, kissing, and cuddling give reassurance that one is loved, revered, and desired as before.

Sexual expression also helps people feel attractive and good about themselves. Physically, it provides excellent exercise, improves circulation, and strengthens the lungs and heart. Emotionally, it brings pleasure and fulfillment. With these advantages, why limit it to the young?

Changes in Response Patterns

The fact that sexual expression in late adulthood remains desirable and possible does not mean that older people respond sexually exactly as they did when they were younger. Sexual response patterns of both men and women show some changes as the body ages.

The older male responds more slowly to sexual stimulation. The time required to achieve an erection takes minutes rather than the seconds characteristic of younger men. Once fully executed, however, the older male can sustain an erection without ejaculation for longer periods of time than when he was younger. This capacity increases his effectiveness as a sexual partner since the woman may require a prolonged excitement or plateau phase to reach orgasm. The lubrication that appears before ejaculation diminishes or disappears completely as men age, but this has little effect on sexual performance. The production of seminal fluid declines, decreasing the need to ejaculate as often.

The orgasm of an older man is generally less explosive. Contractions are weaker and the semen is expelled a shorter distance. These changes, however, do not interfere with orgasmic pleasure. Once ejaculation is achieved, the penis becomes flaccid very quickly, and the older man must wait a longer period of time (from hours to days) before a full erection is possible (Masters and Johnson 1966).

The older woman experiences little deterioration in the physical capacity for sex, but certain physiological changes need to be considered. After menopause, the secretion of ovarian hormones declines, causing gradual shortening and narrowing of the vaginal barrel and thinning, drying, and loss of elasticity of the vaginal walls. Lubrication of the vagina during sexual stimulation takes longer as the woman grows older. Thus, she needs a longer period of foreplay before intromission and, additionally, a vaginal lubricant to prevent painful intercourse. She may also be more susceptible to vaginal and urinary tract infections.

Like the male, the aging female takes longer to become sexually stimulated, although the excitement phase still may total only about five minutes. The incidence and intensity of nipple erection and engorgement of the breasts and the labia may be reduced. However, the nipples may remain erect up to hours after orgasm. Erection of the clitoris, which remains the most sensitive area, continues as before. Contractions during climax may lessen in number and intensity as the duration of orgasm is reduced, but orgasm continues to be an extremely pleasant experience. The genitalia and internal organs associated with sexual excitement return to their nonstimulated state more rapidly than in a younger woman. The important thing is that a healthy woman who was able to have orgasms in her younger years can continue having orgasms until late in life, well into her eighties. In summary, the physiological changes that do occur need not interfere with sexual enjoyment (Masters and Johnson 1966).

Male Capabilities

In the Duke University Studies on Aging, only 10 percent of the men over sixty-five said they no longer had any sexual feelings and only 24 percent said they were no longer having sexual relations (Pfeiffer et al. 1972). A study at the Sleep Laboratory of New York's Mount Sinai Hospital revealed that three out of four men, ages seventy-one to ninety-six, developed erections during sleep. Most evolved out of dreams with sexual content (Lobsenz 1974).

Masters and Johnson (1966) cited six important factors related to the loss of potency in men:

1. Boredom arising from monotony of a repetitious sexual relationship.
2. The male's preoccupation with economic and career pursuits to the exclusion of communication and sexual activity.
3. Physical or mental fatigue.
4. Overindulgence in food or alcoholic beverages.
5. Physical or mental disabilities of either the male or the female.
6. Fear of failure, causing the male to avoid coital activity rather than face the ego-shattering experience of repeated sexual failures.

The most important factor in maintaining sexual ability is the regularity of satisfying sexual expression. The more sexual stimulation, the more improvement in sexual tension and the greater the capacity for sexual performance.

Female Capabilities

Citing again the Duke University Studies on Aging, half of the women over sixty-five said that currently they had no sexual feelings. Three out of four of all the women over sixty-five indicated that they were having no sexual intercourse at all (Pfeiffer et al. 1972). The primary reason for the lack of sexual interest and activity was male attrition. Ninety percent of those who had ceased having sexual relations attributed the reasons to their spouse or to the lack of a spouse.

These data affirm that women overwhelmingly attribute the responsibility for cessation of sexual relations to their husbands. Masters and Johnson also affirmed that "if opportunity for regularity of coital exposure is created or maintained, the elderly woman . . . will retain a far higher capacity for sexual performance than her female counterpart who does not have similar coital opportunities" (1966, 241). Because extramarital partners are usually unavailable to older women, they have few opportunities for sexual expression and their interest may wane.

Unmarried females who have used masturbation for pleasure or relief of sexual tensions during their younger years continue the same behavioral patterns in later life.

SUMMARY

The process of human sexual response can be divided into four stages: the excitement phase, the plateau phase, the orgasmic phase, and the resolution phase. Men and women show similar physical responses as excitement builds, including erection; increases in heart rate, blood pressure, respiration, and perspiration; sex flush; and myotonia. The responses are similar, whether the method of stimulation is masturbation, love play, or intercourse.

In spite of similarities, differences do exist in sexual responses in men and women. Women are more capable than men of multiple and prolonged orgasms. Our culture conditions women to respond to romantic stimuli and men to erotic stimuli, although these differences are not inherent but learned. Women may need longer to become aroused than men, but this difference fades with proper stimulation. The erogenous zones of women are more diffuse.

Sexual interest and activity decrease slightly with age, but there are wide individual differences. Ordinarily, sexual desire continues well into old age. When activity decreases, especially in older women, it is usually due to the unavailability of sexual partners. Masturbation provides physical relief for large numbers of older men and women who lack opportunities for sexual intercourse.

Besides age, a number of important variables affect the level of sexual activity. These include past enjoyment, socioeconomic status, and participation in a warm, loving relationship.

When the human body does not respond sexually in predictable ways, the condition is called a *sexual dysfunction*. The most common sexual dysfunctions in men are premature ejaculation, impotence, and ejaculatory incompetence. Those common in women are orgasm dysfunction, dyspareunia, and vaginismus. Both men and women may exhibit low sexual drive. Dysfunctions have a number of different causes, which can be divided into five categories: (1) ignorance; (2) inadequate stimulation; (3) such psychological blocks as fear, anxiety, emotional illness, embarrassment, or guilt; (4) negative feelings toward one's partner or a disturbance in the relationship; and (5) physical effects of drugs, illness, or disabilities. The possibility of physical causes should be investigated before emotional or psychological causes are suspected.

Four types of help are available for sexual dysfunctions: medical treatment for physical problems, psychotherapy for emotional problems, marriage counseling that deals with the total marital relationship, and sex therapy that focuses on the immediate sexual problem.

Approximately one in ten couples would never be able to have children without medical help. A number of factors influence fertility and conception, including the frequency and timing of intercourse. Such factors as nutrition, anemia, fatigue, physical illness, or emotional stress also affect fertility. To impregnate his wife, a husband requires sufficient numbers of live, healthy sperm; proper amounts and composition of semen; an unobstructed passage from the testicles through the penis to the outside; and an erection that allows ejaculation within the vagina.

To be fertile, a wife must be ovulating. She must also have an unobstructed passage through the Fallopian tubes (down which the ovum must travel), a normal uterus that allows fertilization and implantation, and a vaginal chemical climate suitable for healthy sperm.

The ages of the husband and wife are also important factors influencing conception rates. The mother's age is also important to the health of the baby.

Menopause involves the cessation of menstruation. Physically, the ovaries gradually atrophy so that ovulation, menstruation, and the production of ovarian hormones (estrogen and progesterone) gradually cease. The adrenals secrete some estrogen to compensate for the loss of ovarian estrogen.

The median age of natural menopause in the United States is 49.76 years. All women undergo the change by age fifty-eight. Menopause occurs suddenly when the ovaries are surgically removed. A partial hysterectomy in which only the uterus is removed does not cause menopause, since the ovaries are still intact. A sudden loss of ovarian estrogen disturbs the body, and doctors usually try to alleviate symptoms with hormone replacement therapy. This therapy is used cautiously by some physicians, especially when the unpleasant symptoms are severe. About 75 percent of women do not exhibit typical menopausal symptoms.

Males may also experience a climacteric (but not menopause). The male climacteric is not triggered by a loss of the male hormone testosterone, since the level of this hormone measures in the high-normal range in some eighty- to ninety-year-olds. It is usually a negative psychological reaction to the aging process itself and may result in personality changes.

People continue to need love, affection, and sexual expression even in old age. Unfortunately, society tends to ignore these needs of the elderly. Segregation makes it difficult for the elderly to enjoy normal heterosexual contacts.

Response patterns tend to slow down in old age, but the physiological changes that occur need not interfere with sexual enjoyment if the elderly are in normal health.

8

Drug Abuse, Alcohol Abuse, and Smoking

DRUG ABUSE

Drugs and Extent of Abuse

Few social problems have caused more concern in recent years than drug abuse. One reason has been the dramatic increase in use: first among Vietnam veterans, then among college students, and then among younger adolescents and children. Currently, the greatest abusers of drugs are young adults between eighteen and twenty-five. Table 8.1 compares the use of various drugs by adults from different age groups (Miller et al. 1983). The figures include the total percentages of those who ever used the drug and the percentages who used the drug within the past month.

The *hallucinogens,* or so-called psychedelic drugs, include a broad range of substances. The best known is LSD, a synthetic drug that must be prepared in a laboratory. Other hallucinogens include peyote and mescaline (derived from the peyote cactus plant), psilocybin (derived from a species of mushroom) and four other synthetics, PCP, STP (also known as DOM), DMT, and MDA. Mescaline and LSD are used more frequently than any other psychedelic drug. *Psychotherapeutic drugs* are divided into four different classes: stimulants, primarily amphetamines and various appetite suppressants; sedatives, including barbiturates (used primarily in medicine as a sleep inducement), Dalmane, and others; tranquilizers, including such brands as Valium, Librium, and many others; and analgesics, which are pain killers.

As shown in Table 8.1, young adults eighteen to twenty-five years of age have the greatest percentage of users in every drug category mentioned except alcohol and cigarettes, which have been used by a slightly greater percentage of adults age twenty-six to thirty-four. Young adults also have the greatest percentage of current users (past month) in every drug category mentioned except alcohol and cigarettes, which are used by a slightly greater percentage of adults age twenty-six to thirty-four. More than two-thirds of young adults eighteen to twenty-five years of age report experience with an illicit substance. Two-thirds say they have used *mari-*

TABLE 8.1 Percent Using Drugs, by Age Groups, 1982

Drug	Young Adults 18–25		Adults 26–29		Adults 30–34		Totals for Adults 26–34		Adults 35–49		Adults 50 and Over		Totals for Adults 35 and Over	
	Ever	P. M.	Ever	P. M.	Ever	P. M.	Ever	P. M.	Ever	P. M.	Ever	P. M.	Ever	P. M.
Marijuana	64.1%	27.4%	60%	19%	53%	15%	56%	17%	24%	8%	5%	*%	12%	3%
Hallucinogens	21.1	1.7					19.2	*%					2.0	*%
Cocaine	28.3	6.8					21.7	3.3%					4.0	0.5%
Heroine	1.2	*%					3.5	*%					*%	*%
Any psycho-therapeutic *	28.4	7.0	25.0	5.0	18.0	4.0			11.0	*%	1.0	*%	*%	*%
Alcohol	94.6	67.9					95.8	70.6					85.6	51.8
Cigarettes	76.9	39.5					85.4	43.9					76.3	31.4

P. M. Past Month   *% Less than 0.5%   *Includes stimulants, tranquilizers, analgesics, and sedatives

Adapted from: J. D. Miller et al., *National Survey on Drug Abuse: Main Findings 1982* (Rockville, Md.: National Institute on Drug Abuse, 1983).

juana: 32 percent of this age group report use of marijuana only, and an additional 32 percent report using one or more illicit drugs, such as hallucinogens, cocaine, or heroin, in addition to marijuana. It is also significant that three out of four adults between twenty-six and thirty-four currently use alcohol, and almost half currently smoke. But less than one in five currently use marijuana, less than one in twenty use psychotherapeutic drugs, and only one in thirty use cocaine. A very small number currently use hallucinogens or heroine.

The older the age group, the smaller the percentages of drug abusers. Only 3 percent of adults thirty-five and over are current users of marijuana, and only a fraction of a percent of adults fifty and over use it. However, alcohol and tobacco use by adults thirty-five and over is still widespread.

Trends

This 1982 study indicates a reversal of the upward trends in drug use among young adults (eighteen to twenty-five) that were charted by earlier national surveys conducted throughout the seventies (Fishburne et al. 1980). In comparison to a 1979 survey, fewer percentages of young adults were current users of alcohol, cigarettes, hallucinogens, and heroin in 1982. The widespread increase in cocaine use noted in the second half of the seventies had decreased slightly by 1982. Trends in the use of psychotherapeutics were inconclusive but indicated no radical changes.

This pattern did not apply to adults age twenty-six and over. The young adults of the seventies continued the drug habits developed earlier, so the 1982 survey of adults twenty-six and over showed an increase in lifetime use and current use of every drug category except alcohol and cigarettes. As this cohort continues to age, subsequent surveys will show some increased usage among older and older persons. Older adults grew up in a period when alcohol and tobacco were the preferred drugs. But today's youth have been exposed to marijuana and other drugs. They will carry these experiences with them into adulthood.

DRUGS AND THE ELDERLY

Drugs for Medical Purposes

The figures cited describe the abuse of drugs for nonmedical purposes. But drugs are abused even when legally prescribed by a doctor for medical reasons. In addition, many over-the-counter drugs are taken for other reasons than intended, and in larger amounts or at more frequent intervals than prescribed.

Although national surveys show only small percentages of older persons taking drugs for nonmedical purposes, these same studies do indicate widespread drug abuse among the elderly who report taking them for medical reasons. These drugs are most commonly obtained through prescriptions. Or, they may be nonprescription drugs that are widely available.

Incidence of Abuse

One psychiatrist coined the expression "Spaced-Out Grandma Syndrome" to describe the overchemicalization of older persons (Nelson 1976). To appreciate the extent of the problem, consider that although adults over sixty-five comprise 10 percent of the population, they use 25 percent of the prescribed drugs (Basen 1977). A study of a representative sample of persons over sixty in Washington, D.C., revealed that 62 percent used prescription medication and 69 percent used over-the-counter drugs, half of which were for pain relief (Guttman 1977).

Studies of drug use among institutionalized elderly revealed the use of even greater numbers of drugs (up to eighteen different prescription drugs daily). Ingman and associates (1975) found that among patients in one long-term care institution, 60 percent were exposed to major or minor tranquilizers, 30 percent to sedative-hypnotic agents, and 20 percent to analgesic agents (pain killers).

Types of Drugs

The drugs most commonly prescribed for the elderly can be classified into five groups:

1. *Hypertensives* and *diuretics:* those used to control high blood pressure
2. Heart medicines: those that act either on the heart itself or on the blood vessels
3. *Psychotropics:* mood-altering drugs, such as tranquilizers, antidepressants, sedatives, hypnotics, or stimulants
4. Pain killers: *analgesics* with codeine
5. Miscellaneous: a variety of drugs, including *antacids, antibiotics* (tetracycline is one of the most popular), Diabinese (for diabetes), and Meclizine (for dizziness, lack of balance, travel sickness). (Zawadski et al. 1978)

The widespread use of psychotropics among the aged, especially among institutionalized patients, is causing concern. A major study of the most commonly used drugs among the Medicaid aged in California revealed that five of the ten most used drugs for the institutionalized aged were psychotropics. The cost of the drugs represented 40 percent of all expenditures for drugs for these persons (Zawadski et al. 1978). These figures contrast sharply with those for psychotropic drug use among non-institutionalized aged. In their case, only one of the fifteen most used drugs was a psychotropic drug. This drug accounted for only 5 percent of all drug expenditures. The researchers were unclear as to why the aged in institutions were prescribed many more psychotropics than the noninstitutionalized aged. Either the aged in institutions have more psychiatric problems or develop more while institutionalized, or the drugs are administered more for the benefit of the institutions. Certainly, too many institutions use drugs as chemical restraints in the absence of adequate help. They want to keep patients quiet and avoid trouble. Some patients are so heavily tranquilized, the result is a stupor or coma (Krupka and Vener 1979). To avoid this possibility, Kalchthaler and associates (1977) recommend that long-term care facilities establish aggressive, competent pharmacy committees to evaluate drug use and make recommendations to prescribing physicians.

Dangers

All kinds of drugs are potentially more harmful for older persons than for younger persons. Older adults metabolize drugs more slowly, and because of decreased renal (kidney) and liver functions, the safety margin between therapeutic and toxic doses is considerably narrowed (Krupka and Vener 1979). Drugs taken regularly can easily build up to toxic levels. For example, twenty-four hours after taking Valium, half the drug is still in the system. If another dose is taken at this time, the remaining Valium will escalate the action.

The greater the number of drugs taken, the greater the possibilities of adverse reactions. In one study, hospital patients who were given one to five drugs had an adverse reaction incidence of 19 percent, whereas patients given six or more prescribed drugs had an incidence of 81 percent (James 1976). The more drugs that are taken, the greater the risk of drug interactions (Morselli et al. 1974). Some drugs are antagonistic to one another or potentiate the action of other drugs.

Another factor leading to drug abuse is patients who use the services of different physicians and pharmacists. Prescriptions from several physicians may cause confusion about instruction for individual drugs. Multiple or conflicting explanations may lead to information overload, which could interfere with appropriate drug-taking behavior (Raffoul et al. 1981).

Sometimes the blame for drug misuse falls directly on physicians. Many physicians do not understand the complex effects of drugs, especially when they are taken together. Seventy percent of all drugs now prescribed were unavailable or unknown fifteen years ago. Consequently, few physicians studied them in medical school. Unless they have read journal reports and circulars and carefully researched the drugs they prescribe, they may not fully understand the side effects and interactions of new medications (Green 1978).

Self-Administration

Many drugs the elderly abuse are nonprescription medicines bought over the counter and taken improperly. Heavy consumption of *analgesics* such as aspirin over a period of time can result in toxic levels that cause diarrhea, dizziness or mental confusion, nausea or vomiting, stomach pain, rapid breathing, ringing or buzzing in the ears, sweating, or vision problems (U.S. Pharmacopoeial Convention 1981). *Bromides* have been abused for a long time. An accumulation can mimic a wide variety of psychiatric problems, including organic brain syndrome (confusion and disorientation). *Antihistamines* (including Benadryl, Dramamine, and most cold medications) can cause drowsiness and mental confusion in the elderly. At times, they cause blurred vision, nervousness, unusually fast heartbeat, or stomach pains. They have an even more pronounced effect when taken with aspirin, sedatives, or alcohol. *Anticholinergics* (like scopolamine), found in almost all over-the-counter nerve medications, also cause mental confusion. Stores are also well stocked with over-the-counter psychoactive drugs, such as Compoze, Sleep-Eze, and Nytol. These drugs are essentially antihistamines used to induce drowsiness. Widely used stimulants include No-Doz and No-Nod (Green 1978).

The minority who are senile often forget to take needed medication (Raffoul et al. 1981). One researcher (Lundin 1978) found that the most common type of inappropriate drug use among the elderly over sixty-five was underuse. Twenty-five percent of the elderly were not taking their medication or were not taking it as prescribed. None had adequate information to ensure appropriate use of their medication.

ALCOHOL ABUSE

Alcohol-Related Problems

Alcohol abuse is a generic term that includes both alcoholism (addiction to alcohol) and problem drinking (functional disability as a result of alcohol consumption) (U.S. Dept. of HEW 1980a). There are about ten million alcoholics or problem drinkers in the United States. Five out of six of them are between ages thirty and fifty-five. Each of these persons directly affects the lives of many others—family members, co-workers, employers, friends, and innocent bystanders—so that literally tens of millions of Americans face some of the negative consequences of alcohol abuse. The measurable alcohol-related cost to our society is estimated at $43 billion in lost production, medical expenses, motor vehicle accidents, violent crime, fire losses, and the maintenance of social agencies and resources to deal with the problems.

Alcoholism can destroy the mind and the body. A large percentage of those admitted to mental hospitals are alcoholics. As many as one-third of successful suicides are committed by persons who are drinking or drunk at the time. Alcoholism shortens life expectancy by an estimated ten to fifteen years and contributes significantly to such serious conditions as heart disease, cancer, and liver disease (U.S. Dept. of HEW 1980b).

Alcohol is a major factor in crime. More than 50 percent of all arrests are for public drunkenness, for driving under the influence, or for committing crimes while under the influence. Alcohol is involved in half of all homicides and half of all traffic fatalities. In addition, the majority of pedestrians injured by cars had been drinking at the time of the accident.

Alcohol is now suspected to be a major factor in child abuse and marital violence. In a high proportion of cases in which a parental beating causes a child to be hospitalized, the parent is drunk at the time. Alcohol abuse during pregnancy is also a major problem. Each year, more than 200,000 premature deaths are associated with alcohol misuse (U.S. Dept. of HEW 1980b). Countless thousands of children are born with various defects associated with heavy drinking, especially mental deficiencies.

As more is learned about alcohol and its effects, it becomes clearer that the associated problems are far more extensive than once realized.

Extent of Use

Alcohol is the preferred drug among adults of all ages. However, the daily use of alcohol is most widespread in the twenty-six and over age group. About 11 percent of these adults said they drank on twenty or more days out of the current month (Miller et al. 1983). This represents fairly heavy drinking. No wonder a Gallup Poll revealed that about one-fourth of Americans reported that liquor had caused trouble in their families (Gallup 1979). Current drinkers are also more likely than current nondrinkers to have used marijuana, psychotherapeutics (stimulants, sedatives, tranquilizers, and analgesics), and stronger drugs (hallucinogens, cocaine, and heroin) (Fishburne et al. 1980).

Development of Chronic Alcoholism

Johnson (1973) offers one of the finest descriptions of how alcoholism develops in his book, *I'll Quit Tomorrow*. The following information, presented in abbreviated form, is taken from that book. Johnson divides the process of becoming an alcoholic into four phases.

> Phase one: Learns mood swing.
> Phase two: Seeks mood swing.
> Phase three: Harmful dependence; acute, chronic phase.
> Phase four: Drinks to feel normal.

Phases one and two represented by Figure 8–1 are discovering and learning phases during which people learn that a drink will give them a warm, good feeling and may even cause giddiness, depending on the amount consumed. The initiation is interesting and pleasant, as people learn that drinking can make them feel better. They can turn on a feeling of euphoria anytime they drink, and they can control the degree of mood swing by controlling the amount. It works every time! When people come home tired, depressed, or upset, they take one drink or more. Experience has taught them that alcohol can do the trick. Thus, they develop a relationship with alcohol. It is a positive experience, and they trust it, so they seek mood swings in regular and appropriate ways.

No acute problem exists yet. When the effects of the alcohol wear off, the drinker returns to normal. Unless people drive while drinking and have an accident or get into some other trouble, there is no damage and no emotional cost.

Up to this point, drinkers follow self-imposed rules: for instance, "Don't drink until five o'clock." But one day they look at the time and it's only two o'clock—three hours before work is over. Waiting becomes too painful, so they have a drink with lunch or while watching Saturday afternoon television. From this point on, the feeling of relief may be sought earlier and earlier in the day, with larger and larger amounts of alcohol.

As social drinkers become more dependent on their chemical, getting drunk begins to have a very different effect on them. They are caught in a habit that carries them beyond social drinking. They enter phase three, alcoholism, by becoming harmfully and chemically dependent. They think everything is fine and are unaware they have crossed an invisible line that they cannot recross without help. The index of progression of the disease from this point on is the degree of emotional cost. A significant and progressive deterioration occurs in the personality of alcoholics; eventually physical deterioration becomes apparent.

The more excessive the drinking, the more pronounced the mood swings. Drinkers go from euphoria to negative emotional reactions and pain. They feel remorse for their excesses and their foolish behavior. "I was stupid last night. Nobody stands on a table and leads cheers at the club. I'll have to call Harry and Jane and apologize." Each drinking experience brings more remorse and a reduced self-image. Ego strength ebbs as drinking produces painful and bizarre behavior. They begin to feel self-hatred: "I'm just no damn good."

But no one can live forever with self-hatred, anxiety, guilt, shame, and remorse. Through various defense mechanisms, drinkers build a wall around their negative feelings until they are no longer aware that these destructive emotions exist. For example, they make excuses for drinking and rationalize their behavior. "I don't feel well." "I'm tired." "I'm under pressure at work." "It's my birthday and I need a drink." Every happening becomes an excuse for drinking. Moreover, they begin to blame others for their drinking problem and to project their own self-hate on them.

Alcoholics do not realize this is happening. It occurs unconsciously. Because alcoholics hate themselves, they have to vent their hate by attacking others. Sometimes, the people the alcoholic attacks begin blaming themselves for the drinking and do all they can to try to remedy the situation. They fix dinner earlier; they hide the bottle; they plead; they get angry. But nothing works. As their failures mount, they become more anxious, guilty, frantic, and emotionally distressed. This reinforces the alcoholic's view that others are to blame.

Alcoholics use another defense mechanism to hide their guilt, shame, and remorse. They repress their feelings, which helps them not to feel at all. As a result, they may become apathetic, indifferent, or emotionless about everything—their family and friends, even their own drinking.

As the disease progresses, blackouts may become more frequent. Blackouts are not the same as "passing out," or drinking to the point of losing consciousness. The chemically induced blackout involves a permanent and complete loss of memory for a given period of time. Afterward alcoholics ask: "How did I get home last night?" "Did I hurt anybody?" "Did I make a pass at my boss's wife?" "Where am I? How did I get to this motel room?" Drinkers function during a blackout as though they are aware of what is going on around them, but they actually remember none of it. They suffer amnesia. Other people assume they are in control of themselves and rational. They resume relations with the drinkers following these memory lapses, assuming that they have shared common experiences. Alcoholics are generally embarrassed by their memory loss and try to bluff their way out. Confusion is likely to result.

The loss of memory prevents alcoholics from realizing what they have done. They may have drunk a quart but they honestly remember only two drinks. They may have acted obnoxiously or violently but only remember their euphoria. "I had a few drinks, but I was perfectly all right," is their recollection. It takes a replay of a tape recording of their drinking bout to make them aware of their stammering, nonsensical sentences and obnoxious behavior. Alcoholics cannot understand why others look askance at them or shun them. Friends cannot understand why drinkers do not see what they are doing to themselves and others. The reason is that alcoholics do not remember. Between blackouts and repression, their judgment is seriously impaired. They are acutely ill with a condition that, if not arrested, will impair their constitution emotionally, mentally, physically, and spiritually during their final months or years, and that will ultimately kill them.

In the acute stage, alcoholics are no longer emotionally able to start a drinking episode from the normal point. They no longer feel good or euphoric. They feel chemically depressed on the painful side of the figure (see Figure 8.2) and have to drink just to feel normal. Thus, they drink when they wake up; they drink on the job (if they still have one); they drink at home; and they drink because they have been drinking. Drinking at this stage is compulsive.

Two obstacles prevent alcoholics from getting the attention they need. Most people do not understand their helpless condition and deal with them judgmentally. When alcoholics fail to recognize how sick they are, people react by turning away. They may even have a false expectation that alcoholics will gain insight when they hit bottom. This makes alcoholics even more isolated and defensive. Another reason alcoholics do not get

FIGURE 8.1   Phase One: Learns Mood Swing; Phase Two: Seeks Mood Swing

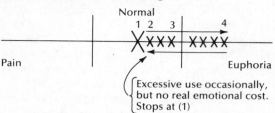

Excessive use occasionally, but no real emotional cost. Stops at (1)

From: V. E. Johnson, *I'll Quit Tomorrow*. New York: Harper and Row, 1973, p. 11, 13. Used by permission of the author.

FIGURE 8.2   Phase Four: Drinks to Feel Normal

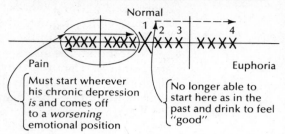

Must start wherever his chronic depression *is* and comes off to a *worsening* emotional position

No longer able to start here as in the past and drink to feel "good"

From: V. E. Johnson, *I'll Quit Tomorrow*. New York Harper and Row, 1973, p. 26. Used by permission of the author.

help is their rigid behavior and distorted memory patterns. Their impaired judgment and chemical dependence lock them into a self-destructive pattern. The sicker they become, the more actively they resent intervention.

Treatment

Alcoholism is a progressive illness that is always fatal unless arrested. But outside intervention by knowledgeable persons is necessary to arrest it.

Treatment consists of several aspects. First, alcoholics must be confronted with the reality of their illness so they can recognize their condition. Even at their worst, they can accept some reality if it is presented to them by persons they trust and in forms they can receive.

Second, once the alcoholic accepts treatment, chemical dependency is treated in a carefully phased detoxification program. Intensive medical treatment is directed at the acute symptoms of the disease.

Third, alcoholics must be taught the facts about their disease, through lectures, films, readings, discussion, and other means. The primary goal is to make them realize intellectually what chemical dependency is, while accurately informing them of the symptoms and consequences of their disease.

Next, individual and group psychotherapy helps them to identify and break down their defenses so they can become feeling persons again. As their defense wall crumbles, they are encouraged to vent their negative attitudes and feelings. Then they can gain realistic insights into their condition and gradually rebuild their own feelings of self-worth as the disease is arrested.

Finally, alcoholics are assisted with the process of rehabilitation: finding jobs, repairing broken family and personal relationships where possible, and becoming accepted members of society again. Rehabilitation must involve those meaningful persons who have suffered because of the alcoholic's illness and help them to develop attitudes conducive to healing.

SMOKING

Consumption

A larger percentage of adults twenty-six to thirty-four smoke cigarettes than do young adults between eighteen and twenty-five or adults thirty-five and over. The latest figures show that 85 percent of adults in the twenty-six to thirty-four age group have smoked cigarettes and that 44 percent are current smokers (used cigarettes the past month). Of those thirty-five and over, only 31 percent currently smoke, indicating that many are able to break the habit. Figure 8.3 shows the recency of cigarette use.

FIGURE 8.3   Recency of Cigarette Use, 1982: Adults 26–34 and 35 and Over

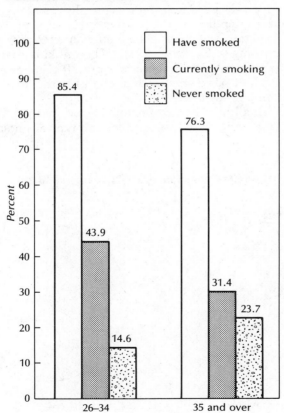

Age Group (Years)

Adapted from: J. D. Miller et al., *National Survey on Drug Abuse: Main Findings 1982,* DHHS Publication No. (ADM) 83–1263 (Rockville, Maryland: National Institute on Drug Abuse, 1983).

Figure 8.4 compares the cigarette consumption of young adults eighteen to twenty-five with all adults twenty-six and over. These figures indicate that a greater percentage of young adults eighteen to twenty-five smoke compared to all older adults. However, adults twenty-six and older who smoke consume more per day than young adults. Twenty-two percent of all smokers age twenty-six and over smoke a pack a day or more, compared to 19 percent of those age eighteen to twenty-five.

Smoking Habits

Smoking is a habit that compounds itself. The longer a person smokes, the heavier the consumption, for two reasons. One, nicotine is physically addicting, so the body craves it (Krasnegor 1979). Two, smokers become tolerant of nicotine and need increasing amounts as tolerance levels rise. Sudden withdrawal produces unpleasant physical symptoms. Twenty to thirty minutes after finishing a cigarette, the nicotine level in the brain declines. The brain sends a signal to the smoker that a fresh supply is needed. According to Russell (1971), "The smoking pattern of the dependent smoker who inhales a cigarette every 30 minutes of his waking life (a pack and a half per day) is such as to insure the maintenance of a high level of nicotine in his brain."

Only a small percentage of smokers can use cigarettes intermittently or occasionally. It is almost impossible for a typical smoker to smoke only

FIGURE 8.4   Cigarette Consumption, 1982: Young Adults 18–25 and Adults Age 26 and Over

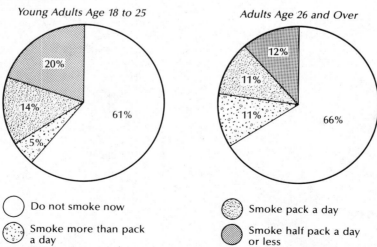

Adapted from: J. D. Miller et al., *National Survey on Drug Abuse: Main Findings 1982*, DHHS Publication No. (ADM) 83–1263 (Rockville, Maryland: National Institute on Drug Abuse, 1983).

a few cigarettes a day. As addiction increases, so does the rate of consumption.

Smoking is a difficult habit to break. Follow-up studies of smokers who have quit show a high relapse rate. One study showed that at the end of four years more than 80 percent of those who had stopped were smoking again (Krasnegor 1979).

Dangers to Health

There is no longer any question that cigarette smoking is harmful. Conclusive evidence shows a positive correlation between smoking and cancer of the lungs, pancreas, and throat, and between smoking and emphysema, bronchitis, and other respiratory diseases. A positive correlation also exists between smoking and cardiovascular diseases, such as high blood pressure, heart attacks, or strokes (U.S. Dept. of HEW January 1974). However, the risks are reduced significantly if a person stops smoking. In spite of these risks, 57 million adult Americans continue to smoke.

SUMMARY

The greatest abusers of drugs today are young adults between eighteen and twenty-five. This abuse includes nonmedical use of all types of drugs except alcohol and cigarettes, which are abused most by adults twenty-six to thirty-four. Two-thirds of young adults age eighteen to twenty-five report experience with an illicit substance: two-thirds have used marijuana; one-third of them have used marijuana only, and the other third report using one or more illicit drugs, such as hallucinogens, cocaine, or heroine, in addition to the marijuana. The older the age group, the smaller the percentages using these drugs. The upward trend in drug abuse noted in the 1970s has been reversed, and fewer adults are current users. However, as the cohort of young heavy users gets older, the percentages of older adults using various types of drugs will likely increase.

A small number of elderly abuse drugs for nonmedical purposes. However, large numbers abuse prescription and over-the-counter drugs taken supposedly for medical reasons. The widespread use of psychotropics (tranquilizers, antidepressants, sedatives, hypnotics, or stimulants) is of real concern, especially among institutionalized adults.

All drugs are potentially more harmful to older than to younger persons because older adults metabolize the drugs more slowly. Also, older adults take a greater number of drugs, which increases the possibility of adverse reactions and drug interactions. Many drugs the elderly abuse are nonprescription drugs they buy over the counter and take improperly. The minority of senile adults may forget how much medicine they have already taken or forget to take their medicine at all.

Alcohol is the preferred drug among adults of all ages. About 11 percent of adults twenty-six and over said they drank on twenty or more days out of the current month. There are about 10 million alcoholics or problem drinkers in the United States. Five out of six of them are between thirty and fifty-five.

Alcoholism is a major problem. It destroys the mind and body; it is a major factor in crime, child abuse, and marital violence; and it is a major health problem during pregnancy.

Chronic alcoholism develops in four phases. In phase one, drinkers learn that alcohol can cause a mood change. In phase two, drinkers seek this change through alcohol consumption. Phase three involves harmful chemical dependency, as drinkers reach acute and then chronic drinking stages. This is accompanied by more pronounced mood swings, from euphoria to negative emotional reactions and pain. As behavior becomes bizarre, drinkers develop more and more self-hatred, guilt, and anxiety, while ego strength ebbs. Drinkers begin to build a wall around negative feelings through such defense mechanisms as rationalization, projection, and repression. In denying the extent of the problem, drinkers become incapable of realizing how sick they are. As drinking progresses to phase four, blackouts occur and drinkers no longer remember how much they drank or how they behaved. By the time drinkers reach stage four, they no longer feel good or even normal; they are chemically depressed and must drink just to feel normal.

Alcoholism is a progressive disease that is always fatal unless arrested. It requires outside intervention to make drinkers realize how sick they are and get help. Treatment consists of detoxification, education, psychotherapy, and rehabilitation.

The largest percent of adults who smoke are in the twenty-six to thirty-four age group. Forty-four percent of this group are current smokers. Smoking is a habit that compounds itself. Because nicotine is physically addicting, smokers develop a tolerance and require larger and larger amounts. Sudden withdrawal causes unpleasant physical symptoms. There is no question that cigarette smoking is harmful. A positive correlation exists between smoking and cancer, respiratory diseases, and cardiovascular diseases. In spite of the risk, 57 million adult Americans continue to smoke.

9

Death and Dying

PROLONGEVITY

Possibilities

Longevity refers to the duration of life, usually implying a long or extended life. The term *prolongevity* was introduced in 1966 by Gerald J. Gruman, a physician and historian, to describe deliberate efforts to extend the length of life by human action (Gruman 1966). Some prolongevitists have been optimistic in their predictions. They assert that the problems of death and aging can be overcome and put virtually no limits on the length of human life. More conservative prolongevitists have proposed a more limited increase in the length of life: usually to age 100 or over. They look forward to breaking the 110-year limit, which is a formidable barrier. Dr. Roy Walford, professor of pathology at UCLA's medical school, asserts that by the end of this century we may be able to retard the rate of aging so people will live to be 100 years of age or more ("How People Will Live to Be 100 or More" 1983).

Opposition

There is some opposition to the idea of life prolongation. Some say it violates divine will; the biblical description of "three score years and ten" is taken as a moral prescription. Some religionists emphasize that life was intended to be immortal, but that death was a punishment for the original sin of Adam and Eve. As long as human beings are under God's judgment, death is the consequence of their sinfulness. To perpetuate life would be to prolong sinful nature: human selfishness, disobedience, and sexual lust. Better for people to leave this life and start over, free of guilt and sin, in the next life.

Other persons suggest that prolongevity violates natural law, which fixes the maximum life span. Another objection holds that because human nature is so defective, prolongevity cannot be attained; or, if attained, it would be accompanied by all the defects and miseries of old age. People question whether prolongevity is desirable. Why perpetuate sickness, disability, and discomfort for the sake of living longer? Psychiatrist Carl Jung was convinced that death was a goal toward which people should strive. To shrink away from it was abnormal and unhealthy. Sociologists, economists, and political scientists point out that the longer people live, the more top-heavy society becomes. Society's greater and greater percentages of older people would tax the medical, economic, and social resources available to care for millions of senior citizens. Even if life could be prolonged, the economic consequences would be devastating. An extended population would consume the earth's resources at accelerated rates, adding to the waste, garbage, and pollution already accumulating.

Implications

Most thoughtful prolongevitists reject the idea that prolonging life is a curse. For one thing, their goal is not simply to increase the maximum life span, but to retard the aging process as well. If people were physically young and healthy, even though advanced in years, heart disease, cancer, and diabetes would practically be eliminated. Instead of being sick, disabled, and dependent, people would have their health and vigor for years and live active, useful lives. Their work careers might extend beyond the age of one hundred. Or, they might have a thirty-year work career, a period of reeducation, and then a second career for the remainder of their lives.

The work force would increase compared to the nonworking population, and such problems as the overburdened social security system would be solved. Seventy-year-old adults would find themsevles in classrooms with twenty-year-olds, increasing the amount of intergenerational interaction. The extended family would become commonplace again, with three, four, or even five generations living together. The elderly would recapture a sense of belonging and a position of leadership. If the old had youthfulness as well as wealth, status, and power, displacing them would be impossible.

Equally important, the wisdom and experience amassed by the young-old could be used to solve societal problems and create a better life for all. There is no telling what a person might become or achieve given a significant number of extra years. Those who live a long time can not only learn more, but also synthesize their learning in new ways to create new systems of thought and ideas. If the lives of some of the world's geniuses were prolonged, what might they achieve?

Life Expectancy

In spite of the exciting possibilities, the maximum longevity of individuals has remained almost unchanged. The average life expectancy, calculated from birth, has increased greatly, but primarily because many childhood diseases and circumstances that caused premature death have been conquered. Figure 9.1 shows the expectation of life at birth from 1920 to

FIGURE 9.1   Expectation of Life at Birth, United States: 1920–1979

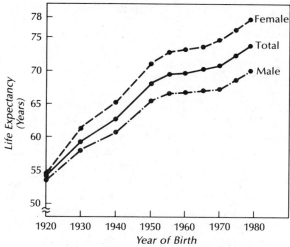

Adapted from: U.S. Department of Commerce, Bureau of the Census, *Statistical Abstract of The United States: 1982, 83* (Washington, D.C.: U.S. Government Printing Office, 1983), 71.

1979 (in the United States) (U.S. Dept. of Commerce 1983). As shown, the average life expectancy from birth has increased from fifty-four to seventy-four years. But for those who survive the younger ages, the chances of a long life are not much greater than they used to be.

Some racial and national differences exist. Blacks in the United States have a consistently higher age-specific mortality rate than do whites, at all ages up to about seventy-five. At this point, there is a crossover of death rates for the two racial groups, that is, the rates for whites become greater than the rates for blacks (Nam and Okay 1977; Rives 1977). The question is why. A biological explanation maintains that if blacks are subject to higher mortality than whites in the early years, then the remaining blacks in older age categories will be relatively more fit. In contrast, the lower early mortality of whites will generate higher proportions of weak individuals at older ages. With advancing age, whites become more vulnerable than blacks and the rates of the two populations converge and cross.

Another explanation is environmental. Because of life style, occupation, social position, and differences in health care, blacks are more prone than whites to circulatory and heart diseases in middle age. But at advanced ages, there is a rapid increase in circulatory and heart diseases among whites that surpasses the slower increase among blacks. The result is a crossover of mortality rates.

How do mortality rates in the United States compare to those in other developed countries? Between sixty-five and seventy-four the death rates among both males and females are lower in Denmark, the Netherlands, Norway, and Sweden than in the United States. Rates are also lower among Japanese males sixty-five to seventy-four and Japanese females sixty-five to sixty-nine than among comparable groups in the United States. The United States has made rapid progress in reducing mortality rates at the oldest age, but not as much progress for those under seventy-five. Also, the death rates are nearly twice as high for males as for females at the same ages, and this differential is increasing due to sharper declines in death rates for females (Myers 1978).

Reports sometimes come from such areas as the Caucasus region of the Soviet Union, the Hunza area of Tibet, or from Ecuador of people who have lived to be 120 years of age or older. These people live in very hilly terrain, eat diets low in cholesterol, drink or smoke moderately, and participate actively in their society. However, the claims of dramatically longer lives are not well substantiated or documented.

Some groups in the United States have life expectancies well below the population average. American Indians have the shortest life expectancy of any group in the United States. Hispanic Americans have shorter life expectancies than white Americans, yet males in Spain live longer than American men (Butler 1976). Much depends on the socioeconomic conditions in which people live and the health care they receive.

Occupational stresses and hazards, or lack of them, also affect longevity. Symphony conductors have unusually long lives, as do clergymen. Those who have been professional athletes do not fare as well. There is speculation that this might be due to an enlargement of the heart from exercise. People engaged in hazardous occupations, such as foundry workers or coal miners, do not live as long as the average person. Farmers enjoy longevity. Some have predicted that as women acquire more managerial and stress-related jobs, their mortality rate will increase. So far, this has not happened (Butler 1976).

Retarding the Aging Process

To prolong life, it is necessary to deal with the factors responsible for death. One approach is to eliminate the diseases that are principal killers. If we cured heart disease, cerebrovascular disease, cancer, pulmonary diseases, diabetes, and the like, the life span would increase from seventy-four to approximately eighty-five by the year 2025 ("How People Will Live to Be 100 or More" 1983). However, besides eliminating disease, we need to retard the aging process itself.

The various biological theories of aging are discussed in chapter 5. Several theories emphasize the importance of DNA in longevity. DNA is a basic substance in human chromosomes that contains the genetic code. But DNA contains strands that wind, unwind, and sometimes break. Longevity correlates very closely with DNA repair efficiency. The body has a series of enzymes that repair defects, and one way to increase the life span would be to increase the repair rate, possibly by manipulating the enzymes.

Heredity plays a part in longevity (Cohen 1976). Some gerontologists refer to *senescence genes,* which accelerate the aging process, and to *longevity-assurance* genes, which speed up the DNA repair rate and increase the life span. Human beings live about twice as long and have twice the DNA repair rate as chimpanzees. As humankind evolved, the life span increased along with the increase in DNA repair rate (Cutler 1975). This evolutionary evidence and modern advances in molecular biology point to the desirability of a concerted search for the positive, genetically controlled functions of molecular protection and repair that underlie our ability to resist aging, disease, and death (Sacher 1978).

One theory of aging describes how the immune system of the body recognizes and rejects foreign organisms and cancer cells. As people get older, the immune system can no longer detect the difference between its own and foreign organisms, and it begins to react against itself. Manipulation of the immune system, possibly through drugs, can increase the life span. Work is also being done with the thymus hormone, which regulates the maturation of the immune system. The thymus begins to deteriorate around thirty-five, and the thymus hormone level declines. Maintenance of the hormone level is a promising approach.

The metabolic waste theory of aging suggests that deleterious substances accumulate within various body cells as by-products of metabolism. These *free radicals* damage body tissues and organs. Scientists have extended the life span of animals by feeding them antioxidants. If the right combinations can be determined for human beings, perhaps damage can be retarded.

The metabolic rate also affects the rate of aging. The higher the rate, the sooner the body wears out and the shorter the life span. This wear and tear theory proposes retarding aging by retarding metabolism. But metabolism is partly controlled by the amount one eats. Body metabolism increases when people eat a lot, as the body struggles to burn up the excess food. It slows down as dietary intake decreases in order to conserve energy. One way to retard aging is by dietary manipulation, by cutting down on the amount of food eaten. Not only does this minimize excess fats and cholesterol, which are killers, but it also slows down body metabolism, and the accompanying aging. This diet requires high nutritional density; that is, one eats only small amounts but still consumes the thirty-two essential nutrients. Caloric intake is reduced gradually over a period of five years until a person reaches 60 percent of normal consumption. However, this diet is so stringent, few people can maintain it.

Undernutrition without malnutrition has other benefits. The immune system stays younger longer, and the self-reject reaction decreases. It is likely that fewer free radicals are generated, and there might be better DNA repair. Studies have shown that this diet increased longevity in laboratory rats by 50 to 100 percent. Biologists believe there is a high order of probability—about 98 percent—that it will work on human beings. A few researchers are on the diet, but as yet no systematic studies support the claims ("How People Will Live to Be 100 or More" 1983).

DEATH RATES

Leading Causes of Death

Figure 9.2 shows the leading causes of death in the United States in 1979. Heart disease was the number one killer. If cerebrovascular diseases and atherosclerosis were added to the total for heart disease, these cardiovascular diseases would account for 57 percent of all the deaths. However, rapid progress in the treatment of these diseases has caused the associated death rate to decrease steadily.

Cancer was the number two killer, and in spite of advances in treatment, the death rate continues to rise. The rising death rate is due primarily to an increase among males, particularly those sixty-five and over. Among females, deaths from cancer actively declined until 1970. Since then there has been a slight rise, but nothing comparable to the increase among older males. Cancer of the lungs has increased drastically in both men and women. Since deaths from most other forms of cancer have declined, the rise in lung cancer deaths is primarily responsible for the total increase.

FIGURE 9.2   Death Rates by Cause and Sex, United States, 1979

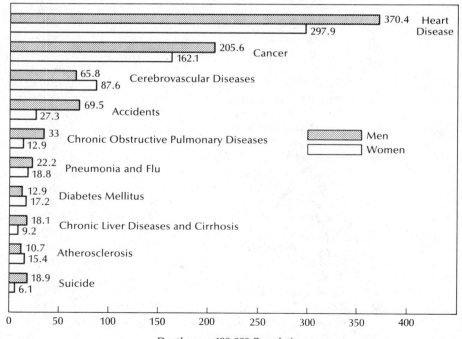

Deaths per 100,000 Population

Adapted from: U.S. Department of Commerce, Bureau of the Census, *Statistical Abstract of The United States: 1982, 83* (Washington, D.C.: U.S. Government Printing Office, 1983), 77.

ATTITUDES TOWARD DEATH AND DYING

Cultural Antecedents

The dominant feature of death in the twentieth century is its invisibility. We try to solve the problem of death by hiding or denying it. We lie to dying people about their condition because death is unmentionable. They, in turn, try to convince us that they are getting better. Or, we use machines to keep organs functioning, even when people are clinically dead. When people die, they are made to look healthy and alive, as though they were sleeping. We discourage mourning and the natural expression of grief at a time of great loss. The denial of death has become the orthodoxy of our culture (Robinson 1981).

Criticisms

These trends have led to increasing examination of our philosophies of death and dying, to a deluge of courses on the subject, and to a flood of literature, much of it protesting modern practices. Tentler (1977) provided a comparative critique of writings about death in American culture, drawn from the fields of psychology, sociology, anthropology, religion, and literature. He observed a common theme in these essays: a "moralist, reformist approach" characterized by criticism of the denial of death. Dishonesty with dying people, lack of care for the aged, and American funeral practices are common subjects of scorn. The point is made that contemporary society needs a philosophy of death it can live with.

Attitudes among the Elderly

The elderly are often more philosophical, more realistic, and less anxious about death than are others in our culture. Many studies underscore these attitudes. Questionnaires were administered to forty volunteer, ambulatory institutionalized residents of the Wyoming Pioneer Home for senior citizens and to forty ambulatory, noninstitutionalized aged persons who were members of the Laramie, Wyoming, Senior Citizen's Center—a center providing meals, nursing services, recreation, and social activities (Myska and Pasewark 1978). Subjects ranged in age from sixty-one to ninety-seven. There were few differences between the institutionalized and non-institutionalized in their views of death. Generally, fear of death was not suggested by the respondents (see Table 9.1).

Although they did not fear death, few of the elderly subjects indicated a resignation to or desire for death. Only 5 percent said they frequently wished for death. Eighty-two percent thought about living things and looked forward to the future. Sixty-nine percent reported that they perceived death as rescuing them from pain and difficulty. However, only 33

TABLE 9.1   Fear of Death among Elderly Rural Residents

Attitude	Percent Affirming Attitude
Strong fear of death	1%
Absolutely unafraid of death	51%
Indifferent toward death	40%
Did not respond	8%

Reprinted with permission of authors and publisher from: M. J. Myska and R. A. Pasewark, "Death Attitudes of Residential and Non-Residential Rural Aged Persons," PSYCHO-LOGICAL REPORTS 43 (December 1978): 1235–1238.

percent looked forward to death for that reason. The one fear of the respondents was that death would be painful (45 percent), but only 6 percent believed this would be the case.

In relation to an afterlife, 62 percent believed it existed but 94 percent said it did not worry them. Seventy-five percent reported they would not change their way of life even if they were certain there was no life after death (Myska and Pasewark 1978). These results indicated an affirmation of life and a realistic acceptance of death, with little anxiety or preoccupation.

Attitudes among Different Age Groups

Detailed studies of groups of adults reveal variations in attitudes toward death among different age groups. One study examined the attitudes toward death of black, Mexican American, and white adults of low, medium, and high socioeconomic status, from three different age groups (forty-five to fifty-four, fifty-five to sixty-four, and sixty-five to seventy-four). It revealed little variation in attitudes toward death with respect to race, socioeconomic status, or sex, but substantial differences according to age (Bengtson et al. 1977). Middle-aged respondents, forty-five to fifty-four, expressed the greatest fear of death; the elderly, sixty-five to seventy-four, reflected the least. The researchers suggested that middle-aged adults are more frightened of death because they experience a middle-aged crisis and become aware of the finitude of their lives.

The researchers also suggested that adults resolve their death fears in old age. This attitude is exemplified by a sixty-seven-year-old widower who said, "I know I'm going to die, it's something that we all have to go through. When it happens, it happens, and there's nothing I can do. I'll cross that bridge when I come to it" (Bengtson et al. 1977).

Attitudes toward death depend partly on attitudes toward life. Keith (1979) surveyed 214 men and 354 women, median age seventy-nine, from small towns in a midwestern state and found that those who experienced continuity in marital status, good health, church involvement, and informal contacts with family and friends viewed life and death more positively.

Continuity in marital status and good health were especially important to men in influencing positive attitudes toward life and death. Continuity in church involvement and informal social participation was especially important to women with positive attitudes toward life and death. Because women are more likely than men to expect widowhood, greater stability in social contacts and friendships would be especially important to them. Among men and women, however, declining social contacts fostered the view that life was over and that the future was a time to wait for death (Keith 1979).

ASPECTS OF DEATH

Determining when a person is dead is not simple. A distinction is made between *physiological* death and *clinical* death. With physiological death, all the vital organs cease to function and the organism can no longer live, in any sense of the word. Deprived of oxygen and nutrients, the cells of the body gradually die. Clinical death is the cessation of all brain activity as indicated by an absence of brain wave. There is no consciousness, no awareness. The organism ceases to function as a self-sustaining, mind-body human, even though the heart and lungs can function with artificial support.

There are other aspects of death. *Sociological death* involves withdrawal and separation from the patient by others. This may occur weeks before terminus if patients are left alone to die. It happens when families desert the aged in nursing homes where they may live as if dead for years. As a resident of one nursing home expressed it:

> What do I have to live for? I have two children who don't care about me. They are so busy with their own lives that they haven't been in to see me for two years. My health is not good. I have arthritis, no appetite, and a weak heart. There is nothing to do here. It's the same old thing day after day. I might as well be dead.

Psychic death occurs when the patient accepts death and regresses into the self. Often this occurs long before physiological death. The acceptance of psychic death can actually cause a person to die. Death comes through the power of suggestion because the will to live is gone.

Figure 9.3 illustrates five different patterns of death (Pattison 1977). In pattern one, the terminal phase begins when the person starts to give up. There is still some element of desirable hope for life, but gradually other people withdraw (sociological death), the patient acquiesces (psychic death), the brain ceases to function (clinical death), and the body dies (physiological death).

In pattern two, other people reject the patient and withdraw (sociological death) long before death occurs. This leads to psychic death, which ultimately results in clinical and physiological death.

FIGURE 9.3   Patterns of Death

1. Ideal Proximity   (note termination of hope)

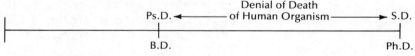

Knowledge
of Death   Terminus

2. Social Rejection of Patient

3. Social and Patient Rejection of Death

4. Patient Rejection of Life

5. Social Rejection of Death with Artificial Maintenance

B.D. = Biological Death*
Ph.D. = Physiological Death
Ps.D. = Psychic Death
S.D. = Sociological Death

*Now referred to as clinical death by physicians

From the book *The Experience of Dying* by E. Mansell Pattison. © 1977 by Prentice-Hall, Inc. Published by Prentice-Hall, Inc., Englewood Cliffs, NJ 07632.

In pattern three, both the patient and others refuse to accept impending death. When death comes, it may precipitate a shocked reaction. The same thing occurs when deterioration is sudden and death occurs contrary to expectation.

In pattern four, the patient rejects life and becomes psychically dead. This is met with social disapproval and efforts by family and friends to motivate the person to live.

Finally, in pattern five, there is social denial of the fact that both psychic and clinical death have occurred, and the patient is kept physiologically alive by artificial means. The morality and ethics of such artificial procedures are currently the subject of much controversy.

VARYING CIRCUMSTANCES OF DEATH

Premature Death

The psychological reactions to death are more extreme when it occurs at a comparatively young age. When a young adult dies, relatives react with frustration, disappointment, and anger. The young adult is on the threshold of life. Career, marriage, children, and a home are yet to come. When this life is snuffed out, it is difficult to reconcile what might have been with what is. A twenty-five-year-old woman with chronic leukemia wanted to be an architect; she had the motivation and talent. But when her condition would not let her complete school and become certified, she would erupt in anger. It seemed so unfair that this had happened to her.

Premature death in middle age can also be tragic, but for different reasons. The middle-ager has assumed responsibilities for a family, job, and home, as well as in the community. Financial obligations are at a peak. There is extensive involvement with spouse, children, relatives, business associates, friends, and neighbors. Death leaves the survivor with continuing obligations and no one to assume the responsibilities. Coping with dying involves coping with obligations already assumed.

Uncertain Death

The person whose death is uncertain faces different circumstances, as do the family members.

> Harvey is lying in a hospital bed in the intensive care unit. He has just suffered a major heart attack. He is hooked up to a machine that beeps and registers a blip on a television screen everytime his heart beats. His wife is beside him holding his hand. He is receiving oxygen. He is scared. His wife is scared. They both know the days ahead are crucial.

The most difficult part about such uncertainty is the waiting: dreading something adverse; hoping for improvement; waiting anxiously for periodic visits from the doctor; and waiting for other family members to arrive. The patient needs to avoid panic, to relax, and let healing take place. The wife and family need relief from the continued anxiety and worry; they need sleep and reassurance that their loved one will be all right.

Irreversible Illness

Pattison (1977) suggests that people live with a potential for death at any moment and project ahead a trajectory of life. That is, they anticipate a certain life span and arrange their activities and plan their lives accordingly. But when irreversible illness intervenes, that potential trajectory is changed. Their life has been foreshortened, and their plans and activities must be rearranged. After they learn of their impending death, they go through a process of adjustment.

One of the best descriptions of the process of dying was given by Kubler-Ross (1969, 1974). Kubler-Ross, a psychiatrist at the University of Chicago, spent considerable time talking with 200 dying patients to try to understand and describe their reactions to terminal illness. She found considerable resistance among medical personnel to the idea of talking with patients about dying; but she also found that the patients were relieved to share some of their concerns.

Kubler-Ross identified five stages of dying that did not necessarily occur in a regular sequence. In fact, she said, "Most of my patients have exhibited two or three stages simultaneously and these do not always occur in the same order" (Kubler-Ross 1974). The five identified stages were denial, anger, bargaining, depression, and acceptance.

The denial response of patients is, "No, not me. It can't be true." Some accuse their doctor of incompetence, and some think a mistake was made in the lab or in diagnosis. Others seek out other physicians, faith healers, or miracle cures. Some simply deny the reality of impending death and proceed as if nothing was wrong. Only a few patients maintain denial to the very end; most accept reality gradually.

As they acknowledge reality, their next reaction is one of anger. "Why me? It's not fair it should be happening to me." Patients in this stage become very hostile, resentful, and highly irritable, often quarreling with doctors, nurses, and loved ones. It is difficult not to take this abuse personally, but patients in this stage especially need to feel cared for and loved, so the situation requires much understanding.

As terminally ill patients begin to realize that death may be coming, they try bargaining to win a reprieve. The patient propositions God, the staff, and family, sometimes just to live a while longer to attend a wedding or complete a task. The patient says to God, "If you'll give me six more months, I'll leave most of my money to the church." If the person lives beyond the bargain period, however, the agreement is usually broken.

Once patients lose hope that life is possible and accept death as inevitable, depression may set in. Depression may be caused by regret at leaving behind everything and everybody that one loves. It may be caused by guilt over one's life. It may result from shame over bodily disfigurement, or because of the inability to die with dignity. Some patients need to express their sorrow in order to overcome it. Others need cheering up and support to improve their morale and to regain their self-esteem.

The final stage of the dying process is acceptance. The patients have worked through denial, anger, depression, and fear of death; they are now peacefully free of negative emotions, generally tired, emotionally exhausted, and weak. This is the time to sit quietly holding their hands, to show that death is not such a frightening experience.

Telling Patients They Are Dying

Should patients be told they are dying? A survey among physicians, nurses, chaplains, and college students concerning their attitudes toward informing patients of their terminal condition revealed that all groups felt the patients had a right to be told (Carey and Posavac 1978–79). Yet, there is a lack of socialization for dying in many hospitals. People are not oriented toward the process of dying and are left to cope with their problems in ambiguity and isolation (Rosel 1978–79). Moreover, not all patients should be approached and told in the same manner. There are no prescribed norms for dealing with dying patients. The basic intent should be to help, not harm, the patient (Gadow 1980). There is no need for a long discussion about the severity of the illness with an acutely ill patient who is barely conscious. That person often knows death is imminent. Care and comfort are the primary concerns. But the patient who is experiencing physical deterioration and who is told there is nothing to worry about may say nothing but wonder much (Pattison 1977). Some people absolutely do not want to know, and some would literally die of shock if they did know. The goal is to ease the dying process, not to apply a dogma of always telling the truth. Patients must be made aware of the significance of their illness and helped to adjust. Respect for their feelings and the use of tact are extremely important (LeRoux 1977).

Socially Accelerated Dying

In the broadest sense, *socially accelerated dying* is allowing any condition or action of society that shortens life and hastens death. This includes industrial pollution, unhealthy mine conditions that lead to black lung disease, asbestos or radiation exposure that causes cancer, and subsidizing tobacco farmers. In a narrow sense, it includes withholding health care from the elderly or abandoning them in nursing homes or other institutions. Hospitals that are unconcerned with geriatric medicine or curing illnesses in elderly people are socially accelerating the dying process.

In the Northwestern Arnhem Land of Australia, a doomed member of the Murngin tribe is socially rejected by other members. All relatives withdraw their sustaining support. Other tribesmen change their attitudes, placing the sick member in a sacred, taboo category. No longer a member of the group, and alone and isolated, the person's only escape is by death. The fact that the community has drawn away from him suggests in countless ways that the condition is irreversible. It takes little imagination to see the institutionalized elderly suffering a similar fate. They too may feel cast aside with little support and condemned to die. No wonder that people relocated to a home often die quickly. About half the deaths take place in the first three months after admission (Watson and Maxwell 1977).

EUTHANASIA

Different Concepts

Some people want to die because they are crippled or in pain and have nothing left to live for, they are terminally ill, or they are physiologically but not clinically dead. What are the moral obligations of society, family, and medical personnel to keep them alive?

The word *euthanasia* conjures up many images, from the senseless slaughter of millions in Nazi Germany, to mercy killing, to pulling the plug when there is no hope of recovery. Euthanasia is sometimes described as a positive/active process (forcing a person to die) or a negative/passive process (doing nothing, allowing death to come naturally). But as medical science advances, these distinctions are no longer clear. There is a difference between doing everything possible to cure a person's illness but allowing death to come if the efforts fail, and using artificial means to prolong life even after ultimate death is certain.

Death with Dignity
Euthanasia includes three different concepts: death with dignity, mercy killing, and death selection. Death with dignity allows a terminally ill patient to die naturally without mechanized prolongation that could turn death into an ordeal. The concept rejects extraordinary means when a person has irrevocably entered the dying process. This is referred to as "pulling the plug." Some families refuse to do this, and physicians have sometimes been forbidden by courts to do it. When asked whether they believed in the right of a patient and/or family to terminate medical care in the case of irreversible terminal illness, three-fourths of 418 persons surveyed (ages seventeen to ninety-one) agreed with this right (Haug 1978). There was a strong belief in the right of self-determination.

Most medical and some church groups have no trouble accepting the concept of death with dignity (Cawley 1977; Nagi et al. 1977; Ward 1980). However, new laws are needed to clarify the concept. California's Natural Death Act of 1977 is viewed as the prototype for such legislation. It "recognizes the right of an adult to sign a written directive instructing the physician to withhold or withdraw life-sustaining procedures in the event of a terminal condition" (Hollowell 1977). Other states have passed similar legislation and it is pending in many others. Shapiro (1977) predicts that "natural death legislation will eventually exist in all 50 states."

Mercy Killing
Mercy killing is positive, direct euthanasia, either voluntary or involuntary. Whereas death with dignity permits a natural death, mercy killing actively causes death or at least speeds up death (as by lethal injection). The nurse who deliberately gives an overdose of medication because she does not want to see her patient suffer is using mercy killing.

Mercy killing also includes abandonment or withdrawal of ordinary medical care: any medical or surgical procedures commonly used to relieve sufferings and problems due to injuries or illness, based on the individual patient, the circumstances, and available medical technology. As medical science advances, the interpretation of this principle becomes more confused. Artificial heart machines and respirators, artificial kidneys, intravenous feeding, and other advanced technologies can keep patients alive for weeks, months, or years. Not too long ago, these patients would have died much sooner. What constitutes ordinary care? Most persons insist that keeping a clinically dead person physiologically alive does not constitute ordinary care. Others feel that sustaining life indefinitely by artificial means is not ordinary care and should not be permitted.

If an elderly person dying of cancer refuses an operation or chemotherapy that would prolong life only a few months, the person's wish is generally upheld. But if an adult refuses proper medical care for an illness that need not be terminal, treatment may still be instituted, especially with family and court consent. The issues are not always clear nor well-defined by the court. No one law can be applied to all circumstances. Difficult questions arise when the outcome of treatment is uncertain and when the treatment may be worse than the disease.

Death Selection

Opponents of euthanasia are especially concerned about death selection, that is, the involuntary or even mandatory killing of persons who are "no longer considered socially useful" or who are judged to be a burden on society. This type of euthanasia poses a real threat to many groups in our society, especially the aged, the severely handicapped, and the retarded. It is strongly opposed by all religious groups.

BEREAVEMENT

No matter how long the death of a loved one has been anticipated through prolonged illness, it still comes as a shock. In fact, people who have watched loved ones suffer through chronic illness and die are sometimes affected as much as or more than those whose loved ones died after a short illness (Gerber et al. 1975).

There are usually three stages of grief (Hiltz 1978). The first is a short period of shock during which the surviving family members are stunned and immobilized with grief and disbelief. The second stage is a period of intense suffering during which individuals show physical and emotional symptoms of great disturbance. Finally, there is a gradual reawakening of interest in life. Physical upsets during the second stage may include disturbed sleep, stomach upset and loss of appetite, weight loss, emptiness in the stomach, loss of energy and muscular strength, and shortness of breath, sighing, or tightness in the chest. Emotional reactions may include anger, guilt, depression, anxiety, and preoccupation with thoughts of the deceased. During intense grief, people need to talk with friends or family about their loss. But since grief and death are uncomfortable subjects, this opportunity is often denied and recovery from the loss is more difficult and prolonged.

One common reaction to bereavement is to purify the memory of the deceased by mentally diminishing that person's negative characteristics. One woman who had hated her husband remarked, "My husband was an unusually good man." If this idealization continues, it can prevent the formation of new intimate friendships. Extended bereavement can result in a sentimentalized, nostalgic, and morose style of life.

Men and women may respond differently to bereavement. Men find it more difficult to express grief but they can accept the reality of death more quickly. Women are more able to continue work during bereavement than are men. Men are more apt to describe their loss as the loss of part of themselves. Women respond in terms of being deserted, abandoned, and left to fend for themselves (Glick, Weiss, and Parkes 1974).

The negative impact of bereavement and the loss of a loved one cannot be minimized. Damage to the self accompanies widowhood, for example, if the spouse was a significant other. The degree and duration of this damage depend on the intensity of the involvement with the departed and the availability of significant others.

SUMMARY

Longevity refers to the duration of life; prolongevity to deliberate efforts to extend the length of life. Some prolongevitists feel that the length of life is almost limitless; others feel that to live beyond one hundred is a reasonable limit. Opponents of prolongevity say it violates divine prescription, that death is a punishment for sinfulness, and that to prolong life is to prolong sin. Others argue that prolongevity violates natural law, prolongs the miseries of old age, and multiplies social, economic, and political problems as our resources become strained caring for millions of senior citizens.

Longevity does have positive benefits. The goal is not only to maximize the life span, but also to retard the aging process, creating young, healthy older people who would lead active, useful, fruitful lives and enjoy extended work careers.

Life expectancy in the United States increased from fifty-four to seventy-four years between 1920 and 1979. This was accomplished largely through the elimination of childhood diseases. Blacks have a shorter life expectancy than whites up to age seventy-five. After that, there is a crossover, with blacks experiencing longer life expectancies. Both biological and environmental reasons may account for the crossover. Death rates are lower in the United States for males above age eighty and for females above age seventy-five than they are in any other developed country. Between sixty-five and seventy-four, rates for males and females are lower in Scandinavian countries and the Netherlands than in the United States. Rates for males of this age group are also lower in Japan. Rates for Japanese females sixty-five to sixty-nine are lower than for the comparable group in the United States. There is little documentation that people live to be 120 or more in certain sections of the world. Some ethnic groups in the United States, such as American Indians and Hispanics, have shorter life expectancies than whites. Work stress and hazards reduce the life expectancies of certain occupational groups.

If all the major diseases were eliminated, life expectancy would increase to about eighty-five. In order to increase more than that, the aging process must be retarded. There are several possibilities for retardation: increasing DNA repair efficiency, manipulating the immune system to keep it from destroying healthy body cells, using antioxidants to reduce the free radicals (harmful substances that accumulate as by-products of metabolism), or slowing the metabolic rate by undernutrition (without malnutrition).

The leading cause of death in the United States is heart disease. Together, all cardiovascular diseases account for 57 percent of all deaths. Cancer is the number two killer, and the death rate continues to rise, primarily because of the increased incidence of lung cancer.

Attitudes toward death have changed gradually during the centuries. Today, it is considered unacceptable and made as invisible as possible, attitudes reflected by modern funeral practices.

These trends have led to the examination and criticism of modern death philosophies and practices. Middle-aged adults experiencing a midlife crisis begin to think about the finitude of their lives and fear death. Most elderly people have resolved their fears of death. In general, those who have the most positive views of life also view death most positively.

There are different aspects of death: physiological death (vital organs cease to function), clinical death (the brain is dead), sociological death (withdrawal and separation from people), and psychic death (the person accepts that he or she is already dead and regresses into the self). Premature sociological and/or psychic death can lead to clinical and physiological death. A patient's rejection of death makes it harder to adjust to the dying process. Societal rejection of death may lead to keeping the patient alive mechanically after clinical death.

The varying circumstances of death each require different adjustments. Premature death may result in frustration, rage, disappointment, and feelings of unfairness and of being cheated. The familial and economic adjustments required are often traumatic and difficult. Uncertain death creates anxiety and worry as people await the outcome. The process of dying as described by Kubler-Ross has five stages: denial, anger, bargaining, depression, and acceptance.

Most experts feel that patients have a right to know the severity of their illness and that they are dying. The difficult decision is how and what to tell them. It requires tact, sensitivity, and flexibility to meet the needs of the individual patient.

Socially accelerated dying is what society does that hastens death. Euthanasia includes three different concepts. Death with dignity means allowing people to die, once death is a certainty, without using extraordinary mechanical and medical means to prolong their lives. It is accepted by most medical and religious groups. Mercy killing that uses active means to hasten death is rejected by most people. But mercy killing also includes abandonment and withdrawal of ordinary medical care to allow people to die. Most people feel that keeping patients physiologically alive when they are clinically dead does not constitute ordinary care, so they oppose it. Whether patients or families have a right to refuse certain medical treatment or to insist on it depends on the particular circumstances. In general, the courts have insisted on treatment when life is possible, but accepted that it may be refused when death is certain and treatment would only prolong life briefly. Certainly, the wishes of the patient must be considered. Death by selection is the involuntary or mandatory killing of persons who are no longer considered socially useful, and it is almost universally condemned.

Most people experience three stages of bereavement when a loved one dies. The first stage is one of shock; the second, one of intense suffering evidenced by both physical and emotional reactions; and the third stage is the gradual reawakening of interest in life and readjustment to it.

Part III

Emotional Development

10

Mental Health

POSITIVE MENTAL HEALTH

Mind and Body

Psychologists have long been concerned with the interrelationship between mind and body. The word *psychosomatic* describes this interaction of the *psyche* (mind) and *soma* (body). What affects one affects the other. Various types of gastrointestinal upsets, for example, illustrate psychosomatic illnesses (physical illnesses with emotional causes).

Emotions are important because psychological factors can influence the body's immunological response. One strain of mice carrying a cancer virus developed cancers 92 percent of the time when exposed to a stressful environment. Similarly infected mice, who were protected from stress, developed cancer only 7 percent of the time ("Cancer: Who Gets It" 1976). This study indicated that the physiological effects of stress led to an impaired defense system and increased the susceptibility to cancer. Usually, cancer cells are weak, vacillating cells often defeated by the body's immune mechanism. People can have cancer cells without knowing it because they are defeated by the body's white blood cells before they can multiply harmfully. Some doctors believe that full medical treatment supplemented by self-healing techniques, such as relaxation, meditation, and biofeedback to mobilize the body's defenses, is more effective than just medical approaches to treatment (Elwell 1975). Positive, relaxed mental attitudes and emotions are thus very important to good physical health as well as to an overall sense of well-being.

Contributing Factors

Many factors contribute to positive mental health. One factor is maintaining physical fitness. The importance of adequate nutrition, sufficient sleep, and physical activity and exercise are discussed in chapter 6. If positive mental health contributes to physical fitness, the reverse is also true—good physical health contributes to positive mental health.

A second factor in positive mental health is forming meaningful relationships. One does not have to have a lot of friends to be contented, but one has to have some. In their study of single men and women, Cargan and Melko (1982) listed having friends as second only to good health as being important to happiness. Friends provided companionship and provided opportunities for shared activities. They were an antidote to loneliness, a source of social support. Close friends were their major source of love, affection, warmth, and closeness. In another study, interviews with working-class grandparents, average age sixty-five, indicated that interaction with friends contributed more positively to their morale than interaction with kin (Wood and Robertson 1978).

A third factor in positive mental health are goals toward which to strive. Most adults are happiest when they are busy accomplishing tasks, whether completing their education, owning a home, creating a happy marriage, raising a family, achieving job success, or pursuing their hobbies. Positive mental health is a by-product of purposeful and fulfilling striving after significant dreams.

Fourth, positive mental health depends on balancing work and leisure activities, with enough variation in each to make life interesting. The workaholic eventually experiences job-related stress, fatigue, burnout and stagnation (see chapter 18). The person who can work hard during employment hours and then relax with completely different leisure-type activities reduces tension build-up and the energy drain that accompanies it. The purpose of recreation is just that—to re-create mind and body, to replenish the physical and psychical energies depleted from physical, mental, and emotional activities. Gleser emphasizes that recreational activities should "literally allow your mind to be free" and help you escape strenuous daily tasks "in a deeply felt way, whether through playing golf, painting a picture, or camping in the woods. . . . The secret of happiness is to get involved doing something you believe in enough to accept yourself completely in the process" ("Recreation for All" 1977, 76).

Finally, mental health develops from positive thought patterns about oneself and others. This is difficult for the person who has been negatively conditioned growing up in a critical, pessimistic, and troubling family environment. Such people develop poor self-images, negative feelings toward themselves and others, and a critical, complaining attitude toward everyone. Some overcome their handicapping start in life through their own efforts. Others require psychotherapy to understand and deal with their feelings and to replace them with more positive emotions. Change is possible if people see the need and take positive action.

STRESS

Most people function adequately and positively during their lives. They may experience difficulty, however, when exposed to large amounts of stress.

Meaning

Stress is physical, mental, or emotional strain or tension caused by environmental, situational, or personal pressures and demands. A woman late for work becomes tense and anxious when caught in a traffic jam. Her boss needs her for an important meeting and paces nervously until her arrival. Her children were upset that morning because she pushed them to dress in a hurry. Her husband exploded when he could not find a clean shirt. These stresses were minor and temporary and soon forgotten by those involved.

Other stresses involve more pressure, tension, strain, and upheaval for longer periods of time: a family member becomes critically ill, a soldier is exposed to violent combat over several months. The amount of stress depends partially on the severity of the circumstances and the duration of the exposure. Generally, more stress occurs when events happen suddenly than when the individual has advance warning and can make preparations. Unpredictable and uncontrollable events cause more stress than those over which individuals exercise more control.

Also, people react differently to stress. Some have a very high frustration tolerance, others a low one. Tolerance depends partially on one's hereditary makeup and past experiences. People raised in tense family environments over a period of years usually react more strongly to stressful situations. The amount of stress experienced depends not only on the severity and duration of exposure, but also on one's previous conditioning.

Causes

Stress arises from various causes. Some stress is job related. Long hours, heavy responsibilities, and continued pressure can make a job stressful. However, these factors do not always cause stress. People who like their occupations, whose work offers opportunities to use their talents and skills and provides status, recognition, and pleasant associations, are less likely to experience job-related stress than those dissatisfied with their jobs (Institute for Social Research 1975).

Work that requires constant vigilance and exposes the worker to uncertainty or danger can result in stress. The work of air traffic controllers is one example. They never know when an accident is imminent. On the job, they must be alert at all times.

Stress can result from role strain. The busy housewife and mother with four young children, constantly under pressure from family members to run errands, provide personal services, supervise children's activities, stay up all night with a sick child, maintain a home, and give moral support to other family members, may find these demands exhausting and stressful over a long period of time.

Mrs. L. prided herself on her ability to run her home, take care of her three children and her husband, and work at the same time. But then things began to pile up. Her aging mother became ill and required daily care and attention. Her boss expected overtime work until his accounts were caught up. Her youngest child became seriously ill and had to be hospitalized. After several weeks, Mrs. L. was physically and emotionally exhausted. She became nervous and distraught. She cried for no special reason. She became so distressed that she had to take a leave of absence from her job to remove part of the pressure on her.

As long as people can manage their situations and feel in control, stress can be kept to a minimum. When the demands placed on one become too much to handle, stress develops (House et al. 1979).

Numerous life crises cause stress. Sarason and colleagues (1978, 1981) developed a Life Experience Survey measuring the impact of various life events. People are asked to check events that occurred during the past year and to evaluate the effect of each on their lives, the extent to which they expected the event to happen, and the extent to which they had control over the event's occurrence. Some of the events listed were marriage, death of a spouse, moving to a new city or town, being fired from a job, divorce, and failing a course in school. Some events, such as death of a spouse, were more stressful than others. People who experienced multiple events, whose troubles "came in bunches," became more depressed, anxious, hostile, and fatigued, performed more poorly, and experienced more of an increase in physical symptoms.

Some stress people experience develops from a series of small events, each of which produces some tension, with the total effect cumulative. Williams tells of one husband returning home from work at the close of an intensely difficult day.

> During the course of the day he lost two big business deals, learned he was being transferred to another department and that the transmission was going out of his comparatively new car. Upon returning home he turns into his driveway and suddenly confronts two bicycles, a tricycle, a go-cart, and a basketball, all of which are directly in his way. He can't park on the street and there isn't a child in sight. He angrily steps from the car, throws the objects quickly and roughly into the yard, gets back into his car, guns the motor, and screams to a stop inches from the garage door.
>
> Following the commotion, his two youngest children innocently appear on the front doorsteps. Instead of his usually friendly tousle of the hair and greeting, father flies into a rage. He yells at the top of his voice about toys and other objects in the driveway, spanks both of them with anger, and tells them to go to their room. By this time he is in the house and begins screaming at his wife about the rough day he has had and her inability to discipline the children.
>
> Little does he know about the day she has had. The washer broke down, the sewer clogged. John fell off the jungle gym and had to be rushed to the emergency room of the hospital to have his arm checked, and she learned that her mother had terminal cancer. One other problem to complicate her day is that she is to host the monthly bridge club that night. (Williams 1974, 223)

In this example, a whole series of events caused frustration, strain, and conflict to increase geometrically.

Stress is likely to arise out of interpersonal relationships that are unpleasant and conflicting over a period of time.

> Mr. and Mrs. S. were married young. She was only sixteen, he was twenty-one when she became pregnant. She dropped out of school to have her baby, and he worked at two jobs to try to make ends meet. After the baby was born, she had no car, little money, and no close friends where they lived. She would become particularly upset if her husband spent his time off going out with his friends, leaving her alone in their apartment to take care of the baby. If she tried to talk to him, he would accuse her of being a nag and storm out the door. They began to argue about everything. No matter what they discussed, it ended up in a fight.
>
> Mrs. S. began to show physical symptoms of the tension she was under. She was exhausted most of the time, frequently sick, and despondent and depressed. Many mornings she didn't feel like getting out of bed. One morning she was shocked when she found herself slapping the baby because he cried. At this point, she realized she needed help and went to a local mental health clinic.

Any kind of transition or change is also stressful for some people. They get along fine if life moves routinely on the same schedule, involving the same responsibilities, the same people, and familiar surroundings. But if something changes that routine, they become upset and confused.

Major transitions in the life cycle, for example, going to school, getting a job, getting married, moving to a new community, becoming a parent, switching jobs, facing retirement, or similar transitions, may require considerable adjustment. Desired changes have a much different effect than unwanted events. However, even happy events can cause stress. People have suffered heart attacks from good news as well as bad. Furthermore, not everyone reacts identically to the same event. Having a baby can be delightful for one couple, but traumatic for the couple who did not plan on children.

Unusually traumatic experiences, such as natural disasters or war combat experiences, create tremendous stress. The eruption of Mount St. Helens on May 18, 1980, created significant stress in thousands of people. Associated Press reports from Washington after the eruption indicated criminal assaults rose 25 percent, suicide threats and attempts doubled, and the number of cases of battered wives increased 45 percent (Blumenthal 1980). The situation was particularly stressful because of the violence of the explosion (500 times the force of the atom bomb at Hiroshima) and the uncertainty of subsequent explosions. People did not know what would happen next or how long it would last. The effect of stress was delayed, however. The greatest increase in spouse-abuse cases did not occur until about thirty days after the major eruption. Stress took that long to take its toll.

The combat experiences and reactions of soldiers during war have been the subject of much research. Soldiers must deal with the fear of death or injury. They witness other people blown up or maimed. There is the strain of combat vigilance against unexpected attack or capture. These situations, plus separation from family, the loss of sleep, physical exhaustion, and exposure to hunger, heat, or cold, produce high levels of stress, sometimes over long periods. So-called "battle fatigue" is common, but long-term negative effects may remain. Combat veterans report terrifying nightmares and other psychological disturbances years after the war ended for them.

Effects of Stress

Stress produces physiological reactions within the body. According to Selye (1976), a Canadian physiologist, the body goes through three stages in adapting to stress. The first stage is an *alarm reaction,* in which the body prepares to cope. Large quantities of the hormones adrenaline (epinephrine) and noradrenaline (norepinephrine) are secreted into the bloodstream to prepare the body for action. This is accompanied by an increase in activity in the sympathetic nervous system, an increase in blood sugar, heart rate, blood pressure, and blood flow to the muscles.

If stress continues, the body enters a resistance stage during which it begins to recover from the initial stress and to cope with the situation. Secretion of adrenaline decreases, as do other body functions. During the final stage, a state of exhaustion is reached as bodily resources are depleted and the body begins to break down.

Repeated stress can result in physical damage and disorders. High blood pressure (hypertension), some types of heart disease, migraine headaches, respiratory problems such as asthma, gastrointestinal disorders such as peptic ulcers, rheumatoid arthritis, and skin disorders such as eczema and dermatitis are stress-related. Stress can play a role in muscle cramps, backaches, and menstrual problems. Stress can adversely affect any part of the body.

Stress can also interfere with psychological functioning. Depression, anxiety, paranoia, aggression, painful guilt feelings, and insomnia are often posttraumatic stress reactions (Vinokur and Selzer 1975).

Coping with Stress

Adults deal with stress in various ways. In a *task-oriented approach,* they make a direct effort to alleviate the source of the stress. A person having financial problems gets an additional part-time job to earn extra money. The parent who is worried about a child consults a specialist for a solution. Couples with marital problems seek marriage counseling. In this way, stress can provide an opportunity for growth.

The task-oriented approach requires reality testing, that is, being aware of what is going on, undistorted by anxiety, hostility, or other negative feelings. The first step in alleviating stress is to discover its roots.

Then, constructive problem solving and objective evaluation must be used to discover methods that will relieve stress.

Another approach to stress is a deliberate, cognitive effort to change one's internal responses. Events alone do not determine the amount of stress. What people strive to do, what they tell themselves, and how they evaluate situations all influence the amount of anxiety they experience.

Meichenbaum (1972) instituted a *cognitive modification program* to help students suffering from high test anxiety. Worries about the tests, fear of failure, and feelings of inadequacy kept these students from doing well on exams. Some would freeze and forget facts they actually knew. Meichenbaum explained to the students what their anxiety was doing to them. He helped them identify their negative thoughts and feelings: "I'm certain I'm going to flunk." "I don't believe I know this stuff." "If I don't do well, my parents will kill me." He instructed the students to restructure their thoughts, to think positively, and to direct their attention to the task at hand: "I can handle this." "I've studied hard." "All I have to do is quit worrying and pay attention to the questions." "Relax, don't be afraid." During group instruction, the students had to imagine test situations and practice eliminating negative self-statements, focusing their attention on the task at hand. As a result, the students reported large decreases in anxiety and improved test performance.

Relaxation training is used widely to cope with stress. One approach is to lie down on a comfortable couch or bed, putting a small pillow under each knee and a large one under each arm. Arms should be slightly flexed alongside the body. Starting with the toes of each foot, make a deliberate effort to relax the muscles. Flex the muscles and relax them, telling each muscle to let go, to relax. Do the same thing with each foot, leg, thigh, and so on up the whole body, ending with the muscles of the neck, face, head, and scalp. By focusing attention on separate parts of the body, it is possible to relax each part and ultimately the whole body. Deep breathing during the process also helps one to relax. Deep relaxation has been used successfully in reducing headaches; in treating insomnia, high blood pressure, and body pains; and in natural childbirth. Some people use techniques like transcendental meditation to accomplish the same purpose. Business executives are encouraged to take catnaps, lie down on the floor, or take a seventh-inning stretch between meetings ("Executive Stress" 1979).

Physical activity and *exercise* are wonderful ways to relieve stress. Dr. G., a dentist, finds his profession tiring and stressful. When he gets very tense, he takes time off to jog, often running six to seven miles before beginning to relax. Other people walk or play tennis, racquetball, or other sports. Some climb mountains; others go fishing or hunting. Physical labor of any kind can be very relaxing after a tense day.

Another way to deal with stress is to *sublimate* it through indirect means, such as psychotherapy, work, sex, hobbies, or recreation. Some people seek counseling to relieve their tensions. Others bury themselves in their work, paint the house, or work in the garden. Others escape through hobbies or through sexual release. One husband who was under great emotional strain at work joined a local theater group and relieved his pent-up emotions on stage. Another would hammer on an old metal water tank in his basement whenever he became upset.

A common way of dealing with stress is to *medicate* it. Judging from the millions of tranquilizers and sedatives sold each year, this seems to be a popular source of relief. Reasonable medication on a temporary basis may provide appropriate and welcome relief. The danger is developing a dependency or addiction that relieves symptoms but never gets to the root of the problem and ends up creating problems of its own.

Seeking social support helps in managing stress. Family members, friends, or counselors who listen empathetically provide moral support and emotional assistance. Some people need support groups when they have problems, and groups like Al-Anon, Parents without Partners, and Divorce Perspectives are very successful. People band together to learn how to cope and to overcome their difficulties.

MENTAL ILLNESS

Incidence

The extent of mental illness in the United States depends partially on which mental and emotional disorders are included. The current system for diagnosing mental disorders used in the *Diagnostic and Statistical Manual of Mental Disorders,* third edition (DSM–III) (1980), issued by the American Psychiatric Association, includes even relatively mild distress. If statistics on mental illness included all emotional disorders, however mild, the figures would be highly inflated. In 1978, the President's Commission on Mental Health estimated that as many as one-fourth of all Americans suffer at least mild to moderate depression, anxiety, or other indications of mental disorder. Even this rough figure is an underestimate in the view of some psychiatrists and psychologists who suggest that everyone suffers some degree of mental illness. Freud wrote, "Every normal person is only approximately normal. His ego resembles that of the psychotic in one point or another, in a greater or less degree" (1959, 337). Psychological abnormality or mental illness is partly a matter of degree. It can be examined from different perspectives: the extent of deviance, the adaptiveness of individuals to their environment, their ability to function, their personal unhappiness. This discussion examines some of the more common and serious illnesses of adulthood that prevent people from functioning adequately.

Figure 10.1 shows the numbers of persons receiving care in mental health facilities, per 100,000 population, during any one year. The total number in 1979 was 2,863 per 100,000 persons, roughly 3 percent of the population (U.S. Dept. of Commerce 1983). Of this total, 72 percent were

FIGURE 10.1   Numbers of Persons Receiving Care in Mental Health Facilities per 100,000 Population, by Type of Treatment Facility—1955 to 1979

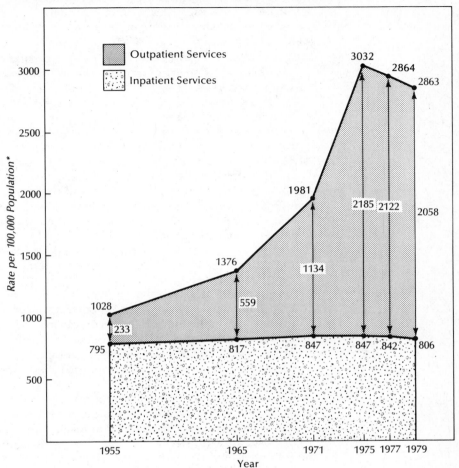

Year

*Excludes private psychiatric office practice.

Adapted from: U.S. Department of Commerce, Bureau of the Census, *Statistical Abstract of The United States, 1982, 83* 103d ed. (Washington, D.C.: U.S. Government Printing Office, 1983), 117.

provided outpatient psychiatric services. The remaining 28 percent received inpatient services. As shown in the graph, the total number of persons receiving outpatient care increased drastically until 1975, after which the figures began to taper off. The numbers receiving inpatient care remained quite constant. However, these figures do not include patients receiving private office care from psychiatrists, psychologists, counselors, and psychotherapists. These numbers far exceed those receiving treatment in mental health care hospitals, clinics, and centers.

Classification

The DSM–III (1980) classifies mental disorders into various diagnostic categories, some of which are included here.

   Organic Mental Disorders. Temporary or permanent brain dysfunction caused by specific organic factors or abuse of substances affecting the brain.

   Substance Use Disorders. Impairment of social or occupational functioning due to abuse of alcohol or drugs, such as sedatives, hypnotics, narcotics, stimulants, hallucinogens, marijuana, tobacco, or other substances such as inhalants.

   Schizophrenic Disorders. Chronic and bizarre behavior characterized by delusions, hallucinations, illusions, incoherence, social isolation, and impairment of personal and role functioning.

   Paranoid Disorders. Persistent delusions of persecution or delusional jealousy without the bizarre delusions, incoherence, or social isolation of schizophrenia.

   Psychotic Disorders Not Elsewhere Classified. This includes schizophreniform disorder, which meets the criteria of schizophrenia except it is of shorter duration (longer than two weeks but less than six months), brief reactive psychosis (longer than two hours but less than two weeks), schizoaffective disorder (an episode of delusions or hallucinations where previous occurrences are unknown), and atypical psychosis (delusions, hallucinations, incoherence, loosening associations, illogical thinking, and disorganized behavior that do not meet the criteria for the other mental disorders).

   Affective Disorders. Includes mania or depression or both.

   Anxiety Disorders. Includes phobias, anxiety states (formerly called anxiety neuroses), obsessive compulsive behavior, and symptoms of posttraumatic stresses without psychotic symptoms.

   Somatoform Disorders. Physical symptoms that cannot be explained by physical disorders, injury, or by ingestion of medication, drugs, or alcohol and that are caused by psychological factors.

   Dissociative Disorders. Sudden, temporary loss of memory, or identity, or unexpected travel from home or work with inability to recall the past; existence of distinct multiple personalities, unexpected episodes of depersonalization, which impair social or occupational functioning.

   Psychosocial Disorders. Deviant sexual thought and behavior, which include the following: gender identity disorders, paraphilias, psychosexual dysfunctions, and other psychosexual disorders. Paraphilias include such things as zoophilia (sexual experimentation with animals), exhibitionism (exposure of genitals to unsuspecting strangers), or pedophilia (actual or fantasized sexual activity with children). (See chapter 7 for a discussion of psychosexual dysfunctions.) Other psychosexual disorders include homosexual arousal that is unwanted and other psychological disturbances related to sexuality.

Factitious Disorders. The production of physical or psychological symptoms voluntarily in order to play the patient role.

Disorders of Impulse Control Not Elsewhere Classified. Failure to resist impulses resulting in pathological gambling, kleptomania, pyromania, or intermittent explosive behavior.

Adjustment Disorder. A maladaptive reaction to stress, which may impair social or occupational functioning or result in symptoms that are in excess of those expected. Symptoms may include depression, withdrawal, anxiety, or disturbed conduct, such as truancy, vandalism, reckless driving, fighting, or default on legal responsibilities.

Psychological Factors Affecting Physical Condition. Psychological stimuli are temporarily related to a physical condition that has demonstrable organic pathology (e.g., rheumatoid arthritis) or a known pathophysiological process (e.g., migraine headache). A condition not due to a somatoform disorder.

Personality Disorders. These include a wide range of personality disorders that cannot be labeled psychoses but that characterize the individual's current and long-term functioning. These personality disorders include paranoid, schizoid, schizotypal, histrionic, narcissistic, antisocial, borderline, avoidant, dependent, compulsive, passive-aggressive, and atypical or mixed personality disorders.

Conditions Not Attributable to a Mental Disorder That Are a Focus of Attention or Treatment. These include a wide variety of problems: malingering, borderline intellectual functioning, adult antisocial behavior, childhood or adolescent antisocial behavior, academic problem, occupational problem, uncomplicated bereavement, noncompliance with medical treatment, phase of life or other life circumstance problem, marital problem, parent-child problem, other specified family circumstances, or other interpersonal problems.

Disorders Usually First Evident in Infancy, Childhood, or Adolescence. These include a wide variety of problems, such as mental retardation, attention deficit disorder, conduct disorder, anxiety disorders, eating disorders, stereotyped movement disorders, disorders with physical manifestations, pervasive developmental disorders, specific developmental disorders, and others.

A complete discussion of all of these illnesses would require another book. The particular ones discussed here were selected primarily because of their prevalence and importance in the lives of adults.

Depression

Depression is the most common functional disorder of adults of all ages. It exists in different degrees (Steuer et al. 1980). Major depressive episodes are characterized by a loss of interest and pleasure in almost all pastimes and activities. The person feels sad, hopeless, low, down in the dumps, and irritable, and these moods are dominant and persistent. To be diagnosed as suffering from major depression, a person must evidence at least half of the following symptoms every day for at least two weeks: (1) poor appetite or significant weight loss; (2) insomnia or hypersomnia; (3) psychomotor agitation or retardation; (4) loss of interest or pleasure in usual activities or decrease in sexual drive; (5) loss of energy and fatigue; (6) feelings of worthlessness, self-reproach, or excessive guilt; (7) diminished ability to think or concentrate, indecisiveness; and (8) recurrent thoughts of death or suicide, or a suicide attempt. Sometimes depression is accompanied by such psychotic features as delusions, hallucinations, or depressed stupor. Depression accompanied by melancholia is especially prevalent in midlife, often in postmenopausal women. In melancholia, the depressed person is usually worse in the morning, often waking up two hours earlier than usual. There may also be marked psychomotor retardation or agitation, significant anorexia or weight loss, and excessive or inappropriate guilt.

Major depression can occur in a single episode, or be recurrent or bipolar (alternating with manic phases). The symptoms of manic episodes are the opposite of depression—the person is in an elevated, expansive, and irritable mood. At least three of the following symptoms must be present for the illness to be diagnosed as *mania*: (1) physical restlessness or an increase in activity socially, at work, or sexually; (2) more talkative than usual; (3) racing thoughts and ideas; (4) inflated self-esteem, grandiose behavior that may be delusional; (5) decreased need for sleep; (6) distractibility; and (7) excessive involvement in such activities as buying sprees, sexual indiscretions, reckless driving, or foolish business investments. Like depression, manic episodes may be accompanied by psychotic features.

When depression or hypomanic symptoms exist but are separated by periods of normal mood lasting months at a time, the person is not considered psychotic. The person who alternates between brief periods of depression and hypomania suffers from what is now labeled a *cyclothymic disorder*. When the predominate mood is periodic depression, the illness is labeled *dysthymic disorder* (formerly called depressive neurosis).

No single theory explains the causes of depression. Some research suggests that depression has a hereditary base (Vinokur and Selzer 1975). Another view emphasizes a relationship to the body's chemical makeup. This theory suggests that depression is caused by a deficiency of norepinephrine at certain receptor sites in the brain, and that mania is due to an excess. This view is currently the best biological explanation for depressed or manic behavior.

Learning theory emphasizes that depressed behavior is learned behavior. It may begin with a loss or stressful event causing temporary depression. Once people are depressed, their friends and family members feel anxious, depressed, and hostile in their presence, causing these persons to avoid them. This, in turn, reinforces the depressed behavior. Depressed persons begin to feel that nothing they do gains social reinforcement, so they withdraw from activity more and more. This, in turn, makes them feel lonely and rejected and increases their depression. Furthermore, depressed people tend to be pessimistic—they are constantly foretelling doom or disaster. Nothing that happens is bright (Lewinsohn and Talkington 1979).

Cognitive theorists suggest that the way a person interprets a situation is important in relation to depression. Their reaction is based not only on the situation, but also on their appraisal of it. They overgeneralize and use inexact labeling; then they respond to the labels and not the actual situation. They see the situation as bad, or themselves as stupid, inadequate, or guilty, and this makes them feel worse.

The more helpless people feel in situations, the more likely they are to feel depressed (Abramson, Seligman, and Teasdale 1978). For example, if a student fails an examination but attributes the failure to a lack of preparation, the depressed mood may be temporary. However, if the student generalizes and attributes the failure to low intelligence, a feeling of helplessness pervades and depression may result. If the failure is attributed to an unfair test, the student reacts with anger, not depression. Thus, the interpretation of the situation is crucial to the emotional response.

Psychodynamic theories of depression emphasize overreactions to events based on early childhood experiences. Thus, prolonged depression following the death of someone close is often related to earlier problems with the person about which the individual now feels guilty.

Humanistic-existential theories of depression emphasize that it is caused by the loss of self-esteem (Wigdor and Morris 1977). The loss of a job, spouse, social status, or money diminishes one's self-esteem. Regrets over the past, accompanied by deep-seated feelings of guilt and unworthiness, trigger the depression.

Actually, each of these theories contributes something to understanding the causes of depression. All or part of the circumstances, situations, or reactions described may be contributing factors. No one theory explains depression in every circumstance.

Bipolar Disorders

In *bipolar disorders* (formerly manic-depressive disorders), the patient alternates between periods of mania and depression. These disorders first appear in early adulthood or even in adolescence (Loranger and Levine 1978). Geneticists suggest that bipolar disorders have a hereditary base, with the defective gene for bipolar disorder carried on the X chromosome. This means that a father with a bipolar disorder would transmit it only to his daughters (only they would receive his defective X chromosome). His sons would receive only his normal Y chromosome. A wife with a bipolar disorder could transmit it either to a son or daughter. However, a few cases of father-son inheritance of the disorder have been found, suggesting causative factors other than inheritance.

One factor is chemical imbalance in the body. Persons who retain sodium and water in particular places in the body are prone to depression. Lithium has been found to prevent both bipolar disorders and mania.

Schizophrenia

Schizophrenia is most common among adolescents and young adults (Bride et al. 1978). There are different types of schizophrenia. The catatonic type is characterized by a disturbance of motor activity. The individual may be completely immobile, so that the muscles are rigid and inflexible and the limbs remain fixed in any position, or the individual may be very agitated, exhibiting excited, purposeless motor activity. The paranoid type is characterized by persecutory delusions, grandiose delusions, delusional jealousy, or hallucinations with persecutory or grandiose content.

> Bill S. believed he had the power to heal anyone by making the sign of the cross and touching them with his fingers on their forehead. He moved about the room slowly, blessing everyone as though he were a priest. He firmly believed that he was able to cure all human ills.

The disorganized type of schizophrenia *(hebephrenia)* is characterized by frequent incoherence, an absence of systematized delusions, and silly, inappropriate emotional responses. Persons suffering from this illness may make strange noises or faces, giggle for no reason, or engage in aimless behavior. The *undifferentiated type* of schizophrenia is characterized by prominent delusions, hallucinations, incoherence, and grossly disorganized behavior, but the illness does not meet the criteria for any of the previous types or it meets the criteria for more than one.

The most common explanation of the cause of schizophrenia traces its history back to early childhood experiences, to frustrating or harmful interpersonal relationships, particularly emotional rejection and a lack of positive emotional ties to parents. Schizophrenics seem to lack warm relationships and social support from others, so they withdraw to avoid hurt.

Neurological, biological, and physical factors have been examined as possible causes of schizophrenia, but in spite of physical abnormalities, it is difficult to determine if these are causes or effects. An excess of dopamine (a chemical involved in the transmission of nerve impulses) has been suspected of causing message flooding to the brain, resulting in confusion, disorganized behavior, and inattention (Iversen 1979). Drugs that block the action of dopamine have antipsychotic effects, whereas stimulants like amphetamines produce schizophrenic reactions.

Research indicates that individuals who have one or more schizophrenic parents have a much higher risk of becoming schizophrenics than do other people (Mednick and Schulsinger 1968). About 10 to 15 percent of children with one schizophrenic parent become similarly ill; 40 to 68 percent of children with two schizophrenic parents do so. Whether this is due to hereditary or environmental factors is a matter of dispute. Both factors may be involved. We do know that if one identical twin has the disorder, there is a 50 percent chance that the other will have it. There is about a 10 to 15 percent chance in fraternal twins or in full siblings (Kety 1979). These figures indicate a strong genetic component in the disease.

Anxiety Disorders

The American Psychiatric Association now groups in this category a number of disorders that used to be called neuroses. The most common are the phobic disorders (phobic neuroses). *Phobias* are persistent, irrational fears that may restrict particular activities. Simple phobias of animals, dirt, heights, or closed spaces are out of proportion to reality.

Psychoanalysts say that phobias indicate repression of unacceptable basic urges. When people repress unwanted urges, their anxiety is transferred to an undeserving object or situation. They fear the symbolic substitute and avoid dealing with it, rather than fearing the impulse. Thus, the phobia protects them from having to accept the real problem.

Behaviorists suggest that people's fears are conditioned; that is, they learn to fear objects or situations. Phobias develop out of similar unpleasant experiences. The object or situation need not be identical to the one that first stimulated the fear, but it is similar enough to trigger a fear response. Thus, the child shut up in a dark closet for punishment becomes the adult who fears closed spaces. People can be reconditioned by gradual exposure under pleasant circumstances until their fears subside.

Anxiety disorders also include panic disorders in which the individual has periods of extreme apprehension or fear. At least four of the following symptoms appear during each attack: labored breathing, palpitations, chest pain or discomfort, choking or smothering feelings, dizziness or vertigo, feelings of unreality, tingling in hands or feet, hot and cold flashes, sweating, trembling or shaking, faintness, fear of dying or going crazy, and fear of doing something uncontrolled (DSM–III 1980).

In *generalized anxiety disorders,* people manifest symptoms in three of the following categories: motor tension (such as shakiness), autonomic hyperactivity (such as sweating), apprehensive expectation (worry), and vigilance and scanning (hyperattentiveness). From a psychodynamic point of view, anxiety disorders stem from unconscious impulses, motivations, conflict, and guilt. When individuals struggle with inner fears and pressures that they cannot manage completely, they overreact in self-defeating attempts to cope with their high anxiety level. Once they understand the source of their difficulties and have therapeutic opportunities to vent their fears, they can learn effective ways of dealing with their problems. Psychiatrists often use antianxiety drugs temporarily to reduce tension.

Obsessive compulsive disorders (formerly called obsessive compulsive neuroses) are characterized by obsessions (persistent ideas or thoughts not voluntarily produced) or by compulsions (uncontrolled desires to perform repetitive, often senseless acts). Knocking on wood and avoiding cracks in the sidewalk are compulsions. Washing one's hands repetitively dozens of times a day (as a symbolic act of cleansing) is another compulsive behavior.

Posttraumatic stress disorders are also included under anxiety disorders. In this type of disorder, the person may recurrently experience the traumatic event, acting as though it were actually happening again, or the person may have disturbing, recurrent dreams of the event. For example, a person whose loved one has died starts attending funerals daily. One husband dresses in his best clothes and goes each day to his wife's grave. These unusual reactions to stress indicate posttraumatic stress disorders.

Organic Brain Syndromes

The discussion so far has focused on functional disorders, that is, disorders that originate from emotional problems related to peoples' personalities and life experiences. As noted, many of these disorders may have a hereditary base or may be influenced by organic factors such as chemical balances of the body.

In other mental disorders, the primary cause is organic (related to disease, injury, or aging of tissues). The most important are the *organic brain syndromes* (OBS), mental disorders caused by or associated with impairment of brain tissue function.

One syndrome is *dementia,* commonly called *senile dementia* in older people. The distinguishing features of dementia are: (1) disturbance and impairment of memory, (2) impairment of intellectual function or comprehension, (3) impairment of judgment, (4) impairment of orientation, and (5) shallow or labile effect (Lawson et al. 1977). These five signs may not appear together or in the same degree. The signs may be barely perceptible, with decline coming gradually or suddenly, depending on the cause. Some older persons evidence impairment of mental functions, but their basic personality and behavior remain unchanged. They often sense what has happened to their intellectual abilities and make suitable adjustments, especially in the early stages of the illness. One example would be the older woman who writes notes to remind herself to do things, who puts letters on the doorknob so she won't forget to mail them, or who attaches glasses to a chain around her neck so she won't misplace them.

Sometimes, intellectual functioning becomes so impaired that the person cannot live alone and requires constant care and attention. Memory deficits are the most noticeable symptom. The older person may remember past events but not what happened in the past few moments, today, or yesterday. Disorientation about the time of day or year and the loss of a sense of place (where the person is) are common. In advanced stages, persons may not recognize family members or even know their own names.

OBS is sometimes accompanied by emotional symptoms and psychotic, neurotic, or behavioral disorders that complicate the picture. Anxiety, irritability, and loss of inhibitions are often present, particularly in the early stages. Hallucinations, delusions of persecution, and severe depressive or manic manifestations are typical psychotic symptoms.

The reversible form of organic brain syndrome is called *reversible brain syndrome* (RBS) or *acute brain syndrome*. One symptom is a fluctuating awareness level, which can vary from mild confusion to stupor or active delirium.

Some persons with reversible brain syndromes recover completely if given proper and prompt treatment before permanent brain damage results (Branconnier and Cole 1978). Some recover partially, whereas others die, usually from a serious physical illness that initially caused the syndrome.

Some organic brain syndromes are chronic (CBS) or irreversible because of permanent brain damage. Often, all brain syndromes are categorized as such and left untreated when they could benefit from treatment (Barnes and Raskind 1981). Even when damage is permanent and irreparable, some of the emotional and physical symptoms can be treated and functioning improved (Zeplin et al. 1981).

The two major types of chronic brain syndrome are *senile psychosis* and *psychosis associated with cerebral arteriosclerosis*. Senile psychosis is caused by the atrophy and degeneration of brain cells, independent of vascular change, which causes an even and progressive decline in mental functioning (Yamaura et al. 1980). The disorder is more frequent in women, and the average age of onset is seventy-five. Eventually fatal, senile psychosis has an average survival rate of five years beyond the onset of symptoms. Many persons can remain at home throughout most of the course of the illness if given adequate care and assistance.

Psychosis associated with cerebral arteriosclerosis is caused by a hardening and narrowing of the blood vessels preventing sufficient oxygen and nutrients from reaching the brain. The onset of the disorder occurs in middle and late adulthood, between fifty and seventy, with an average age of sixty-six. Men are afflicted three times as often as women. The progress of the disease is uneven and erratic, with symptoms more pronounced at various times. A person may be unable to remember one minute and regain total capacity the next. The degree of insight and judgment may be spotty, and hallucinations, deliriums, and paranoid reactions may occur when cerebral circulation is insufficient.

Alzheimer's Disease

Alzheimer's disease was first identified in 1907 by A. Alzheimer. It is characterized as a *presenile dementia,* since it often occurs in the forty- to fifty-year age group. However, it also occurs in older people, accounting for perhaps one-half of the older people admitted to nursing homes (Butler 1980). Individuals seldom live longer than four or five years after onset, although remissions occur occasionally.

The disease is characterized by rapid deterioration and atrophy of the cerebral cortex. There is a characteristic neurofibril change in the nerve cells, which shrink and diminish in number. There is an increase of plaque and tangle (PT) formation and lipoid deposits throughout the cortex. The EEG shows significant slowing (Muller and Schwartz 1978).

In its early stages, Alzheimer's disease can be mistaken for a behavioral disorder with symptoms of depression and anxiety as mental deficits and a tendency toward agitation appear. Gradually, the person becomes more incoherent, loses the ability to use or understand spoken or written language *(aphasia)*, loses the ability to recognize objects through use of the senses *(agnosia),* and loses the ability to perform purposeful movements *(apraxia).* The person develops a parkinsonian-like gait and convulsive seizures. Gradually, the person becomes rigid, unable to stand or walk, incontinent, and eventually helpless (Burger and Vogel 1973).

Pick's Disease

Pick's disease is much less common than Alzheimer's disease. Although clinical appearances of the two may be similar, Pick's disease is different pathologically. It involves severe atrophy and cell loss in the outer layers of the frontal and temporal regions of the cortex, but no senile plaques or neurofibrillary tangles as in Alzheimer's. The most complex mental functions fail first, followed by sensory loss. The patient may move about aimlessly, quit work, commit sexual follies, steal, contract debts, become silly and child-like, make jokes, repeat the same stories, and lose initiative and drive. Frequent whimpering, screaming, monotonous singing, laughing, grimacing, and kicking occur. Eventually, the personality is completely devastated as the individual becomes helpless. The prognosis is always fatal, with survival rates of two to fifteen years. The illness is progressive, and only the symptoms can be treated.

SUICIDE

Incidence

Suicide is an acting out behavior often indictive of severe emotional upset. It is a leading cause of death in the United States. The rate is highest among males over sixty-five, with the rate increasing steadily from age fifteen. Among females, the rate is highest among those forty-five to sixty-four. Figure 10.2 shows the rates (U.S. Dept. of Commerce 1983). Although representing only 18.5 percent of the population, people sixty and over commit 23 percent of the suicides in our country (Miller 1978).

Although more women than men attempt suicide, a greater number of men succeed because they use more violent means. Also, more whites than blacks of comparable sex commit suicide, perhaps because whites are

FIGURE 10.2   Suicide Rates, United States, by Age and Sex, 1979

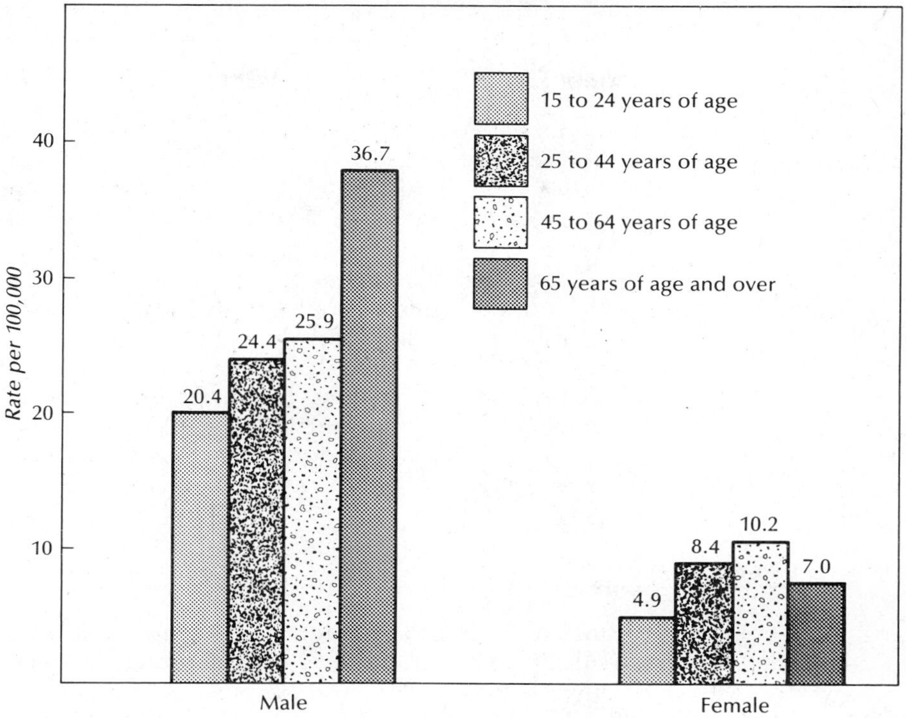

Adapted from: U.S. Department of Commerce, Bureau of the Census, *Statistical Abstract of The United States, 1982, 83,* 103d ed. (Washington, D.C.: U.S. Government Printing Office, 1983), 77.

affected more by the loss of status with age, whereas blacks suffer loss of status all their lives.

Motivations and Reasons

There are a variety of motivations and reasons for suicide other than alienation (through loss of status). One is mental illness, especially depression, which involves losing all desire to live. Schizophrenics may even hear voices that urge self-destruction. Many senile persons kill themselves in such a way that intention cannot be proven. They forget to light the gas stove after turning it on, or they overdose with medicine, having forgotten how much they have already taken. Often, young people commit suicide to get even, to call attention to themselves, to manipulate others, to cry for help, or to hurt a loved one who has been cruel or rejecting, so that person will feel sorry. The elderly, however, quietly and methodically take their lives by the thousands each year (Miller 1978). Sometimes the elderly make a deliberate and rational decision to end their lives, rather than die a slow death or live alone and penniless. Married couples may make a pact to commit suicide together or to commit mercy killing and suicide.

More single males commit suicide than married ones. Often, they have been forced into unwanted retirement because of poor health or because an employer has gone out of business. It appears that poor planning for retirement and poor adjustment to it are major factors in the suicides of older men (Miller 1978). Very low income seems to have a significant impact on aged white males who commit suicide (Marshall 1978).

Older people who attempt suicide fail much less often than younger people, and any threats or symptoms must be taken seriously. Relatives and friends should be especially alert to signs of depression or suicidal preoccupation. Few human beings can sustain a meaningless life, and suicide is evidence of that fact. Some people do not attempt to take their lives with one act; rather, they neglect themselves, refuse to eat, or show other self-destructive behavior as an alternative to suicide (Nelson and Farberow 1980).

SUMMARY

Psychosomatic (*psyche* for mind and *soma* for body) refers to the interrelationship of mind and body. Psychosomatic illnesses are physical illnesses with emotional causes. Negative emotions are important causative factors in physical illnesses such as cancer since stress breaks down the body's natural immune system.

A number of factors contribute to positive mental health. One is maintaining physical fitness through proper nutrition, sufficient sleep, physical exercise, and preventative medicine. Four other important factors are forming meaningful relationships, having goals to work for, maintaining a balance of leisure time and work activities, and forming positive thought patterns about oneself and others.

Stress is strain or tension that develops because of pressure. How a person reacts to stress depends partly on heredity and past experiences. People raised in tense environments usually react more strongly to stressful situations later in life.

Stress may be caused by job-related pressure, role strain, life crises, a series of small events that cause pressure to build up, interpersonal relationships, transition or change, and such traumatic experiences as natural disasters or war.

People react to stress in three stages, the first of which is an alarm reaction. Next they experience a resistance stage and finally a stage of exhaustion. Repeated stress can result in physical damage and disorders and can also interfere with normal psychological functioning.

There are various ways of coping with stress: alleviate the source; make a deliberate effort to change one's internal response through relaxation training, physical activity, and exercise; sublimate it; medicate it; or seek social support in managing it.

The incidence of mental disorder in the United States depends on what types of illness are included and how serious the distress. The President's Commission on Mental Health estimated that one-fourth of all Americans suffer from some type of mental disorder. The numbers may be much greater if mild distresses are included. The number of persons receiving outpatient psychiatric care has grown tremendously, even though the number of persons receiving inpatient care has remained fairly stable.

The present classification of mental disorders is outlined in the *Diagnostic and Statistical Manual of Mental Disorders,* third edition, 1980 (DSM—III), issued by the American Psychiatric Association. Depression is the most common functional disorder of adults of all ages. It can be present in varying degrees, from major to mild. When alternating with manic phases, the illness is described as bipolar.

No single theory explains the causes of depression. Some causes are physical. Heredity or an imbalance in the body's thermal makeup are the two most plausible explanations. Learning theory suggests that depression is learned and perpetuated through reinforcement. Cognitive theorists emphasize that the extent of depression depends on how people interpret a situation and react to it. The more helpless people feel, the more likely they are to become depressed. Psychodynamic theories emphasize the influence of early childhood experiences. People who have lost their mothers early in life are especially prone to depression later on. Depression can also be caused by a loss of self-esteem. Actually, each of these theories contributes to an understanding of the causes of depression. Bipolar disorders, where the patient alternates between mania and depression, have a strong physical base. Both heredity and chemical imbalances are significant factors.

Schizophrenia is most common among adolescents and young adults. There are four major types: catatonic, paranoid, disorganized, and undifferentiated. The most common explanation of the cause traces its origin back to early childhood experiences; frustrating, harmful, and rejecting relationships teach the person to withdraw to escape stress and hurt. Chemical factors and heredity also play important causative roles.

Anxiety disorders can be grouped into five major categories: phobic disorders, panic disorders, generalized anxiety disorders, obsessive compulsive disorders, and posttraumatic stress disorders.

Organic brain syndromes are mental disorders associated with impairment of brain tissue and function. They can be acute (reversible) brain syndromes or chronic (irreversible because of permanent brain damage). Their distinguishing features are memory impairment and impairment of intellectual function. Sometimes these disorders are associated with a variety of other symptoms: anxiety and fear, dazed expression, aggressiveness, lack of cooperation, disorientation, hallucinations, and delusions of persecution. Some persons with reversible brain syndromes can recover completely if prompt treatment is instituted. Two major types of chronic brain syndromes are senile psychosis, caused by atrophy and degeneration of brain cells, and psychosis associated with cerebral arteriosclerosis.

Two types of presenile dementias that often occur in middle age are Alzheimer's disease and Pick's disease. They both involve cell loss and atrophy of the cerebral cortex, which lead to a rapid decline of mental functioning and loss of physical abilities, accompanied by marked changes in behavior. The illnesses are progressive and fatal, although remissions occur occasionally.

Suicide is one type of acting out behavior often indicative of severe emotional upset. The suicide rate is highest in males over sixty-five and in females forty-five to sixty-four. More women than men attempt suicide, but men succeed more often. There are various reasons for suicide, such as alienation and mental illness (especially depression). Some people want to call attention to themselves, manipulate others, cry for help, or hurt a loved one. Others make a deliberate rational decision to commit suicide. Unwanted retirement because of poor health and a very low income can be important causative factors.

Part IV

Intellectual and Cognitive Development

11

Intelligence: Meaning, Measurement, and Change

THE MEANING OF INTELLIGENCE

Definitions

Intelligence has almost as many definitions as experts who try to measure it. Some definitions describe it as an innate capacity to learn, think, reason, understand, and solve problems: an attribute genetically determined and with a theoretical limit when health, educational opportunity, social background, and motivation do not detract from performance.

Other definitions focus on mental ability that one possesses at any particular time, but that has no biological limit. Early researchers sought to identify and describe various factors that made up mental ability. *Two-factor* theories of intelligence described a general factor and specific factors. General ability, as measured by the general factor, is required for performance on mental tests of all kinds. Specific abilities are measured by specific factors or subfactors. Horn (1968) states that current factor analytic studies have identified twenty-five to thirty abilities, labeled as primary mental abilities. He rejects the view that each of these abilities is a distinct aspect of intelligence. Some distinctions among them are trivial and many correlate positively with one another, suggesting a higher level of ability organization that may be more useful to the individual than the specific abilities measured. Besides, primary mental abilities often are poor predictors of such factors as on-the-job success and have limited practical value.

Crystallized versus Fluid Intelligence

One difficulty of some research studies on intelligence is that the tests do not account for developmental considerations. Major exceptions are the work by Cattell (1963) and Horn (1967, 1968). Cattell described two dimensions of intelligence: *crystallized* and *fluid*.

Crystallized intelligence includes knowledge and skills measured by tests of vocabulary, general information, and reading comprehension. It arises out of experience and represents the extent of acculturation. It is both a person's ability to learn or profit from experience and the experiential knowledge actually acquired.

Fluid intelligence is a person's ability to think and reason abstractly as measured by reasoning tests, such as figural analogies, figural series completions, and figural classifications. It involves the processes of perceiving relationships, educing correlates, reasoning inductively, abstracting, forming concepts, and solving problems as measured by tasks involving figural, symbolic, and semantic content. Fluid intelligence has a hereditary base in neurophysiological structures; therefore, it is not influenced as much as crystallized intelligence by intensive education and acculturation.

Three-Factor Description

Sternberg (1981) and his colleagues at Yale conducted a survey in which intelligence experts were asked to rate (on a 1 to 9 scale) either how important each of 158 behaviors was in defining their concept of an "ideally intelligent person," or how characteristic each of these behaviors was of each person. Factor analysis of the 142 responses resulted in three major groupings or constellations of scores that correlated highly with one another. The three groupings were:

> Verbal intelligence: included general learning and comprehension abilities, such as good vocabulary, high reading comprehension, intellectual curiosity, rapid learner, easily conversant on a wide variety of subjects, and widely read.
> Problem-solving ability: included abstract thinking or reasoning in the integration of information, such as ability to apply knowledge to problems at hand, to pose problems in an optimal way, to solve problems well, to plan ahead, to get to the heart of problems, to approach problems thoughtfully, and to consider the end result of actions.
> Practical intelligence: included adaptive behavior needed in the real world, such as ability to size up situations, to achieve goals, to be aware of the surrounding world, and to display interest in the world at large.

Sternberg (1981) found that the concepts of intelligence held by these experts, all of whom held doctoral degrees in psychology and were employed at major universities or colleges, differed little from the concepts of intelligence held by the general adult population.

TESTS, TESTING, AND AGE CHANGES

Any attempt to measure intelligence with advancing age depends on the types of tests used and what they purport to measure. Some intellectual functions increase with age; some peak early and are maintained well into old age; others show decline beginning in early adulthood. Clearly, conclusions regarding changes in intellectual ability will differ, depending on which functions are evaluated.

Wechsler Adult Intelligence Scale (WAIS)

The *Wechsler Adult Intelligence Scale (WAIS)* is the most widely used measure of adult intelligence (Wechsler 1955). It includes eleven subtests. Six of these tests, Information, Comprehension, Arithmetic, Similarities, Digit Span, and Vocabulary, comprise the verbal scores. The other five tests, Digit Symbol, Picture Completion, Block Design, Picture Arrangement, and Object Assembly, comprise the performance scores. In general, verbal scores tend to hold up with increasing age, whereas performance scores tend to decline after the mid-twenties. The decline of performance scores is partially due to a loss of speed and psychomotor coordination (Erber et al. 1981).

Figure 11.1 shows the curves for young adults on eleven Wechsler subtests (Bayley 1968). The findings are taken from the longitudinal Berkeley Growth Study (Bayley 1968). Since only fifty-two subjects were available for retesting at ages sixteen, eighteen, twenty-one, twenty-six, and thirty-six, the findings must be interpreted cautiously. As shown, scores on five of the first six subtests, representing verbal scores, tended to increase through age thirty-six. The scores on Information, Comprehension, and Vocabulary were still increasing rapidly at that age. Only the arithmetic subtest score peaked by age twenty-six and declined after that. However, all scores on the last five subtests, representing performance scores, peaked in the early or mid-twenties and declined thereafter. A continuation of the study to age forty showed that the average IQ gained 3.8 points between ages eighteen and forty.

Cross-Sectional versus Longitudinal Measurements

It must be emphasized that the results obtained from the Berkeley Growth Study were longitudinal measurements. As discussed in chapter 1, longitudinal measurements tend to minimize intellectual decline with age, whereas cross-sectional measurements tend to maximize it. However, both methods of measurement show that verbal scores remain the most stable and performance scores decline the most. Figure 11.2 shows the cross-sectional scores on the verbal and performance portions of the WAIS as a function of age (Wechsler 1955). Scores on Information, Vocabulary, and Comprehension from the verbal section remained the most stable. Scores on Block Design, Object Assembly, and Digit Symbol from the performance section declined the most with age.

Some longitudinal studies emphasize that intellectual decline of a number of abilities is not inevitable, even by age fifty and over. Owens (1966) gave the Army Alpha Intelligence Test to 363 students entering Iowa State College. He retested 127 of them thirty years later, and 97 of

FIGURE 11.1   Curves of Mean Scores for Young Adults on the Eleven Wechsler Subtests, Berkeley Growth Study

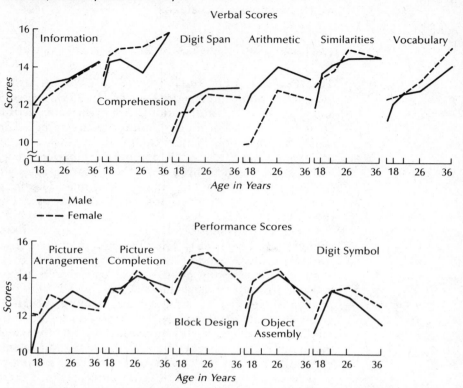

From: N. Bayley, "Behavioral Correlates of Mental Growth: Birth to Thirty-Six Years," *American Psychologist* 23 (1968): 1–17. Copyright 1968 by the American Psychological Association. Reprinted by permission of the publisher and author.

them eleven years after that. He was thus able to test them at ages nineteen, forty-nine, and sixty-one. He reported that all scores on the eight subtests (except Arithmetic Problems) increased from ages nineteen to forty-nine, and that the Numerical Factor showed a slight decline between ages forty-nine and sixty-one. However, the factors labeled Verbal and Reasoning showed nonsignificant improvement from ages forty-nine to sixty-one. Owens labeled this improvement *cultural change*. When he considered the cultural change when calculating scores, he found that between ages nineteen and sixty-one the Verbal Factor score showed a gain and the Numerical and Reasoning Factor scores showed some loss.

Extreme care must be taken when interpreting the results of any testing or faulty conclusions will be drawn. Figure 11.3 shows the full scale WAIS scores of subjects who were aged 60 to 69 and 70 to 79 at the start of a longitudinal study (Eisdorfer and Wilkie 1973). The solid lines represent the scores of those tested four times during a ten-year period and the dashed lines those of subjects tested seven times during a

FIGURE 11.2   Scaled Scores on the Verbal and Performance Portion of the WAIS as a Function of Age

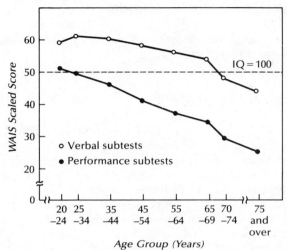

Reproduced by permission from the Manual for the Wechsler Adult Intelligence Scale. Copyright © 1955 by The Psychological Corporation. All rights reserved.

FIGURE 11.3   Full-Scale WAIS Scores of Elderly Subjects Tested Four Times During a Ten-Year Period and of Subjects Tested Seven Times During a Fifteen-Year Period

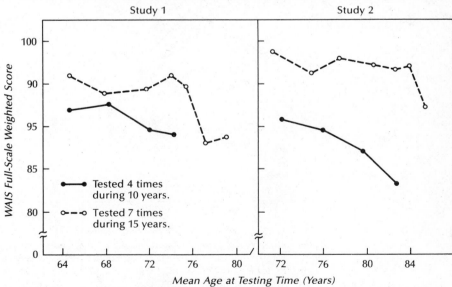

Adapted from: C. Eisdorfer and F. Wilkie, "Intellectual Changes with Advancing Age," in *Intellectual Functioning in Adults,* L. F. Jarvik, C. Eisdorfer, and J. E. Blum, eds. (New York: Springer, 1973), 21–29. Used by permission.

fifteen-year period. Note that those available over a fifteen-year period showed no decline the first ten years, whereas the group tested four times did. Those tested over fifteen years apparently were healthier, since they were available five years beyond the initial four testings. Decline was not apparent until much later in life. As the longitudinal research continued, selective subject dropout obscured decline patterns that otherwise might have been present earlier.

Primary Mental Abilities (PMA)

Thurstone's (1949) *Primary Mental Abilities Test (PMA)* is constructed so scores are derived from five subtests: Word Fluency, Number, Reasoning, Space, and Verbal Meaning. Each score represents a different mental ability relatively unrelated to the others. Schaie and colleagues (1973, 1974) used the Primary Mental Abilities Test (PMA) to test subjects so comparisons could be made between cross-sectional and longitudinal results. The cross-sectional data were obtained by testing 500 people, fifty in each of ten five-year intervals. The results of the cross-sectional comparisons are given in Figure 11.4. The scores peaked at age thirty-five, with a very

FIGURE 11.4   Composite Primary Mental Abilities As a Function of Age (Cross-Sectional Studies)

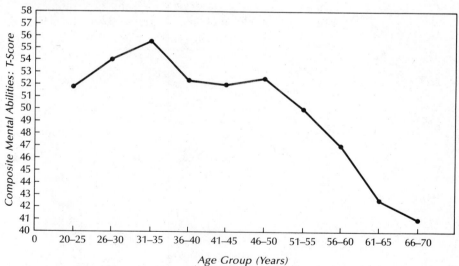

Age Group (Years)

Adapted from: K. W. Schaie and G. Labouvie-Vief, "Generational versus Ontogenetic Components of Change in Adult Cognitive Behavior: A Fourteen-Year Cross-Sequential Study," *Developmental Psychology* 10 (1974): 305–320, and K. W. Schaie, G. V. Labouvie, and B. U. Buech, "Generational and Cohort-Specific Differences in Adult Cognitive Functioning: A Fourteen-Year Study of Independent Samples," *Developmental Psychology* 9 (1973): 151–166. Copyright 1973, 1974 by the American Psychological Association. Adapted by permission of the publisher and authors.

slight decline over the next fifteen years. Overall, however, there was little decline between thirty and fifty. The decline from fifty to seventy was still only 22 percent.

The longitudinal data were obtained by dividing the subjects into seven age cohorts and testing them during a fourteen-year time span (in 1956, 1963, and 1970). The results of the longitudinal testing are shown in Figure 11.5. The findings suggest no significant age decline at all in cohorts I through IV during the fourteen-year span. Decline began in the mid-fifties and continued progressively in cohorts V through VII. The greatest decline was in the oldest cohort, ages sixty-seven to eighty-one, but it was still only 16 percent over the fourteen-year span. It is evident that intellectual decline was less when measured longitudinally than when measured cross-sectionally. It is also apparent that decline does not always occur. When it does, it usually takes place after age fifty. Feier and Gerstman (1980) made cross-sectional measurements of sentence comprehension abilities of adults throughout the adult life span and found this ability remained stable until the sixties, with decline occurring only after that age.

FIGURE 11.5   Composite Primary Mental Abilities As a Function of Age (Longitudinal Studies)

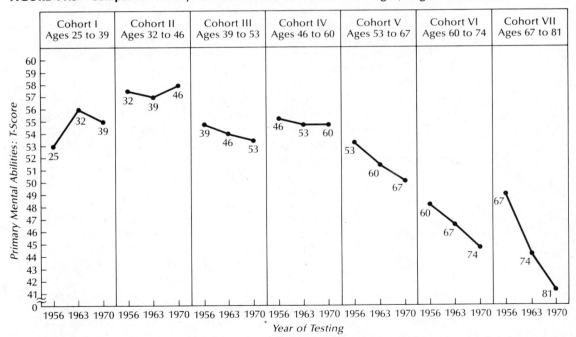

Adapted from: K. W. Schaie and G. Labouvie-Vief, "Generational versus Ontogenetic Components of Change in Adult Cognitive Behavior: A Fourteen-Year Cross-Sequential Study," *Developmental Psychology* 10 (1974): 305–320, and K. W. Schaie, G. V. Labouvie, and B. U. Buech, "Generational and Cohort-Specific Differences in Adult Cognitive Functioning: A Fourteen-Year Study of Independent Samples," *Developmental Psychology* 9 (1973): 151–166 Copyright 1973, 1974 by the American Psychological Association. Adapted by permission of the authors and publisher.

Fluid and Crystallized Intelligence

Horn (1967) felt the reason the studies of Schaie and colleagues (1974) showed a plateau in intelligence test scores during the early adult years was that the data for fluid and crystallized intelligence were averaged together. Horn found that fluid intelligence declined after age fourteen and that the sharpest decline came in early adulthood. The decline in fluid intelligence was evidenced by poorer performance on tests requiring abstract thinking, inductive reasoning, relational thinking, and short-term memory, and on tests requiring figural classification, analogy, and the completion of logical series. Horn also reported that at least twenty studies, both cross-sectional and longitudinal, showed increases in crystallized intelligence throughout adulthood. He reasoned that learning through experience and acculturation continues for many years; therefore, intelligence, defined as knowledge, increases until at least age sixty. However, when the scores on the tests for both fluid and crystallized intelligence were combined, the composite intelligence score remained substantially the same or increased very slightly from age fourteen to sixty.

Schaie (1978) did not accept Horn's arguments as valid, since the data were based on cross-sectional studies. He felt the apparent decline in fluid intelligence was due to generational differences: older subjects were more poorly educated and had less exposure to intellectual stimulation and fewer opportunities to grow during their lifetime than did the younger subjects. The increase in crystallized intelligence could be expected since a greater number and variety of life experiences would increase their knowledge over many years.

Taken together, these findings show that the measurement of intelligence is a complex undertaking and that it is difficult to sort out age-related differences from other causes. Some intellectual functions decline, others improve. But the two-factor model of Cattel and Horn, helpful as it is, may oversimplify the complexity of intellectual change over the life span (Cunningham et al. 1975).

Criticisms

The WAIS and other tests have been criticized in recent years primarily on the basis that they are not relevant for the purposes for which the tests are used. Scores on the WAIS can be converted into *IQ* using a table in the test manual. But IQ is only one important factor necessary to carry out responsible tasks. To succeed, a successful business person needs drive and motivation, social adeptness, courage, patience, self-confidence, practical wisdom, organizational and administrative ability, and a variety of skills, in addition to intelligence. People should not be selected for a job on the basis of intelligence alone. It would be a mistake to assume that people of any age could be successfully evaluated for responsibility only by test scores.

Another criticism of adult intelligence tests is that the test items are more familiar to children or very young adults than to older adults. When tests are constructed comprising practical information items related more to the needs of adults, scores rise through the middle and older adult years. Furthermore, intelligence tests show a cultural and ethnic bias. They are more suited to middle-class adults than to minority and low socioeconomic groups, who tend to score poorly because they are unfamiliar with the vocabulary and examples used.

The original WAIS (1955) is outdated and no longer used. It was tested originally on only a very small adult sample. The new, revised WAIS-R (1982) was tested on a much larger adult sample and is an improvement over the original.

Intelligence Quotient (IQ)

IQ can be quite misleading. It does not measure innate capacity; it measures the score on a test at a particular time with reference to one's own age group. Thus, an IQ of 100 at age fifty indicates an average level of performance relative to other adults the same age. But the fifty-year-old woman actually has performed less well than a twenty-year-old, because an age correction is added to the score. The older person is given a handicap in expectation that his or her score will decline.

Figure 11.6 indicates the corrections made with age. Twenty- to twenty-four-year-olds have 10 points subtracted; people seventy-five and older have 32 points added to attain average IQs of 100 (Wechsler 1955). If one matched the IQs of older and younger subjects for research purposes, the results would be completely misleading. Studies to ascertain absolute levels of intellectual functioning at different ages should use scaled scores, not IQs.

Factors Affecting Scores

How, by whom, to whom, and under what circumstances tests are administered can affect scores (Schaie 1978). Adults score better if test items are relevant to their daily lives. For example, the Block Design subtest of the WAIS requires the rearranging of assorted red and white blocks according to a design on a printed card, while the examiner checks a stop watch. If adults find this activity irrelevant, their scores will be lower than on tests they consider more meaningful.

Other factors, such as the degree of motivation, affect performance. Such personality traits as cautiousness, rigidity, or dogmatism negatively affect test scores. Self-confidence can improve scores, as can experience and practice in taking tests (Beres and Baron 1981). Physical factors, such as fatigue, health, eyesight, hearing, motor ability, and reaction time, are especially important on subtests measuring performance. Furthermore, such emotional factors as low morale, depression, learning apprehension, and tension may result in lower scores. One study showed that hypertension

FIGURE 11.6   Full-Scaled Scores As a Function of Age

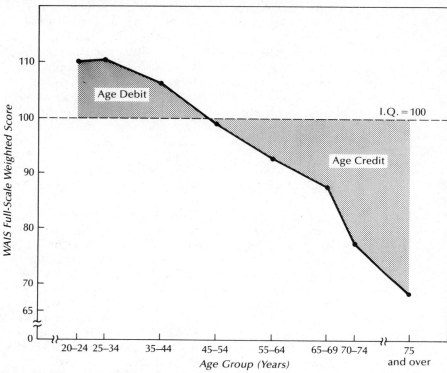

had a more negative effect on the WAIS scores of young adults than on the scores of older subjects (Schultz et al. 1979).

The relationship between the test administrator and the test takers also affects performance. In general, the administrator who develops good rapport, puts subjects at ease, and offers supportive comments can maximize test performance. General intellectual level and years of school completed are also related to test performance. People with superior intelligence and education show little decline or they show improvement, at least to age sixty. Those of average intelligence show increasingly poorer performance between forty and sixty (Kangas and Bradway 1971).

PHYSICAL FACTORS AND COGNITION

Physical Fitness, Activity

Clinical observations of men and women of advanced ages (89–105 years old) in Japan showed a positive correlation between physical fitness and intellectual ability (Karasawa et al. 1979). Other studies have shown the same relationship. Elsayed and colleagues (1980) measured fluid and crystallized intelligence differences among high-fit and low-fit young and old groups. Neither age nor physical condition effected crystallized intelligence, but the high-fit of each age group had higher fluid intelligence than did the corresponding low-fit groups. Also, regardless of physical condition, the young groups scored higher. When subjects were given a vigorous exercise program (three ninety-minute sessions each week for four months), all age groups scored higher on the posttest. The researchers offered the following explanation: (1) physical training has a positive effect on the physiological and biochemical process that produces energy and makes it available to different parts of the body, including the brain; (2) exercise enhances feelings of self-worth and decreases psychological stress which, in turn, could improve performance on complex psychological tests.

Brain Functioning

Some studies have tried to ascertain the role of changes in brain structures and functions in intellectual decline. There are various ways to measure changes in the brain. One is simply to make quantitative measurements of brain size. Yamaura and colleagues (1980) made quantitative measurements by computer tomography and found that brain volume decreased after the mid-thirties, with brain atrophy advancing drastically with increasing age, especially after age fifty.

Measurements of brain activity are even more significant in explaining intellectual functioning. Michalewski and colleagues (1980) found reduced electrical activity in the frontal areas of the brain with advancing age. They suggested this was due to cellular loss as a result of aging, which in turn might be linked to performance deficits. Thompson and Wilson (1966) found that reduced cortical reactivity was associated with poor learning; poor learners tended to slower brain waves than did good learners.

Researchers in the Duke Longitudinal Study of Aging (Obrist et al. 1962) sought to compare the scores on the Wechsler-Bellevue test (W-B) and the Wechsler Adult Intelligence Scale (WAIS) of 245 community volunteers living in Durham, North Carolina, with the scores of 115 residents of Moosehaven, a fraternal home for the aged in Orange Park, Florida, and the scores of 37 psychiatric patients in a state hospital in North Carolina. The subjects ranged in age from sixty to ninety-four and represented a wide range of socioeconomic and educational backgrounds. Both the community and Moosehaven groups had mean IQs average for a normal population. The hospital psychiatric patients averaged 20 points lower in IQ. Measurements of brain waves of the community volunteers on an *electroencephalogram (EEG)* showed no significant relationship between EEG and intelligent test scores (Obrist et al. 1962). This confirmed previous findings showing little or no relationship between EEG and intelligence test performances in elderly community subjects leading normal lives. In contrast, the hospital subjects and residents from the old-age home with diffuse slow activity (as measured on the EEG) scored consistently lower on the intelligence tests compared with patients and residents with normal EEGs. This relationship was attributed partially to general health status, as measured by the presence of arteriosclerosis. Subjects with clinical evidence of arteriosclerosis revealed consistently higher correlations with poor test performance than those showing no signs of the disease. Cardiovascular disease contributed to the relationship between EEG and intelligence test scores.

Further investigation in the Duke Longitudinal Study revealed a relationship between cortical blood flow and changes in the WAIS scores. Low blood flow was associated with a decline in scores, with performance scores declining more than verbal scores (Wang et al. 1970).

Intellectual functioning can be affected by any type of organic brain damage or abnormal brain deterioration in old age. As people age, they are more susceptible to heart attacks, infections, accidents, strokes, and other events that increase the possibility of brain damage.

Cardiovascular Disease

The Duke Longitudinal Study of Aging sought to demonstrate a relationship between heart disease and brain impairment of aged persons (Wang and Busse 1974), and between intelligence and hypertension as measured by blood pressure (Wilkie and Eisdorfer 1971). Figure 11.7 shows the relationship between heart disease and WAIS verbal and performance scores (Wang and Busse 1974). Verbal and performance scores were significantly higher for persons with no heart disease than for those with compensated heart disease (those who have received remedial treatment) or decompensated heart disease. This difference in scores was due partly to the fact that subjects with heart disease were slightly older than those without. When age, race, and education differences were considered, however, WAIS scores of the diseased group were still slightly lower, particularly on performance tests.

An analysis between WAIS scores and blood pressure over a ten-year period revealed that people with heightened *diastolic blood pressure* showed the most decline in WAIS scores (verbal, performance, and full-scale scores) during these years (Wilkie and Eisdorfer 1971). People with normal blood pressure declined some. Sixty- to sixty-nine-year-olds with borderline elevated pressure showed some improvement in WAIS performance scores (see Figure 11.8). Other studies have suggested that mild elevations of blood pressure may be necessary to maintain adequate cerebral circulation among the aged (Karasawa et al. 1979). However, seventy- to seventy-nine-year-olds with borderline elevated pressure still showed a decline in WAIS performance scores, indicating that other factors compromised cerebral circulation. However, many drugs currently used to treat hypertension had not been developed at the time of this study. Prompt diagnosis of hypertension and early treatment, especially with drug therapy, may

FIGURE 11.7   Mean WAIS Verbal and Performance Scaled Scores

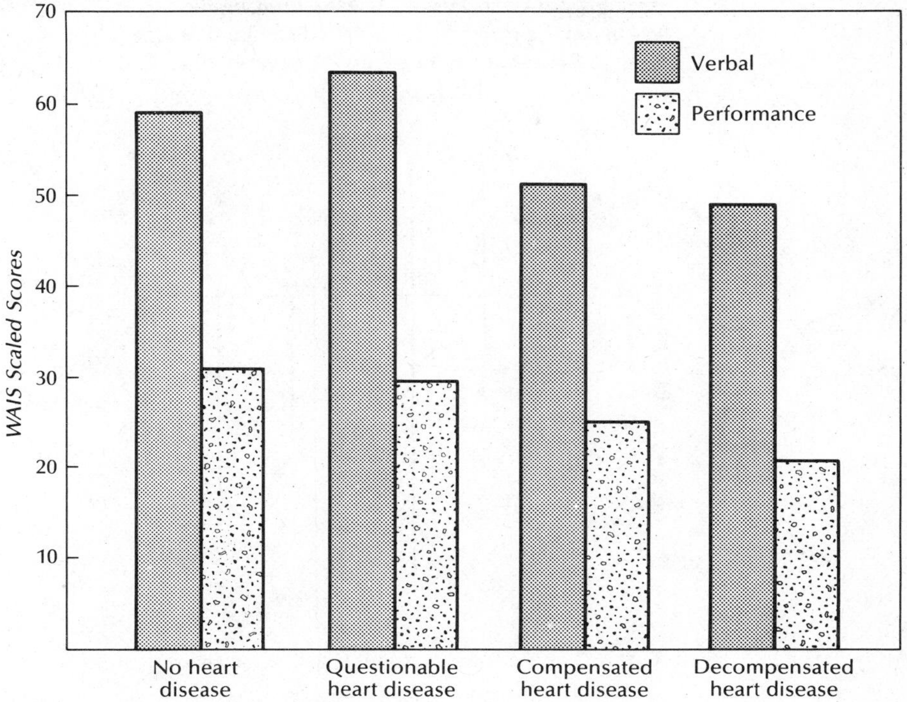

From: "Heart Disease and Brain Impairment among Aged Persons," by H. S. Wang and E. W.
  Busse, in *Normal Aging II,* editor E. Palmore (Durham, N.C.: Duke University Press, 1974).
  Copyright © 1974 by Duke University Press.

alleviate many symptoms and the consequent cognitive impairments already reported.

Auditory Factors

One explanation for the decline of cognitive functioning of the aged, particularly verbal comprehension, is a decline in hearing acuity. Even a slight hearing loss imposes handicaps in receiving and understanding verbal messages. Many older people show poor intelligibility of fast speech and low volume speech. Research has shown a fairly clear-cut relationship between auditory acuity and a decline in level of cognitive functioning.

Granick and associates (1976) studied the relationship between cognition and mild hearing loss in persons in their seventies. Hearing losses at various frequency levels were correlated with performance on cognitive tests such as the WAIS. With age effects discounted statistically, the results revealed substantial associations between hearing losses and test scores. These findings suggest that aged subjects may be more intellectually ca-

FIGURE 11.8   Intellectual Change (Delta Scores) during a Ten-Year Period As Measured by the WAIS among Individuals Initially Examined at Age Sixty to Sixty-nine and Seventy to Seventy-nine

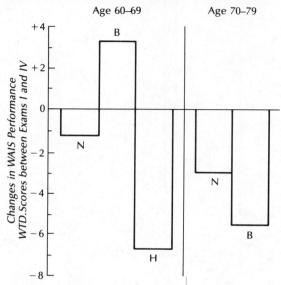

Diastolic Blood Pressure, Initial Examination

N = Normal
B = Borderline elevated
H = Heightened

From: F. Wilkie and C. Eisdorfer, "Intelligence and Blood Pressure," *Science* 172 (1971): 959–962. Copyright 1971 by the American Association for the Advancement of Science.

pable than their test scores suggest, and that a decline in measurements of their verbal abilities may be due to reduced auditory acuity.

Sleep

Human sleep patterns undergo changes with advancing age. Sleep becomes more fragmented; awakenings during the night are longer and more frequent. EEG measurements of the sleep stages indicate that with advancing age there is a significant reduction in *rapid eye movement (REM) sleep*. EEG measurements of sleep also indicate a sharp decline in the deepest stage of sleep. All studies agree that impaired sleep occurs with advancing age.

What is the effect of both these sleep patterns on cognitive functioning? Feinberg (1974) and Prinz (1977) found a correlation between the amount of REM sleep and performance scores on the WAIS. Moreover, subjects who had maintained stable intellectual function during the preceding eighteen years displayed greater amounts of REM sleep, whereas subjects with a previous history of cognitive decline displayed lower REM sleep levels. The important implication for mental functioning is that senescent sleep patterns may have important influences on brain function, as inferred from mental performance test scores.

PERSONALITY, BEHAVIOR, AND MENTAL IMPAIRMENT

To what extent is the decline in intellectual functioning with age related to personality factors? Unfortunately, only limited objective information is available to answer this question. Part of the problem is the difficulty of classifying and measuring personality types and trying to describe personality changes with age. Older people have been described as turning inward, becoming more withdrawn, passive, introverted, isolated, and depressed. Some are characterized as dogmatic, stubborn, more cautious, conformist, and rigid. Others are labeled hostile, irascible, irritable, touchy, and difficult to please or get along with. Do these stereotypes, valid or not, have any relationship to cognitive factors?

Emotional Health

In general, there is a positive relationship between mental health and cognitive ability. The emotionally healthy seem to show less cognitive decline with age than the emotionally ill. The extreme example is the seriously depressed person whose severe withdrawal precludes any type of testing. In comparison to subjects exhibiting declines in functioning levels, Kleban and associates (1976) found that the stable subjects comprehended their situations better (more awareness, coherence, verbalization, better memory), were more socially reactive, manifested fewer neurotic conditions, and had greater control over impulses and aggression.

Personality Types

Personality indirectly affects intellectual functioning by influencing life cycle (Karasawa et al. 1979). People who are more open and imaginative, outgoing and highly interactive socially, more open to new ideas, curious, and highly motivated to learn are likely to accumulate a great variety of cognitive experiences over a lifetime. Therefore, they score higher on measures dependent on accumulated knowledge and abilities, such as crystallized intelligence measures.

Personality changes with old age, for example, becoming short-tempered, stubborn, or suspicious, cause maladaptations in the elderly. These changes are frequently observed together with distinct intellectual decline. Sometimes organic brain pathologies underlie such personality changes.

Cautiousness and Rigidity

Individuals become more cautious with advancing age. They take longer to answer questions on cognitive tests because they want to avoid mistakes. As their response time increases, they do progressively worse on timed tests. But, conversely, cautiousness in later life is a function of intellectual decline, making either interpretation tenable.

Rigidity involves a person's resistance to change and it may influence changes in one's ideas, attitudes, habits, and tasks. The rigid person refuses to relinquish attitudes, opinions, or tasks, despite plentiful evidence that this persistence is wrong or unrewarding.

There is no such thing as *global rigidity,* that is, inflexibility in all aspects of one's personality or life. The notion that one's whole being or life-style can be characterized as rigid or flexible is not supported by research results. There are a variety of rigidities. An engineer who is very rigid in his ideas of marital roles can be very open-minded about the results of his scientific research. A person with inflexible habits may show tolerance to new ideas.

The statement that rigidity increases with age is simplistic. Rigid behavior in older people tends to be marginal. Many studies that indicate increasing rigidity with age fail to differentiate among other deficits in cognitive performance. For example, older people have difficulty shifting from one task to another, but this is partially due to slowness, to the increased time they require to switch. This slowness results in higher rigidity scores. When given step-by-step instructions regarding which function to perform next, their slowness in shift performance is minimized and the elderly score higher.

Some studies also fail to consider cultural change factors. Cross-sectional studies comparing older and younger subjects show the former to be more rigid. But longitudinal studies fail to show consistent results or extensive rigidity (Schaie and Labouvie-Vief 1974). Thus, rigidity may or may not be intrinsic to *maturational age changes.* Rigidity is influenced greatly by intelligence and educational level. The person with more intelligence and education will exhibit less rigidity.

SOCIOENVIRONMENTAL EFFECTS

Stimulating Environment

Older adults exposed to intellectually stimulating environments maintain a higher level of cognitive ability with increasing age than those not exposed. Social contacts with family, friends, social groups, or at work, interesting activities, a variety of experiences in different settings, and opportunities to look at books, magazines, art, or television all help maintain cognitive powers. A person who is isolated from other people, with little opportunity for meaningful interpersonal contacts, becomes generally divorced from social interaction. In all probability, that person's mental abilities will evidence decline.

Weinstock and Bennett (1971) found that newcomers to a progressive residence home for the aged scored higher on tests of cognitive ability than did those on the waiting list or those who had lived in the home longer than a year. Apparently, the opportunities for social and intellectual stimulation in the home, and the active involvement in adjusting, had a beneficial effect on cognitive functioning. However, after being in the home for a year or more, the stimulation decreased, routines were established, and cognitive functioning declined. The researchers suggested that if meaningful learning experiences and positive goals were provided throughout a resident's tenure in an institution, the elderly might show fewer decrements.

Education and Socioeconomic Status

People with high education levels and superior socioeconomic status show less decline in cognitive abilities with age, especially verbal abilities, than do those with less education and lower socioeconomic status. Superior education and socioeconomic status are both causes and effects. The most educated people have superior intellectual abilities to start with, regardless of age. In fact, educational level is as important to intellectual functioning as is age. Those with high status and education are also more likely to maintain an active interest in learning and remain involved in various rewarding activities. They also have more opportunities and resources to participate. As a result, they manifest fewer signs of mental deterioration in old age. In fact, they may show improvement, at least to age sixty. Although they decline in perceptual-integrative abilities and in performance functions, the extent of the decline is not enough to reduce them to the level of their less intellectually capable age peers (Kangas and Bradway 1971).

Life Crises and Stress

Mental deterioration is also related to the frequency and intensity of people's life crises. The greater and more frequent the stress, the greater the probability of mental deterioration. Amster and Kraus (1974) found the elderly females from sixty-five to ninety-five who showed mental deterioration had been exposed to almost twice as many crises as the women in a control group who showed no deterioration.

Education

Learning is a lifelong endeavor. There is no specific age at which people can or should cease learning.

> Learning is not something outside life. It is something within life waiting to be understood. Learning is a kind of big umbrella over everything else that happens to you. And it can help you whether you are buying a house, reading about heart trouble, studying your social security rates, or even trying to understand what's happening in congress. (Schuckman 1975, 85)

Increasingly, serious consideration is being given to adult education. Many opportunities exist to learn through adult courses in high schools, vocational schools, community colleges, universities, and self-taught or directed home study programs. In addition, thousands of older adults attend regular university classes with younger students. Some universities provide gold card registrations that offer free tuition to people over sixty-five. The *New York Times* reported that the number of colleges and universities offering courses to retirement-aged people multiplied twenty-five times in the 1970s. A variety of nonacademic organizations also offer courses for older people, notably, The Institute for Lifetime Learning sponsored by the American Association for Retired Persons (AARP) and the National Retired Teachers' Association (NRTA).

In spite of the progress, the total number of older persons with a secondary or college education is limited. Figure 11.9 shows the percentages of people fifty-five and older who complete various levels of education (U.S. Dept. of Commerce 1983). The number of older people taking some type of formal education is also limited. The National Council on Aging (1975) reported that only 2 percent of all persons over sixty-five were enrolled in some type of course. The major reasons older people give for not participating in educational courses are lack of interest (45 percent), being too old (27 percent), poor health (22 percent), and lack of time (13 percent). Other barriers are vision and hearing problems and lack of transportation. For handicapped adults, courses must be carefully planned, considering numerous learning, personality, and environmental factors.

The concept of lifelong education is taken seriously today by educators and administrators. Exposure to schooling throughout life will enable adults to maintain their cognitive skills, morale, self-image, and abilities to deal with the complex problems of the future. The rate of change of our knowledge base in most fields is so rapid that workers need refresher and retraining courses several times during a career.

Training

Efforts have been made to improve the cognitive abilities of older adults through training. Such efforts reflect the philosophy that reduced intellec-

FIGURE 11.9   Years of School Completed by Adults, Fifty-five Years of Age or Older, 1981

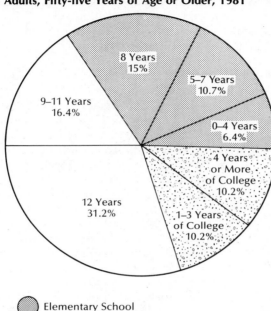

8 Years
15%

5–7 Years
10.7%

0–4 Years
6.4%

9–11 Years
16.4%

4 Years
or More
of College
10.2%

12 Years
31.2%

1–3 Years
of College
10.2%

Elementary School

High School

College

Adapted from: U.S. Department of Commerce, Bureau of the Census, *Statistical Abstract of the United States, 1982, 83,* 103d ed. (Washington, D.C.: U.S. Government Printing Office, 1983), 145.

tual performance is an experiential or performance deficit that can be reduced by training in certain component skills. However, current opinion emphasizes that the extent to which different intellectual abilities are trainable differ markedly, depending on the degree to which they represent the effects of acculturation or of the individual's biological-maturational well-being. Those abilities most dependent on acculturation, such as the components of crystallized intelligence, are considered the most trainable.

To show that other abilities may also be trainable, Labouvie-Vief and Gonda (1976) attempted to improve the ability of sixty females, ages sixty-three to ninety-five, to solve complex problems requiring inductive reasoning. The results showed that training could produce significant increments in intellectual performance of the elderly, even with skills linked primarily with biological-maturational factors (i.e., fluid intelligence). Plemons and associates (1978) tried to determine to what extent fluid intelligence could be modified in aged subjects (fifty-nine to eighty-five). A training program was devised to enhance the Figural Relations component of fluid intelligence. Posttraining assessments after one week, one month, and six months showed improved performance as a result of training. This improvement carried over to other tasks related to fluid intelligence. These significant findings suggest that intellectual performance on fluid intelligence tests is more modifiable through short-term intervention than traditionally assumed.

Several studies have also shown that scores on performance-type tasks requiring speed and motor coordination can also be improved with practice (Grant et al. 1978). Beres and Baron (1981) administered the Digit Symbol Substitution subtest of the WAIS to older women (mean age sixty-nine) and to younger women (mean age twenty-three) on each of five training days. The older women improved substantially, but equally large gains were made by the younger women. Therefore, age differences were not reduced by training. As a consequence of practice, scores of the older women on this subtest increased from the twenty-fifth to the ninetieth percentile, relative to norms for young adults in general. These scores were maintained during a follow-up test ten days later.

The notions that adults cannot or will not learn and that little can be done about the decline of cognitive abilities are fallacious. The fact that a variety of performance deficits typically observed in the elderly are amenable to intervention suggests that adult cognitive functioning can be more proficient if adequate environmental support is provided (Sanders and Sanders 1978). Moreover, the degree of plasticity revealed in intervention studies (Baltes and Schaie 1976) has contributed to a deeper, more positive understanding of adult cognitive potential.

TERMINAL DECLINE

The theory of *terminal decline* holds that many human functions are not primarily related to chronological age, but show marked decline during a period of a few weeks to a few years before death (Palmore and Cleveland 1976). The theory assumes that whatever genetic and environmental factors cause death also cause marked functional decline prior to death.

Some evidence suggests that within one to five years a decrement in intellectual performance is associated with death (Siegler, Roseman, and Harkins 1975). The Duke Longitudinal Study of Aging (Wilkie and Eisdorfer 1972) showed that survivors and nonsurvivors achieved the same WAIS scores in initial testing, and that there was no significant relationship between the actual scores and nearness to death. However, two nonsurvivor groups (deaths occurred thirteen to twenty-four and twenty-five to thirty-two months after initial testing) showed significantly greater losses in scores between the first and second tests than did the survivor groups.

These results partially support previous findings of terminal decline in intellectual performance. The groups that died within thirteen to thirty-two months after testing showed greater intellectual losses than the survivors. However, the group that died within one year after the first test showed intellectual changes similar to the survivors. Thus, the magnitude of observed intellectual changes was not related to distance from death. Also, not all individuals experienced a marked decline before death. Non-survivors who sustained both acute and chronic illnesses showed the greatest intellectual decline. If acute illnesses could be treated, intellectual loss might be minimized.

An additional analysis of this study attempted to distinguish between the relative effects of aging declines and terminal declines. The analysis showed substantial aging declines in intelligence and substantial terminal declines in physical functions. Longitudinal analysis showed no substantial terminal declines remaining after aging declines were controlled. Cross-sectional analysis, however, showed a small but significant terminal decline in intelligence after aging decline was controlled (Palmore and Cleveland 1976). Although the reality of terminal decline was confirmed, it was much less than previously supposed when age was taken into account. Age and physical condition were more important factors in intellectual decline than a person's distance from death.

SUMMARY

Intelligence has been defined as mental capacity: the ability to learn, think, reason, and understand, and to solve problems. Two-factor theories of intelligence describe it as mental ability, including a general ability plus specific abilities. Cattell and Horn differentiated crystallized intelligence (knowledge and skills arising out of experience) from fluid intelligence (the ability to think and reason abstractly that has a hereditary base). Three-factor theories of intelligence describe verbal intelligence, problem-solving abilities, and practical intelligence.

Various tests have been used to measure adult intelligence. The Wechsler Adult Intelligence Scale (WAIS) is one of the most widely used. It includes eleven subtests, of which six comprise the verbal scores and five the performance scores. In general, verbal scores hold up with increasing age, whereas performance scores decline. However, findings depend on whether the study is cross-sectional or longitudinal. Cross-sectional measurements tend to maximize age trends and longitudinal measurements minimize them. Subjects who survive to be tested repeatedly over a period of years usually show very little decline in WAIS scores until late in life (the seventies or eighties). The healthiest subjects who remain to be tested are also the most intellectually capable.

The Primary Mental Abilities Test (PMA), consisting of five subtests, is also widely used. Schaie's cross-sectional results show scores peaking at age thirty-five and some decline between thirty-five and fifty. But scores at age fifty were still higher than at age twenty. Longitudinal scores showed no significant decline until the late fifties. The greatest decline was in the oldest cohort (ages sixty-seven to eighty-one), but it was still only 16 percent over the fourteen-year age span. Horn suggested that Schaie's findings would have been more meaningful if he had separated fluid intelligence from crystallized intelligence. Horn found that fluid intelligence begins declining in early adulthood, and that crystallized intelligence increases until at least age sixty.

The WAIS and other tests have been criticized as irrelevant for the purposes for which they are used. Test scores and IQ are only one ingredient in carrying out responsible tasks. IQ scores can be misleading because they are adjusted according to one's age and thus do not measure innate capacity. Test items are also more familiar to children and young people than to older adults and reflect cultural and ethnic biases. Many other factors affect scores: factors of administration, relevance of the questions, degree of motivation, personality factors, physical factors, experience and practice in taking tests, emotional factors, and educational level of the subjects.

A positive correlation exists between physical fitness and intellectual ability. Brain functioning, as measured by brain volume, brain atrophy, and brain activity, is related to intellectual functioning, especially after age fifty. Brain waves, as measured by an electroencephalogram (EEG), do not necessarily correlate with intellectual test scores, except on subjects with peripheral artery disease (arteriosclerosis and atherosclerosis) or circulatory problems. Low blood flow to the brain impedes intellectual functioning, as does organic brain damage or abnormal brain deterioration. Other cardiovascular diseases, such as coronary heart disease and hypertension, may also diminish intellectual functioning. Prompt diagnosis and treatment can alleviate many symptoms and cognitive impairment.

Cognitive functioning is also affected by a decline in hearing acuity, insufficient sleep, poor mental health, and personality. Adults open to new ideas, imaginative, curious, social, and motivated to learn may show improvement in test scores that depend on accumulated knowledge such as crystallized intelligence. Adults who are cautious, rigid, and resistant to change may show declining intelligence test scores with age. However, not all older people become more rigid with age. Adults with superior education are usually less rigid and have more opportunities for intellectual growth. They are less likely to show intellectual decline. People exposed to a stimulating environment maintain a higher level of cognitive ability with increasing age than those who are not. Those exposed to the greatest and most frequent stress have a greater probability of mental deterioration.

Learning is a lifelong endeavor. Continuing education and training of adults better enable them to maintain their cognitive skills. In 1981, only about half of the United States population fifty-five or older had twelve or more years of education. Only 20 percent had any college training; only 10 percent had four or more years of college. Only a small percentage (2 percent) of adults sixty-five and older were enrolled in any kind of course. Even abilities linked with biological-motivational factors (such as those comprising fluid intelligence) and formerly considered untrainable have been improved through carefully designed training programs. Scores on performance tests requiring speed and motor coordination can also be improved with practice. The notion that adults cannot or will not learn is fallacious.

Although there is some evidence of terminal decline, that is, a decline in cognitive functioning before death, such decline is not always related to the time period before death. Age and physical condition are more important factors in intelligence decline than how close a person is to death.

12

Memory and Learning

MEMORY

What Memory Involves

The ability to remember is basic to all learning and intellectual and social functioning. Studies of memory during adulthood are extremely important because they enable us to determine what happens to this basic process throughout the adult life cycle. All studies of memory recognize three basic processes: *acquisition, storage,* and *retrieval.*

The process of acquisition begins with exposure to stimuli so information can be learned. It involves making an impression on memory receptors and registering and recording information. Acquisition is the learning or input phase of memory. Unless something is acquired, it cannot be remembered.

In the process of storage, information is cycled, processed, organized, rehearsed, and stored until needed. The most popular concept of memory storage is a three-fold model: *sensory storage, short-term storage,* and *long-term storage.* These stores are also referred to as *sensory memory, short-term memory,* and *long-term memory.* Figure 12.1 illustrates this three-stage model of memory (Murdock 1974).

Information is seen as passing from one compartment to another, with decreasing amounts passed on at any one time to the next stage. Information is first received and transduced by the senses. It is held only

FIGURE 12.1 Three-Stage Model of Memory

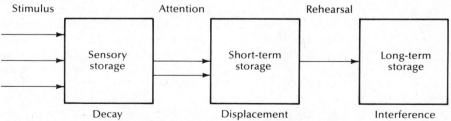

Adapted from: B. Murdock, *Human Memory: Theory and Data* (Potomac, Md.: Lawrence Erlbaum Associates, 1974).

briefly (as little as a fraction of a second) before the image begins to decay and/or is blocked out by other incoming sensory information. Information that has not already faded from the sensory store is *read out* to the short-term store. Because of the limited capacity of the short-term store, information to be held longer must be further rehearsed and transferred to the relatively permanent long-term store. For all practical purposes, long-term storage capacity is infinite.

In the process of *retrieval,* stored information is obtained by searching, finding, and remembering, either through *recall* or *recognition.*

Memory efficiency depends on all three of these processes. Loss of memory represents a decline in the efficiency of these processes. In general, memory ability tends to decline with advancing age. This is true whether learning is measured in terms of speed or by the amount revealed or recognized. However, there are many exceptions to this generalization. If ample time is given for registering, assimilating, coding, categorizing, rehearsing, and reinforcing short-term holdings, many older persons do as well as or better than younger ones. This is true even when no extra time is given for recall or recognition.

Sensory Memory

Sensory memory abilities of older adults depend partially on the extent to which their sensory receptors are functioning at normal levels. Those who show some decrement in visual or auditory functioning cannot be expected to remember what they have not acquired (Arenberg 1982). Less information is passed from sensory to short-term stores.

Information received by the senses is held very briefly in one of several specific sensory stores. For example, auditory information is held in an auditory sensory store; visual information is held in a visual sensory store. The auditory sensory store is referred to as *echoic memory,* the visual sensory store as *iconic memory.* Other sensory stores include those for tactual information and for smell.

Most investigations of visual or iconic memory have shown a rapid decay in less than a second. But other studies have confirmed that the durability of a memory trace depends on how intensively the stimulus was presented and how deeply it was processed. The more processing and analysis that are carried out, the longer lasting the trace (Craik and Lockhart 1972). In one experiment by Abel (1972), subjects were exposed to visual stimuli for a full half second. Only a little decay of recall ability occurred as *probe delay* (the time elapsing between stimulus and required recall) was increased from 0 to 1200 milliseconds. It may be that the long duration of the stimuli actually tested very short-term memory rather than sensory memory. Although middle-aged subjects (forty-six to fifty-two) did slightly poorer overall than younger subjects (nineteen to twenty-seven), they showed no more decay of information than the younger subjects as the time delay for recall was increased.

Studies of auditory or echoic sensory memory as contrasted with visual or iconic sensory memory and *tactual sensory memory* show variable results (Riege and Inman 1981). All three sensory memory stores show some decline with age, but tactual memory seems to decline the fastest (Riege and Inman 1981). Figure 12.2 shows the average performance of groups of volunteers divided on the basis of age decades. Visual sensory memory did not decline much before age sixty, but did so fairly rapidly after that. It also declined faster than auditory memory after sixty. This is particularly true in older subjects if any interference or disruption occurs while the stimuli are being presented. Visual memory tasks require close attention while the images are being presented; auditory inputs can be heard and held briefly whether they are attended to or not.

However, the durability of an audio memory trace depends on the attention given it when heard, and therefore the depth at which the stimulus is *processed*. When attention is diverted during a stimulus, older subjects in particular remember less because the information is processed less deeply. Thus, if they are asked to listen to two things at once, or to hold some information while reporting other, or to receive some input while recalling and reporting information previously given, older subjects tend to concentrate on only one task. Performance on the other task deteriorates badly. Older subjects are penalized more when they must divide their attention.

Short-Term or Primary Memory

There is some confusion in various studies about the difference between short-term and long-term memory. One helpful distinction was given by Waugh and Norman (1965). They used the terms *primary memory* (PM)

FIGURE 12.2   Average Performances (d') on Nonverbal Recognition Tests, by Age Group

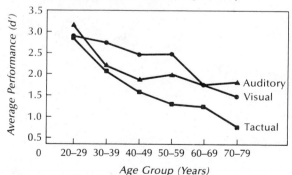

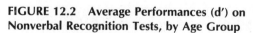

Adapted from W. H. Riege and V. Inman, "Age Differences in Nonverbal Memory Tasks." Reprinted by permission of *Journal of Gerontology* 36 (January 1981): 51–58.

and *secondary memory* (SM). Primary memory (PM), considered synonymous with short-term memory, involves information still being rehearsed and focused on in one's conscious mind. Secondary memory, or long-term memory, is characterized by how deeply the information has been processed, not by how long the information has been held. Deep processing, in which perceived information has been passed into layers of memory below the conscious level, constitutes secondary memory. For example, when a subject memorizes a word list, the words under immediate consideration are at the primary or short-term memory stage. Words already looked at, memorized, and tucked away are at the secondary or long-term memory level, even though they were learned only a short time before. Specific words recalled several days or months later are recalled from secondary memory. Secondary memory can last for thirty seconds or for years. These two layers of memory are used synonymously in this discussion with short-term and long-term memory, even though some secondary memory stores may be recalled after relatively short time intervals.

In measuring primary or short-term memory, the subject is presented a short string of digits, letters, or words and then tested for the total that can be recalled immediately. When measured in this way, primary memory span does not change with age or it decreases only slightly, unless ability has been seriously impaired by physical deterioration (Friedman 1974; Wright 1982). Botwinick and Storandt (1974) found no loss of memory span for letters presented auditorily until the subject reached age sixty. However, primary memory span capacity ranges only from 2.6 to 3.4 words. If subjects are asked to recall longer lists, some secondary memory ability (SM) is required, and performance begins to decline with age. This is supported by other studies showing that age differences occur during the transition from primary to secondary memory (Poon and Fozard 1980). Also, if the time required for response is measured, aging begins to have an effect. The time taken to recall an item from primary memory increases most markedly after age sixty. Furthermore, older subjects do not acquire (or *encode*) information as efficiently as younger subjects. Charness (1981) found that recall of chess diagrams was less accurate for older players (median age fifty-four) than for younger players (median age twenty), particularly because the older subjects were less efficient in initial encoding. Older players slow down in the sense of encoding less accurate information per unit of time.

Long-Term or Secondary Memory

Retention of initial segments of a free recall list longer than three or four words depends on secondary memory (SM). However, SM is not an intermediate memory store or process. The qualitative characteristics of SM performance after thirty seconds of activity are identical to those observed after months or years. Thus, SM and long-term memory are equivalent.

Many studies show that older subjects perform less well than younger subjects when secondary memory (SM) is involved. For example, if subjects are asked to recall a list of twelve to thirty words in any order, no age differences appear in the recall of the last four items (retrieved from primary memory). However, older subjects recall fewer words from the beginning and middle of the list where secondary memory is involved.

Many factors can partially eliminate age differences. Material organized, categorized, or associated with what is already familiar is remembered more readily, because acquisition is enhanced (Mueller et al. 1979; Rankin and Kausler 1979; Sanders et al. 1980). Also, if a list of words is presented in one category (for example, animals), age differences in recall are slight, suggesting that grouping words under one concept offers cues that enhance retrieval. Furthermore, other studies have shown greater age losses in free recall than in recognition performance, suggesting that retrieval from storage without any cues constitutes a special problem for older subjects (Kausler and Puckett 1981; Riege and Inman 1981). Recognition does not require retrieval, since cues are given, so smaller age decrements are found in recognition than in recall (Harkins et al. 1979; Perlmutter 1979).

Older subjects are at their greatest disadvantage when materials to be learned are meaningless or unfamiliar, or cannot be associated with what is already known. Thus, it is more difficult to remember nonsense syllables than meaningful words. Also, if random materials can be sorted out or arranged in some logical order, such as alphabetically, they are easier to remember. Recall ability decreases with age (Hultsch 1971).

Extremely Long-Term Memory

The ability to remember over a long period of time depends partially on how often the material is recalled and used in the intervening years (Botwinick and Storandt 1980). For example, if words are periodically recalled, held in working memory, and then tucked away again, they can be remembered more easily than if they were never used after initial learning took place (Howard et al. 1980). Retrieval from very long-term memory is also enhanced if the information is familiar. In one experiment, twenty-year-olds remembered the names of unique contemporary pictures faster than the older subjects, but the sixty-five-year-old group retrieved the names of unique but dated pictures faster. The speed of fifty-year-old subjects fell between that of the two other groups (Poon and Fozard 1978). Each age group recalled best pictures with which they were familiar.

It is commonly assumed that older people are not good at recalling recent events, but that their memory for remote events is unimpaired. One flaw in this assumption is that childhood events usually have been recalled many times since they occurred; the older person is remembering from the time of the last rehearsal, not from forty years ago. Even so, objective studies show that older subjects are poorer than younger controls at recalling and recognizing events from the past (Bahrick, Bahrick, and Wittlinger 1975). Performance declines with the remoteness of events and with increasing age. When subjects of various ages were asked to list the names of high school class members and to associate names with faces, the recall both of names and names associated with faces declined with time. From three to four years after graduation to forty-seven to forty-eight years after graduation, recall of names declined 60 percent and recall of names associated with faces declined more than 70 percent (Bahrick, Bahrick, and Wittlinger 1975).

It must be emphasized, however, that decline is very slow. Warrington and Silberstein (1970) found that adults under forty were able to recall 32 percent of news items one and one-half years after they had happened. Adults over fifty-five were able to recall 26 percent of the items. No differences were found in recognition performance between the two different age groups.

The ability to recall may depend partially on the subjects' ages when the events occurred. Botwinick and Storandt (1974) found that subjects of all ages (twenty to seventy-nine) could best remember sociohistoric events that occurred when the subjects were fifteen to twenty-five years old. These ages may be the most impressionable years, so persons of sixty remember events that occurred thirty-five to forty-five years earlier better than they recall events that happened before or after.

Acquisition, Recording, Encoding, and Processing

Before something can be remembered it must be learned. There is some evidence that older subjects show *acquisition deficits,* reflecting declining abilities in *recording, processing, encoding,* and *storing* material. (Adamowicz 1976; Nebes 1976; Misler-Lackman 1977; Puglisi 1980). Essentially this is due to a lessened ability to organize materials into mental groups and hierarchies, and they do better when given instructions that help them organize the material to be learned. They also make less effective use of verbal or imaginal mediators (mental images) or association to enhance their level of learning. Because older subjects fail to perform those mental operations that result in deeper, elaborative encoding of the material to be learned, their retention is poor (Eysenck 1974). However, some researchers have shown that there is little age difference in retention if the amount of initial learning is equated (Moenster 1972).

Search and Retrieval

Search and retrieval involve finding information in the memory stores and remembering it. Free recall requires search and retrieval, and older people perform these tasks more poorly than younger persons.

Figure 12.3 shows age-related differences in recognition and recall (Schonfield 1965). The graph shows the number of words recalled (out of a total of twenty-four) by free recall from one list, and by recognition from the other. There was no decline with age in recognition scores, but there was a consistent decline in the recall scores.

**FIGURE 12.3   Mean Recall and Recognition
Scores As a Function of Age**

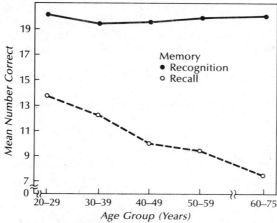

Adapted from: D. Schonfield, "Memory Changes with Age,"
Nature 28 (1965): 918. Reprinted by permission from
Nature, Vol. 28, p. 918. Copyright © 1965 Macmillan
Journals Limited.

As people get older, they require more time to search memory stores
and retrieve information (Fozard and Popkin 1978). In one experiment,
healthy adult male subjects, varying in age from thirty-one to seventy-
five, were asked to memorize a list of six letters (Thomas et al. 1978). In
one condition, the letters were presented alphabetically: *abcdef*. In another
condition, the letters were presented in an unfamiliar sequence: *pgktri*.
After memorizing a list, subjects were shown individual letters and asked
whether each letter was in the memorized list. They were to respond yes
or no. Older subjects took longer to respond in both conditions, but particularly in the case of the unfamiliar list. Apparently, the older subjects
were less efficient at search and retrieval than the younger subjects. It must
be emphasized, however, that most of the age differences related to the
unfamiliar sequences did not occur until after age fifty; regarding the familiar sequences, there was little difference before age sixty.

Memory Training

Can the memory of older adults be improved with training? Evidence
indicates that it can. Recall ability, in particular, can be improved if adults
are trained in such recall strategies as repetition, association, and categor-
ical material arrangement (Schmitt and McCroskey 1981). In one experiment, training classes were held weekly for four weeks during which
institutionalized adults, sixty to eighty-nine years of age, were exposed to
ninety-minute training sessions (Zarit et al. 1981). At the end of the training, retesting revealed considerable improvement in their ability to recall

related items, names and faces, and unrelated items. No improvement was found in the recall of paragraph materials or in recognition performance. Training did cause some decline in subject complaints about their memory ability, regardless of whether performance improved. This finding indicates that elderly complaints about memory may not be related objectively to actual memory decrements.

LEARNING

Importance

Most people maintain the ability to learn throughout adulthood. Such capacity is vitally necessary since each new event in an adult's life requires new knowledge and abilities. Getting married, becoming parents, assuming a new job, moving to another house or community, retiring, and adjusting to a rapidly changing world all require learning.

Learning, Memory, and Performance

Learning and memory are inextricably intertwined. Unless individuals learn well, they have little to recall. Conversely, if their memory is poor, they cannot learn much. Learning is the acquisition of knowledge; memory is the storage, retrieval, and processing of knowledge. Each ability depends on the other.

A distinction must be made between learning as an internal process and performance as an external act. If performance declines, we assume, often incorrectly, that learning has decreased. Performance, not learning ability, may decline because of many environmental factors, lack of motivation, or psychological disturbances. Before making definitive statements about changes in learning ability as one ages, it is necessary to sort out factors that affect performance. Much of what was previously regarded as learning ability deficiency in later life is now seen as a problem in the ability to express learned information—as a difficulty older people have in adapting to a task and demonstrating what they know. There is little disagreement regarding performance declines in later life, but controversy exists about how much learning ability declines with age.

Verbal Learning

Verbal learning research uses two different types of tasks: *paired-associate learning* and *serial learning* tasks. In paired-associate learning tasks, subjects must learn associations between pairs of verbal items (for example, *book-car*), and then be able to supply the correct word to complete the pair when a particular stimulus word is given. Paired-associate verbal learning ability is measured by the number of trials required for perfect recitation, or to reach a designated level of proficiency, or by the number of errors made per trial. In serial learning tasks, subjects must learn a list of simple words, usually in the exact order presented. Learning ability is measured by the number of errors per trial or by the number of trials required for one or more perfect recitations of the list.

Motivation, Relevance, Meaning

Every teacher knows that the desire to learn (the degree of motivation) is an important key to success. Intrinsic motivation comes from within, from physical and/or psychological drives. Thus, a person who has an emotional need to excel is driven to learn; so is a person who wants to learn to achieve status. These people are driven by personal needs for ego satisfaction and strive harder than those who have lesser needs and desires.

Motivation is also enhanced through outside incentives. The promise of promotion or increased financial rewards, even verbal praise, may stimulate greater efforts. However, no amount of incentive works unless the subjects feel the rewards are attainable. Prizes seen as virtually unattainable result in lower peformance scores, since the subjects do not try. Even among students of high ability, there is no significantly different effect between virtually unattainable prizes and no prizes at all.

Motivation is also enhanced if assigned tasks are more meaningful and personally relevant. Laboratory investigations that tend to involve highly abstract tasks may not be meaningful at all. As a result, subjects may refuse to exert themselves to learn. The most meaningful tasks are those that are also familiar. In paired-associate learning tasks, for example, older learners do better with familiar pairings. With nonsense combinations, such as combining the letters *tl* with the word *insane,* older subjects either have more difficulty or they do not try.

Associative Strength

The degree of association, or so-called *associative strength,* also affects learning. Some words go together naturally. For example, *table* goes with *chair* more than with *hat.* Thus, *table-chair* has greater associative strength. The higher the associative strength, and the more meaningful and familiar the word lists, the less likely older adults are to show a decline in learning ability.

Autonomic Arousal

Autonomic arousal is stimulation of the autonomic nervous system. The degree of autonomic arousal has been measured in a number of ways: by the level of free fatty acids (FFA) in the blood (the higher the level the greater the degree of arousal) and by heart rate, blood pressure, and skin conductance. It was assumed in the past that older persons showed less autonomic arousal during learning tasks because they did not get as involved as younger persons. Consequently, they did not learn as much as younger subjects. Actually, just the opposite may occur. Powell and associates (1980) showed that the blood pressure of older subjects (between fifty-five and seventy) increased during serial learning tasks, and that this increase was positively related to serial learning ability and better performance on the easier tasks. If, however, learning tasks became too complex, the positive relationship to an increase in autonomic arousal was obscured. Subjects did less well because of anxiety. Older adults can become so emotionally aroused and anxious that their energies are dissipated in undifferentiated, haphazard ways, and learning performance declines. When given a drug that suppresses the action of the autonomic nervous system (hence, anxiety and upset), learning performance improves (Eisdorfer et al. 1970).

Pacing, Speed

Pacing refers to the time intervals between stimuli. In paired-associate tasks, subjects must learn a series of paired words or letters, such as *ball-bat* or *boy-girl*. These paired associates may be presented at two-second, four-second, or longer intervals. It has been found that it takes more time for older adults to learn than it does younger adults. When allowed to study paired associates on a slower or a self-paced schedule, the learning ability of older adults improves. The total time to learn continues to increase with advancing age.

Once the pairs are learned, older adults also take longer to respond to the stimulus word. Thus, if the word *ball* is presented, older adults take longer to respond with the correct word *bat*. Older adults need more time to show what they have learned; otherwise it appears they have not learned as well as younger adults.

Summary of Learning and Age

The most extensive body of longitudinal data on adult learning appears in the Baltimore Longitudinal Study of Men (Arenberg and Robertson-Tshabo 1977). For the most part, these were well-educated men of high socioeconomic status. The data consisted of paired-associate and serial-performance learning data measured at two different speed intervals for each task. Cross-sectional analysis showed small age differences before age sixty and large age differences thereafter, particularly at the faster pacing speeds. Analysis of the longitudinal data for both the paired-associate and serial-performance learning tasks showed similar results; the greatest increases in learning errors occurred after age sixty, using both the slow-

and fast-paced intervals. The youngest group of men (initially between thirty and thirty-eight) either showed a slight improvement in scores or the smallest mean decline (depending on the speed of pacing) over a seven-year period. The two groups of men between thirty-nine and fifty-four years of age showed moderate mean declines; the two oldest groups, initially sixty-one to seventy-four, showed the largest mean declines. Even among men who learned at the slower pace, the earliest born cohorts showed the most decline and the latest born cohorts the least. Mean errors were consistently greater for older subsamples within each cohort, indicating that they performed less effectively than younger subsamples from the same cohort. This evidence indicates a verbal learning deficit in the later years of life.

Enhancing Learning

One purpose of research is to provide practical knowledge that can be used. The research on adult learning can be beneficial to adult education. People who teach adults and adults who seek to learn can benefit from understanding and practicing the following important principles:

1. Task performance and learning improve as adult anxiety regarding proficiency decreases. Establishing rapport and offering assurance, moral support, and assistance help reduce anxiety.
2. Adults need opportunities to express what they do know and to exhibit their talents. They often know and are capable of more than they show. A natural cautiousness about doing something wrong makes them wary of exhibiting their skills.
3. Careful instruction and directions help overcome adult cautiousness and stimulate performance.
4. Adults do much better with materials and tasks that are relevant and meaningful to them. They can hardly be expected to show their intelligence on tests or tasks they consider stupid (Ridley et al. 1979; Barrett and Wright 1981).
5. Adults are able to perform better with materials and tasks that are organized into logical categories or sequences. They benefit from organizational aids and suggestions that help them categorize and group materials into meaningful associations.
6. Motivation is increased if adults comprehend the reasons for learning or for performance. Offering explanations about the relevance of the material or task and providing rewards and incentives, within the realm of possibility, stimulate effort (Hartley and Walsh 1980).
7. Because adults value accuracy more than speed, tasks must be paced to allow maximum learning and performance. Self-paced assignments are often accomplished more proficiently than those with severe time limitations.

8. Maximum and repeated exposure to material or tasks to be learned encourages deeper processing and enhances learning and performance.

9. Reducing all forms of interference and distracting stimuli enhances learning. If present materials and tasks are completely learned before new ones are introduced, interference effects are minimized and learning enhanced (Arenberg 1976; Parkinson et al. 1980).

10. The use of both visual and auditory presentations in the teaching process enhances learning more than the use of only one method.

11. Adult performance declines as fatigue increases. Offering appropriate breaks and rest periods may actually improve learning and performance.

SUMMARY

Memory involves three major processes: acquiring information, storing it, and retrieving it. The three-fold memory model describes three levels of storage: sensory, short-term, and long-term. Information passes from one compartment to another. It is received by the senses and held briefly. Part of it is then passed to the short-term storage. Because short-term storage has a limited capacity, the information is further rehearsed and transferred to long-term storage. Memory efficiency depends on the three processes of acquiring, storing, and retrieving information.

Information received by the senses is held briefly in several specific sensory stores. The two most important are the auditory or echoic memory store and the visual or iconic memory store. Other sensory stores include tactual information and smell. Adults of all ages show a decay of auditory, visual, and tactual memory stores in less than a second. Tactual memory seems to decline the fastest. Visual memory does not decline much before age sixty and declines faster than auditory memory after age sixty. The durability of a memory trace depends partly on the attention given to it. When adults are distracted during a stimulus, the information is processed less deeply and they remember less.

Primary or short-term memory does not change with age, or it decreases only slightly, unless the ability has been seriously impaired by physical deterioration. Age differences occur after the information has been transferred from primary to secondary or long-term memory, which shows decline with age. Age differences can be partly eliminated if information is grouped in categories and if information is meaningful and relevant. There is less age loss in recognition performance than in free recall. The ability to remember over a long time depends partially on how often the material has been recalled and used in the intervening years. Retrieval from long-term memory is enhanced if the information is familiar. Overall, older subjects are poorer than younger subjects at recalling and recognizing events of the past. Subjects of all ages remember best those sociohistorical events that occurred when the subjects were fifteen to twenty-five years old.

Some evidence exists that older subjects show acquisition deficits, especially in encoding and processing information. As people age, they also require more time to remember, that is, to search memory stores and retrieve information. Memory training can improve recall ability.

Learning and memory are inextricably intertwined. Unless individuals learn, they have little to recall. However, older people often know much more than they can express. What has been regarded as a deficiency in learning ability is primarily a problem in the ability to express information.

Many numerous factors affect learning: motivation or the desire to learn, the associated strength of the information, anxiety, the degree of autonomic arousal of the subject (too little or too much effects learning negatively), and the pacing and speed with which information is presented. The greatest increase in learning errors occurs after age sixty, using both slow- and fast-paced intervals.

Adult learning can be enhanced in many ways: reduce their anxiety, give them opportunities to express what they know, provide careful instructions and directions, and present materials that are relevant, meaningful, and organized. Also, adults must comprehend the reason for learning. Teachers must present assignments at an appropriate pace, give maximum and repeated exposure to the material, reduce interference and distractions, and use both visual and auditory presentations. Finally, if appropriate breaks and rest periods are provided, learning and performance will improve.

13

Thinking, Problem Solving, Problem Finding, Comprehension, and Creativity

THINKING

Concrete versus Abstract Thinking

The word *concrete* implies something actual or real, existing in reality as an actual substance, thing, or instance; something that is *abstract* exists only as an idea or thought, conceived apart from concrete realities, specific objects, or actual instances. Thus, the word *man* is concrete, whereas *masculinity* is abstract. Laws are concrete, but justice is often an abstraction.

Concrete thought concerns what is real, for example, objects that can be seen, identified, manipulated, classified, and arranged or combined in various ways; concrete ideas grow out of actual experiences. Abstract thinking goes beyond the real to the possible. It enables thinkers to project themselves into the future, to distinguish present reality from possibility. Abstract thinkers generate new and different ideas and thoughts and become inventive, imaginative, and original.

Concrete Operational Stage

Jean Piaget contributed more than any other psychologist to our understanding of the qualitative changes in cognitive processes that occur as children grow to adulthood. The last two stages of cognitive development, according to Piaget, are the *concrete operational stage* and the *formal operational stage* (Inhelder and Piaget 1958; Piaget 1972; Piaget and Inhelder 1969). The concrete operational stage of development relies on logical means to solve problems involving concrete objects or experiences. This involves a number of abilities: seriation, classification, symmetry, associativity, negation, and conservation.

Seriation involves the ability to group objects according to increasing or decreasing size or weight, or to arrange them alphabetically. Classification involves the ability to group like objects together. Thus, all yellow objects, or all flowers, or all dogs are grouped together. Objects can also be arranged into hierarchical classifications. For example, dogs and cats can be put into separate classes, and then dogs further subdivided according to breed, color, or size. Objects can belong to more than one class. An animal can be a dog, a Labrador retriever, male, and black, at the same time. Also, two or more classes can be combined into a larger, more comprehensive class. All men and women equal all adults. But what is grouped together can also be taken apart, so that the process of combining classes is reversible. All adults except all men equal all women.

Symmetry involves understanding that some relationships are reciprocal—two brothers are brothers to each other. A parent has a child, and the child also has a parent. Associativity requires recognizing the association between things to reach the same conclusion in different ways. For example, (2 plus 3) plus 5 equals 10; and (5 plus 2) plus 3 also equals 10. Different substitutions can be made to produce the same result. Thus, (5 plus 4) plus 1 also equals 10.

Negation combines an operation with its opposite or inverse operation to cancel the whole thing out. Thus, $+A - A = 0$. People learn they can add or subtract objects or make decisions and then reverse the process.

Conservation involves the realization that the configuration of objects can be changed while maintaining sameness. Conservation applies to volume, substance, weight, length, or to wholes. The conservation of volume is demonstrated by pouring the contents of glass A into a narrower glass B, resulting in a higher liquid level in glass B. Early school-age children reason that because the liquid is higher in B, the liquid has increased in volume, regardless of the fact that they saw it poured from one container to another. But a person at the concrete operational stage of development reasons that the amount of water is the same because nothing has been added or taken away. The situation is also reversible. By pouring the water from B back into A, you restore the original situation.

In a conservation of substance experiment, a ball of clay is shown and then rolled into a long, thin shape or into a few smaller balls. The person watching, who is operating at a concrete operational stage of thinking, knows that the original amount of clay remains the same, even though the shape is distorted. In a conservation of length experiment, a long, straight line is shown and then broken into two or more lines. In conservation of wholes, the spatial arrangements of objects are changed, giving only the appearance of change.

Changes in Concrete Operational Abilities with Age

Various experiments have been conducted with adults to show how their concrete operational abilities change as they age. For example, one cross-sectional study compared the categorizing or classification behavior of seven groups, ages five, six, seven, nineteen to twenty-one, sixty to sixty-nine, seventy to seventy-nine, and eighty to eighty-nine (Cicirelli 1976). All subjects were asked to sort the drawings of fifty common objects (fork, chair, cup, book, etc.) into groups that belonged together and to separate those that did not fit any group. Significant age changes were observed. In relation to younger age groups, elderly subjects tended to divide the objects into fewer groups, leave more objects ungrouped, and make less use of logical bases for groupings.

Since the study was cross-sectional rather than longitudinal, the question arises whether those differences represented true age differences or generational, educational, and occupational differences. However, the finding that differences in occupation or educational level did not account for observed age differences supported a hypothesis of regressive age changes. These results were similar to those of other studies that showed that the elderly have diminished categorization skills, forming fewer and less abstract categories than middle-aged subjects (Denney 1974; Kogan 1974).

However, the question remains whether this represents a true loss in ability or merely a preference for certain types of response. Denney (1974) found that the ability to use similarity as a basis for grouping was not lost when elderly subjects were first exposed to a brief modeling procedure. Certainly, their ordinary environment did not require logical classification, so they saw no need to do this in the test unless they first saw it demonstrated. Kogan (1974) felt the elderly were prone to try something more adventurous, which accounted for their different groups.

A number of studies have measured the abilities of different age groups to make correct judgments about conservation problems. Rubin (1976) found no differences between middle-aged and healthy older adults in solving conservation problems, even after false, disconfirming examples had been given. Both age groups were less adept than college students, but relative ability over a major portion of the adult years was confirmed.

Chance and colleagues (1978) compared the ability of college students with that of elderly subjects, aged sixty-five to ninety-four, to solve a number of conservation tasks: conservation of substance, weight, volume, and area. They found no support for the hypothesis that cognitive regression occurs as part of the normal aging process. They emphasized, however, that careful interviewing and discussion made all subjects as comfortable and responsive as possible. Also, their elderly subjects were not medically ill or severely sensory impaired. Although some were infirm, they lived in a supportive environment (a private retirement home) that allowed maximum personal freedom and activities within the home or outside in community affairs.

The outcome of studies depends somewhat on the use of realistic, practical problems. Elderly adults are more likely to understand conservation of substance when given material common to their experience—hamburger and a lump of ground beef, a glass of whiskey and several shot glasses, or a ball of pie dough divided into several smaller portions.

Formal Operational Stage

The formal operational stage of cognitive ability implies the capability to separate the content of a problem or set of statements from the form itself. It includes the ability to think abstractly about meaning and content, to go beyond the actual object or situation in solving problems. This type of ability extends beyond concrete operations, which sort classes, relations, or numbers into logical groupings but never integrate them into a single, logical system. Formal operations superimpose *propositional logic* on the logic of classes or relations and give meaning to relationships.

Formal operations also employ *hypothetico-deductive reasoning*, which includes formulating a hypothesis or explanation of a phenomenon, deducing a prediction, and then testing it with other propositions and against reality to establish its validity. By varying a single factor while keeping others constant, the experimenter can sort out cause and effect to discover the reasons for things and factors that correlate with them. This type of deductive reasoning is basic to all scientific theory.

One of Piaget's experiments, which led to discovering the strategies used in solving problems, involved a pendulum (Inhelder and Piaget 1958). The selected subjects were shown a pendulum suspended from a string. The problem was to discover what factors would affect the oscillatory speed of the pendulum. The subjects were to investigate four possible causes: changing the length of the pendulum, changing its weight, releasing the pendulum from various heights, and starting the pendulum with various degrees of force. The subjects were allowed to solve the problem in any way they chose.

Those using formal operational thought showed three basic characteristics in their problem-solving behavior. First, they planned their investigations systematically. They began to test all possible causes for variation in the pendulum swings: long or short string, light or heavy weight, high or low heights, and various degrees of force. Second, they recorded the outcomes accurately and with little bias under the different experimental conditions. Third, they were able to draw logical conclusions.

For example, they observed that height of drop and degree of force did not effect oscillatory speed. Believing that pendulum weight or length of string might be involved, they tried different combinations of weight with different combinations of string length, only to find that whatever the weight, the oscillatory speed remained the same. They discovered, however, that changing the string length altered the oscillatory speed. They were able to conclude that pendulum length alone determined the speed of oscillation. The methods and results of this experiment have been replicated by other researchers (Mecke and Mecke 1971).

Other subjects given the same problem may obtain the right answer by trial and error but fail to use systematic and scientific procedures or to be able to explain the solution logically. They tend to form conclusions that seem warranted by the facts. But often these conclusions are premature and false because they have not considered all important facts and cannot reason logically about them. Even when presented with contrary evidence, they tend to hold tenaciously to their initial hypothesis and try to make the circumstances fit these preconceived notions.

An important difference between concrete and formal operations is that people using the latter are able to orient themselves toward what is abstract and not immediately present. This facility enables them to project themselves into the future, to distinguish present reality from possibility, and to think about what might be. Some adolescents and adults have not only the capacity to accept and understand what is given, but also the ability to conceive of what might be possible or what might occur. Because they can construct ideas, they have the ability to elaborate on what they receive, to generate new or different ideas and thoughts. They become inventive, imaginative, and original in their thinking and let *possibility dominate reality*. This ability to project themselves into the future has many important consequences.

In summary, several characteristics of formal thought become evident. These are the ability to consider two or more variables in complex relations, the ability to determine the effect of one or more variables on another when a certain relationship is suspected among the variables, and the capacity to combine and separate variables in a hypothetical-deductive framework (if this is so, this will happen) so that a reasonable possibility is recognized before the test is made in reality. The fundamental property of formal thought is this reversible maneuvering between reality and possibility. In formal thinking, people can think about thought (propositional logic) and distinguish the real from the possible by formulating hypotheses and testing them against reality.

Another feature of formal thought is that it does not deal with objects directly but with such symbols as numerical or verbal symbols. When verbal statements are substituted for objects, for example, data are translated into representational imagery. Through propositional logic, people can deal with many more operations than is possible with simple groupings of classes and relations. All possible combinations can be explored in various testable hypotheses. In some cases, symbols may be used for symbols. In metaphorical speech or algebraic equations, for example, symbols are used for other words or numbers. The capacity to symbolize symbols makes formal operational thought much more flexible than concrete operational thought. Words can carry double or triple meanings. Cartoons can represent a complete story that would otherwise have to be explained in words. It is no accident that algebra is not taught to elementary school children or that children have difficulty understanding political cartoons or religious symbols. Until approximately junior high age, they do not have the capacity for formal thought.

Achieving Formal Operational Thought

Piaget described his concept of the formal operational stage of cognitive development in this way.

> All normal subjects attain the stage of formal operations of structuring if not between 11–12 to 14–15 in any case between 15 and 30 years. However, they reach this stage in different areas according to their aptitudes and their professional specializations (advanced studies or different types of apprenticeships for the various trades). (Piaget 1972, 10)

This suggests that solving the types of physical and logical problems Piaget used to investigate formal operations depends on a person's skill and interests, which have been learned while preparing for a profession or trade or while practicing it. Thus, a sociology or political science student may be able to deal with abstract social or political problems at a formal level but not with problems requiring a knowledge of science. Specialized aptitude or training prepares one to solve certain types of problems in formal operational tests.

Piaget also admits "that perhaps in extremely disadvantageous conditions, such a type of thought will never really take shape" (1972, 7). Not all adults reach the level of formal operational thinking. One researcher, using Piaget's III–A level to measure the percentage of females achieving formal operational thinking, demonstrated that 32 percent of eleven-year-old girls, 67 percent of college women, and 54 percent of adult females had reached that level (Tomlinson-Keasey 1972). But when the more advanced III–B criteria were used in measurements, the percentages were 4 percent for girls, 23 percent for college women, and 17 percent for adult females (364). According to Piaget, being able to think abstractly and use formal operational thinking is the highest, most inclusive level of adaptation to the environment, and it enables people to consider alternative solutions to situations. Not all adults develop this ability.

Actually, no adult needs to rely exclusively on formal operational thinking. Carpentry skills are more dependent on sensorimotor skills and concrete abilities. Designing an imaginative house or estimating the value of the house in twenty years, based on real estate values, inflation, and depreciation, requires formal operational thinking. Having the ability to conceptualize, theorize, symbolize, and reason logically is important in many aspects of life.

Formal Operational Abilities and Age

One theory suggests that aging adults use their Piagetian abilities in the order opposite to their acquisition during childhood and adolescence. In other words, they regress to the earlier cognitive levels of childhood. But this theory has little basis for support. Papalia and DelVento Bielby (1974) reviewed the published Piagetian research and found some regression among elderly adults, but the research itself had too many problems to justify drawing similarities between children and elderly adults in their operational levels of cognitive thinking. Many studies have no controls for differences in living environments, education, overall health status, or occupational experiences. Certainly, age is no more important than these other factors. Furthermore, many of the Piagetian tasks seem totally irrelevant to adults. They are not familiar with them because they never use them in their daily activities. Those adults whose activities require a lot of abstract thinking, using logical reasoning and symbols, do very well because they are practiced and because they are motivated to perform well on familiar tasks.

PROBLEM-SOLVING ABILITIES

Abstract Abilities

Overall, some adults show decrement of abstract problem-solving abilities with age. Four groups of adults were tested on their abilities to solve a problem requiring deductive reasoning (Hartley 1981). The four groups were younger adults (mean age 20), middle-aged adults (mean age 41.4), older adults (mean age 65.4), and community-dwelling older adults (mean age 71.5). The younger adults were enrolled in college; the middle-aged adults and younger groups of older adults were college graduates; the community-dwelling older group had completed an average of 14.33 years of education. Figure 13.1 shows that a significantly smaller number of adults in the older age groups were able to solve the problem than among the younger and middle-aged groups. One reason was that the older non-

FIGURE 13.1   Percentage of Problem Solvers As a Function of Age Group

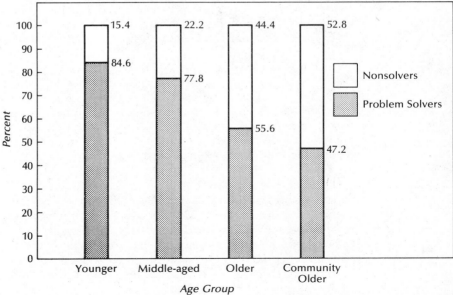

Adapted from A. A. Hartley, "Adult Age Differences in Deductive Reasoning Processes." Reprinted by permission of *Journal of Gerontology* 36 (November 1981): 700–706.

solvers were not as capable of differentiating relevant from irrelevant information. (See also Hoyer et al. 1979.) They based solutions on hunches rather than on available evidence and were inflexible in their thinking. They seemed able to process information on only one dimension at a time, perhaps because of reduced ability to do formal operational thinking. They probably also differed in general experience. This finding is consistent with other laboratory experiments that showed a decline in abstract reasoning abilities with advancing age (Hayslip and Sterns 1979; Hoyer et al. 1979).

Practical Problem-Solving Abilities

The finding is not consistent, however, with older adults' feelings about themselves. When individuals over sixty-five were asked how they thought their abilities to reason, think, and solve problems had changed throughout their adult lives, 76 percent thought their abilities had increased with age, 20 percent reported no change, and only 4 percent reported that their abilities had declined with age (Williams et al. 1980). But these oldsters were talking about practical problems of everyday living, not about abstract reasoning problems traditionally used in laboratory experiments. Denney and Palmer (1981) found a diminution with age in capacity to do abstract problems but an improvement in the ability to solve practical problems that might actually be encountered. Denney and Palmer (1981) presented two types of problem-solving tasks to adults between twenty and seventy-nine years of age. The first task was a twenty question type of test typically used in problem-solving research. The test results showed that such ability peaked in the late twenties. The second task was designed to measure the ability to solve problems presented in real-life situations. The following are three examples of the real-life situations.

> Let's say that one evening you go to the refrigerator and notice that it is not cold inside, but rather, it's warm. What would you do?
> Let's say that you live in a house with a basement. One night there is a flash flood and you notice that your basement is being flooded with water coming in the window wells. What would you do?
> If you were traveling by car and got stranded out on an inter-state highway during a blizzard, what would you do? (Denney and Palmer 1981, 325)

The test results showed that the ability to solve such practical problems increased during early adulthood and did not peak until the late forties. The researchers cautioned that this was a cross-sectional study so one must be careful about drawing strong conclusions with reference to age. Since cross-sectional studies usually overemphasize decline with age, the fact that the ability to solve practical problems actually increased is even more significant.

Other problem-solving research shows similar results. Young adults do not appear to solve the practical problems of everyday living any more efficiently or even as efficiently as older adults, although they do better on tests that are age-sensitive (discriminate among age groups). Problem-solving abilities may also be improved with training (Denney 1980; Sanders and Sanders 1978).

PROBLEM-FINDING ABILITIES

A Fifth Stage

Recent investigations of the Piagetian stage of formal operations suggest that progressive changes in thought structures may extend beyond the level of formal operations. The suggestion is that formal structures may not be the final equilibrium; they may be building blocks for new structures that might be identified as a fifth stage of cognitive development. The implication is that cognitive growth in adulthood is continuous; there is no end point beyond which new structures may appear. Researchers continue to seek these new structures (Arlin 1975; Arlin 1977; Commons, Richards, and Kuhn 1982; Getzels and Csikzentmihalyi 1970; Gruber and Barrett 1973).

Although the results of investigations are still tentative, there is some evidence that a fifth stage of development can be differentiated. It has been labeled a *problem-finding stage* (Arlin 1975). This new stage characterizes creative thought, the envisioning of new questions, and the discovery of new heuristics in adult thought. The traditional formal operations stage is a problem-solving stage. The new fifth stage represents an ability to discover problems not yet delineated, to formulate these problems, or to raise general questions from ill-defined problems.

Problem Solving and Problem Finding

The relationship between formal operational thinking (the problem-solving stage) and the new stage of problem finding should be such that subjects successful in problem finding should also be characterized as Piagetian formal operational thinkers. However, not all subjects in the problem-solving stage should be characterized as having reached the problem-finding stage. The establishment of the relationship would satisfy the stage criterion of sequencing.

Arlin (1975) generally found this sequencing in her research with female college seniors. All subjects high in problem finding had reached formal operational thinking, but not all subjects who had reached formal thinking were high in problem finding. Furthermore, none of the subjects who had failed to reach formal operational thinking were high in problem finding.

Questions

Even though it is significant, this exploratory study raises more questions than it answers. If only a certain percent of the adult population ever attains formal operational thinking, which is a necessary but not sufficient condition for developing problem-finding operations, what proportion of the population can be expected to reach this hypothesized fifth stage of development? If this fifth stage can be delineated exactly, research ought to be able to define the processes of inventing, discovering, interacting, and constructing knowledge in terms of the fifth stage. There is certainly a need for further research efforts.

COMPREHENSION

Word Familiarity

A number of studies have been conducted to determine age-related abilities of adults to comprehend linguistic meanings of individual words, sentences, or paragraphs. Tests of word familiarity have shown that adults generally show performance improvement to ages fifty through fifty-nine (mean age fifty-five), after which scores decline (Monge and Gardner 1972). However, as shown in Figure 13.2, the scores of people with high education (above high school) were never as low as the scores of those with

FIGURE 13.2 Performance on Word Familiarity As a Function of Age Cohort and Education

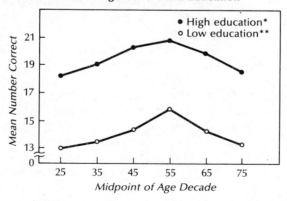

*Beyond High School
**High School or below

Adapted from: R. H. Monge and E. F. Gardner, *A Program of Research in Adult Differences in Cognitive Performance and Learning: Backgrounds for Adult Education and Vocational Training*. Final Report (Project N. 6-1963, Grant No. OEG 1–706193-0149), 1972.

low education (high school or less), regardless of age. Thus, educational level was found to be more important than age itself.

Sentence Comprehension

Sentence comprehension research has revealed that the ability to comprehend relativized sentences (complex sentences with a number of relative clauses) remains stable until the sixties, after which ability declines with age (Feier and Gerstman 1980). However, comprehension of sentences presented auditorily depends partially on the rate of presentation. Material presented either too rapidly or slowly is not comprehended as readily as material presented at a normal rate (Schmitt and McCroskey 1981).

Prose Comprehension

Belmore (1981) tested the ability of adults to process and comprehend linguistic meanings of short prose passages they were asked to read. Older adults (mean age 66.5) were able to comprehend the meanings almost as well as younger adults (mean age 18.3). The older subjects were correct 83 percent of the trials, the younger subjects 91 percent of the trials. However, when testing for levels of comprehension was delayed, older adults showed impairment in retaining the information over a period of time. They comprehended almost as well initially, but they could not remember the material as long as the younger subjects could.

CREATIVITY

Meaning

Creativity implies two different concepts. One is of originality of thought or expression. A creative writer writes with a unique or different style, or about a subject others have not covered, or deals with a familiar subject in a new and fresh way. An imaginative artist may create a new style of painting. The same principle applies to other fields, for example, science, medicine, and architecture. The really creative person makes a unique contribution, discovers something, or does something no one else has done.

The second concept implied in creativity is productivity: creating a quantity of new products or services. The person who has original ideas is a creative thinker, but unless those ideas are developed or put into practice, they are not meaningful. Creativity is acting on an idea to translate it into something useful. An architect may conceive a new type of construction, but unless it is developed, drawn up, and used in a building, nothing has been created except the idea.

Creativity in Late Adulthood

Much has been written about developing creativity in children but little about creativity in adulthood. Do educators and psychologists equate creativity with youthfulness? If so, the notion is fallacious. Outstanding contributions have been made by many people during late adulthood, as the following examples show.

- Will and Ariel Durant completed their eleven-volume *The Story of Civilization* when he was ninety and she was seventy-seven.
- Sophocles wrote *Oedipus Rex* at seventy-five.
- Sigmund Freud wrote his last book at eighty-three.
- Von Benden discovered the reduction of chromosomes at seventy-four.
- Mahatma Gandhi launched his movement to gain India's independence at seventy-two.
- Cecil B. DeMille produced *The Ten Commandments* at seventy-five.
- Claude Monet began his *Water Lily* series at seventy-three.

Creativity As Quality of Production

The lack of attention to creativity in adulthood has resulted in a paucity of research. The work by Lehman (1962, 1966) is usually cited as the most important on the subject, even though it is now more than twenty years old. Lehman is still cited because little subsequent research is available to supplement his work. Lehman measured creativity by the quality of work achieved by adults in the various fields of science, medicine, philosophy, psychology, art, invention, and other areas. His method was to tabulate by age groups the frequency with which high-quality productions were listed in historical accounts covering a period of more than 400 years. He found that in most fields people produced the greatest proportion of superior work during their thirties. After that there was a decline in high quality production. About 80 percent of superior work was completed by age fifty. The rate of lower-quality work peaked somewhat later. He also found some fields of endeavor peaked earlier than others. However, in all fields, individual variations were so great that Lehman emphasized that usefulness was not limited to age and that age was not always a causative factor in the decline of creative quality. People made valuable contributions at all ages.

Zusne (1976) investigated the age at which eminent psychologists published their most significant works. A comparison of his findings with those of Lehman (1966) showed remarkably similar results.

Creativity As Quantity of Work

Lehman has had his critics. Dennis (1966) maintained that it is almost impossible to make objective judgments of the quality of a person's work.

A person's early, pioneering work is more likely to be mentioned than later work. Older work is usually designated masterwork more often than recent work. Thus, investigations tend to show that earlier work at younger ages is superior. Besides, competition increases as the years pass, making it difficult for a person's later work to be labeled superior. Dennis (1966) maintained Lehman's analysis of quality through bibliographies and citations favored early work and distorted the findings. He insisted that quantity of output, not quality, is a far better measure of creativity.

Dennis's research revealed that peak performance years occurred much later than Lehman maintained, that performance often continued over many years of the life cycle, and that the quantity of output at each age varied depending on the field of endeavor. Output in creative arts and science peaked in the forties and declined thereafter, with artistic output declining the most and scientific output falling only a little. Output of adults in the humanities continued to rise from the thirties to the sixties, with little decline even through the seventies. Figure 13.3 shows the data presented by Dennis and represented graphically by Botwinick (1967).

Individual Variations

Why individuals in the humanities remain creative into late adulthood, whereas the output of artists and scientists declines, remains a question. Certainly, individual variations exist in every field. Some people remain intellectually alive, active, and inventive, continuing to question, search, and participate fully in life. Others become stagnant at an early age. What happens depends partly on individual attitudes about oneself and the aging process. Life can be a fascinating challenge throughout the adult life span.

FIGURE 13.3   Creative Output of People in the Humanities, Sciences, and Arts over the Life Cycle

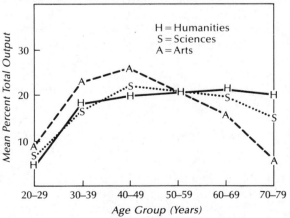

Adapted from: Botwinick, *Cognitive Processes in Maturity and Old Age* (New York: Springer Publishing Co., Inc., 1967).

The creative person, young or old, can contribute much to human endeavor.

SUMMARY

Concrete thinking concerns something real or actual. Abstract thinking concerns something that exists only as an idea or thought, something that is possible rather than actual.

The last two stages of cognitive development, according to Piaget, are the concrete operational stage and the formal operational stage. The concrete operational stage is the ability to use logical means to solve problems involving concrete objects or experiences. This requires several abilities: (1) seriation or the ability to group objects according to size and so forth, (2) classification or the ability to group like objects together and arrange them into hierarchical classifications, (3) symmetry or an understanding of reciprocal relationships, (4) associativity or the ability to see relationships so that any substitutions made still produce the same results, (5) negation or combining an operation with its opposite or inverse operation to cancel the whole thing out, and (6) conservation or the realization that the configuration of objects can be changed and sameness maintained.

In classification experiments. elderly people tend to arrange objects into fewer and less abstract categories than do middle-aged subjects. Whether this can be attributed to age itself is uncertain. The elderly may not see any reasons for logical classifications or they may be more adventurous than younger subjects. Other research shows no differences between middle-aged and older subjects on solving conservation problems. There is no support for the thesis that elderly subjects regress to a lower stage of development. The elderly do best on realistic, practical problems using familiar objects.

The formal operational stage of cognitive development includes three abilities: the capacity to use propositional logic to show relationships and to solve problems; the ability to combine and separate variables in a hypothetico-deductive framework so a hypothesis can be formulated and tested; and the ability to escape the concrete present and think abstractly about the possible. In formal thought, reality is secondary to possibility. Formal thought also uses symbols or symbols of symbols to impart meaning and explore all possible combinations in various hypotheses tested.

Not all adults reach the formal operational stage of development. However, not all activities require formal thought; sensorimotor skills and concrete abilities are often used. To think abstractly and to conceptualize, theorize, symbolize, and reason logically requires formal operational thought. Adults whose activities require abstract thinking are more likely to do well on formal operational tasks than are those who never use this type of thinking in their daily activities.

Some adults show some decrement of abstract problem-solving abilities with age, but the ability to solve practical, everyday problems may not peak until the late forties and it remains fairly high thereafter. Problem-solving abilities can also be improved with training.

The ability to comprehend linguistic meanings of words, sentences, and prose passages increases to the late fifties or to the early seventies before gradual decline occurs. However, at all ages, the scores of adults with education above high school are never as low as those with less education, indicating that educational level is a more important factor than age.

Creativity implies two things: originality of thought or expression and productivity (creating a quantity of new products or services). Many adults remain active and creative well into late adulthood. When measuring creativity as quality of production, Lehman found creativity peaked in the early thirties, with 80 percent of quality work completed by fifty. Dennis felt that quantity of output was a more important measure of creativity than quality. When measured in this way, he found that output in the creative arts and sciences peaked in the forties and declined thereafter, but the output of adults in the humanities continued to rise through the sixties. Certainly, wide individual variations exist in every field. Some people remain active and inventive well into old age, continuing to contribute much to human endeavor.

Part V

Individual and Family Living

14

Never-Married Adults

NEVER-MARRIED VERSUS DELAYED MARRIAGE

Trends

For most people, becoming an adult means getting married, having children, and raising a family (see chapter 2). A small minority (about 5 percent), however, never marry. Figure 14.1 shows the percentages of each age group who have never married (U.S. Dept. of Commerce 1983). According to this figure, large numbers of persons remain unmarried until fairly late in life. Among the twenty-five to twenty-nine-year-olds, one-third of males and one-fifth of females were unmarried. More than 16 percent of males and 10 percent of females between thirty and thirty-four had never married. This means there are many unmarrieds in the young adult population. By ages forty to forty-four, however, the percentages of those remaining unmarried were cut in half.

Figure 14.2 shows a marked trend to marry at later and later ages. In 1960, somewhat more than 50 percent of males and 28 percent of females between twenty and twenty-four had not married; by 1981, those figures had risen to 70 percent for males and 52 percent for females. Getting married in the early twenties had become the exception, not the rule.

Reasons for Delay

The reasons for the delay in marriage are social, economic, and personal. One particular reason is the changing attitude toward single life. Existing prejudices against single persons, especially against unmarried women, are declining. It is no longer as unacceptable for a woman in her thirties to be unmarried, especially if she has a flourishing career, an active social life, and an outgoing personality. She may be admired by married female friends and pursued by male friends who find her interesting and attractive. However, both family and friends continue to expect that ultimately she will marry. The attitudinal change accepts her decision not to marry young, but not necessarily the idea of remaining single permanently.

The lengthening of the period of education and economic dependency

FIGURE 14.1   Never-Married Persons As Percent of Total Population, by Age and Sex: 1981

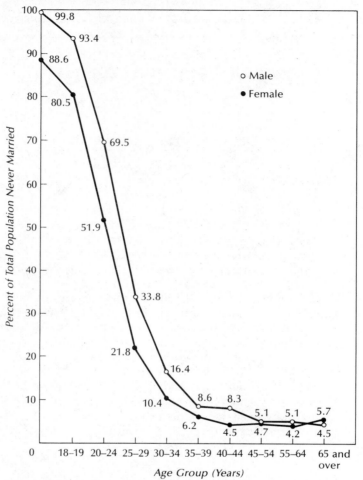

Adapted from: U.S. Department of Commerce, Bureau of the Census, *Statistical Abstract of the United States: 1982, 83,* 103d ed. (Washington, D.C.: U.S. Government Printing Office, 1983), 41.

has greatly influenced the delay of marriage. Long years of education and the accompanying financial drain necessitate postponing marriage for some people. Young adults who go on to higher education are more likely to delay marriage. One study of women in their twenties showed that those who had career aspirations married later in life than those who planned to be housewives (Cherlin 1980). Lower socioeconomic status individuals, with lower educational and vocational aspirations, are more likely to marry at earlier ages (Carlson 1979).

The sexual revolution has also influenced the age at first marriage. An increasing acceptance of premarital sexual intercourse has made sexual

FIGURE 14.2   Never-Married Persons As Percent of Total Population, by Age and Sex: 1960 to 1981.

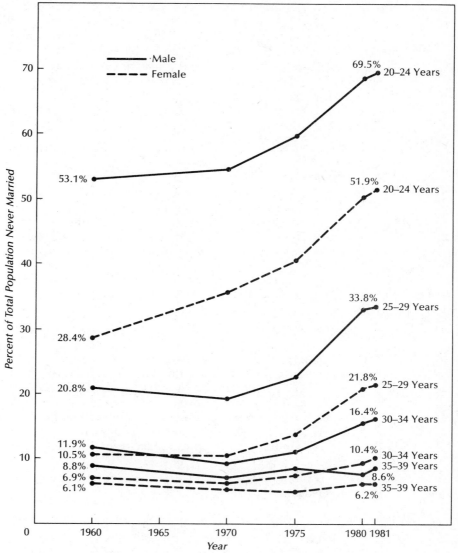

Adapted from: U.S. Department of Commerce, Bureau of the Census, *Statistical Abstract of the United States: 1982, 83,* 103d ed. (Washington, D.C.: U.S. Government Printing Office, 1983), 41.

expression possible at young ages without necessitating marriage. An increase in the acceptance of nonmarital cohabitation also provides some benefits of marriage without the commitment; for example, companionship, sex, and shared housing, living expenses, and physical services. This practice has become appealing to increasing numbers of young adults who see the life-style as a temporary marital substitute or an intermediate step between being single and married.

The women's movement has also influenced views of marriage. Women are encouraged to seek their own identity, apart from a marital identity, and to find career fulfillment and economic self-sufficiency. Marriage has been devalued as the best life for all women. Feminists are not opposed to marriage, but women are encouraged to explore opportunities in addition to family fulfillment. At the least, this attitude has led to marital postponement as women search out and explore other options.

WHY SOME PEOPLE REMAIN SINGLE

Deliberate Choice

For some of the small minority who never marry, this is a matter of deliberate choice. The clearest example is members of religious orders who take vows of chastity. Another example is people who perceive marriage as incompatible with their careers.

Lack of Opportunity

At the other extreme are people who would prefer to marry but never have the chance. Included are people with marked physical or mental handicaps that preclude marriage. Also included are women who are caught in the marriage squeeze, that is, who have difficulty finding eligible male partners (Glick 1977). Until 1940, the male population in this country exceeded the female population. Since then, adult women have outnumbered men. The older the age group, the greater the discrepancy in numbers. As a result, larger and larger numbers of women are competing for marriage partners from a smaller group of men.

Personality Problems

Stereotypically, people do not marry because they have personality problems. They are considered hostile toward the opposite sex or are homosexual. Some are regarded as immature, unwilling to assume responsibility, neurotic, or emotionally fixated on a parent; others are deemed socially inadequate or fixated on a lost love. Certain stereotypes focus on economics: people are too poor to marry or unwilling to share their wealth with others (Cargan and Melko 1982). These stereotypes imply that marriage is a desired state, and that the single person has not attained it because he or she is unfit, incomplete, or abnormal. Although common in years past, this view is oversimplified. At the least, it applies only to a small percentage of singles.

Circumstances

For many people, remaining unmarried permanently is not necessarily a matter of deliberate choice but rather a result of such circumstances as family situations, geography, social isolation, or financial condition.

> Mary lived with her widowed father, who was very possessive and protective of her. He made her feel she had an obligation to take care of him. Her father was also very critical of every young man she dated or brought home. None were ever good enough for her according to him. She had several chances to marry but was always dissuaded by her father. She vowed that she would marry after her father died. But the years slipped by. Her father lived until his mid-eighties. By this time, Mary was in her sixties and has remained single.

A comparison of the life histories of twenty never-married men over the age of thirty-five with the experiences of twenty men who first married after the age of thirty-five showed that bachelorhood is primarily a situational rather than a psychological condition (Darling 1976). All the bachelors had been insulated against the usual pressures to marry early, but those who eventually married had experienced changes in their social situations, including shifts in reference groups, changes in their familial relationships (for example, a parent died), and greater exposure to social pressures to marry.

Timing was a crucial factor. Many bachelors married at turning points in their careers: at times of promotion, career changes, or geographical moves. Some married after times of stress, when they felt vulnerable and received the support of significant others, particularly the women they eventually married. Darling concluded that any social state, whether singlehood or marriage, develops as the end point of a series of "situational contingencies, turning points, and commitments" (1976, 3).

Pushes and Pulls

The decision to remain single or to marry involves complex factors. Stein (1978) described the negative and positive influences on this decision as *pushes* and *pulls*. Pushes are negative factors in a situation. For the single person, pushes are influences to marry; for the married, they are influences to leave the situation. Pulls are positive attractions. The single person is pulled to remain so; the married person is pulled to remain married. Table 14.1 shows the pushes and pulls (Stein 1978, 4).

The strength of these pushes and pulls is affected by a number of variables, including age, stage of the life cycle, sexual identification, extent of involvement with parents and family, availability of friends and peers, and perception of choice. For some people, dating patterns, parental pressures, and an acceptance of the cultural script leads to early involvement and marriage. Those who postpone marriage find greater pulls toward

TABLE 14.1   Pushes and Pulls toward Marriage or Singlehood

Toward Marriage

Pushes (negatives in present situations)	Pulls (attractions in potential situations)
Socialization	Approval of parents
Pressure from parents	Desire for children and own family
Desire to leave home	Example of peers
Fear of independence	Romanticization of marriage
Loneliness	Physical attraction
No knowledge or perception of alternatives	Love, emotional attachment
Job availability, wage structure, and promotions	Security, social status, social prestige
Social policies favoring the married and the responses of social institutions	Legitimation of sexual experiences

Toward Singlehood

Pushes (to leave permanent relationships)	Pulls (to remain single or return to singlehood)
Lack of friends, isolation, loneliness	Career opportunities and development
Restricted availability of new experiences	Availability of sexual experiences
Suffocating one-to-one relationship, feeling trapped	Exciting lifestyle, variety of experiences, freedom to change
Obstacles to self-development	Psychological and social autonomy, self-sufficiency
Boredom, unhappiness, and anger	Support structures: sustaining friendships, women's and men's groups, political groups, therapeutic groups, collegial groups
Role playing and conformity to expectations	
Poor communication with mate	
Sexual frustration	

From: P. J. Stein, "The Lifestyles and Life Chances of the Never-Married," *Marriage and Family Review* 1 (July/August 1978): 4. Copyright © 1978 The Haworth Press, Inc., New York.

satisfying careers, work colleagues, and developing friendships, all of which are possible outside marriage (Stein 1978).

SINGLES AND THEIR PARENTS

Staying versus Leaving Home

One stereotype of singles is that their failure to marry is due to immaturity. A man is considered still tied to his mother's apron strings; a woman living at home is still dependent on parents.

Actually, many single men and women are anxious to leave home. They want their independence, the freedom to do as they please without having to answer to parents. Living at home can mean curfews or restrictions against smoking, drinking, or using pot. People living at home imagine the social scene passing them by. Some feel their parents try to influence their love life or intrude into their politics. Lieberman, an associate professor of education at Columbia University Teachers College, commented:

> I have seen a marked difference between the woman who lives at home and other single women in the way they relate to issues and what's happening in the world. . . . If a woman makes an accommodation to stay at home, she is making an accommodation not to try other lifestyles. (Barclay 1976)

Most singles who strain for independence are embarrassed or ashamed of living at home. Their friends make them feel they have not really grown up.

Relationships with Parents

One question that arises is whether a significant percentage of never-marrieds remain single because of unresolved conflicts or problems with parents. The research evidence is somewhat contradictory. Spreitzer and Riley (1974) found that among men and women who never married, very poor relations with mothers were far more characteristic than good or even poor relations. Men who never married were twice as likely to report very poor relations with fathers as men who did marry.

A different relationship existed between girls who never married and their fathers. Twice the percentage of never-married women had good relations with their fathers as had poor relations. Except for the relationships between girls and fathers, Spreitzer and Riley's findings do not support the apron-strings image. The majority of findings indicate singles may have been discouraged by unpleasant family situations. Apparently they were not deterred from marriage by family bonds but by the lack of them.

According to Cargan and Melko (1982), married people were much more likely than single people to have warm, stable current relations with parents. Single people were more likely to report cool relations and arguments with parents. As a result, singles did not visit their parents as often as marrieds. Some singles avoided their parents because of parental pressure to get married, which caused hard feelings and arguments.

LIVING ARRANGEMENTS

Singles' Communities

The stereotyped fantasy pictures groups of singles occupying apartments or condominiums that cater especially to their needs. A case in point is Carl Sandburg Village in Chicago, transformed from a skid-row neighborhood with rundown apartments, greasy spoon taverns, and transient

hotels into nine high-rise buildings surrounded by townhouses and reno-
vated apartments. Nearly three-quarters of the residents eighteen and older
are unmarried. Occupants enjoy an indoor swimming pool, gymnasiums,
restaurants, and other built-in amenities. Rents have sky-rocketed, but
people who cannot afford the leases often get roommates, increasing the
number of unwed couples living together ("The Ways 'Singles' are Changing U.S." 1977).

One of the most popular singles areas on the West Coast is Marina
del Rey, adjacent to Los Angeles, where 9,500 apartment dwellers live on
400 acres of the Pacific waterfront. Singles outnumber marrieds by almost
two to one. Residents live amidst office buildings, restaurants, and bars
and enjoy swimming pools, tennis, and handball courts, a facial salon, and
limousine, bodyguard, and charter-jet services. They also have the largest
man-made pleasure harbor in the world, which moors 6,000 sailboats,
yachts, and cruisers ("The Ways . . ." 1977).

More people are criticizing the life-style epitomized by Marina del
Rey as rootless and superficial. The aging baby boom generation of post-
World War II is beginning to look for a more stable life-style oriented
more toward family and career. In many communities, singles are settling
easily and quickly into traditional family neighborhoods.

Singles' living areas have had their problems. As singles flooded into
new and restored apartments in the Yorkville section of Manhattan, cases
of venereal disease increased dramatically, as did the numbers of prosti-
tutes and burglaries. Skyrocketing rents and taxes drove out many older
ethnic groups.

Sharing Living Spaces

Although large numbers of unmarrieds live in singles' areas or apartments,
more live with the general population. The majority occupy individual
apartments, usually with roommates. The usual pattern is to share apartments and living expenses with one or more persons who provide emotional support and companionship. One college woman lives with three
men, none of whom is her lover. She prefers their company to that of
females. She has become the group leader, requiring a strict rotation of all
responsibilities, including cooking, cleaning, and laundry, and making sure
each person contributes his weekly financial share.

Living Alone

Table 14.2 shows the percent distribution, by age group, of singles living
alone (U.S. Dept. of Commerce 1983). However, this table includes divorced, separated, or widowed people, as well as never-marrieds. As illustrated, greater numbers and percentages of males than females in the
fourteen to twenty-four and twenty-five to forty-four age groups live alone.

TABLE 14.2   Persons Living Alone, by Age and Sex: 1981

Age Group	Numbers of Persons (1,000)			Percent Distribution		
	Both Sexes	Male	Female	Both Sexes	Male	Female
14–24	1,651	899	752	8.7%	4.7%	4.0%
25–44	5,138	3,189	1,949	27.1	16.8	10.3
45–64	4,663	1,715	2,948	24.6	9.1	15.6
65 and over	7,484	1,415	6,034	39.5	7.9	31.9
All ages	18,936	7,253	11,683	100.0	38.3	61.7

Adapted from: U.S. Department of Commerce, Bureau of the Census, *Statistical Abstract of the United States: 1982, 83,* 103d ed. (Washington, D.C.: U.S. Government Printing Office, 1983), 41.

With each succeeding age group (forty-five to sixty-four and sixty-five and over), the relative numbers and percentages of females living alone increase rapidly. This is due to the greater numbers of older females in the population.

SOCIAL LIFE AND LEISURE TIME

Singles versus Marrieds

Is it true that singles have more leisure time and more fun than marrieds? It is easy for married persons to envy their apartment-dwelling single friends. Singles may not have to mow the lawn, clean out the garage, take the children to the zoo, attend PTA meetings, or coach the little league team. They can read, listen to stereos, bicycle along the river, visit an art gallery, or play poker in the evening. It sounds ideal.

But singles who work all week still have to clean house, make beds, cook, and do laundry. They may go bicycling or to an art gallery, but if they want company, they have to call friends and probably encounter some rejections before plans are completed.

In spite of this, singles do have more time for optional activities. They can make more choices and devote more time to leisure activities if they choose. Marrieds are more likely to have houses and children requiring time and attention (Cargan and Melko 1982).

The extent of a single's social life depends partially on the age group being discussed. Cargan and Melko's (1982) study of singles revealed that greater percentages of those in the once married, over thirty age group went out socially than did never-marrieds of the same age. However, at younger ages (eighteen to twenty-nine), greater percentages of never-marrieds went out than did those who were married once. At all ages, never-marrieds who went out socially went out more frequently than those who were married once, confirming the stereotype that they did more roaming.

Types of Social Activities

Visiting friends was the preferred social activity of never-marrieds, followed (in declining order of preference) by going to the movies, restaurants, nightclubs, and theaters, visiting relatives, or going to social clubs (Cargan and Melko 1982). Couples married once preferred going to restaurants or visiting relatives. The entertainment preference of never-marrieds was more a preference of youth. Both never-marrieds and marrieds spent a lot of time watching television. Never-marrieds spent more time on hobbies.

Fun and Happiness

Despite the fact that singles spent more time on social activities, a greater percentage of marrieds than never-marrieds said they got a lot of fun out of life and that they were happy (Cargan and Melko 1982). Marrieds may derive happiness and fun in different ways. Gardening or taking the children on a picnic can be fun. When asked what was most important to their happiness, marrieds mentioned health first, then marriage, children, love, religion, and friends, in that order. Only the category of friends was more important to singles than to marrieds. Surprisingly, success and money were not listed as important to happiness (Cargan and Melko 1982).

Singles' Bars

Studies of singles' bars revealed that they function as social centers, as places to meet potential dates or sexual partners and to enjoy a casual evening with acquaintances and friends. But most popular bars are noisy and crowded and arranged to discourage sitting or prolonged conversation. Starr and Carns (1972), who studied Chicago's singles' community, found that most singles did not establish dating relationships in bars. Most dates resulted from work contacts or from friends introducing friends.

LONELINESS AND FRIENDSHIPS

Contradictory Views

The greatest need of single people is to develop interpersonal relationships with other people, networks of friendships that provide emotional fulfillment, companionship, and intimacy (Verbrugge 1979). Single people value freedom and varied activities, but they also place a high value on enduring, close friendships.

The picture we have of singles is contradictory. They may go out more, but marrieds say they have more fun and are happier. Most singles have friends, but they are perceived as being lonely, having to initiate social relationships, and having no permanent, sharing relationships.

Loneliness versus Aloneness

There is a difference between being alone and lonely. Many never-marrieds do not perceive themselves as especially lonely. Two-thirds of them still live at home or with roommates of either sex (Cargan and Melko 1982). Most have many friends with whom they spend considerable time. Loneliness is partly a psychological state, independent of whether a person is in the company of someone else. Married people who are estranged from their mate may be quite lonely, even though they still live together. Many people enjoy being by themselves. A frequent complaint of busy housewives is that they never have an opportunity to be alone.

The popularity of singles' clubs, bars, and organizations evidences the need of singles to seek companionship. But does getting together in a bar, club, or church automatically signify loneliness? Or does it indicate gregariousness? On any one night, most singles are more likely to be home watching television, working on a hobby, baking, or reading than at a bar or church group. Even married people at home may be engaged in separate activities in different rooms, seldom touching or sharing. Married people frequently comment that they don't really talk to one another. On the other hand, singles who get together occasionally may stay up half the night talking.

Loneliness is not related to doing things with someone, but rather to having someone to turn to, to call or touch when the need is there. "You are lonely when you feel there is nobody upon whom you can rely to augment you, especially in conditions of stress or threat" (Lear 1980, 202).

The Importance of Companionship

When Cargan and Melko (1982) asked both marrieds and singles to describe the greatest advantage of being married, most replied in terms of shared feelings: "Companionship and someone to share decisions with," "companionship," "love and companionship," "the opportunity to converse with someone every day," "being able to share your life with someone you love," "togetherness is very important to me," "love is caring and having children and sharing things, and doing things together." The concept that turned up most frequently was companionship. Apparently the lives of a majority of singles meet this need.

A minority of singles feel the lack of sharing with someone. A physician (now married) commented:

Med school for me was the loneliest period of my life. I lived alone, studied alone, and was alone most of the time. I didn't really have any friends or anyone with whom to socialize. I think I married Chris soon after I met her because I was so terribly lonely. At last, I had someone to talk to and to do things with.

One woman remarked, "I'm not lonely everyday, only when I have something to share, or want to do something with someone. The rest of the time I'm perfectly content."

Some singles, however, feel that solitude is synonymous with loneliness. One young adult gave his rationale for visiting singles' bars. "It's better to be surrounded by people you don't want to talk to . . . than to be drunk alone in your apartment." Margaret Mead asked, "Are we so afraid of loneliness that we flee from solitude, fearing emptiness?" She continued, saying, "The reason we cluster together with such determination is because nowhere in childhood or youth is there any training or any practice is self-sufficient isolation. . . . Who wants to be free when it means being alone?" (O'Brien 1973, 39, 40, 62).

Males versus Females

Loneliness is a problem for a significant minority of never-marrieds. Some evidence suggests that among single young adults, male-male friendships are less intimate and spontaneous than female-female friendships. Single males are more isolated and have fewer intimate relationships than do single females. Although men sometimes exceed women in the number of voluntary associations in which they hold memberships, they spend less time in group activities and their participation is less stable (Booth 1972). The norms of competition and fear of homosexuality have hindered the development of male friendships. Yet, males as well as females need close, caring friendships that develop into a sense of mutuality and constitute a major source of social support. In departing traditional family structures, single adults express a strong need for substitute networks of human relationships that provide the basic satisfactions of intimacy, sharing, and continuity (Stein 1978).

AFFLUENCE AND MONEY

Figures

One stereotype is that singles are richer than marrieds. They have no spouses or children to support, they do not require expensive homes, and they can live more cheaply than marrieds.

Actually, marrieds are financially better off than never-marrieds. The median income of married, male householders in 1981 was $25,169; for single, male householders it was $15,640. The median income of married, female householders in 1981 was $23,702; for single, female householders it was $11,496. Figure 14.3 shows the comparison (U.S. Dept. of Commerce 1983).

According to these figures, greater percentages of married householders are in high income brackets compared to never-married householders.

Reasons

There are a number of reasons for these differences. Slightly more than half of all married women are employed outside the home, contributing substantially to the total household income. The combined incomes of two wage earners is likely to be greater than the income of one wage earner.

FIGURE 14.3   Median Income, by Household Type and Marital Status: 1981

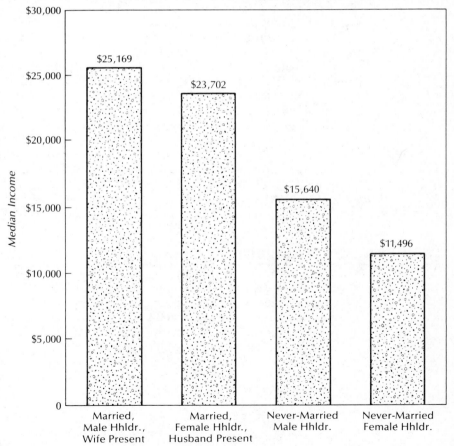

Adapted from: U.S. Department of Commerce, Bureau of the Census, *Statistical Abstract of the United States: 1982, 83,* 103d ed. (Washington, D.C.: U.S. Government Printing Office, 1983), 430.

Another reason is that employers are prejudiced in favor of married persons. There are only certain kinds of jobs for which employers would prefer a single person. Employers assume that married people are more stable, will stay on the job longer, and are more qualified for promotions than single people. Married people do receive higher wages and more promotions than single persons. It is assumed that married couples will become an integral part of the community and fit into the corporate structure; single people are sometimes considered outsiders, occupying their own worlds apart from the corporate family.

A third reason for the income discrepancies is that singles comprise a younger, less experienced age group and so earn less money. However, when age differences are considered, singles still earn less than married people.

A fourth reason is a practical one. Married people, especially those with families, have to earn more money because their needs are greater, and they are more highly motivated to earn higher incomes. Despite the many exceptions to this principle, it is generally true. Many marrieds are forced to work more than one job to provide sufficient incomes for their families.

Finally, the discrepancies reflect deep-seated prejudices against women. Overall, the average female with education, experience, and position comparable to that of a male is paid only about 61 percent as much for the same work (Rice 1983). As shown in Figure 14.3, the never-married, female householder earns a median income of $11,496 per year compared to $15,640 per year for the never-married, male householder. This clearly reflects the disadvantage under which women work. More than 43 percent of never-married, female householders earn less than $10,000 per year as opposed to only 30 percent of never-married, male householders (see Figure 14.3) (U.S. Dept. of Commerce 1983).

THE OLDER, NEVER-MARRIED ADULT

The major differences between older adults who have never married and younger ones is that most younger singles consider their status temporary, whereas older singles are usually well adjusted to their situation. They may not be interested in dating, but they usually have some social life and a variety of things to do with a few friends. A study of older singles between sixty and ninety-four found that they saw nothing special about being married: it was "just another way of life" (Gubrium 1976). They valued being independent, were relatively isolated (but not lonely), and were generally satisfied with their activities. They did not have to face widowhood or divorce and tended to accept and take for granted their life-style. They were unique persons, not misfits, who had adjusted to life differently than most.

The following comments from a seventy-one-year-old male are typical:

I have been single all my life (seventy-one years). I am living alone now and have a beautiful well-furnished, two-and-a-half-room apartment. I work at home and keep the apartment clean. I don't think I would like to live together presently. I'd rather not be married, even though I have plenty of opportunities.* (Hite 1982, 266)

It is pretty hard to find fault with this man's point of view or life-style. The important thing is that he was happy and satisfied.

SUMMARY

There is a marked trend to get married at later and later ages, but by age forty-five about 95 percent of men and women are or have been married. The reasons for delaying marriage include social, economic, and personal factors, for example: changing attitudes toward remaining single, lengthening of the period of education and economic dependency, greater premarital sexual permissiveness, and women's struggle for personal fulfillment in addition to marriage.

People remain single for a variety of reasons: deliberate choice, lack of opportunity, personality problems, and special circumstances related to family, geography, social isolation, or finances. There are many negative and positive influences, pushes and pulls, to be married or remain single.

One stereotype is that single persons do not marry because of close dependency on parents. Actually, more singles are eager to leave home. Men and women who never marry are more likely to report very poor or poor relationships with their mothers than those who do marry. Similarly, men who never marry are twice as likely to report very poor relations with their fathers than men who did marry. Adults do not seem to be deterred from marriage by family bonds but by the lack of them. However, greater numbers of never-married women report good relations with their fathers than those who have poor relations. It is a mistake to conclude that family background factors alone determine whether people ever marry.

Some of the more affluent singles live in communities like Carl Sandburg Village in Chicago or Marina del Rey in California. These communities are occupied primarily by unmarried persons. However, more singles are mixed in with the general population, occupying apartments with or without roommates, living alone, or living with other family members.

Singles have more leisure time and go out socially more than do marrieds, but marrieds report that they are happier and have more fun than singles. Marrieds and singles may derive happiness in different ways. Marrieds report that their happiness comes from health, marriage, children, love, religion, and friends. Singles list friends as most important to their happiness.

*Shere Hite, *The Hite Report on Male Sexuality,* copyright 1982, Alfred A. Knopf, Inc., p. 266.

Singles need to develop a network of friendships to find emotional fulfillment, companionship, and intimacy. Many never-marrieds live alone but do not consider themselves lonely. Most have many friends with whom they can spend considerable time if they choose. However, the popularity of singles' clubs, bars, and organizations is evidence that singles need to seek the companionship of other people. Both marrieds and singles report that the greatest advantage of being married is companionship.

Loneliness is a problem for a significant minority of never-marrieds. Single males are often more isolated and have fewer intimate relationships than do single females. The norm of competition and fear of homosexuality have hindered the development of male friendships.

One stereotype of singles is that they are richer than marrieds, when actually most are poorer. One reason is that more than half of married women work, and the income of two wage earners is likely to be greater than that of one person. There are other reasons for the lower income of singles: employers are prejudiced in favor of married persons, singles are younger and less experienced, married people are motivated to earn more because of greater need, and deep-seated prejudice exists against women (they are paid only about 61 percent as much as a man for the same work).

Older, never-married adults are usually well adjusted to their situation. They value their independence, generally are not lonely, are satisfied with their activities, and are happy. To them, being single is just another way of life.

15

Marriage, Family Living, and Widowhood

MOTIVES FOR MARRIAGE

Adults get married for a variety of reasons. Some reasons are positive; others are negative reactions to undesirable circumstances in their lives.

Positive Motives

The desires to have children, a home, and family are some of the strongest motives for marriage. The desire for children varies among people. Some people do not want children; others who have them wish they never had. Some people who already have children, but who have lost their spouse through divorce or death, marry again to find a substitute father or mother.

Other people marry for financial security. The author asked a class of college women how many would rather marry a physician with an income of $75,000 per year, who was never home, than a school teacher with an income of $20,000 per year, who was home most of the time after work and in the summer. About 10 percent of the class said they would rather marry the physician. Because doctoring is a more prestigious profession than school teaching, the desire for status has to be considered. The fact remains, however, that some women and men marry for money and economic security. Being a good provider is still considered one of the most desirable qualities in a husband. As women become more independent economically, the desire for financial security from a husband becomes a less important motive for marriage. Many women today do not want to be financially dependent; in fact, they insist on full economic parity.

There are still many men who marry women they feel will be good housekeepers, good cooks, and fine mothers, and who will take care of home and family. As unromantic and unglamorous as these motives are, thousands of men since pioneer days have wanted to marry domestic, healthy women. In fact, women were considered failures unless they could capably perform household duties. Although this motive is no longer considered a central one, it still must be included. Similarly, many women desire men who can do the heavy work, take care of the traditional men's chores, and who are willing to share the household chores.

Some people marry to gain status and recognition in a society that places a premium on being married. Marriage is also a means of social mobility, a way of changing status. People who marry partners in higher social positions are able to improve their own status.

The most important reasons that people in our culture marry are to love and be loved. Ask people "Why do you want to get married?" They will invariably reply, "Because we love one another."

Human beings above all seek to love and be loved. There is a universal and primitive longing to be attached, to relate, to belong, to be needed, and to care (Nuebeck 1979). Men and women can have companionship outside of marriage with persons who share common interests and enjoy their company. Such companionship fills a real need. But most people have an even more personal need: the need for intimacy, what Kennedy (1972) calls "the profoundly reaffirming experience of genuine intimacy." In a highly impersonal society, where emotional isolation is frequent, a close relationship with an individual is vital to a person's identity and real security.

> What men and women seek from love today is no longer a romantic luxury; it is an essential of emotional survival. . . . For in today's world, when men and women are made to feel as faceless as numbers on a list, they want intimate love to provide the feelings of worth and identity that preserve sanity and meaning. They hunger for one pair of eyes to give them true recognition and acceptance, for one heart that understands and can be understood. Only genuine intimacy satisfies these hungers. (Bach and Deutsch 1973, 157)

Negative Reactions

People get married not only because they have positive needs, but also because they are reacting against persons and circumstances. The primary reason students marry is pregnancy. It is difficult, however, to succeed in such a forced marriage. The couple must deal with "triple crises"—youth, early marriage, and parenthood. As a result, about half the youths who marry because of pregnancy divorce within five years.

Other people marry to escape an unhappy home, school failure, personal insecurity, or an unhappy social adjustment with peers. But people take their unhappiness and problems with them into marriage, making escape futile. Sometimes people marry to hurt others, for example, parents, a former boyfriend or girlfriend, or even themselves. People even show contempt for themselves by marrying a completely unsuitable partner (Rice 1983).

Other individuals want to prove their worth or attractiveness.

Sue grew up under the constant criticism of her older sisters. They made her feel that she was homely, that no man would ever look at her, that she would never marry, and that it was her responsibility to stay home to look after their sick mother. But Sue was determined to prove her sisters wrong. When she was twenty, she married a man seventeen years her senior, not because she loved him, but to prove to herself that some man did want her and that she didn't have to remain single.

It is not unusual for people to believe they are in love with someone who has helped them. Clients often "fall in love" with their counselors, patients with their doctors, parishioners with their clergy, and students with their teachers. They mistake gratitude for love.

Similarly, paternal or maternal types of people are attracted to those for whom they feel sorry. Some men marry women who seem defenseless, alone, in trouble, or in need of a strong shoulder on which to lean. Such marriages build the male egos. Some women are invariably attracted to men who are maladjusted and problems to themselves and others. One woman married an alcoholic because she thought he needed her and she wanted to take care of him.

In a society that overromanticizes marriage, it is difficult to resist the temptation to get married simply to avoid condemnation. Well-meaning friends and relatives ask the eligible bachelor: "When are you going to get married? Why don't you find yourself a nice wife and settle down?" When people marry because other people think they should, because other people are married, or because they are pressured into it, success becomes difficult. Sometimes people never really make a conscious decision to marry; they just drift into it because it is expected.

The motives for marriage are extremely important to marital success or failure. Those who marry for the wrong reasons are more likely to marry hastily and to wed the wrong person, decreasing the chances for success.

ADULTS VIEW MARRIAGE

Happy with Marriage

Ask any group of adults what they think of marriage and you will get conflicting answers. A majority, however, have positive opinions of marriage. In one nationwide survey, two-thirds of married adults reported being very happy in their marriages (U.S. Dept. of Commerce May 1980). The comments of one middle-aged husband are typical. "As far as I'm concerned, marriage is great. Having someone to come home to, to share my life with, is the most important thing in my life."

Marriage Plus Careers

Other adults like being married but accept it as only one part of their lives. A physician explained:

> I don't know why everyone seems to make so much about men and women and marriage. Of course I'm married and if anything happened to my wife, I'd get married again. I think it's the proper way to live. It's convenient, orderly, and solves a lot of problems. But there are other things in life. I spent nearly ten years preparing for the practice of my profession. The biggest thing to me is the practice of that profession, to be of assistance to my patients and their families. I spend twelve hours a day at it. (Cuber and Harroff 1965)

This view is shared by a great number of women who want marriage, children, and careers. One wife recalls her conversation with her fiancé before their marriage.

> I made the point—which he completely agreed with and obviously understood—that a career was my way of life. And, that although I wanted a family also, I in no way considered this a matter of alternatives or substitutes, but a matter of both. And he completely agreed. (Holmstrom 1973, 17)

A survey of male and female readers of *Psychology Today* showed that marriage was a major source of happiness for these persons, but the happiest women were those who were both married and employed outside the home (three out of four wives) (Shaver and Freidman 1976). They were happier than single women and had fewer psychological problems. These and other findings indicate that contemporary women want the best of all possible worlds—marriage, career, and children—and are happiest if they succeed at all three.

Disappointed with Marriage

Other adults have been disappointed by marriage. One young wife complained:

> Marriage is not what I expected it to be at all. I thought I'd be able to go back to college after the baby was born, but I'm too tired and busy. My husband has to work nights and Saturdays at a second job just to make expenses, so we never get to see one another, except on Sundays. I'm alone a lot in our apartment; I don't have any way to go anywhere or any money to do anything if I did. I keep hoping things will get better, but in the meantime, I'm not very happy.

The Paradox

In spite of the dissatisfaction with marriage, one paradox is that among those whose marriages end in divorce, almost nine out of ten eventually remarry (Carter and Glick 1970). They feel marriage can meet their needs and are highly motivated to make their second marriages succeed.

In focusing on marital failure, the important fact is often overlooked that two out of three persons who marry remain in the same relationship for a lifetime. Not all of these persons are happy, but the majority indicate that they are.

Trends

Some criticisms of modern marriage are offered by the disillusioned, those who tried marriage and found that it did not work for them. Some attacks come from the unorthodox who live on the fringes of society and criticize those in the mainstream. In spite of these attacks, the percentage of people marrying has varied little during the past five years. Figure 15.1 shows the trends.

THE FAMILY LIFE CYCLE

The Cycle

What people think of marriage depends on the existing circumstances. Marriage relationships are not static; they change over the years as people

FIGURE 15.1   Marriage Rate per 1,000 Population

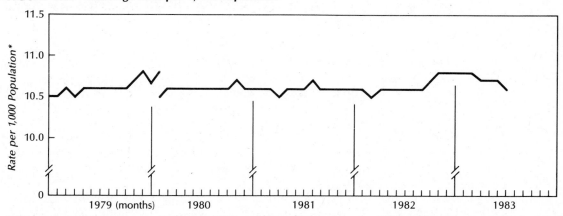

* Rates before 1980 were computed using 1970 population figures. Rates for 1980 and later were computed using 1980 population figures, so the data are not comparable.

From: U.S. Department of Health and Human Services, "Births, Marriages, Divorces, and Deaths for June 1983," *Monthly Vital Statistics Report*, Vol. 32, no. 6 (September 21, 1983): 2.

mature and share experiences together. Even the happiest couples admit to some difficult times together.

One way to understand the various phases and changes in marriage is to use the family life cycle. This cycle divides the marriage experience into various stages, from the beginning to the end of marriage. The most commonly used family life cycle is one divided into eight stages (Duvall 1977).

I. Beginning families. Married couples without children.
II. Childbearing families. Oldest child: birth to thirty months.
III. Families with preschool children. Oldest child: thirty months to six years.
IV. Families with schoolchildren. Oldest child: six to thirteen years.
V. Families with teenagers. Oldest child: thirteen to twenty years.
VI. Families as launching centers. First child gone to last child leaving home.
VII. Families in the middle years. Empty nest to retirement.
VIII. Aging families. After retirement.

Figure 15.2 shows the comparative length of time in each stage. Note that the length of stages II through V is based on the age of the oldest child. Obviously, the cycle does not apply to childless couples, to those who delay marriage and childbirth to much later than these averages, or to those who divorce and remarry (Nock 1979; Norton 1980). Variations have been found among people of different educational levels (Spanier and Glick 1980). The length of stage VII, the *empty nest period,* has been extended greatly due to improving survival rates and smaller families (Glick 1977). Stage VIII represents the total number of years from retirement until the death of both spouses. According to Figure 15.2, the number of years that adults live after the last child leaves home equals the total number of years of marriage that have gone before.

Changes in Marital Satisfaction

How does marital satisfaction change during these various stages of the family life cycle? Studies consistently show a decline in marital satisfaction during the early years of marriage, particularly following the birth of the first child, continuing to the end of stage III or IV (preschool or school-age children). A few studies show the decline extending to the end of stage V (teen-age children). Practically all studies show an overall increase in marital satisfaction after stage IV or V (after school-age or teen-age children). Some also show a slight decline in satisfaction before stage VIII (retirement) (Feldman and Feldman 1975; Rollin and Cannon 1974; Spanier, Lewis, and Cole 1975; Uhlenberg 1974). The general trend for marital satisfaction is somewhat curvilinear—high at the time of marriage, lowest during the child-rearing years, and higher again once the oldest child is beyond the teen-age years (after stage V) (Schram 1979).

FIGURE 15.2   The Family Life Cycle

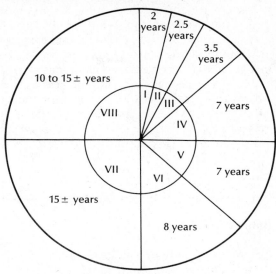

I   *Beginning families*—married couple without
      children
II   *Childrearing families*—oldest child: birth–30
      months
III   *Families with preschool children*—oldest child:
      30 month–6 years
IV   *Families with school children*—oldest child: 6–13
      years
V   *Families with teenagers*—oldest child: 13–30 years
VI   *Families as launching centers*—first child gone to
      last child leaving home
VII   *Families in the middle years*—empty nest to
      retirement
VIII   *Aging Families*—after retirement

From: Figure 7–2 [p. 148] in *Marriage and Family Devel-
      opment,* 5th ed., by Evelyn Millis Duvall (J. B. Lippincott
      Company). Copyright © 1957, 1962, 1967, 1971, 1977
      by Harper & Row, Publishers, Inc. Reprinted by per-
      mission of Harper & Row Publishers, Inc.

The common assumption that couples, and particularly wives, are
affected negatively when children leave home cannot be substantiated by
research. In fact, data from six United States surveys indicated that women
whose children had left home were happier, enjoyed life more, and had
greater marital satisfaction than women whose children were still at home
(Glenn 1975). Among women forty to forty-nine years of age, a 1973
survey showed that 93 percent of postparental women indicated that they
had very happy marriages, as compared to only 57 percent of parental
women. Similar results were obtained for women fifty to fifty-nine years
of age (National Opinion Research Center 1973).

As to why marital satisfaction is at an ebb when the children are of school age, the most plausible explanation is that the greatest demands are placed on the couple during these years. There are increased financial pressures to meet the needs of a growing family. Usually, career responsibilities are at a maximum. The children make increasing demands as they get older. Community responsibilities also increase during the middle years of marriage. Thus, the number and intensity of social roles of an individual gradually increase until the middle years. As a result, the couple experience greater role strain because of the discrepancy between role expectations and performance. This discrepancy leads to dissatisfaction with the marital relationship. After the children are grown, however, role expectations and strain decrease and marital satisfaction increases.

THE EARLY YEARS

Marital Adjustment Tasks

After marriage, most couples must make many adjustments to live together harmoniously and achieve maximum satisfaction in the relationship. The areas of adjustment can be termed *marital adjustment tasks* and divided into nine areas, as shown in Table 15.1 (Rice 1983, 174).

After Marriage

The number of adjustments the couple are expected to make and the heavy responsibilities they assume often create disillusionment and disenchantment for naïve, immature couples who do not realize what marriage really involves. Some couples are unaware until the honeymoon that marriage is such an intimate relationship. The primary focuses of the honeymoon are on sexual expression and relationships, on learning to express affection, and on developing physical and emotional intimacy. The majority of couples have slept together before marriage, but even for some of them, being together constantly and sleeping together in the same bed every night are very different experiences. For some couples, this physical intimacy is a new adventure. Sometimes sexual intercourse at the beginning of marriage does not prove to be the wonderful experience that was expected, leaving the couple disappointed, bewildered, doubtful, or hurt.

Tremendous Trifles

In the beginning, couples notice every minute detail of how the other person walks, talks, dresses, eats, sleeps, bathes, and so on. The newness of the experience makes the two people very observant and sometimes critical.

Some couples complain about a variety of little things. One husband

TABLE 15.1   Marital Adjustment Tasks

Intimacy

Adjustments to personal habits: cleanliness, dress, manners, eating and sleeping habits, habits relating to smoking, drinking, drugs

Adjusting to temperamental differences

Developing physical and emotional intimacy

Learning to fulfill ego needs of one another

Learning to express affection

Satisfying needs for love, physical contact

Finding, using acceptable means of birth control

Material Concerns and Economics

Selecting a residence: geographical area, community, neighborhood, type of housing

Equipping and maintaining a household

Finding, selecting, and maintaining employment

Adjustments to type, place, hours, conditions of employment

Establishing husband-wife roles in relation to material concerns in and outside the home

Agreement on division of labor

Power, Decision Making

Achieving desired balance of status, power

Learning to make, execute decisions

Learning cooperation, accommodation, compromise

Learning to accept responsibility for actions

Extrafamily Relationships

Establishing relationships with parents, in-laws, relatives

Learning how to deal with families

Establishing, maintaining husband-wife job-related relationships

Establishing, performing community, voluntary responsibilities

Children

Adjusting during pregnancy and childbirth

Reorientation of roles, responsibilities, allocation of time, resources

Companionship

Learning to think in terms of "we" rather than "I"

Getting used to living together

Learning to work, play, talk, eat, sleep together

Learning to share space, time, belongings, ideas, interests, work

Learning to communicate ideas, worries, concerns, needs

Achieving privacy and togetherness

Social Life

Selecting, relating to friends

Learning to plan, execute joint social activities

Learning to visit, entertain as a couple

Deciding on type, frequency of social activities as individuals and as a couple

Conflict

Learning to understand conflict causes, circumstances

Learning to cope with conflict constructively

Learning when, how to obtain help if needed

Mores, Values, Ideology

Understanding and adjusting to individual mores, ethics, values, beliefs, philosophies and goals in life

Establishing mutual values, goals, philosophies

Accepting one another's religious beliefs and practices

Decisions in relation to religious affiliation, participation

From: F. P. Rice, *Contemporary Marriage* (Boston: Allyn and Bacon, Inc., 1983), 174.

complained because his wife never wanted to sleep with a window open, whereas he liked a lot of fresh air. One meticulous wife discovered that her husband never liked to take a bath or use deodorant. Another discovered that her husband always threw his dirty socks and underwear in a corner. One husband was annoyed because his wife lounged around the house in her bathrobe until after lunch. Gradually, couples get used to one another, overlook some of the little things, and learn how not to annoy one another. Early in the marriage, however, these trifles can be tremendously aggravating.

Marital Roles

One major adjustment relates to husband-wife roles in the marriage. Traditionally, these roles clearly distinguished between "man's work" and "woman's work." The husband's chief role was that of breadwinner; the wife's that of housekeeper and mother. Today, with more than 50 percent of married women employed outside the home at any one time, these distinctions can no longer be made. If the wife shares in earning income, it is only right for the husband to share in child care, in housekeeping, and in food preparation. Each couple has to work out a division of responsibilities that satisfies them.

Earning an adequate income is not easy. If the couple hold stereotyped concepts, this burden falls heavily on the husband, who begins to realize what an enormous responsibility he has accepted. One husband told his counselor:

> After we got back from our honeymoon . . . I sat with my head in my hands. I wanted Janet. I still do. But I felt like the walls were closing in. Already we owe thousands—on a car, furniture, the whole bit. I see myself in ten years with a mortgage, a power lawn mower and kids that need braces. It's like *my* life is over. (Maynard 1974, 136)

The wife who holds traditional views assumes the daily responsibility for cooking and homemaking. Many modern women have never done these tasks regularly at home, so they become major chores. As one wife said, "I spent the first year of our marriage with my nose in a cookbook." When the husband and wife observe less traditional sex-role separations, they can help one another in earning income and performing household duties.

Dual-Career Marriage

Special problems arise when both the husband and wife pursue full-time careers, especially after children are born. One problem is overwork (Keith and Schafer 1980). The demands of the marriage, career, children, and home are great and often leave couples tense and exhausted (Voydanoff 1980). Most couples have to learn to budget their time very carefully. Most try to increase the efficiency of housework and to streamline tasks.

Where to live and whether to move become important considerations. Most career people are expected to move frequently as they progress up the corporate ladder (Gilliland 1979). If the husband or wife is transferred, whose job takes precedence? Most couples try to consider the occupational needs of both and to make career decisions allowing both to find employment in one locality.

Another major task is finding suitable child care when both parents work. Parents who work days, seldom travel, and are usually home weekends often hire a baby-sitter during the week and care for their children at other times. If the husband and wife travel often, they may have to hire a live-in baby-sitter.

Independence, Decision Making

Some young people who have never lived away from their parents before marriage become homesick and want to visit their parents often. It is a major task to become emotionally independent of one's parents and to learn to depend on each other for guidance, moral support, and emotional fulfillment (Gendzel 1974). Learning how to make joint decisions is an important step in the early months of marriage. In so doing, the couple work out a balance of power and status and develop a process for decision making.

Communication and Conflict

When differences and conflicts arise, the couple must deal with them constructively, not only to solve the problems but also to strengthen their relationship. This involves learning how to communicate in a way that eases tensions. Good communication has been called the key to family interaction and the lifeblood of the marital relationship (Powers and Hutchinson 1979). But the act of communication itself does not always lead to a resolution of problems. Talking things over and expressing feelings in hurtful ways can make things worse. Constructive communication is best accomplished by rational discussion that attacks the issues and not one another. It involves careful listening in an effort to understand one another's point of view and a willingness to be flexible and make compromises.

Friends and Social Life

Selecting and relating to friends and establishing the type and frequency of social life sometimes cause trouble. A common complaint is, "I don't like his (or her) friends." Being married does not mean giving up one's old friends, but neither does it mean maintaining one's single social life. Young wives often complain, "After we were married my husband wanted to spend most of his spare time with his buddies and to run around with them just like he used to." Yet, these same wives may be expected to stop seeing many of their old friends and to stay home and take care of the house and children.

Sharing and Cooperation

It is not easy for individuals who have been single and independent for a number of years to begin thinking in terms of "We" instead of "I." Even deciding such things as time schedules, for example, when to go to bed and when to get up in the morning, involves some degree of cooperation and consideration (Adams and Cromwell 1978; Darnley 1978). Couples now share belongings, space, work, and time; they have to get used to adjusting to individual differences. Throughout it all, they also need some individual privacy and space in their togetherness.

PARENTHOOD

Parenthood As Stress

"First pregnancy," said psychiatrist Eldred, "is a nine-month crisis. Thank God it takes nine months, because a child's coming requires enormous changes in a couple's ways of adjusting to each other" (Maynard 1974, 139). In recent years, the addition of a first child has been regarded as less of a crisis and more as a period of stress and transition (Bell et al. 1980; Boss 1980; Miller and Sollie 1980). The amount of stress varies among couples. If a couple's marriage is stressful before parenthood, they are more likely to have difficulty adjusting to the first child. Middle-class parents seem to find the transition to parenthood more stressful than do lower-class parents (Russell 1974).

Sometimes stress arises because the pregnancy is not planned (Hobbs and Wimbish 1977). Even couples who plan the pregnancy slowly realize that tremendous adjustments are required. Roles have to be realigned, heavier responsibilities assumed, and social activities curtailed. Often the couple living on two incomes must make the difficult adjustment to three people living on one income.

Some stress occurs because couples are inadequately prepared for parenthood. One mother stated, "We knew where babies came from, but we didn't know what they were like." One study showed that 81 percent of middle-class, working women reported absolutely no experience in caring for infants at the time of the first child as compared to 63 percent of lower-class respondents (Jacoby 1969). Another study showed that men who had been prepared for parenthood by attending classes, reading books, and so forth found far greater satisfaction in being a parent than those who had not been so prepared (Russell 1974).

Stress varies with each child, depending on the child's temperament and how easy it is to care for the child. Some children are no trouble. Others, such as hyperactive or sick children, require an abnormal amount of care (Balkwell and Halverson 1980; Roberts and Miller 1978).

Adjustments of the Wife

Parenthood affects the wife and husband differently. The wife, who has to carry the child for nine months, experiences varying degrees of physical discomfort or difficulties, and sometimes anxiety about impending child-birth. Women with rewarding jobs may resent taking time away from work to bear and care for a child. At this point, some women suffer an identity crisis similar to that of men who are retiring. The necessity of giving up their jobs—even temporarily—plus the long hours of constant physical work and confinement to the home with a demanding infant create an intellectual and social void in the lives of women who participated in multidimensional social roles before their children were born. Some women feel tied down. "My life is not my own. The demands of the children take time and I have less time for myself. When I worked, there was no nervous strain. I wish I could be out more." Others complain about the lack of privacy or feel they have been "lost in the shuffle" or are "vegetating" because of the endless repetition of physical tasks and lack of social interaction. One of the biggest changes for the mother is the added work and responsibility. One mother remarked, "I never realized how much work is involved in caring for one small child."

Another important change is the realignment of the woman's wife-mother roles. Even middle-class women in companionate marriages experience a decrease in the time, attention, and social activities previously shared with the spouse. Many couples report that having a baby gave them something in common and brought them closer together, but their combined attention is now focused on the child rather than on one another. Despite the common bond of their child, there is usually less husband-wife companionship and communication (Rosenblatt 1974). Some husbands feel rejected, especially when sexual relations are medically discouraged or when the wife is too tired to attend to her husband's desires.

Some wives also feel rejected, especially if they feel unattractive during and after pregnancy. Wives worry about their personal appearance and loss of figure (Russell 1974). One study emphasized that a woman accepts pregnancy well when it brings her closer to her husband, but she rejects pregnancy when she feels it excludes her from her husband. If the wife feels confident of her husband's ability to provide for the baby, she also feels better about having a child. Other women enjoy their motherhood role and report that having a baby was a great source of satisfaction in their lives.

Adjustments of the Husband

After the first surge of phallic pride ("I did it"), expectant fathers experience different reactions. Some men become angry and take out their hostility on their wives. Other husbands welcome this responsibility, which confers a new and valued status. Such men identify closely with all the stages of pregnancy, feel excitement when the baby moves, enthusiastically prepare a room for the baby, and complete other arrangements before the actual birth (Maynard 1974).

All first-time fathers, however, experience a prolonged period of strain following the birth. New fathers report interrupted sleep and physical weariness. Most men complain about the work involved and about being tied down. In one study, 53 percent indicated having a baby increased their money problems and the amount of work required (Russell 1974). Young husbands find parenthood more of a crisis than those who are older and who have been married longer. Insecure husbands may be jealous of the time their wife devotes to the baby and grow to resent their offspring.

THE POSTPARENTAL YEARS

Time Span

The postparental years usually refer to the period after the last child leaves home until the husband's retirement. If a woman marries at the median age of twenty-one and has children, she is fifty-one when the last child leaves home. The husband who marries at the median age of twenty-three and has children will be fifty-three when the last child leaves. Some writers prefer to use the term the *empty-nest years,* because if one has children, one is always a parent.

Fact and Fiction

Fictional literature presents a depressing picture of this period. The stereotype of middle age suggests a loss of companionship, sexuality, and purpose for the aging female and a time of overwork, disillusionment, and womanizing for the male.

According to recent research, however, such concepts are only partly factual (Harkins 1978; Robertson 1978; Targ 1979). Some women are going through menopause during these years, but often with a minimum of physical or psychological disturbance because of greater understanding and better medical care. The biggest adjustment for the wife whose life has been wrapped up in her children is to fill the gap their departure leaves.

> My daughters were both nineteen when they married. I didn't want them not to marry, but I missed them so much. I felt alone. I couldn't play golf. I couldn't even play bridge. I don't have a profession, and I couldn't take just any job. I just didn't have a chance to learn anything. (Einzig 1980, 158)

Although these comments are not unusual, greater numbers of women breathe a sigh of relief when the last child leaves (Rubin 1979). These women are now free to live their own lives.

Husbands at this age are at the height of their careers, assuming more responsibility and making more money than ever. The decreased financial burdens and increased income enable the couple to take longer and more expensive vacations, buy expensive jewelry or automobiles, and eat at expensive restaurants. Couples do not feel too great a loss when the children leave, especially if they are proud of them and their accomplishments (Lewis, Freneau, and Robert 1979).

Considerable evidence indicates that adults in the postparental period are happier than those in earlier or later periods. Described as a time of freedom, the empty-nest years may require adjustments, but they offer increased opportunities to enjoy life as a couple.

THE LATER YEARS

Husband-Wife Relationships

People who are retired spend more time at home with their mate. This may put a strain on the marriage because the couple must now interact more. Some wives complain of additional work when they and their husbands retire. The couple sometimes annoy each other. Studies show that retired husbands take on a few additional household tasks, but not much more than when they were working (Arling 1976). Much of a retired husband's time at home is spent in his own pursuits.

One advantage of retirement is that couples who enjoy one another's company can spend more time together. They are free to pursue mutual interests, to travel, or just to be better companions. Retirement can bring years of carefree fun and relaxation.

Relationships with Grown Children

A national survey revealed that the nearest child of more than three-fourths of the aged respondents was located within a thirty-minute drive, and that two-thirds had seen one of their children in the twenty-four-hour period preceding the interviews (Stehouwer 1968). A study of older persons living in two small Wisconsin communities found only a third who did not have at least one child living in their community. Of those with children in the same town, two-thirds saw at least one child each week. Only one-tenth of all the elderly studied did not have at least one child living in the same state. Elderly migrants to retirement communities in Florida or Arizona were somewhat more isolated, but 36 percent of the elderly migrants to Florida and 43 percent of those to Arizona saw their children more than once a year. Those who saw their children infrequently were also unlikely to see them often even if living in the same community (Bultena and Marshall 1970).

Most elderly people see their children frequently, but only a minority turn to their children for help in meeting many daily responsibilities. Several studies have shown that older people are more likely to turn to their daughters rather than their sons for help. Help comes in many forms:

providing living accommodations (about 10 percent of married elderly couples and about 17 percent of previously married elderly people live with a married child); providing economic support, personal care, transportation, and gifts of cash and food; performing housekeeping, yard, and home chores; and providing help for outings and holidays (Shanas 1967). Understandably, most older people dislike turning to their children for help. They prefer independence. Sometimes the older person provides the help: caring for grandchildren; giving gifts of food, cash, clothing, and household furnishings; and assisting with home repairs, yard work, or housework. Generally, white-collar parents more often provide help to their children than do blue-collar parents; blue-collar parents more often need help from their children than do white-collar parents. About 18 percent of elderly people in the United States have no surviving children.

Housing and Living Conditions

It is usually very important to the elderly to keep their own home. This may mean moving to a smaller house, but one that is theirs. This provides independence and contributes to satisfactory relationships with children. A home allows the elderly to live as they choose, which is important. Furthermore, the elderly prefer to remain in one place among familiar faces and surroundings. Younger people often have occupations that require them to move a great deal. If their parents live with them, the parents must discard important roots of their past. Almost three out of four households maintained by persons sixty-five and older are owned by them. The remaining households are rentals. Of course, large numbers of older people (about one out of ten men and one out of five women, sixty-five and older) live with their married children and are not heads of households (U.S. Dept. of Commerce May 1980).

There is an increasing trend for older people to sell their homes and move to retirement communities. But these people are usually leisure-minded, in good health, and financially secure. Housing developments for the elderly are increasingly popular, but little research is available on the effects of segregating people by age groups. Usually, older people prefer to have young people around them. A number of elderly Americans (almost a million) live in nursing homes or convalescent facilities. The trend is increasing, and nursing homes now provide more beds than do hospitals. Some of these homes maintain high standards and strive to provide for the social and emotional needs of residents, besides offering custodial care. Other homes are shockingly inadequate. Many are understaffed, and patients are tranquilized or restrained to keep them quiet. Some lack basic sanitation and provide inadequate nutrition, nursing, and/or medical care. Such abuses have led to corrective legislation and licensing requirements in some states. As might be suspected, residence in nursing homes or homes for the aged is rare for elderly persons whose marriages are intact (Carter and Glick 1970).

WIDOWHOOD

Sex Ratios

A couple who marry and have children in the 1980s, and whose marriage is not broken by divorce or separation, can expect to live together for forty-seven years. From birth, the female's life expectancy is age seventy-seven. If the wife dies at that age and her widowed husband is seventy-nine, he can expect to live seven more years. From birth, the male's life expectancy is age seventy. If the husband dies at that age and his widow is sixty-eight, she can expect to live for sixteen years (U.S. Dept. of Commerce 1983). These are long periods to be alone and they require significant adjustments.

The greater longevity of women means that the number of widows exceeds widowers at all age levels. Table 15.2 shows the ratios at different ages (U.S. Dept. of Commerce 1983). Partly as a result of these ratios, the remarriage rates for widows is lower than for widowers. The younger a person is when a mate dies, the greater the chances of remarriage. More than 75 percent of women widowed before age thirty remarry, but only 6 percent of those widowed after age fifty remarry. Also, widows who have many children are less likely to remarry than those who have fewer children (U.S. Dept. of Commerce 1977).

Relationships with Friends and Family

Older people, especially widows, have a consistently high degree of contact with other family members, including married children. Usually, the elderly female is closer to her children, especially daughters, than is the elderly male. However, the woman is more likely to depend on them for material aid. The more dependent elderly people become, and the more that helping roles are reversed, the lower their morale. Arling (1976) found that widows with children living nearby had morale no higher than respondents who either had no living children or had none within an hour's drive. Similarly, the frequency of contact with children had no significant

TABLE 15.2   Ratio of Widows to Widowers at Different Ages

Age	Ratio of Widows to Widowers
45–54	5.1 to 1
55–64	5.2 to 1
65–74	6.4 to 1
75 yrs. and over	5.3 to 1

Adapted from: U.S. Department of Commerce, Bureau of the Census, *Statistical Abstract of the United States: 1982, 83,* 103d ed. (Washington, D.C.: U.S. Government Printing Office, 1983), 39.

association with morale. Widows having family members nearby were just as likely to worry and to feel lonely.

One reason for this finding was that even though the children visited their widowed mothers regularly, affective ties were not always close. Therefore, the married children provided relatively little emotional support. Because the children and their elderly mothers had contrasting interests, they often made poor companions. Another study of widows in Chicago revealed that only about 10 percent received any economic support or physical services (transportation, house repairs, or yard work) from siblings or other relatives. Only about one in ten shared social activities with them. Having relatives nearby does not necessarily mean they can be counted on for emotional, physical, or social support, or that the elderly would be happier if support were given (Lopata 1978).

All research findings stress the positive importance of peer support in helping widows and widowers adjust. Morale is positively associated with involvement with friends.

Problems of Widows

An in-depth study of seventy-two women of middle socioeconomic status, all widowed for fewer than five years, showed that the most frequently cited problem was loneliness (Wyly and Hulicka 1977). Widows miss their husbands as companions and partners in activities (Kivett 1978). This problem is accentuated if the woman has low income and cannot afford many social activities outside the home. Younger widows report that social participation is a problem because so many activities are couple oriented. Sexual frustration is common among the widowed (Goddard and Leviton 1980). The problem of loneliness is accentuated because more than half of widowers and widows live alone (U.S. Dept. of Commerce 1983).

A second problem cited by the widows in Wyly and Hulicka's study was home maintenance and car repair. Other problems cited frequently by younger widows were decision making, child rearing, and financial management. Widows in the oldest group mentioned such problems as learning basic finance, lack of transportation, and fear of crime. The only advantages of widowhood, mentioned by the younger women, were increased independence and freedom of choice (Wyly and Hulicka 1977).

Financial problems plague both widows and widowers. In every age category, however, widowed females earn less than widowers. The most impoverished females are widows older than sixty-five, even though they may be receiving social security or pensions of some sort (Sass 1979; Tissue 1979). Blacks and other minorities in rural areas or areas of urban blight are the poorest. If they are to have the basic necessities of life, a variety of social supports are needed (Scott and Kivett 1980).

Widows indicate that one of their major adjustments is related to role changes. Widowhood, at all ages, changes the basic self-identity of a woman. This is especially true of the traditionally oriented woman whose role of wife was central to her life. This woman has to reorient her thinking to find other identities. The widow whose primary role was that of mother and who still has dependent children at home is not forced to change her role as drastically, except to that of provider if necessary. Therefore, specific role changes depend on what roles were emphasized before widowhood. The childless career wife who was not very close to her husband may not have to change her role performance at all. In fact, she may welcome the increased freedom.

Widowers

Whether the adjustments for widowers are easier or more difficult than for widows is a matter of dispute. Men with dependent children may have difficulty caring for them. Bischof feels that widowers without parental responsibilities, however, have a greater degree of freedom than widows without dependent children (Bischof 1976). The loss of a wife does not directly affect occupation or income, unless, of course, the wife was earning a considerable share of the family income. Their primary disruptions are learning to cook, keep house, and care for themselves, although many men already do these things. Or, they may be able to hire help. In such cases, the major adjustment is to the loss of their wife's companionship and love.

SUMMARY

People marry for positive and negative reasons. Positive motives include the desire to have children, a home and family, and financial security; the need for physical care and services; and the desire to gain status and recognition. The most important reason in our culture is to love and be loved (the need for intimacy). Negative motives for marriage include pregnancy; the desire to escape, to hurt others, or to prove one's worth and attractiveness; gratitude or self-pity; the need to avoid social condemnation; and social pressure.

Views of marriage differ. The majority who marry have very positive views. Others like being married but consider it just another part of life in addition to their career. The happiest women are those who are both married and employed outside the home. Still other adults have found marriage disappointing. Even among people whose marriages end in divorce, almost nine out of ten eventually remarry. The marriage rate has varied little during the past five years.

The marriage experience can be divided into various phases of the life cycle. Most young couples experience a period of disillusionment and disenchantment after marriage as they face many adjustment problems. Marital satisfaction decreases to its lowest point during the child-rearing years, as the number and intensity of social roles increase and cause role strain. After children are grown and gone, role strain decreases, resulting in an increase in marital satisfaction. Women whose children have left home are happier and enjoy life more than those whose children are still at home. The retirement years can also be a time of decreased satisfaction, depending on the total circumstances.

Adjustments after marriage include developing physical and emotional intimacy and learning to express affection; learning to overlook and/or adjust to tremendous trifles; working out marital roles and dealing with the special problems of dual-career marriage; becoming emotionally independent of parents and learning to make decisions; dealing with conflict constructively and developing the art of communication; relating to friends and establishing the type and frequency of social life; and learning to share, cooperate, and show consideration for one another.

First pregnancy is a time of stress for most couples, especially if tension already exists in the marriage, if the pregnancy is unplanned, or if the couple are unprepared for parenthood. Part of the stress is due to the abrupt transition to parenthood. Stress varies with each child, depending on the child's temperament and how easy it is to care for the child. Some women, especially those who have to leave a good job, suffer an identity crisis, complain of being tied down, or resent having so much work and responsibility. During and after pregnancy, some feel unattractive and rejected by their husbands.

Husbands react to fatherhood with awe, resentment, excitement, or anxiety over the responsibilities involved. First-time fathers, especially young husbands, find fatherhood a period of prolonged role strain.

The picture of the empty-nest years as a period of lost companionship, sexuality, youthfulness, and purpose in life is only partly factual. The majority of women and men breathe a sigh of relief after the last child leaves home. Most adults are happier during the postparental years than they are earlier or later in life.

The retirement years can be a time of crisis because of lack of money and reduced social status. After retirement, couples spend more time with their mate, which offers more companionship but also requires additional adjustments. Most older people have at least one child living in their community or in their home state. As a result, most elderly people see their children frequently. Only a minority turn to their children for help.

Most elderly want to keep their own homes, even if it means buying a smaller house. Only one out of ten men and one out of five women, sixty-five and over, live with their married children. There is an increasing trend for older people to move to retirement communities. Others live in federally subsidized housing developments for the elderly. Only a small minority live in nursing homes or convalescent facilities.

Because of the greater longevity of women, the number of widows exceeds widowers at all age levels. Widowhood represents a major adjustment for both men and women. Major problems include loneliness, finances, and changing roles and responsibilities within and outside the family. Peer support is of major importance in enabling adults to adjust to their new life situations. People who have been the most independent and have led full, well-rounded lives before widowhood seem to adjust most easily.

16

Divorce and the Reconstituted Family

DIVORCE AND THE HUMAN LIFE CYCLE

The Early Years

As discussed in chapter 1, various writers have described the psychosocial tasks of early adulthood in relationship to marriage. Buhler (1977) argues that the basic human tendency is toward fulfillment, primarily through creativity. But this creativity can include developing loving understanding with a marital partner. Erikson (1968) describes the chief psychosocial task of early adulthood as the development of intimacy. Havighurst (1972) describes a dual task: selecting a mate and then learning to live with that marital partner.

According to probability statistics, about 60 percent of people who marry in the United States today will remain married for a lifetime. How many people have unhappy marriages is difficult to determine, but the fact remains that many find personal fulfillment in their married relationships.

A significant minority, however, about 40 percent, divorce. The early years of marriage are the most difficult in relation to the probability of divorce. This probability is greatest two to four years after first marriage for males and one to four years for females. Considering that months may pass between the beginning of marital discord and when the couple separate, seriously considering divorce, the first year or so of marriage is certainly most difficult. In the United States, about 10 percent of divorces occur in the second year, and about 8.6 percent in the third year, with the rate diminishing after that. Among those who divorce, the median number of years of first marriage is 6.8 years (U.S. Dept. of Commerce 1983). The duration of first marriage is greater for whites than for blacks.

Later Crises

Many couples who survive the early years of marriage experience a crisis later. As discussed in chapter 1, Gould (1978) suggested that the years between twenty-nine and thirty-five may be a time of role confusion, during which the individual begins to question self, marriage, and other aspects of life. Between thirty and forty, the percentage of people who believe marriage is a good thing declines. The period from thirty-five to forty-three is a time of goal realignment and may include serious thought about divorce. Levinson (1978) talked about the age thirty transition, during which individuals modify their life structures after sensing the need for change. For some people, a mid-life crisis beginning at age forty or so is a period when individuals seek to reappraise their lives and modify the unsatisfying aspects. This reappraisal may also include divorce. About 40 percent of all broken marriages last ten or more years; 13 percent last more than twenty years (Freed and Foster 1972).

FACTS AND FIGURES ON DIVORCE

Divorce Rates

It is necessary to examine divorce itself before discussing its effects on the people involved and the adjustments that are required. Why are divorce rates so high? Numerous and conflicting explanations have been offered: the declining influence of religious organizations, the breakdown of morals, more lenient divorce laws, changes in marriage functions and roles, and a declining interest in traditional family forms. Probably all of these are valid reasons (Glick 1975, 1977).

The most meaningful divorce statistics are obtained by indicating age-specific rates, that is, rates per 1,000 married women of certain ages. The divorce rate in 1981 was 23 per 1,000 married women fifteen and older. Figure 16.1 shows the trends in first marriage rates and divorce rates for women fifteen years and older, and remarriage rates for women fourteen years and older (U.S. Dept. of Commerce 1983). As indicated, the rate of divorce has risen dramatically whereas the rate of first marriage has decreased. There does seem to be some indication, however, that the rise in divorce rates and the decline in marriage rates are now leveling off.

Age Factors

Divorce rates vary greatly according to the age of the wife. Divorce rates are highest among women fourteen to twenty-four, with the probability of divorce decreasing as the woman gets older (England and Kuntz 1975).

Socioeconomic Factors

Divorce rates vary according to a number of socioeconomic factors. In general, college-educated men have a greater chance of their marriage surviving the first five years than do men with less education. Also, those

FIGURE 16.1   Marriages, Remarriages, and Divorces: United States

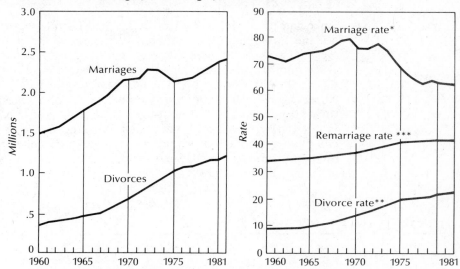

*Rate per 1,000 unmarried women, 15 years old and over.
**Rate per 1,000 married women, 15 years old and over.
***Rate per 1,000 widowed and divorced women, 14 years and over

From: U.S. Department of Commerce, Bureau of the Census, *Statistical Abstract of the United States: 1982, 83* 103d ed. (Washington, D.C.: U.S. Government Printing Office, 1983), 124.

with higher incomes have more stable marriages. The differences in rates between those with more education and income and those with less generally disappear after ten years of marriage (Glick and Norton 1971).

Family Background

Persons raised in unstable and unhappy homes are less likely to marry. If they do marry, their marriages are more likely to end in divorce than the marriages of people raised in stable and happy homes (Riley and Spreitzer 1974).

Variations by States

Divorce rates vary greatly from region to region in the United States. Generally speaking, the rates increase moving from the East to the West. This variation has been attributed partly to the frontier atmosphere of the western states, and particularly to their higher migration rates, which result in relaxed norms and lower social costs attached to divorce. The lower divorce rates in New England can be attributed to the high percentage of foreign born and Catholics in the total population, coupled with a low migration rate.

Number of Children

Since half of all divorces occur in the first seven or eight years of marriage, it is inevitable that many children, especially young children, are involved. Nearly two out of three divorces involve couples with children. The average number of children involved per divorce is about 1.2, which means that more than one million children were affected by divorces that occurred in 1979 (U.S. Dept. of Commerce 1983). It is estimated that more than 30 percent of all school-age children do not live with a father and mother who are in a continuous first marriage (Glick 1975). In some cases, one parent is deceased or the parents are separated, but in most instances the parents are divorced. Such situations look to become even more commonplace in the future.

DIVORCE AND THE LAW

No-Fault Divorce

In 1960, the National Conference of Commissioners on Uniform State Laws promulgated the new Uniform Marriage and Divorce Act (Kargman 1973). This act is now a law; it is a model for state legislatures to accept or deny in part or completely. It rejects *fault grounds* (the question of who is to blame) as a precondition for access to courts and recognizes instead the rights of the individual who petitions for a divorce on the grounds of irretrievable breakdown of the marriage (Monahan 1973).

Some states now have no-fault grounds for divorce as the only ground. Other states, such as California and Florida, recognize irreconcilable differences in addition to incurable insanity or mental incompetence. Other states have merely added no-fault grounds. In these states, one spouse can still threaten to sue for divorce on grounds other than no-fault if his or her demands are not met. If this is possible, divorce can be a bitter contest between partners who want to hurt or to win something from the other. All but one state now have no-fault divorce laws.

The possibility for vengeance is removed when no-fault divorce is the only course. California was one of the earliest states to pass a no-fault divorce law. Under California law, divorce is referred to as the dissolution of marriage. The law removes all fault and reduces the grounds to (1) irreconcilable differences or (2) incurable insanity. Because of community property law, in California the property is usually divided equally, unless the couple request otherwise. If the petitioner seeks spousal support (not called alimony), the final decision is based on the needs of the petitioner, ability to pay, the standard of living, and similar considerations.

The California law did not solve all the problems of divorce. The sensitive issue of child custody is supposed to be settled according to the best interests of the child, although sentiment favors the mother when the child is young. The petition for divorce itself can still be contested. If needed, the court can call witnesses to establish the existence of irreconcilable differences. Although the purpose is to give information rather than find fault, it can still lead to ugly testimony. To avoid a California "divorce mill," a six-month residency requirement was established.

One of the most criticized provisions of the California law was the establishment of an interlocutory period of six months, a period of time that must elapse between the decree of dissolution and the final granting of it. The intent was to offer a "cooling-off" period, but this should come before the decree, not after. Delaying final action usually prolongs the couple's agony, adds to the expense of the divorce, adds to the tension between the spouses, and delays the time when they can begin to readjust their lives as divorced persons. Most authorities oppose any interlocutory provision in a decree (Weitzman, Kay, and Dixon 1974).

No-fault divorce is a great improvement over the older adversary system, but some critics contend that divorce should be awarded to any person, without the possibility of its being contested. Cantor writes, "No one should have the right to force the legal continuation of a marriage that has ceased to exist in fact" (Cantor 1970).

An uncontested divorce is extremely easy to obtain. It usually requires only a brief, superficial court hearing. But the harm comes in the process of trying to work out the agreement. Couples fight bitterly, using the promise not to contest as a leverage for benefits. The possibility of contest creates havoc. The interests of the children and the lives of people are traded in the negotiations. Eliminating the possibility of contest eliminates most of the fighting.

The Adversary Approach

A number of states still allow an *adversary approach* to divorce. This means that one party must bring charges and prove the other guilty of cruelty, desertion, nonsupport, habitual drunkenness, or some other fault. If the accused proves his or her innocence, or if the court finds that both spouses are guilty, the divorce may not be granted. In some states, no matter how incompatible the partners are, or how miserable they are together, if both spouses are at fault, the divorce can be denied. Some states, recognizing the folly of denying a divorce when both parties were guilty, introduced the doctrine of comparative rectitude, which recognizes that the court can grant a divorce to the party least at fault.

The worst aspect of the adversary approach is that it forces spouses to become combatants, each trying to defeat the other. This creates tremendous hostility and anger, even when couples are trying to settle amicably (Wylie 1975).

The adversary approach pressures one party to grant concessions in exchange for not delaying a divorce or for not contesting it. The consequence is bargaining. The divorce itself becomes an object of trade in exchange for alimony, child custody, visitation rights, and/or the allocation of property.

THE HIGH COST OF DIVORCE

Property and Finances

Nowhere is the injustice of adversary divorce law more evident than in matters of property and money. One crusader for women's rights pointed out that wives in many states, unless they have joint deeds to property, are legally entitled on divorce only to whatever income and property they themselves have earned or acquired. A minority of states have *community property laws* that entitle a wife on divorce to an equal share of family income and property (Wylie 1975). In actual practice, many husbands turn over the house to their wives, especially if children are involved. By law, many do not have to.

The husband is responsible for the support of his wife and children while they wait for the divorce to be granted. If the wife is vindictive, or if the divorce drags out for months or years, the husband may be deeply in debt by the time the divorce is granted.

As a result, some husbands try to close all charge accounts to protect themselves. Husbands can be vindictive, especially if their wives have money. One actress announced that she paid her husband $75,000 as part of her divorce settlement, in exchange for her freedom.

Alimony and Child Support

Alimony and child support, referred to as "the high cost of leaving," are usually expensive. Normally, a husband with two small children pays one-third to one-half of his after-tax income in alimony and child support (Porter 1975). Costs will vary, depending on the family's standard of living, whether the wife is able to work, the amount of her independent wealth, the number and ages of the children, and the overall financial status of the husband. Some women now reject alimony as demeaning and a symbol of feminine dependency. Others try to sue their husbands for as much as they can get. In some states, a wealthy woman may be ordered to pay alimony to her husband, particularly if he is not able to work. Alimony payments are usually made only until the former spouse remarries; child support payments continue until children reach legal age. Sometimes, an escalator clause is added, which boosts payments as the husband's income increases. Often, the husband agrees to finance his children's college education. If the husband remarries, he is still obligated for the payments awarded to his former wife and children. This means he must help support both the new family and the former one.

Legal Fees

Most husbands are surprised to learn that they may be responsible for the legal fees of both lawyers (their own and their wife's). Fees vary according to income bracket and the amount of time and work a case demands. Many families never recover their former standards of living.

> Whatever your financial situation, a divorce is one of the most costly economic ventures you can undertake—with expenses which few to-be-divorced couples weigh in advance. (Porter 1975, 715)

CHILDREN AND DIVORCE

Children As Pawns

In the most tragic cases, children become pawns in the battle. As one appalled judge put it, children "are treated as negotiable debris from the marriage, not much different from the hi-fi or the family car" (Wylie 1975). Couples may fight over custody, each trying to win the children. In one case, the wife would not agree to a divorce unless the husband promised to give her custody of the children and move at least 1,000 miles away. Since judges often consider the wishes of the children in deciding parental custody, parents may try to influence the children to side with them or to reject the other parent. One husband related: "My wife has done everything she can to turn my son against me. She told him so many lies, which he believed, that whenever anyone comes to the door of the house where my wife and son are living, my boy answers the door with a shotgun in his hands, just in case it's me at the door."

Much of the upset and turmoil children experience because of divorce arises because parents are upset and force the children to take sides. The children love both parents; which one are they to believe or to defend? If parents become embittered, these hostilities are deeply disturbing. The adversary bargaining process prevents justice, destroys whatever semblance of friendly feelings might still exist between couples, and often works great harm on children (Cantor 1970).

Child Custody

Traditionally, custody of the children has been granted to the mother, unless she is found unfit. Actually, the children might be closer to the father; he might be the one who can better afford them and care for them. Most wives have to work after a divorce, as does the husband. More and more, therefore, the overriding consideration is what the court considers the best interests of the children (Dullea 1975).

In some cases, *joint custody* is awarded with both parents responsible. The children may reside alternately with each parent or primarily with one, visiting the other often. In theory, the children should have complete access to both parents. Such arrangements require great maturity and forbearance of both parents. Otherwise, numerous squabbles create continual tension.

Visitation Rights

Ordinarily, visitation rights are given to the parent not awarded custody. These rights may be unlimited (able to visit the children at any time) or they may be restrictive (limiting visitation to several hours or days a month or a year). A vindictive spouse can make life miserable by managing to be away with the children at visitation time, by poisoning the children's minds against the other parent, by refusing to allow the children to phone or write, or by using visitation rights as a weapon against the other person.

One of the most difficult adjustments for a parent with no custodial rights is being away from the children. One Marine sergeant was sued for divorce, with the wife asking for custody of their two sons. When informed by his attorney that the wife is ordinarily given custody, the sergeant expressed his anguish.

> Parting with either of my two sons would be like his death to me. If they (the lawyers and the court) part them, they might as well kill me. . . . I stand to lose my own son through a dirty, nasty experience in court. I have never been afraid of a thing in my life, but I'm afraid of the court. (Wylie 1975, 224)

Faced with the possibility of losing their children, some fathers are driven to violence or to kidnapping their own children.

Effects on Children

In spite of the harmful effects of a bitter divorce, a divorce that is uncontested and fairly amicable may be better for the children than an unhappy marriage (Shideler 1971). An independent survey by Nye and Berardo (1973) compared children from happy, broken homes with children from unhappy, unbroken homes. It showed either few differences or that the children from the happy broken homes had made better personality adjustments and showed less stress, less psychosomatic illness, and less deviancy than those from the unhappy, unbroken homes. An analysis of eleven studies of the relationship between broken homes and juvenile delinquency showed the correlation between the two factors was small (Rosen 1970).

Not all studies agree. A study of 5,376 juveniles showed that children from broken homes were more than twice as likely to be charged with offenses as would be expected by their numbers in the population (Chilton and Markle 1972). In another study, Rosenberg (1965) found that New York high school juniors and seniors from broken homes showed less self-esteem and more psychosomatic symptoms than those from unbroken homes. The unbroken homes in these two studies, however, were not necessarily unhappy and the self-esteem of the children in Rosenberg's study was greatly affected by the age of the mother at the time of the divorce. The younger the divorced mother, the greater the children's loss of self-esteem. Younger mothers were not as able to cope with the upset of the divorce and the added responsibility of raising their children alone. The greater the trauma of the mother over the divorce, the more negative the effect on the children.

Divorce does not always have the tragic impact on children that was once suspected. The long-term effect depends to an extent on how happy the situation is after the divorce. Children who are forced to live in an unhappy home, broken or unbroken, will be affected negatively. Children will find relief in a divorce that removes them from a highly conflicting family; but they will be distressed by a divorce if previously unaware of parental conflict. For this reason, it is important to help children understand the reasons for divorce.

ADULT ADJUSTMENTS AFTER DIVORCE

The problems of adjustment after divorce can be grouped into eight categories.

1. Getting over the emotional trauma of divorce.
2. Dealing with the attitudes of society.
3. Loneliness and the problem of social readjustment.
4. Finances.
5. Realignment of responsibilities and work roles.
6. Sexual readjustments.
7. Contacts with ex-spouse.
8. Kinship interaction.

Emotional Trauma

Under the best of circumstances, divorce is an emotionally disturbing experience. Under the worst conditions, it can result in a high degree of shock and disorientation. Krantzler (1974) referred to divorce as an emotional crisis triggered by a sudden loss. He spoke of the emotional turmoil before and during the divorce, the shock and crisis of separation, a time of mourning as the relationship is laid to rest, and a period of disruption as one attempts to regain balance. Sometimes the emotional trauma of divorce comes primarily from an extended and bitter legal battle. In these cases, the actual divorce decree comes as a welcome relief from this long, painful period.

The trauma is greater when only one spouse wants the divorce, when the idea comes unexpectedly, when there is little time to consider the idea, when one continues to be emotionally attached to the other after the divorce, or when friends and family disapprove of the divorce.

A definite relationship seems to exist between age at the time of divorce and the amount of trauma. Younger people in marriages of long duration experience the highest trauma. For older people, divorce after a long marriage seems less traumatic. The greatest trauma usually occurs at the time of final separation, not at the time of the final decree. After the decree, there is a long period of realization that the relationship is over emotionally as well as legally (Krantzler 1974). The fact that the suicide rate for divorcees is three times that of married women, and four times as great for divorced males as for married men, indicates that being divorced is emotionally unsettling.

Attitudes of Society

Part of the trauma of divorce results from society's attitudes toward divorce and divorced persons (Brandwein, Brown, and Fox 1974; Honig 1974). To some people, divorce represents moral failure, evidence of personal inadequacy or of deviant behavior, which society condemns. A lot of courage is needed to reveal that one has failed, because it exposes that person to social ridicule and condemnation. As a result, some persons who should divorce never do. Or if they do, they retreat from family and friends for a considerable period of time. Some discover that the people they thought they could count on have deserted them. "Friends," one woman remarked bitterly, "they drop you like a hot potato."

Research indicates that, in the beginning, the majority of divorced persons are ashamed of their divorce and try to keep it from new friends. Their children feel stigmatized and try to hide the fact of divorce, primarily because of the attitudes of teachers and other parents. Negative attitudes make the fact of divorce harder to live with, but such attitudes are lessening as divorce becomes more common.

Loneliness and Social Readjustment

Even two married people who do not get along keep one another company. At least someone else is in the house. After divorce, people realize what it is like to live alone. This adjustment is especially difficult for people without children or whose children live with the other spouse. Holidays are particularly difficult for the lonely. Krantzler related, "I celebrated Christmas one day late with my daughter. As on Thanksgiving, I was alone on Christmas and wept without shame over my solitary state and for the past I would never know again" (1974, 24).

Divorced persons complain about the difficulty of rebuilding their social life. "I can't seem to meet any women who are right for me." "How on earth do you get back into circulation after nine years of marriage?" "Where are all those divorced men I used to hear about?" Many authorities suggest that the friendship and companionship of other people is one of the most essential ingredients for a successful adjustment after divorce.

Finances

Most divorced persons suffer financial hardship and have to lower their standard of living. Men who must meet heavy alimony and child support payments may have little money left. Wives who have never worked or who have no special education or skills and who now have the custody of one or more children find themselves impoverished.

This is especially true since only about one-third of ex-husbands contribute at all to the support of their ex-wives and children (Kriesberg 1970). One study in Wisconsin showed that only 38 percent of fathers were in full compliance with the support order. Four years after the divorce, 67 percent of the fathers had ceased providing any money (Citizens Advisory Council 1972). As a consequence, many mothers with children need welfare assistance. The effect of this is a lowered standard of living, with less income and the necessity of moving to poorer housing and a poorer neighborhood, which often means more delinquency, poorer schools, and other concomitant social conditions that affect the family (Weisman and Psykel 1972).

Realignment of Responsibilities and Work Roles

The divorced woman with children faces the prospect of work overload. She must perform all the family functions once shared by two persons. If she works outside the home, she faces an eighteen-hour day, seven days a week. She also has to readjust her parenthood role, taking over functions formerly handled by her husband.

The roles of the divorced man also change, especially if he is a traditional male used to depending on his wife for household care and personal maintenance. If a father also has custody of his children, his responsibilities are total. Whether male or female, the single parent has to fulfill all the family functions, with no relief from the burden.

Sexual Readjustments

A 1982 study revealed that most divorced persons are sexually quite active (Cargan and Melko 1982). More than one-half of divorced persons said they had intercourse twice a week or more. More than one-third reported intercourse at least three times a week. Almost a third of these divorced persons had had more than ten different sexual partners. Apparently, the complaint of sexual frustration common among divorced people a decade ago has been partially eliminated. In addition, formerly married men and women masturbate frequently to release sexual tensions when other sexual outlets are unavailable (Masters and Johnson 1970).

This does not mean, however, that all of these sexual contacts are emotionally satisfying. Some divorced persons speak of meaningless sex, using sex to find companionship, to prove sexual attractiveness, or as an escape from problems. Divorced women complain frequently that they are the targets of sexually aggressive males who believe that experience denotes promiscuity.

Contacts with Ex-Spouse

The more upsetting the divorce and the more vindictive the spouse, the less the other person desires postdivorce contact. This is particularly true in the case of remarriage. Most second wives or husbands object to contacts with former spouses because such contacts usually lead to resentment and conflict. A bitter ex-spouse may try to cause trouble for the new couple.

Contacts that are maintained are usually in regard to the children and/or support money. When the children have problems, both parents become concerned and sometimes correspond or talk to one another about these problems. In this case, an amicable relationship helps them to work things out. Amicable relationships are easier on the children, but they are infrequent. Occasionally, couples end up remarrying. Westman and Cline (1973) mention one extreme case in which a couple separated from each other seventeen times, with three divorces and eighteen reconciliations.

Kinship Interaction

Contacts with parents and siblings usually remain about the same after a divorce. One study showed that almost one-fifth of the divorced individuals increased their contacts with relatives, primarily because of affectional needs and sometimes because of the need for assistance (Spicer and Hampe 1975). Bernard wrote, "Assistance such as money or clothing, was vital, but having people who could give advice, encouragement, and understanding was even more central to the respondent's morale" (1971, 39).

REMARRIAGE

Who Remarries and When?

At the present time, about one in three marriages are second marriages for one or both partners (U.S. Dept. of Commerce 1983). About 87 percent of all divorced men and about 86 percent of all divorced women eventually remarry. About one-fourth of the remarriages take place within a year, one-half within three years, and three-fourths within nine years of the divorce. The median duration between the divorce and second marriage is a little more than three years. Black men and women usually wait longer than whites to remarry. The median age of remarriage is the early thirties for women and the middle thirties for men (U.S. Dept. of Commerce 1983). The younger people are when they get divorced, the greater their chances of remarrying.

The majority of people remarrying are divorced rather than widowed. Part of the difference is due to the younger ages of the divorced as compared to those whose mates are deceased. Only after fifty-five does the number of widowed people remarrying exceed the number of divorced remarrying (U.S. Dept. of Health, Education and Welfare 1973).

Partners

Most persons marry those of like marital status. More than 90 percent of single men and women marry other single persons. More than half of divorced men and women marry divorced partners, and about half of widowers and widows select each other (U.S. Dept. of Health, Education and Welfare 1973).

The Success of Remarriage

The research on marriage and divorce contains little data on the outcome of remarriage, and some contradictory findings have yet to be resolved. One issue concerns whether remarriages are more unstable than the first marriages of divorced persons. The only valid method of resolving this issue is to follow the marital history of a representative population group. This was done by Riley and Spreitzer (1974), using a sample of 1,445 white males and 520 white females, from three different sections of the country, who were in the forty-five to fifty-four age bracket. This sample had somewhat higher rates of separation and divorce than the general population because it represented those who had applied for disability benefits with social security (disability introduces stress into the marital relationship). The data are significant for the population studied, however, and show that the second marriages of both the divorced and widowed were no more likely to end in divorce or separation than the first marriages. Other data also show that remarriages, especially of males, are no more likely to end in divorce than are first marriages (Glick and Norton 1971).

Quality of Remarriages

Divorce statistics tell only part of the story about remarriages. What about the quality? Most studies indicate that remarriages are happier. An overwhelming majority of remarried people indicate that their second marriages are better than their first. One reason is that remarried couples are older, more experienced, and highly motivated to make their marriages work. "The most distinguishing characteristic of second marriages," says a New York marriage counselor, "is sweat. They really work at it" (Rollin 1973, 493).

Stepchildren

This does not mean that remarriages have no problems. One of the biggest problems arises when children live at home. Adolescent stepchildren, particularly, have difficulty accepting their stepfather or stepmother (Rice 1978b). A typical reaction of a stepchild to a stepparent is rejection. "You're not my father," or "You're not my mother." This rejection is difficult for the stepparent to accept, and sometimes leads to a battle of wills, a contest over authority, or to resentment and bitterness. Infant children usually grow up accepting the stepparent as a substitute mother or father.

Adjustments to stepfathers are usually easier than to stepmothers, primarily because stepmothers play a more active role in relation to the children and spend more time with them (Duberman 1973). Also, fairy tales and folklore have fashioned the stereotype of the cruel stepmother, a myth difficult to overcome. Problems are also greater if the parent without custody encourages a child to dislike the stepparent. If stepsiblings live together, trouble ensues if the natural parents show favoritism to their own children. Resentment and jealousy are likely to occur.

In contrast, other examples show very satisfactory stepchild-stepparent relationships. One mother spoke of her husband's relationship with her child.

> He's always referred to her as his daughter rather than as his stepdaughter. He never made any issue of her being a stepchild. There are times when I think she is closer to him than she is to me. He is more her father than her real father ever was or is now. (Duberman 1973, 285)

Relationships among stepsiblings can also be harmonious.

> Our boys are the same age to the day. They are just like brothers. His son and my son are more alike than the two real brothers are. They all refer to each other as brothers; they are like one family. (Duberman 1973, 286)

Out of a total of eighty-eight couples who had remarried and had stepchildren, Duberman found that 64 percent of the families could be judged excellent, as measured by a parent-child relationship score. However, in these reconstituted families with two groups of children—hers and his—the relationship between the stepsiblings was excellent in only 24 percent of the cases and poor in 38 percent. Apparently, stepparents and stepchildren have an easier time adjusting to one another than do stepsiblings. (For additional information, see *Stepparenting* by Rice.)

SUMMARY

Developing intimacy, selecting a mate, and learning to live happily with a marital partner are important psychosocial tasks of early adulthood. According to probability, about 60 percent of those who marry in the United States today will remain married for a lifetime. The remaining 40 percent will divorce some time in their lives.

The earliest years are the most difficult in relation to the probability of divorce, with the chance of divorce greatest during those years. Among those who divorce, the median number of years of first marriage is 6.8 years. Some who survive the early years experience a crisis in the late twenties, early thirties, or at age forty, during which time they reappraise their lives and seek to modify unsatisfactory aspects. For some, divorce is the chosen route. About 40 percent of all broken marriages last ten or more years before the break; 13 percent last more than twenty years.

A number of factors relate to divorce rates. One factor is age. The divorce rates are highest among women fourteen to twenty-four. Men with a college education have a greater chance of their marriage surviving during the first five years than do those with less education. However, differences related to education and income generally disappear after ten years of marriage. Divorce rates are higher in the western part of the United States, and among people who grew up in unstable, unhappy homes. Two out of three divorces involve couples with children (an average of 1.2 children per couple).

The grounds for divorce vary from state to state. All but one state now offer no-fault divorce, which is an improvement over the old adversary approach. However, where no-fault is simply added to existing fault grounds, one spouse can still threaten to sue unless demands are met. The possibility for vengeance is removed when no-fault is the only alternative. In California and many other states, the property is usually divided equally, unless the couple request otherwise. Child custody is supposed to be settled in consideration of the best interests of the child. The worst aspect of the adversary approach is that it forces spouses to become combatants and attack one another.

Divorce is expensive. The husband is responsible for the continuing support of his wife and children while waiting for the divorce to be granted. Meanwhile, living apart can be expensive. The husband with two small children may pay one-third or one-half of his after-tax income in alimony and child support. Legal fees, especially if agreements are not reached easily, can run into thousands of dollars.

In the most tragic cases, the children become pawns in the battle between the parents. Children's upset can be minimized if they are not forced to take sides. Traditionally, child custody has been granted to the mother, but joint custody is becoming more common. Custody battles are upsetting to children. After divorce, full visitation rights are ordinarily given to the noncustodial parent.

The effects of divorce on children vary, depending on the total circumstances. A good divorce may be better for children than an unhappy marriage. Younger mothers generally have a more difficult time adjusting to divorce, so the effects on children are more negative than when the mother is older. Upset can be minimized if children understand the reasons for the divorce and if divorce offers freedom from tension and relief from a highly conflicting family situation.

Divorce is emotionally traumatic to most adults. The trauma is greater when only one spouse wants the divorce, when the idea comes suddenly, when one spouse continues to be emotionally attached to the other, or when friends and family disapprove. Part of the trauma is experienced because of society's negative attitudes toward divorce and divorced persons, although these negative viewpoints are being moderated.

Divorce requires many adjustments: learning to live apart and/or alone, rebuilding one's social life, overcoming financial hardships, realigning work roles and responsibilities, readjusting sexually, minimizing the upset from contacts with an ex-spouse or payment of support money, and relating to relatives and family members.

Almost 90 percent of divorced men and women remarry. The median duration between divorce and second marriage is slightly more than three years. Most persons remarry those of like marital status. Second marriages are no more likely to end in divorce or separation than are first marriages. Often the quality of remarriages is considerably better than that of first marriages.

The biggest problem in remarriage involves children and stepchildren. Both stepparents and stepchildren may have considerable difficulty adjusting to one another. Adjustments to stepfathers are usually easier than to stepmothers. Relationships between stepsiblings can be conflicting or harmonious but often take time to work out. Most couples are able to work out their problems in remarriage, enabling them to fulfill their dreams of living happily ever after.

Part VI

Vocational and Career Development

17

Career Establishment

IDENTITY AND VOCATION

Identity and Vocational Achievement

Two major psychosocial tasks of early adulthood are to mold an identity and to choose and consolidate a career. These two goals are intertwined, because vocational choice is one way to establish identity. Adults are associated with their work. "She is branch manager of the bank." "He is superintendent of schools." Vocational achievement is important in a society that emphasizes individualism, personal fulfillment, and material success. Success and job satisfaction reaffirm one's identity and provide social recognition. One important task of this period, therefore, is to become established in an occupation (Levinson et al. 1978).

Women and Identity

Before the women's movement, choosing a satisfying vocation and achieving success made a positive contribution to identity achievement in men, not in women. In fact, women who had achieved vocational identity showed lower self-esteem than those who had not (Marcia and Friedman 1970). The vocational achievements of the women were in opposition to stereotyped, cultural expectations. Their success carried feelings of anxiety and lowered self-esteem because of social stigma. Since 1972, however, studies have indicated that this situation is slowly changing. Females who have achieved vocational identities report less ego diffusion and an ability to function at the highest ego levels (Ginsburg and Orlofsky 1981). A study in 1982 showed tht women holding nontraditional views of themselves had achieved a clearer sense of identity than women with traditional views (Stein and Weston 1982). They showed the positive psychological growth necessary for mental health.

Work and Negative Identity

Not all work builds a positive identity, however. Work can be a major source of disappointment and frustration and even create a negative image.

Dan Turner, thirty-eight, worked as a physical therapist and coach and chairman of a physical education department of a state college in New York. He worked hard to develop imaginative, Outboard-Bound-type programs. Then the state legislature started cutting back on funds. One by one, members of his staff were dismissed. He was told to "make do." He felt his professional world was being pulled out from under him "by a bunch of bureaucrats." He described the budget cuts and staff reductions as "eating my guts out. My own job is secure, but my life's work was being undone."

Rather than swallow his frustration, as his Dad had done all his life, he retired a quarter century before he intended and moved with his family to a small parcel of land in Vermont, where he had built an A-frame vacation cottage. The family has cut back on living expenses. He works part-time as a physical therapist in a mental hospital nearby; his wife works part-time in a doctor's office. The family is having a hard time adjusting to rural life and their low income.

Most of the time, Dan is satisfied with his decision, but it was one that was forced on him against his will. He misses the challenge of the work he had been doing. (Yankelovich 1981)

Vocation and Life Satisfaction

Discontentment with jobs or money also affects other aspects of life. Rubenstein (1981) found that discontent with one's work is also strongly associated with unhappiness at home. People most troubled about money or deriving little pleasure from their work are most unhappy with their love and sexual relationships. But marital satisfaction is not necessarily greatest when income is highest (Jorgensen 1979). Satisfaction comes from feeling that income level is adequate. If the husband feels he cannot do his part to support his family, he experiences frustration and failure, since one measure of a successful husband in American culture is his adequacy as a breadwinner. If the wife is not earning as much as she feels she needs, and if she and her husband consider their earnings inadequate, their marital dissatisfaction increases because of financial pressures and tension.

Vocational success, or lack of it, affects everyone. A physically handicapped man in his thirties had been looking for a job unsuccessfully for five years. He commented, "The worst part about being out of a job is I feel so useless. When I get up in the morning, I don't have anything more exciting to do than decide which shirt to put on that day. I went to college four years, yet no one wants me. It makes me feel like a nobody."

The more affluent the society, the more isolated people feel if they do not keep up with the standard of living.

Different Levels of Aspiration

One goal of early adulthood is to succeed according to individual criteria with which one feels comfortable within the context of one's community.

Everyone has to be somebody—somehow, somewhere, sometime. It is important to strive toward personalized goals and experience some success. The boy whose parents have only an elementary education, who graduates from high school and attends vocational school, and who gets a good job after graduation is certainly successful when compared to his parent's achievement level. Most parents want their children "to go farther" than they did. Levels of aspiration are determined partly by the role modeling of significant others, but also by individual preferences and personalities, and by peer and societal socializing influences. A positive identity is built into the personality structure when reality approximates possibility and when achievement approximates aspirations.

VOCATIONAL DEVELOPMENT

Timetables

No one timetable for vocational development applies to all persons. Super and associates (1963) assigned general age divisions to each of five major sequences of vocational development.

> *Crystallization*—formulation of ideas about work that are in accord with the individual's self-concept: fourteen to eighteen years.
>
> *Specification*—signifying a vocational preference by narrowing one's choice and taking the first steps to be able to enter an occupation: eighteen to twenty years.
>
> *Implementation*—solidifying vocational preference by finishing training and entering employment: twenty-one to twenty-four years.
>
> *Stabilization*—settling down to the appropriate career choice: twenty-five to thirty-five years.
>
> *Consolidation*—advancement and attainment of status: after age thirty-five.

Super's research indicated that much vocational development occurs after the individual leaves high school. In some cases, this process is not completed for ten or more years. Some adults continue to change vocations throughout adulthood.

In general, the process of developing vocational maturity is delayed in highly complex, industrialized societies where youths are dependent during long periods of education and vocational preparation. In the nineteenth century, the Harvard student body consisted largely of boys aged fourteen and fifteen. Adolescent youths worked twelve to fourteen hours a day in mills and on farms. Today, a student may not complete a higher degree until the late twenties. Many young adults in their late twenties and early thirties work at various jobs as they try to become established in a vocation. Selecting and becoming established in a vocation is a complicated process that usually occurs over a period of many years.

One study of the career aspirations and achievements of a group of women, conducted seven years after college graduation, revealed the following:

- 41 percent showed a positive correlation between aspirations and life accomplishments.
- 28 percent exhibited a working-class pattern, finding whatever employment they could, in whatever place they lived, fitting work periods around family experiences.
- 32 percent showed inconsistencies between goals and what they were doing. They were either career aspirants with family styles, or family aspirants with career styles. For some reason, they were not able to pursue their personal goals according to their preferences. (Almquist and Angrist 1977)

Five Groups of Vocational Development

During the years of early adulthood, primarily the twenties, adults can be grouped into five different categories according to the status of their vocational development.

One group consists of *vocational achievers*. They are highly involved in a vocation of their choice and are actively pursuing established career goals. They have completed their formal education and training and are applying their knowledge and skill in their work. They are fairly contented with their work and look forward to continued development.

A second group are the *vocationally frustrated*. They have in mind particular vocational goals they have not been able to attain, at least at present. This group includes a large number who want to go on to higher education or some type of post-secondary training, but they are hampered by economic, family, or personal circumstances. Also included are those who dropped out of school to get married and those locked into jobs they dislike because they cannot afford to leave them to pursue other goals.

Many young adults have fairly clear-cut vocational plans but find it difficult to pursue their goals because of practical considerations. Many young adults also are doing work they dislike because they cannot find employment in their chosen field.

Steven graduated from the University of Miami, having majored in movie directing. He moved to Hollywood, expecting to find employment. One year later, he still had not found employment and was back home in Connecticut, living at home and selling used cars.

A third group consists of the *noncommitted:* people who are still uncertain what they want to do. They are confused and anxious, unable to decide which direction to pursue (Marcia and Friedman 1970). Some are still in school. They change majors frequently, trying a lot of different courses, but they cannot select a preference. Some of these persons are interested in so many things they are unable to narrow down their interests to one program. Some are not particularly interested in any one thing. They take job after job but never find one type of work they prefer. They are concerned and confused. Some are so emotionally insecure that they have trouble making decisions about anything.

People in the fourth group are *vocational opportunists*. They do not have a clear-cut vocational plan or specific goals. In fact, they have not selected any particular occupation or profession. They accept jobs as opportunities arise. If they can get a job as a salesperson, they take it. If they find a better job doing factory work, they try that. Their employment record is usually erratic, with no real planning involved.

Members of the fifth group are *social dropouts*. Some of them do not care whether they work. They have no occupational goals and little personal ambition. Most of the time they are unemployed. Or they work long enough to be eligible for unemployment and then get fired to collect. Some beg, some steal, some live off of others; some have drug problems. Others live at home, expecting their parents to support them. Certain people have a nonmaterialistic philosophy of life, rejecting the work ethic, or preferring to work as little as possible to maintain themselves. Some young adults move in with others who have adopted a "hang-loose" ethic. For many, this is a phase to be worked through before they become established members of society.

THE WORLD OF WORK

Work Adjustments

Newly employed persons have to make a number of important adjustments if they are to succeed. One is to learn the specific requirements of the job. Job descriptions, if available, may or may not be accurate outlines of what the work entails. Sometimes employees are asked to develop their own job descriptions, especially for newly created positions. Many times, employees do not know in advance exactly what responsibilities their work encompasses. Or, they may find the performance of those responsibilities completely different than imagined. Employees may have a somewhat idealized preconception of their work. Their educational preparation and training emphasized only the positive aspects, overlooking the more distasteful, routine tasks. Workers often suffer reality shock when they learn that their idealized image does not match the day-to-day demands of the occupation (Mortimer and Simmons 1978). These individuals experience a period of disillusionment as more accurate perceptions develop.

After the worker knows what the job entails, he or she must adjust to doing it. Management Decisions, Incorporated, decided to follow the careers of 2,154 professional employees of a large technical corporation over a period of five years to determine who was fired and why. The study showed some surprising results. One-third left the company within five years. Of these, 27 percent were fired. About 40 percent of the entire group of employees who left, and the same percentage of those who stayed, had graduated in the top quarter of their college classes.

A greater percentage of the terminated workers were self-confident about their abilities than were those who stayed. About half of the terminated workers rated themselves in the top 5 percent in terms of job ability, compared to 38 percent who stayed. Nearly 60 percent of the fired employees had high hopes of rising in management, compared to 46 percent of the remaining group.

But management fired these self-confident employees because they did not perform on the job. The fired employees' performances were appraised much lower than those who stayed, both after the first year and after five years ("Who Gets Fired—and Why?" 1980, 8).

In a highly competitive society, employees who tend to be lazy or who expect to get promotions easily and quickly without working for them are going to be disappointed. Whatever the work, the employee must produce or get fired. Getting a job is only the first step. Competence is required to keep it and advance in it.

A third adjustment is to become a part of the firm or organization for which one works. This requires a knowledge of the basic philosophy, structure, services or products, and operating procedures. Each organization is different. Gradually, as the individual worker discovers the employer's idiosyncracies and begins to feel at home in the organization, commitment and loyalty to the company develop. This is a necessary step if the employee is going to be happy in that firm.

A fourth adjustment is getting acquainted with supervisors and fellow employees and learning to work and to get along with them. The ability to work with others is more important than competence and skill. Many competent people create havoc in plants or offices because of their personality problems and social maladjustments. The ability to get along, to like and be liked by others, is an asset in any job or profession.

Finally, the employee must learn to balance the demands of home and job so the needs of both are fulfilled. Every person who cares about home and work feels conflicting demands and loyalties. The wife who is committed to her homemaking tasks but who neglects her work usually gets enough pressure from her superiors so that she feels unhappy with her performance and discontented with the situation. The workaholic husband, who devotes all of his time and energy to his job, has nothing left to give his wife and children and usually gets complaints from them that make him feel uncomfortable about his family performance. Learning to sort out priorities and keep things in balance is difficult. It means learning how to say no to unreasonable or excessive pressures from either quarter.

Job Satisfaction

Much research has been done to determine what factors are important to job satisfaction. Cohn (1979) divides them into two major categories:

extrinsic work satisfactions and *intrinsic work satisfactions*. Extrinsic satisfactions are derived from economic and material rewards given for work. A national survey of *Psychology Today* readers revealed that 74 percent of respondents agreed with the statement, "In America, money is how we keep score" (Rubenstein 1981).

However, income level is not the only criterion. People who earn a lot of money but who are dissatisfied with their income level still feel frustration and failure. A young stockbroker represents this attitude. "I am among the top ten in the country in terms of commissions earned for my company. Last year, I netted $200,000. But my goal is $100,000 more." No matter how well they do, some people are still dissatisfied and unhappy and they suffer terribly when they compare themselves with others.

Intrinsic satisfactions are derived from intangible, emotional, ego-building components accompanying work pursuits. Individuals who find their work interesting and who gain personal enjoyment, status, self-esteem, pleasure, and the opportunity for self-actualization and creativity from it are receiving intrinsic rewards. One study of 652 currently employed males revealed that slightly more than 80 percent said they would continue to work even if there were no financial necessity (Campbell et al. 1976). This means that they were motivated in part by intrinsic rewards. A sampling of 1,992 men, aged eighteen to forty-nine, revealed the importance of nonmaterial rewards (Miller and Simon 1979). These men considered it important that their work provide opportunities for challenge, autonomy, growth, and making a meaningful contribution. In comparing age groups, more younger men than older ones reported a gap between their desires and the realities of their work experience. The younger men were more impatient to attain their goals, had an intense need for self-realization, and felt frustrated that it was not happening fast enough.

EDUCATION AND VOCATION

Amount of Education

What one achieves and the level one attains depend partly on the amount of education received. Although some individuals "pull themselves up by their boot straps," without benefit of much formal education or vocational preparation, the vast majority need and depend on as much schooling as possible. Table 17.1 shows the relationships between occupation and education. The need for a college education is especially pronounced among professional and technical workers. Seventy-two percent of men and 62 percent of women employed in this category had four or more years of college. Among blue-collar workers, 33 percent of the men and 40 percent of the women had less than four years of high school. Overall, a majority of both white- and blue-collar workers had a high school education, but those occupying the least skilled positions had the least amount of education (U.S. Dept. of Commerce 1984).

TABLE 17.1 Occupation of Employed Workers, by Educational Attainment and Sex: 1982

| Sex and Occupation | Less Than 4 Years High School | | 4 Years of High School | | 4 Years or More of College | |
	Male	Female	Male	Female	Male	Female
TOTAL WORKERS	20.1	16.5	35.8	45.0	26.6	20.0
White-Collar Workers	6.3	6.3	24.3	43.5	49.1	27.5
Professional, technical	1.7	1.8	11.3	14.8	71.7	62.3
Managers, administrators, except farm	9.1	8.4	30.0	43.2	39.0	25.7
Sales workers	7.0	13.5	25.3	49.4	37.7	16.2
Clerical workers	11.8	7.0	43.6	59.9	18.1	9.1
Blue-Collar Workers	32.7	40.4	48.3	48.2	4.5	4.0
Craft workers	26.3	21.3	50.6	52.6	5.8	11.5
Operatives, except transport	37.6	46.5	47.8	45.9	2.7	2.2
Laborers	43.7	36.0	39.5	50.8	4.1	3.8
Service Workers	30.1	35.8	42.1	47.3	10.2	5.0
Farmers and Farm Workers	42.7	23.0	36.9	60.4	10.7	6.7

*Percentages do not add up to 100 since those with 1–3 years of college have been omitted from the table.

Adapted from: U.S. Department of Commerce, Bureau of the Census, *Statistical Abstract of the United States: 1984*, 104th ed. (Washington, D.C.: U.S. Government Printing Office, 1984), 418.

Income

The amount of education has an important influence on the level of income attained. Figure 17.1 shows the percent distribution of households by income level and educational attainment of the householder in 1982. Forty-five percent of those with only eight years of schooling earned less than $10,000 in 1982; only 1.8 percent of those with this education earned $50,000 or over. But among those with four years of college, only 8.4 percent earned less than $10,000, and 20 percent earned $50,000 and more. Those with four years of high school fell in between these two extremes. Thus, there was a high positive correlation between education and income.

ETHNIC AND RACIAL CONSIDERATIONS

Education

Unfortunately, considerable discrepancies exist in education, employment, and income when race or ethnic origin is considered. Fewer blacks than whites completed college. Hispanic adults had considerably less education

FIGURE 17.1   Percent Distribution of Households by Income Level and Educational Level of Householder: 1982

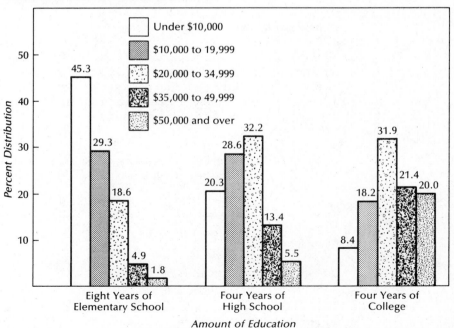

Amount of Education

Adapted from: U.S. Department of Commerce, Bureau of the Census, *Statistical Abstract of The United States: 1984,* 104th ed. (Washington, D.C.: U.S. Government Printing Office, 1984), 460.

than either whites or blacks. Only a little more than a third of Hispanics graduated from high school, and only one-tenth completed college. However, a further breakdown of Hispanic adults according to national origin revealed considerable variations. Table 17.2 shows the percentages with fewer than five years of school and with four years of high school or more. As shown, those from Cuba and those from Central or South America were the best educated. Those from Mexico had the lowest level of education.

Employment

There are even greater racial discrepancies in employment. Unemployment continues to be a major problem, particularly among blacks. Even educated blacks have trouble finding employment, especially during recessions. They are the last hired and the first laid off. The younger the age of blacks, the higher their unemployment rate. Even young Hispanic adults have less trouble finding employment than blacks, in spite of their lower level of education. This situation reflects deep-seated prejudices that have yet to be overcome. In spite of the civil rights laws that make it illegal to discriminate according to race, inequalities and injustices remain.

Income

Considerable racial differences also exist in relation to income. From 1970 to 1982, the gap between black and white income actually increased. Table 17.3 shows the discrepancies. These years also brought an increasing discrepancy in income between whites and Hispanics (U.S. Dept. of Commerce 1984, 459). Rather than decreasing, income differentials are becoming greater. The decline in real income of minority groups has inflicted increasingly greater hardships on those involved.

TABLE 17.2   Percent of Spanish Population, Age 25–34, with Fewer Than 5 Years of School and with 4 Years of High School or More, by National Origin: 1982

National Origin	Fewer Than 5 Years of School	4 Years of High School or More
Mexican	9.5%	52.7%
Puerto Rican	2.3%	59.5%
Cuban	1.9%	73.8%
Other (Central or South America or Other Spanish Origin)	2.7%	73.7%
All Spanish Combined	6.9%	58.3%

Adapted from: U.S. Department of Commerce, Bureau of the Census, *Statistical Abstract of the United States: 1984* (Washington, D.C.: U.S. Government Printing Office, 1984), 146.

TABLE 17.3   Differences in Median Income between Black and White Households, 1970 and 1982, in Constant (1982) Dollars

| | Median Income | | |
Year	White	Black	Income Differential
1970	$22,613	$13,764	$8,849
1982	$21,117	$11,968	$9,149

Adapted from: U.S. Department of Commerce, Bureau of the Census, *Statistical Abstract of the United States: 1984* (Washington, D.C.: U.S. Government Printing Office, 1984), 459.

INCOME AND LIFE-STYLE

The Very Poor

There are important implications and consequences of these facts and figures on income. The very poor live restricted, colorless lives. Lack of money restricts them generally to their neighborhoods, in turn limiting their possibilities and opportunities. They have only minimal necessities and certainly nothing that would make their lives easier or more enjoyable. They are at the mercy of life's unpredictable events: sickness, loss of work, injury, legal problems, problems with children, family difficulties, and others. Because they lack resources, they have little social or political power and cannot protect themselves against adversity. Any minor crisis can become an emergency: missed rent payments bring eviction, a problem with police ends in court, a slight illness develops into a major medical emergency. The poor strive to stay out of trouble; they strive for security because they feel uncertain about their lives; and they strive just to provide themselves with the basics of life.

The Lower Middle Class

Just above the poor are the lower middle class, who face other considerations. They have the necessities of life but little else. They cannot afford to buy a home so they rent. They would like to advance their education but schooling has to be postponed. They cannot afford to change jobs or take a nice vacation. They would like braces for the children's teeth, some clothes besides jeans, a newer car, the chance to eat at better restaurants, and more money for recreation, sports events, or hobbies. They look forward to the day when they can have or do the things they always wanted.

The Middle Class

Many middle-class Americans are fairly well off but still "money poor." They struggle to pay for a house they can barely afford or a car that cost more than they intended. Their credit cards and charge account balances are out of control. No matter how much they earn, the demands for money seem almost insatiable. They spend their lives working to meet their obligations, under a great deal of strain to pay their bills.

The Money Conscious

In a survey by *Psychology Today,* Americans at all levels of income up to $50,000 per year felt they needed more money than they earned in order to live comfortably (Rubenstein 1981). Those people earning less than $10,000 felt they needed $10,000 to $20,000. Those earning $10,000 to $20,000 said they needed $20,000 to $30,000. Those earning $20,000 to $30,000 said they needed $30,000 to $50,000, and so on. Only those earning $50,000 to $100,000 a year and more said their incomes were already sufficient to live comfortably. Apparently, needs and desires rose geometrically with income. For some people, money was a critical passion. Some of them had grown up in rich families, some in poor; their fathers were either extravagant or penny-pinching. Money was often discussed at home, and they were taught to believe it was all-important. As a result, more than three-fourths of them viewed income as a prime indicator of success (Rubenstein 1981).

WOMEN AND VOCATIONS

Labor Force Participation Rates

The numbers and percentages of women in the labor force continue to rise. Figure 17.2 shows the labor force participation rates of women, aged twenty to twenty-four and twenty-five to thirty-four, from 1960 to 1982. As shown, there was a considerable increase over this span. The Bureau of Labor Statistics forecasts that the female labor force will continue to grow in the next fifteen years. By 1995, women will make up 47 percent of the total labor force, reflecting their greater job activity as well as a decrease in male participation ("Women at Work" 1981).

One significant fact about these participation rates is the high percentages of working women with dependent children. Even among married women with husbands present, 49 percent with children under six and 63 percent with children six to seventeen work. These percentages continue to rise.

Another significant fact about the participation rates of women is related to the types of jobs they hold. Although significant progress has been made, women continue to be a minority in the managerial and administrative occupations. More than half of all female workers (54 percent) are in two major occupational categories: clerical and service work. An additional 13 percent hold blue-collar jobs (crafts, operatives, and

FIGURE 17.2   Labor Force Participation Rates of Women, Aged 20–24 and 25–34, 1960–1982

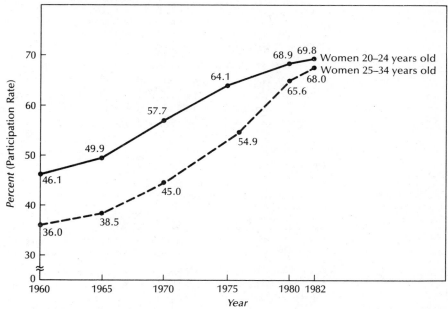

Adapted from: U.S. Department of Commerce, Bureau of the Census, *Statistical Abstract of the United States: 1984,* 104th ed. (Washington, D.C.: U.S. Government Printing Office, 1984), 407.

laborers). The real problem is that women are employed primarily in low-status, low-paying jobs. However, real progress has been made in some occupations. The percentages of female bank officers and financial managers have approximately doubled in ten years, as have the percentages of insurance agents and pharmacists. The percentages of female lawyers and judges have multiplied four times. Progress in other occupations, such as accounting, college teachers, physicians, social and recreation workers, school administrators, writers, artists, entertainers, and real estate agents or brokers, has been less spectacular but nevertheless significant. Although engineering continues to be one of the most segregated, male-dominated professions, the percentage of female engineers has increased seven times in the last ten years. These figures indicate less and less segregation of women in occupations.

Discrimination and Income

Despite the increasing acceptance of women in various occupations, discrimination is evident when their income is compared with that of men in identical occupations. A number of factors influence earnings differentials.

As already discussed, men have higher-status jobs than women, thus higher incomes. A greater percentage of men go on to higher education. Men are about twice as likely as women to be working full time, twelve months a year. Men have about twice the work experience as women of comparable age. But if these factors are adjusted statistically so that women are assumed to have the same occupational status, education, full-time working hours, and worker experience as men, the income level of women is still only 61 percent of the male income level (Rice 1983). The conclusion of discrimination is inescapable. Women are not receiving equal pay for equal work. Nationally, a female chemist with a Ph.D. averages less income than a male chemist with a bachelor's degree.

Role Strain

The increasing participation of women in various occupations has its disadvantages. One is the increased *role strain* as women seek to fulfill their responsibilities at home and at work. Because women are assuming greater responsibilities outside the home, one would reason that husbands are assuming a proportionate share of the homemaking and child-rearing tasks. This is not always the case.

One United States Department of Agriculture study gave a detailed analysis of what husbands and wives actually do around the house ("How Much Does He Do Around the House?" 1971). According to this study, husbands averaged a total of one and one-half hours a day on yard and home care, car upkeep, food preparation and/or cleanup, child care, and all home tasks combined. This was true regardless of whether the wife was a full-time homemaker or full-time job holder (thirty or more hours a week). Women who held full-time jobs still spent an additional four and one-half hours daily on homemaking tasks, or three times the amount of time spent by their husbands. Although *egalitarian* and democratic marriage ideals emphasize that the husband and wife share everything fifty-fifty, in actual practice, the wife still assumes primary reponsibility for housekeeping and child care.

Role strain is especially evident in the lives of women who have full-time careers (Gilbert et al. 1981). Research on dual-career families indicated that conflict between professional and parental roles was especially stressful for the female spouse (Bryson and Bryson 1978; Holahan and Gilbert 1979; Johnson and Johnson 1976). Conflict arises over numerous events, for example:

- The need to take a child to a mid-day dentist appointment when an important committee meeting is scheduled.
- The need to care for children's emotional concerns and to listen to them when one is under tremendous pressure at work.
- The need to care for a sick child.

Most women in dual-career families have a high degree of commitment to both the maternal and professional roles (Holahan and Gilbert

1979). As a consequence, most career women generally feel guilty about not being a good parent or spending enough time with their children (Gilbert et al. 1981, 424). At the same time, these women feel that their increased role conflict is more than offset by the increased resources and privileges and the enhanced sense of personal worth accrued from the professional role.

SUMMARY

An important way to achieve identity is through one's vocation. People become known by the work they do. Since the women's movement, establishing a positive identity through one's vocation has become as important to women as to men. However, work that becomes a major source of disappointment can also create a negative image for both men and women. People dissatisfied with their own level of achievement who feel frustration and a sense of failure become discontented with their jobs. This, in turn, affects their marriage and family life and other aspects of life as well. A positive identity is built into people's personality structures when achievement approximates aspirations.

Young adults can be divided into five categories according to the status of their vocational development: vocational achievers, vocationally frustrated, noncommitted, vocational opportunists, and social dropouts. The vocational achievers are involved in a vocation of their choice, are fairly content with the work they do, and look forward to continued development. No single timetable of vocational development applies to all persons. Because of the necessity of long years of preparation in a highly complex, industrialized society, many young adults may not become established in their vocations until their late twenties or early thirties.

Newly employed persons must make a number of adjustments in order to succeed in their work. These adjustments include learning the specific requirements of the job, doing the work, becoming a part of the company, getting acquainted with other persons and getting along with them, and learning to balance the demands of home and office so the needs of both are fulfilled.

Job satisfaction depends both on extrinsic or material rewards and on intrinsic or intangible, ego-building components of a job. Dissatisfaction sets in if either extrinsic or intrinsic rewards are not as great as anticipated.

Vocational achievement depends partially on the amount of education received. In general, the more education, the higher the level of vocational attainment, and the greater the level of earned income. Members of minorities have lower levels of education, higher rates of unemployment, and lower levels of income.

Income is important since it affects life-style. The very poor have only minimal necessities. The lower middle class have some basic necessities but little else, so they cannot buy a home or do many other things they would like to do. The middle class are fairly well off but money poor, usually struggling to pay for purchases they cannot afford. Only those earning incomes of $50,000 to $100,000 a year say their incomes are sufficient to live comfortably.

The percentages of women in the labor force continue to rise, even among married women with dependent children still at home. A greater percentage of divorced women work than those who are either separated or married. But because of many factors, including discrimination, women continue to occupy a disproportionate share of low-status, low-paying jobs. Progress is being made, however. The percentage of women in high-status, high-paying jobs continues to rise, but the income level of all women is still only 61 percent of the male income level when occupational status, education, full-time working hours, and work experience are adjusted statistically to the level of men. The conclusion is inescapable: the primary reason for the lower income of women is discrimination.

The increasing participation of women in various occupations has increased their role strain as they seek to discharge both home and work responsibilities. Their plight has not been eased as much as it might because their husbands still expect them to assume the major responsibilities at home, even if they work full-time. If wives are to work outside the home, husbands need to assume a greater proportion of homemaking and child-rearing tasks. Women with full-time careers are especially strained because of the heavy responsibility they carry. But they feel their increased role conflict is more than offset by the increased resources and privileges their careers bring, as well as the enhanced sense of personal worth they derive from their professional role.

18

Mid-Life Careers and Employment

A TIME OF FRUITION

Achievement and Honors

For most people, middle adulthood is the fruition of a long period of professional work, when years of training and experience culminate in positions of maximum authority and responsibility (Buhler 1977). People appointed to leadership positions usually achieve these positions by their early fifties. Executive search firms, which place people in top positions in industry, usually prefer individuals in their late forties or early fifties. Such people are old enough to have adequate experience to assume maximum responsibilities but young enough to have the vigor and drive to do their best work. As a consequence, the average age for chief executives and members of corporate boards is about fifty-five ("Middle Age, The Best of Times" 1982).

One study compared the ages of individuals who had won academic or professional honors (between 1901 and 1975) as Nobel prize winners, as presidents of scientific or professional associations, or as presidents of major research-oriented universities (Shin and Putnam 1982). The mean age for Nobel prize winners in science was 52.2 years; it was 62 years for winners in literature. The fact that scientific prize winners were an average of ten years younger than literature winners indicated that achievement of scientists and the recognition of that achievement occurred at younger ages than that of literary winners.

Association presidents included presidents of such organizations as the American Society of Civil Engineers, American Medical Association, American Psychological Association, and the American Sociological Association. The mean age of association presidents was 56.8 years. Candidates elected to these positions were judged worthy by peers to represent the total profession. This judgment certainly was based not only on individual contributions to the field, but also on such personal considerations as the ability to exemplify those ideas that formed the basic tenets of the scientific and professional ethos.

The mean age of university presidents was 50.8 years. The median age of presidents at Harvard and Princeton was 47; at Stanford it was 47.7. The oldest mean age of presidents was 52 years at the University of California at Berkeley. University presidents were generally younger than either Nobel prize winners or association presidents (Shin and Putnam 1982).

In chapter 13, it was concluded that peak performance as measured by the quantity of creative output varied according to the field of endeavor. According to Dennis's (1966) study cited in that chapter, the output of those in the creative arts and science peaked in their forties and declined thereafter. The output of those in the humanities continued to rise until their sixties. This study agrees with Shin and Putnam's (1982) study, which showed that proficiency in fields involving literature and verbal skills did not peak until the early sixties, whereas proficiency in fields involving scientific skills peaked much earlier. Studies of cognitive development also show that verbal skills tend to hold up until about sixty years of age, whereas numerical abilities decline earlier (see chapter 11).

A difference exists, however, between productivity and the recognition of that productivity. National or international recognition of ability does not come until some time after the actual work has been accomplished. This is why most honors, even in science, go to recipients in their fifties, and literary honors to those in their early sixties. The important point is that the middle years of the forties and fifties are years of high productivity. They can be quite satisfying to those who gain widespread recognition of their accomplishments.

Income

On the average, income peaks during the middle years. Figure 18.1 shows mean family income (not individual income) as a function of the age of the householder. As shown, income peaks between forty-five and fifty-four years of age (U.S. Dept. of Commerce 1984). These figures include people in all types of occupations. Generally speaking, those involved in work requiring physical labor do not earn as much in late middle age as they did earlier. As physical capacity wanes, so does income. This contrasts with people in white-collar occupations, whose average earnings continue to increase, at least for a while. The net result is a peak in mean wages during the middle years.

With family income at a peak, middle age can be a time of affluence. Major financial commitments, such as buying and financing a house, are fulfilled. Many have a large discretionary income for leisure and travel. The current group of middle-aged adults has also benefited from being a relatively small generation born during the depression years. They enjoyed a wealth of job opportunities in the booming 1950s and 1960s, and bought their first homes at interest rates of 4 to 6 percent, before the enormous increase in housing prices. This led one advertising executive to remark that "there's gold in them thar middle ages," meaning a rich harvest awaits

FIGURE 18.1   Mean Family Income, by Age of Householder, 1981

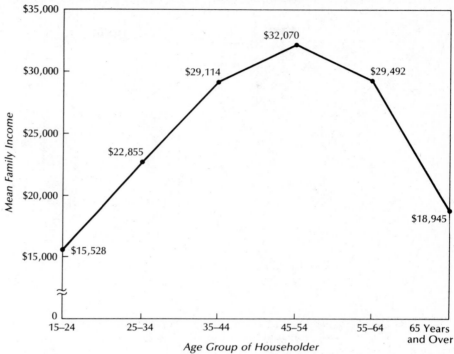

Adapted from: U.S. Department of Commerce, Bureau of the Census, *Statistical Abstract of the United States: 1984* (Washington, D.C.: U.S. Government Printing Office, 1984), 465.

the marketer who taps the affluence of today's middle-agers ("Prosperity Looks 50–Plus" 1979).

UNEMPLOYMENT

The unemployment rate of middle-agers is also quite low. Figure 18.2 shows the rate by age and sex in 1982 (U.S. Dept. of Commerce 1984). There are, however, some middle-aged adults who find it difficult to hold their present jobs. Two recessions forced scores of companies to lay off white- and blue-collar workers who had twenty to thirty years of experience. For many adults, this was the first snag in their careers.

Other middle-agers lose their jobs to younger, ambitious workers moving up the employment ladder. Supervisors pressured to cut expenses find it cheaper to hire younger people and pay them less. Followers of older mentors suddenly turn into carnivores. Sometimes middle-aged people do not keep abreast in our increasingly technological society, where change is so rapid you become completely outdated unless you attend

FIGURE 18.2   Unemployment Rate of Civilian Labor Force, by Sex and Age, 1982

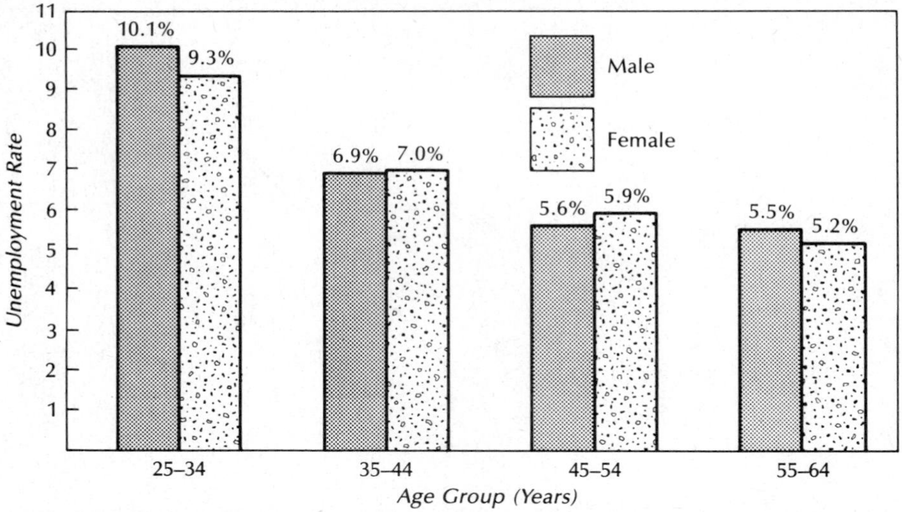

Age Group (Years)

Adapted from: U.S. Department of Commerce, Bureau of the Census, *Statistical Abstract of the United States: 1984* (Washington, D.C.: U.S. Government Printing Office, 1984), 409.

refresher courses every several years. Companies are forced to hire new employees who are familiar with the latest technology.

SECOND CAREERS

Americans with Second Careers

When a person is shut out of a career or at a dead end, one answer is to begin a second career. Thousands of middle-agers make mid-life career changes, sometimes voluntarily after months or years of reevaluation and thought, or other times because of losing a job.

Opera star Beverly Sills gave up her active singing career at fifty to take on a second career as general director of the New York City Opera. "I may be considered old as an opera singer," she remarked, "but I'm thought of as a young manager. That's one of the corporate perks of this job" (Heymont 1980, 64).

Lesser known Americans have also undertaken second careers.

Teddy Colbert, age fifty-one, of Los Angeles, after raising a family of seven children, turned her long-time hobby of gardening into a busy and rewarding new life. She went back to college to take journalism and began writing gardening tips for the local paper. This led to a regular gardening column in the Sunday edition of the *Los Angeles Times*. (Shuman 1979, 11)

Overcoming Doubts

Part of the problem of establishing a second career is that many middle-agers feel they are too old to learn or return to school and start over. The important motivators are a desire to learn and to grow and a realization that one can change and make provisions for doing something different and interesting. Dr. Jacob commented, "I don't believe in reincarnation, but I do think we have many lives within one life" (Freese 1977a, 38).

Mothers

Mothers who have launched their last child from the nest and need to fill their lives with something other than children's problems are important candidates for second careers. The most devoted mothers have the most difficult time adjusting, unless they establish new goals to fill the gap. A second career is the answer for many such women. However, getting a good job is difficult for women who were unemployed during the child-rearing years.

In such cases, a woman may find it necessary to return to school to update her skills. In other instances, a woman may have to create her own job (Deakin 1977a).

Widows and Divorcees

Many women seek work out of necessity because their marriages break up or because their husbands die at a comparatively young age. These women assumed that they would always be married and have adequate support. Suddenly, they find themselves alone, with little income and accumulating bills. A typical situation is the widow who is too young for social security (she must be sixty unless she is disabled) and with no dependent children to generate benefits. The following example illustrates the problem.

> In the employment office of a middle-sized business in New England, the personnel director called a woman to his desk: "Mrs. Middleton."
>
> Edith Middleton, 52, slim and younger looking than her years, got up from a bench and walked over to him.
>
> The personnel man looked at the job application she had filled out. "I see you worked as a secretary in 1943, '44, and '45. Have you been gainfully employed since then?" Gainfully employed! Edith felt like screaming.
>
> Everywhere she had gone to look for a job, she had been asked the same question.
>
> She wanted to tell him: "I've raised two children, parents themselves now, and both decent, law-abiding, fine human beings. I quit that secretarial job thirty-three years ago to marry John Middleton. He had a traditional view of marriage, and so did I—so did most people then. I was sure I'd be

a homemaker all my life. I never dreamed—and neither did John—that he would be dead at fifty-four."

Had she been gainfully employed recently? Quietly, Edith replied, "No."

"Thank you for coming in," the personnel director said, "but I'm afraid we have nothing for you." (Deakin 1977, 28)

It is estimated that four to six million *displaced homemakers* have been forced to fend for themselves by divorce or the death of a husband (Downey 1981). In many cases, these women went from incomes of well over $25,000 to under $5,000 per year. If their children are still at home, their only money may be an unstable child-support check. They usually need help with financial, legal, medical, and social assistance matters. Some of these women are battered wives who need a place to stay. More than thirty-two states have passed displaced homemaker legislation to provide assistance for such women. Dozens of programs have been set up with the help of federal grants. With additional training, many such women can find remunerative and satisfying jobs.

OCCUPATIONALLY RELATED STRESS

Work and Emotional Stress

Whereas the middle years can be productive and rewarding for many, they can also be years of upset and anxiety for others. Job-related emotional problems are common among middle-agers. One source of stress, which was discussed earlier, is being laid off or fired. Although the economic impact of job loss may be severe, the emotional impact may be even more serious. Such psychosomatic symptoms as diarrhea, headaches, sleep disturbances, or depression are common. Middle-aged persons whose main gratifications in life came from work may panic when they find their primary source of emotional support terminated.

The frustration of unfulfilled expectations is a source of stress for some people. It may be inevitable for the ambitious because only a few can reach the upper levels. Women who determine what they want to become and then fail, feel bitterness and resentment. Business women who aspire to top positions are in an especially difficult position. If they undertake challenging new roles but are grudgingly accepted, they may become more and more frustrated. Their achievements come only with much effort and emotional cost. Psychological and occupational counseling for both men and women is often helpful to assist them through rough periods.

The Workaholic

Workaholics are people driven to overwork, not because of the job situation or job pressure but because of personal drives that compel them to work rather than relax. They have overly strict consciences that make them feel guilty if anything is left undone. Their job becomes all-consuming and they forego normal outlets such as vacations, sports, and parties.

Not only corporate executives become workaholics. A construction worker can be inwardly driven to put in long hours of overtime. Such drives usually originate in the family background. A child brings home four A's and one B, but the parents berate the child for the B rather than giving praise. If parents constantly pressure their children to excel, be perfect, and do things to please them, the children soon develop the feeling that striving and working are the only things that matter (Norborn 1979).

Initially, workaholics may appear quite successful on the job. They work hard and are usually productive. But many spend twelve hours doing eight hours of work, because they are constantly running on depleted resources. They never refresh themselves through recreational activities or stop to regenerate themselves. Consequently, they work longer hours less efficiently.

One problem with workaholics is that their all-exclusive attention to work affects their families. As one wife said, "He gives all he has to his job, so he has nothing left for me." Anniversaries, holidays, and birthdays are glossed over or forgotten. Family vacations never take place. Wives sometimes end up depressed and unhappy, feeling that something must be wrong with them since their husbands spend no time with them.

Long hours of overwork often result in chronic health problems, commonly, headaches, fatigue, depression, and insomnia. These people are also prime candidates for heart attacks or bleeding ulcers. Like the person addicted to alcohol or drugs, the workaholic usually needs outside counseling to overcome the problem (Norborn 1979).

Burnout

Burnout is a term describing the condition of a person emotionally and physically exhausted from too much job pressure.

A typical example is that of a fifty-one-year-old principal of a ghetto neighborhood school in a large Eastern city. She can't control the students who constantly present severe discipline problems. Teachers are beaten on campus. Because of violence and salary issues, faculty members themselves are in an ugly, rebellious mood. Some resign, others are forced out by an economic squeeze that also leaves the school short of other resources and supplies. District administrators meanwhile are pressuring the principal to deliver more for less.

Nor is there any respite for her at the end of the day. She goes home each night to care for a seriously ill, invalid husband.

As the stresses mount, she confides in no one. After all, she tells herself, she's a strong, competent person who ought to be able to handle it.

But as the inner turmoil builds it must come to the surface. She is sarcastic and quick to anger over the slightest irritation. She slams doors and tells people to go to hell. One afternoon a colleague finds her at her desk weeping profusely. Fortunately, she is persuaded to visit a psychologist for help. Diagnosis: severe depression precipitated by burnout. (Briley 1980b, 36)

Burnout can occur at any stage of adult life, but middle-agers seem particularly prone. They have devoted their efforts to their careers and families, often not finding the replenishment they hoped for. Burned out men and women describe their overwhelming depletion saying: "I don't care any more," "I have nothing left to give," "I'm drained," "I'm exhausted."

People with certain personality characteristics are more susceptible to burnout than others, for example: those who have shaky self-confidence to start with; those who depend on constant validation from others to build their self-esteem; and those who drive themselves in overcompensation, becoming exhausted in the process. Pessimistic people, who always dwell on the negative rather than the positive aspects of daily activities, find themselves under constant stress. These people find the glass half empty rather than half full (Briley 1980b).

Burnout can come from a variety of job situations. It is common among frustrated workers doing monotonous work. High rates of stress and burnout occur in working environments where employees are over-controlled and granted little autonomy, where there is little trust of a management that tends to manipulate workers, where there are threats and fear of authority, or where there is insufficient delegation of authority, inevitable stagnation, and little or no opportunity for job or career growth. Unnecessary pressure, long hours, monotony, poorly defined responsibilities and goals, conflicts among employees, favoritism, departments working at cross purposes—all foster stress and burnout.

Job pressures often combine with personal and family circumstances to create an overload. Added together, family tensions and conflicts, financial pressures, illness, and problems with children or other family members can create stress. Poor health habits over a period of time can cause havoc. Unless people take time off for rest and relaxation and diversionary social activities, they forget how to relax and their stress builds up.

One problem with burnout is that it develops insidiously, becoming real before the victim knows what is happening. It can be prevented by following several rules:

- Look for cues and do something about them.
- Talk out job stresses with colleagues to solve the problems.
- Take time out at work
- Look after physical health.
- Separate job stresses from home life.
- Replenish yourself through leisure-time pursuits.
- Rest, relax, and recreate. (Briley 1980b, 39)

When burnout becomes advanced and prolonged and turns into severe depression or chronic anxiety, then psychotherapy or counseling is in order.

SUMMARY

Middle adulthood is ordinarily a time of generativity, when adults reach the peak of success. The mean age of Nobel prize winners in science is 52.2 years, and in literature it is 62 years. The mean age of appointment as president of a professional association is 56.8 and as university president 50.8 years, indicating that most adults do not gain outstanding recognition until fairly late in life. Income also peaks between forty-five and fifty-four.

Unemployment is quite low among middle-agers, although some are forced out of jobs they have held for twenty or thirty years. This creates not only financial crises but also emotional ones. A mother whose last child has left home may find that a second career will fulfill a need to feel important and useful. Other women must return to work out of necessity because their marriages break up or because their husbands die at a comparatively young age. To get a good job, they may have to upgrade their training and skills by returning to school. With additional education, these women can find jobs that are remunerative and satisfying.

Work can be productive and rewarding but a source of anxiety and stress as well. Stress increases slowly if expectations are not fulfilled. Workaholics are driven to overwork, not from external pressure, but because of inner drives. Many times, these drives originated in childhood from unreasonable parental pressure. As workaholics exhaust themselves, they become less efficient, working more and accomplishing less. They often develop such chronic health problems as headaches, depression, or insomnia.

Burnout describes the condition of a person emotionally and physically exhausted from too much job pressure. People who have to compensate for shaky self-esteem or who are pessimistic are particularly prone to burnout. Burnout can also arise from a variety of job situations: monotony, lack of autonomy on the job, management that manipulates or threatens employees, insufficient delegation of authority, stagnation, pressure, long hours, poorly defined responsibilities, conflict, favoritism, and competition among departments. Family tension, financial pressures, and illness combine with job difficulties to create stress. Burnout can be prevented by following a few important rules, but once it becomes advanced, it usually requires professional intervention and help.

19

The Older Worker
and Retirement

THE OLDER WORKER

Increased Numbers

Because of increased longevity, better health care, and recent legislation extending the mandatory retirement age, the possible span of an adult's working life in the United States is increasing (Fozard and Popkin 1978). The mandatory retirement age of seventy will allow millions of workers to remain on the job. Workers in certain types of jobs can remain even longer if they desire. Accordingly, the numbers of older workers in the work force may increase in the years ahead.

Misunderstanding and Discrimination

Employers, fellow employees, and even older adults themselves often misunderstand the capabilities of the older worker. This misunderstanding causes widespread discrimination against older workers and underuse of their talents in the job market or on particular jobs (Greene 1978). Even though Congress passed the Age Discrimination Employment Act (ADEA) in 1967, more than 9,000 complaints of age discrimination were filed with the Equal Employment Opportunity Commission in 1981 ("More Age Bias?" 1982).

Capabilities

What are the capabilities of older workers? This question is difficult to answer because of the widespread differences among employees regardless of age. However, some generalizations can be made.

Studies of the job records of older workers generally have shown that they demonstrate better attendance and report fewer instances of injury or absence because of illness than their younger colleagues (Bartley 1977).

Older persons generally place a lower priority on outside interests and are more settled in their work habits than younger workers. Some employers prefer to hire older people because they consider them more dependable and responsible.

Verbal abilities of older adults tend to hold up with advancing age, whereas performance abilities tend to decline. Thus, the competence of the older worker cannot be ascertained on the basis of age alone but depends partially on the job requirements. If the job requires physical and motor skills, such as fast reaction time, motor ability, coordination, manual dexterity, or superior strength, older adults will be at a disadvantage. If the job requires verbal skills or experience in practical problem solving or personal relationships, older adults may be superior to younger people. However, even physical performances of older adults can be improved greatly by instruction and practice. Because some older adults with superior health and fitness may evidence physical performance abilities superior to those of younger persons, individual differences should be considered. Also, work environments and demands can be adjusted to suit the special needs of the elderly. Adults with poor vision need extra illumination; adults who work steadily but not as fast may still produce more if speed requirements are modified. The adult on an assembly line who completed fewer production units but has a smaller number of units rejected because of errors may demonstrate a greater unit-per-hour production rate.

Task performances of older adults are greatly influenced by motivational and psychological factors. Like everyone, older adults do better on tasks that interest them, that offer opportunities to use their abilities and talents, and that offer rewards and social incentives (Levendusky 1978). However, job situations that are too competitive, demanding, or anxiety-producing reduce performance because they inhibit positive response and performance (Lair and Moon 1972). Psychological factors, such as self-confidence and emotional well-being, are especially important positive influences on task performance.

Any evaluations of job performance of the elderly will depend partially on the attitude and/or prejudices of the persons doing the evaluating. Evaluators with positive attitudes and feelings toward the elderly tend to give more positive evaluations than those with prejudiced, negative feelings. One study of the attitudes of undergraduate and mid-life adults toward older job applicants revealed that even though participants felt older subjects were as competent as younger workers, they less often expected the older persons to be hired and more often expected them to fail on the job (Connor et al. 1978; Locke-Connor and Walsh 1980).

Retraining

Increasing industrial technology requires that adults have opportunities to upgrade their knowledge and skills to keep pace with their job demands. This means continued education and retraining, whether on-the-job or in special classes. An older worker who has operated a particular machine for twenty years needs help to learn how to operate a new replacement machine. Learning can take place at any age if people are in reasonably good health and motivated to try.

One important factor is the desire to learn. Friedman (1978) studied the composing room printers of New York City's three largest newspapers to gauge their response to the trade's increasing automation. He found that whereas younger workers generally underwent retraining, three out of five older printers did not, considering it unnecessary since they planned to retire soon.

Job Satisfaction

Most research has pointed to a high and positive correlation between job satisfaction and age; that is, job satisfaction tends to increase with the worker's age (Quinn et al. 1974; Wright and Hamilton 1978). There are several explanations for this satisfaction. The most plausible one is that older workers have better jobs with higher incomes, more occupational prestige, and greater skills. Also, older workers more likely have remained in jobs they liked and for which they were best suited (Phillips et al. 1978). They left unsatisfactory jobs earlier in their careers.

Even though older workers indicate overall satisfaction, there may be particular facets they do not like, for example, pay, supervision, co-workers, or promotion aspects (Muchinsky 1978). Few people like every facet of their job, and those in late adulthood are no exception. There is also some evidence that morale and satisfaction decline as the individual approaches retirement. Even though the quality of the work experience does not change, the job as a source of satisfaction becomes less important as the individual approaches retirement. Some begin to think of early retirement, since they no longer consider their work as important as it once was (Cohn 1979).

Unemployment

Unemployment among the elderly who want to work is the lowest for any age group. In 1982, only about 3 percent of men and women sixty-five and over who were in the labor force were unemployed. The highest percentage of those sixty-five and over who were unemployed were blacks, but even their rate was 9 percent for the men and 4.6 percent for the women (U.S. Dept. of Commerce 1984).

One reason for these low figures is that the elderly hold on to jobs they have worked at for years. But once they are unemployed, they use up their employment insurance benefits, become discouraged over their inability to find a job, and eventually drop out of the labor market. Their names are removed from the unemployment records, but not because they were able to find jobs (Taylor 1977). Actually, workers sixty-five and older have never accounted for more than about 3 percent of the total labor force during the past ten years (Graney and Cottam 1981).

THE RETIREMENT PROCESS

Origin

Retirement has become an established institution in modern societies for people nearing age sixty-five. Yet, when the social security system was enacted in 1935, the selection of age sixty-five was purely arbitrary and uncontroversial. It simply copied a German legal precedent set in 1889 (Monk and Donovan 1978–79). Furthermore, the social security system was not set up primarily to meet all the retirement needs of older people. The original benefits were too modest. Social security was established during the depression years as a way of removing older persons from the job market to open more jobs to younger workers. Presumably, families would continue to provide for the elderly as they always had. The net result was that even the able elderly began to retire from the job market. In 1900, two-thirds of all males sixty-five and over were in the labor force; by 1982, these figures had declined to 18 percent of the men and 8 percent of the women over sixty-five (U.S. Dept. of Commerce 1984).

Since 1961, the law has allowed workers to retire early (from sixty-two to sixty-four years of age) and still draw partial benefits. As a result, the percentage of those eligible for benefits who have accepted them has risen continually. It is now over 50 percent. This has placed a strain on the social security system.

Private Pension Plans

As the practice of retirement grew, it became obvious that social security was inadequate. Not all workers were covered, and benefits for those included were minimal. So the law was broadened to include more workers, and benefits were increased and financed by ever-increasing payments. In addition, unionized workers began to pressure employers to set up private pension plans to supplement their retirement income. Most of the pension growth has taken place since World War II. Today, about 40 percent of all male workers and about 60 percent of males in manufacturing industries are eligible to receive benefits from private pension plans (Burkhauser and Tolley 1978).

As private pension plans grew, many laws were passed to regulate the practices. Under most plans, employees must now work ten years before becoming *vested,* that is, before they can quit or change their jobs without losing all pension benefits (Carlson 1980). This requirement discriminates particularly against women. The pressure continues to pass laws allowing employees to transfer all pension credits no matter how long they have worked. Other laws regulate employers' contributions, divorced and widowed spouses' benefits, and so forth.

Compulsory Retirement

For years, the principle of compulsory retirement was challenged. In 1978, Amendments to the Age Discrimination and Employment Act raised to seventy the minimum age at which workers could be forced to retire solely because of age. In federal government employment, age can no longer be considered a criterion for forced retirement (Burkhauser and Tolley 1978). There is continued pressure to eliminate forced retirement at any age for all employees.

IRAs and KEOGH Plans

Another significant advance in retirement planning was the passage of the 1981 Economic Recovery Tax Act, which allowed all working Americans under the age of seventy and one-half years to establish an *individual retirement account (IRA)*. This permits people to make tax-deductible contributions to their own retirement plan and earn tax-deferred income, regardless of whether they are covered by another pension plan. At present, the law allows a maximum yearly contribution of $2,000 each for an employed husband and wife, or $2,250 when only one spouse is employed. Similarly, self-employed persons can put tax-deferred income into a *KEOGH plan* up to a current maximum of 20 percent of yearly income, but totaling no more than $30,000 per year (Block 1984). These plans allow workers to spread taxable income across their working years in much the same manner as job-related pensions.

Result

The net result of the retirement system has been to provide financial incentives not to work. But forces are already operating that may counteract this trend. If inflation grows and living costs soar, some employees will be forced to stay on the job longer to build up retirement income. Other retirees will want to return to the job market to supplement pensions eroded by inflation. Some people are psychologically unprepared for retirement. As the population slowly ages, the number of dependent persons in relation to employed persons will increase, taxing the social security and pension systems. Future laws will be enacted to encourage people to work beyond normal retirement age, continuing as contributors to pension plans and social security.

TIMING OF RETIREMENT

Early Retirement

The number of persons retiring between sixty and sixty-four has increased sharply during the last twenty years (Barfield and Morgan 1978). There are a number of reasons for this. The most obvious is the growing financial ability to retire early, due to improved social security benefits and private retirement plans. Prospective income is the major determinant of whether a worker can retire. If a potential retiree's principal source of income is social security, that worker is more likely to suffer hardship. But when private pension funds are added to social security, retirement becomes financially feasible (Zalusky 1977).

The person with health limitations who is eligible for social security and pension payments is a likely candidate for early retirement. Millions of people are able to retire early by claiming disability benefits. This provision in the social security law allows maximum payments to those who can prove they are disabled.

Some people retire earlier than they otherwise would because they hate their job, feel disillusioned, or no longer feel challenged. They cannot wait to leave (Hellebrandt 1980).

Some people retire early because they have developed, or want to develop, interests outside their work-related responsibilities. A study of early retirement among college professors revealed that half of them had planned a specific project, such as finishing a book or a research project (Kell and Patton 1978). They were not retiring completely. They left one job to devote time to other work or interests (Patton 1977).

In some cases, workers retire early because they are fired, others because of induced retirement (management offering financial incentives to retire early). Those who anticipate working for a number of years but who are laid off are especially hard hit. They are forced to retire from their job whether they want to or not. Those who receive financial inducements to retire early have an easier time adjusting.

An increasing number of workers retire before sixty-five because their pension plans provide full benefits after twenty or thirty years of service. Government employees or military service personnel enjoy these benefits. They can work at one job for a period of time, receive full pension, and then apply for another job with another agency. This practice of double dipping is under examination by the government in an effort to cut expenses. One survey of 641 United States manufacturers showed that 96 percent of private pension plans had early retirement provisions. The minimum age was usually fifty-five, although in some cases it was fifty or lower. Some companies require thirty years of work, regardless of age (Lowe 1978). Such plans encourage early retirement and make it feasible.

Another reason for early retirement may be a subtle attitudinal change toward the work ethic and what people consider important in life. One study showed that younger cohorts of workers favored an earlier age of retirement than did their older colleagues (Ekerdt et al. 1980). This indicates a possible generational shift in attitudes toward work, a trend substantiated by other studies (Rose and Mogey 1972). However, the longer people work and the older they get, the older the preferred retirement age. Apparently, preferences of retirement age increase over the life cycle, so that preferences more closely correspond with actual probabilities (Ekerdt et al. 1980).

What has been the effect of early retirement on individuals involved? Despite the broad individual differences, the effects generally seem positive when early retirement has been a matter of choice. Do people age more quickly and die sooner after they retire than they would otherwise? One study investigated the survival rates of 3,971 United States rubber tire workers. Part of the group had retired early (sixty-two to sixty-four). Others had retired normally (at sixty-five) (Haynes et al. 1978). The results showed no significant mortality excesses or differences between the two groups, based on time of retirement. Other factors were more important: preretirement health status was the only significant predictor of survival after early retirement. Some correlations also exist between mortality and socioeconomic status. Among age sixty-five retirees, lower-status workers were more likely to die within three years of retirement than higher-status workers.

In interviews with fifty-two college and university professors who had been induced to retire early, it was obvious that the overwhelming majority (73 percent) were *very* satisfied with their decision. In addition, 24 percent said they were satisfied (Kell and Patton 1978).

A number of factors contributed to this satisfaction. The most important was their financial well being. Eighty-eight percent of the respondents said there had been no change in their standard of living since retirement. Their gross income was lower, but spendable income was higher, since they had no deductions for social security and did not pay income tax on their social security checks or after-tax contributions to retirement funds. Also, all but two of the retirees were extremely satisfied with the induced retirement arrangements.

Another important factor was that they continued their professional activities, mostly on a part-time basis. This reflected the marketability of their professional skills. The scientists in particular were in demand.

A majority of respondents also said they were happier after retirement than they had been before. They were more contented and relaxed, had greater freedom, and were no longer subject to the pressures and tensions of academic life.

A large number (39 percent) of the early retirees said they had made specific financial preparations for early retirement. Forty-six percent had made nonfinancial preparations, such as relocating their residence, making trips to study retirement communities, or phasing out their work activities. Others had consciously developed outside interests and arranged for postretirement activities (Kell and Patton 1978).

Although the subjects of this study and the conclusions drawn are not typical of the general population of early retirees, the findings are significant because they reveal important components of any successful retirement plan: adequate finances, continued activity, voluntary and willing acceptance of retirement, and adequate preparations.

Another study of retirement satisfaction of auto workers in Michigan revealed two contributions to retirement satisfaction: family income (those with the highest income had the greatest satisfaction) and good health, which made continued work possible if desired (Barfield and Morgan 1978).

Mandatory Retirement

Mandatory retirement forces people to retire at a certain age (now age seventy) whether they want to or not, even if they are physically and intellectually capable of working. Mike Shapiro, a worker forced to retire, commented:

> It just doesn't make sense to me. The Social Security Administration says it's running out of money, and has to keep raising payroll taxes to support all the old folks. Meanwhile there's plenty of us old-timers hanging around who'd like to earn our own living, and they won't let us keep on working. . . . It just doesn't make any sense. (Shapiro 1977, 36)

The idea that retirement is necessary so that older people can "take it easy" in their later years is increasingly irrelevant in this era of white-collar work. Unless a job requires heavy physical labor or unless the older person has become intellectually incapacitated, most people can continue to be productive. They should have the opportunity to work if they desire. Professor Ben Duggar retired from the University of Wisconsin at age seventy, after a mildly distinguished academic career. After retirement, he became a consultant to Lederle Laboratories. At the age of seventy-three, he isolated the antibiotic Aureomycin and then Tetracycline, which has become the world's most widely prescribed antibiotic (Shapiro 1977). The fact that the government has set seventy as the minimum age for mandatory retirement does not preclude companies from keeping employees beyond that age, if they desire.

Forced retirement compels many older people to live near or at a poverty level. Social security alone is not an adequate income. Furthermore, only half the workers in the United States are covered by private pension plans. Most of these plans have fixed income provisions, so as inflation decreased buying power, the recipients become poorer. Working women are especially hard hit by forced retirement; their wages were lower and consequently their social security and pension payments are lower than those of men (Campbell 1979). Also, because they live an average of seven years longer than men, they are more likely to suffer from the effects of inflation over this period. Allowing people to continue working as long as they can and want to, or permitting them to work part-time to supplement their retirement incomes without penalties can make the difference between living well and living at a subsistence level. Of persons sixty-five and older who were living below the poverty level in 1981, blacks were the poorest, followed by females not living in families. Males living in families had the smallest percentage with incomes below the poverty level.

Adjustments

Forced retirement has been ranked among the top ten life crises in terms of the amount of stress it causes the individual (Fritz 1978; Sarason 1981; Shapiro 1977). People who elect retirement, plan for it, and look forward to it feel that they have directed their own lives and are not being pushed or manipulated. They have some adjustment problems, but far fewer than those who retire unwillingly. For people who want to continue working, forced retirement is a bitter pill to swallow. The resulting stress can precipitate various physical and emotional problems. Morale drops, the mortality rate jumps as disillusionment sets in, and individuals who identified very closely with their work sometimes suffer prolonged depression and other ailments. Without the stabilizing influence of work, old emotional conflicts can reemerge, and the person often acquires feelings of inadequacy and worthlessness that generate behavior sometimes regarded as "senile" (Brickfield 1980a).

The real issue of retirement is whether people have a choice (Miller 1977). They should be able to decide for themselves. Actually, the earlier fears of industry that large numbers of less efficient workers would remain on the payrolls have not materialized. Workers with good health and superior performance are the ones most likely to stay on the job.

Delayed or Partial Retirement

Altogether, an average of 18 percent of males and 8 percent of females sixty-five and over worked during any one month in 1982 (U.S. Dept. of Commerce 1984). Since these are monthly averages, the total number of persons who worked at any time during the year would be much greater. One summary of 6,000 workers revealed that only 11 percent reported making recent changes in retirement plans after the mandatory retirement age had been raised to seventy. Of those 666, only 10 percent decided to delay retirement explicitly because of the 1978 amendment ("See No Evil" 1982).

Even if they retire officially, a large number of retirees return to work, mostly part-time. The Labor Department reports that more than 20 percent of all retired Americans work at least part-time.

Partial retirement has several advantages over full retirement. It serves as a transition between full-time work and complete retirement. The person used to working full-time must make a significant adjustment to not working at all.

In addition, partial retirement provides supplemental income, without the loss of too much of one's social security benefits. As of 1982, a person sixty-five or over could earn $6,000 per year without any reduction in social security benefits. This amount is a substantial addition to an income consisting solely of social security.

The only way to have maximum income until age seventy is not to draw social security and to continue earning as much as possible. At seventy, one can earn as much as possible and still receive full social security benefits. In the meantime, accrued social security benefits increase, but only at the low rate of 3 percent per year (plus increases for cost-of-living raises). In times of high interest rates, one is really penalized by not drawing benefits at age sixty-five.

Clearly, a tug-of-war exists between the forces encouraging retirement and those encouraging an extended work life. Partial retirement and part-time work ease the dilemma for millions of workers who do not want to continue working full-time or retire completely.

FINANCIAL PLANNING AND MANAGEMENT

Insufficient Income

Many older people, some of whom thought their retirement income would be sufficient to meet their needs, find themselves in financial difficulty. This situation is due to several causes. One is the lack of proper financial planning. Some simply did not determine their monetary needs and anticipated resources. Those who tried to plan often did not have accurate information available on which to base realistic decisions. Or, they held unrealistic expectations about sources and amounts of potential additional income in retirement. This lack of information and unrealistic expectations constrain one's ability to plan finances (Morrison 1976).

In addition, despite resolves to save more for retirement, current workers fail to allocate significant amounts of current income for this purpose. If this continues year after year, retirement approaches with the prospect of completely inadequate savings. One study of 7,000 males, ages forty-five to fifty-four, employed by a large manufacturing corporation in the northeastern United States, revealed fairly small savings (half had less than $5,000 saved) in spite of the fact that most said they were saving for retirement (Morrison 1976). Most found that saving money was difficult and that the pressure to spend all or most of their money was great. Since this study, IRAs have been established to allow employed persons to save, tax-free. However, people with the highest incomes are the most likely to establish IRAs. Those with the lowest incomes are the least likely, and they will have the lowest retirement income.

A third cause of financial difficulty is inflation, which decreases the buying power of retirees. Money they thought would be adequate for retirement turns out to be inadequate.

Suppose a couple retires at the beginning of 1986 with a fixed income of $20,000 per year and savings of $50,000, tax-deferred. Inflation averages an annual 5 percent. The couple earns 10 percent interest on their savings. If the husband retires at sixty-five, he has a life expectancy of fourteen more years. Table 19.1 shows what happens during the fourteen-year period. Income exceeds expenses for the first seven years, resulting in a maximum savings of $70,532 by the end of 1992. But because of inflation, expenses exceed income from that point on. By the time the husband dies in the year 2000, the savings are nearly gone. If the wife is two years younger than her husband (age seventy-seven if the husband dies at age seventy-nine), she can expect to live ten more years in poverty. Inflation not only wipes out their entire savings, but also makes it impossible for the wife to enjoy the same standard of living after her husband dies, even assuming she continues to get the entire $20,000 per year from the fixed pension. This analysis substantiates the findings of studies showing that as the age of couples increases, their expenditures increase and net worth decreases (Plonk and Pulley 1977). These findings have given rise to pressure to make pensions indexed to the increase in cost of living, which is the case with social security.

Retirement Fund Growth

Suppose a twenty-five-year-old single person establishes an IRA account and pays the maximum into it ($2,000 per year or $166.67 per month). The money is invested at 10 percent interest, compounded monthly, over a forty-year period. All the money and the interest are left in the account for the entire forty years. At that point, the person will be a millionaire! The retirement fund will have grown to $1,070,701.30. Table 19.2 shows the net worth of the fund each year during the forty years. If the rate of return received was more or less than the average of 10 percent, the total fund would change accordingly. Certainly, the table illustrates the phenomenal results of saving regularly and letting the interest accumulate tax-

TABLE 19.1 Effects of Inflation on Income and Savings

Year	Income	Expenses	Net	Savings
1986	$25,000	$20,000	+ $5,000	$55,000
1987	25,500	21,000	+ 4,500	59,500
1988	25,950	22,050	+ 3,900	63,400
1989	26,340	23,152	+ 3,187	66,587
1990	26,658	24,310	+ 2,348	68,936
1991	26,893	25,525	+ 1,368	70,304
1992	27,030	26,801	+ 1,228	70,532
1993	27,053	28,142	− 1,088	69,444
1994	26,944	29,549	− 2,604	66,839
1995	26,683	31,026	− 4,342	62,496
1996	26,249	32,577	− 6,328	56,168
1997	25,616	34,206	− 8,589	47,578
1998	24,757	35,917	−11,159	36,419
1999	23,642	37,712	−14,070	22,348
2000	22,234	39,598	−17,363	4,985

TABLE 19.2   Growth of IRA at 10-Percent Interest over a 40-Year Period

End of Year	New Worth of Fund
1	$2,260.97
2	4,407.91
3	6,963.78
4	9,787.28
5	12,906.44
6	16,352.21
7	20,158.80
8	24,364.00
9	29,009.53
10	34,141.51
11	39,810.88
12	46,073.90
13	52,992.74
14	60,636.08
15	69,079.77
16	78,407.63
17	88,712.24
18	100,095.87
19	112,671.52
20	126,564.00
21	141,911.21
22	158,865.47
23	177,595.05
24	198,285.88
25	221,143.32
26	246,394.21
27	275,789.24
28	305,105.18
29	339,147.98
30	376,755.51
31	418,301.04
32	464,196.93
33	514,898.71
34	570,909.65
35	632,785.65
36	701,140.88
37	776,653.79
38	860,073.91
39	952,229.19
40	$1,070,701.30

free. Only $80,000 has been invested out-of-pocket in an account valued at over one million dollars.

SUMMARY

The possible span of the adult working life in the United States is increasing due to better health care, increased longevity, and an increase in the mandatory retirement age from sixty-five to seventy.

Yet there is often misunderstanding of the capabilities of older workers. Investigations have revealed that they demonstrate better attendance, have fewer absences because of injury or illness, and are more dependable than younger workers. Verbal and practical problem-solving abilities tend to hold up with age, as do skills in working with people. Physical performance abilities decline. The latter handicap can be overcome partially through instruction, practice, and by adjusting work requirements to meet the special needs of older workers. The task performances of older workers are greatly influenced by psychological factors; self-confidence and a sense of emotional well-being are important. Sometimes people are unjustifiably prejudiced against older workers.

Industrial technology requires that adults upgrade their knowledge and skills through retraining programs. Some older workers resist retraining programs, especially if they are approaching retirement age. Job satisfaction tends to increase with the age of the worker.

Unemployment among the elderly seems low (about 3 percent), but this is because many who have not found jobs drop out of the labor market and are no longer classified as unemployed, even though they would prefer to work.

The retirement system in this country began with the enactment of social security in 1935. The selection of age sixty-five for retirement was purely arbitrary, based on a German legal precedent set in 1889. The primary motive when the system was established was to retire older adults to make room for younger ones during the depression years. The net result was to phase more and more older people out of the job market. The law now allows early retirement, many private pension plans, and the establishing of IRAs and KEOGH plans; mandatory retirement is set at age seventy. These factors provide financial incentives not to work.

The number of persons retiring early continues to increase. They do so for various reasons: they can afford to retire, they have health limitations, they hate their job, they want to pursue other interests, they are fired or induced to retire, they can draw full pension after twenty or thirty years of service or at a fairly young age, or they reject the work ethic. The overall effect has been positive for workers who elect to retire early. However, satisfaction comes from having adequate finances, continuing to work part-time or at another job, making adequate preparations ahead of time, and enjoying good health.

Mandatory retirement forces people to retire at age seventy, whether they want to or not. Many workers deeply resent it. It cannot be justified from a medical standpoint because many workers are in excellent health, nor can it be justified from a financial standpoint. It forces many elders to live at near poverty levels. Forced retirement has been ranked among the top ten life crises in terms of the stress it causes. People should not be forced to retire, but should have a choice.

Many workers delay retirement or only partially retire, choosing to work part-time after their official retirement. There are several advantages. It allows a time of transition from full-time employment to no employment, and it provides supplemental income, allowing a worker to receive social security if earnings are not higher than $6,000 per year. (At age seventy, earnings can be unlimited with no penalty.)

Many retirees find they have insufficient income after retirement, primarily because of the effects of inflation on fixed incomes. People need to plan ahead to provide for their needs within a certain number of years.

Part VII

The Future

20

Adults and the Future

AGING OF THE POPULATION

Demographic Trends

The steady aging of the population is one of the most important factors to consider when examining what the future holds. This aging is due largely to two childbearing cycles. The high birth rate during the early 1900s was followed by a large decline during the late 1920s and the great depression of the 1930s. This was followed by a baby boom after World War II and a baby bust that drove birth rates sharply downward after the 1960s. Figure 20.1 illustrates these cycles.

These cycles generated one small cohort (people born between 1930 and 1945) and two age cohorts that are much larger than the generations surrounding them. The older large cohort, born between 1910 and 1925, were sixty to seventy-five years old in 1985. They are retiring by the millions, putting great strain on the economic and social resources available to meet their needs. The even larger cohort born between 1945 and 1960 are now young adults. By the year 2000, this group will be middle-aged and will represent over one-fourth of the population in the United States. By the year 2020, the cohort will be sixty to seventy-five years old: the largest group of older adults in the history of this country. Figure 20.2 shows the aging of this cohort.

Implications

These cycles have important implications. The small cohort born between 1930 and 1945 (the depression babies) are now middle-aged. They have little job competition and enjoy an exceptionally high degree of prosperity and social stability. As a generation, they succeeded primarily because of their small numbers and superior opportunities.

But the teeming ranks of baby boomers have had a more difficult time. They were the restless generation in the 1960s and early 1970s, the activists, protestors, and hippies rebelling against society and unwilling to accept the status quo handed down by their prosperous parents. They attended college in huge numbers but had to compete for jobs. Many

FIGURE 20.1   Birthrates: 1910–1983, United States

Source: U.S. Department of Commerce.

remained unemployed or underemployed, forced to accept lower-level positions than those for which they had been trained. They married later than their parents, often not until their late twenties or early thirties. Once married, this cohort exerted great pressure on the housing market, which resulted in sky-rocketing rents and housing prices. The competition they have faced has made them more materialistic than they were fifteen years ago. Their pressures are reflected in high divorce rates and continued high drug use. As this group moves up the career ladder, many will be blocked by a glut of fellow employees competing for senior positions. The view of America as a land of opportunity is going to fade for many of them, especially for those in minority groups.

What happens when this group reaches age sixty and beyond, beginning in the year 2005, is of great concern. The prospects are staggering. Because the elderly get a disproportionate share of health care, medical costs will keep soaring unless drastic measures are taken. Already, people sixty-five and older consume more than half of tax-supported health expenditures, although they are only one-tenth of the population. The pressure on the nation's social security and pension systems is already surfacing

FIGURE 20.2   Aging of the Postwar Baby Boom Generation

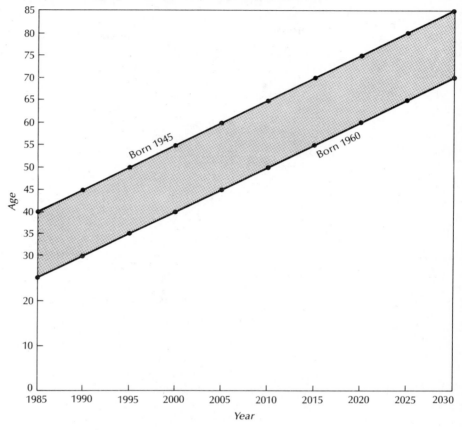

with the retirement of large numbers of pre-depression babies. What will happen to the system when the postwar, baby boom generation retires? Within fifty years, one beneficiary will be drawing social security for every two workers paying into the system. The ratio stands at one to three today. If revenue sources remain unchanged, the social security tax rate, already high, will become exorbitant.

The problem will beome more complicated because as larger numbers of Americans move into older adulthood, their political power will increase. If society tries to infringe on their rights or reduce their benefits and services, they will present formidable opposition. The American Association of Retired Persons (AARP) currently has twelve million members. Other senior citizen's groups increase their total political power. Some sociologists predict a war between the ages that will make the protests of the 1960s seem mild. This generation has always fought for its rights and will continue to do so. As high expectations collide with reality and possibilities, some degree of frustration is bound to set in. People in minority groups, who have always been shortchanged, will be especially hard-pressed.

SOME POSITIVE DEVELOPMENTS

As a result of these demographics and other social and political forces shaping our lives, some positive changes are taking place.

The incidence of crime is decreasing, primarily because the number of youths (who have the highest crime rate) has been decreasing since 1980. Similarly, traffic accidents should decrease as the number of teen-age drivers decreases. The divorce rate, which peaked in 1979, has leveled off and is decreasing slightly as the baby boom generation moves through the crucial early years of marriage. The birth rate has dropped sharply since 1970 and now remains fairly static, averaging a little less than two children per family. With fewer dependent children, employed couples will have more money to spend on themselves and to care for elderly parents. Women will continue to enter the labor market in increasing numbers, giving them more status, independence, and greater emotional well-being. Moreover, as women continue to outlive their husbands, they will have considerably more financial security in their old age if they are employed.

The aging of the population has caused a shift from a youth-oriented culture to an adult-centered society. Clothing styles are increasingly geared to the needs of young and middle-aged adults. Demands for automobiles reflect the practical requirements of adults and their families. Even tastes in music have become more conservative, with increasing emphasis on the big-band sound and the love ballads of the 1940s and 1950s. The food industry, which for years catered to the demands of the young, now courts middle-aged and older adults who want to stay healthy and trim and add years to their lives. Aerobic classes and fitness centers enroll adults by the millions. The recreational industry, after years of emphasizing the sports pursuits and leisure-time activities of the young, now appeals to adults to take up tennis, golf, fishing, or skiing, or to rent or buy a recreational home. Travel agencies cater to adults who prefer tours or more leisurely cruises. Because of increasing housing costs, more and more adults are moving into condominiums and other group housing arrangements. This frees them from some of the responsibilities of home ownership, allows them more time for leisure-time pursuits, and offers companionship and camaraderie to those who enjoy social living.

As colleges experience a drop in enrollments due to the declining numbers of teen-agers, they are expanding continuing education and other programs for adults. As a result, the average level of education of adults continues to rise. Adults can now upgrade their knowledge and skills and even retrain themselves for a second or third career. The more educated they become, the less likely they are to face obsolescence and the greater their chances to continue working throughout their life.

SOME CHALLENGES

Age-Appropriate Norms and Values

Some real challenges remain. One is to alter our age-appropriate norms of behavior and make the necessary psychological adjustments to living a longer, more active life. The stages of the life cycle have been delayed. Adolescence is prolonged, entry into adulthood comes later, and the ages of vocational establishment, marriage, and parenthood have been delayed. Yet, America still suffers from a rocking chair syndrome, a special notion that disengagement should come early, even though poor health and death come later and later. A man conditioned to early retirement, who decides to retire at age sixty, still has an average of eighteen more years to live; a woman has twenty-three. These are long periods of time to live without working regularly and to be supported by the rest of society. Society will not be able to support the whole generation of baby boom dependents. For the most part, they will have to continue to struggle to look after themselves.

Society needs a new orientation to the concept of who is old. A person of sixty should no longer be considered old. Perhaps eighty is old, but in a short span of time, this concept may be outdated and eighty-year-olds may be considered young-old. We know that sexual enjoyment can continue into this age, that a high proportion of intellectual capacity is retained, that an ability to learn remains, and that many health problems of late adulthood are being solved, allowing the majority of people to be healthy, active, and productive throughout their lives. Therefore, we need to revise our age norms, our social age clock. We have to rethink the time schedule of life—the time to go to school, the time to work, the time to marry, the time to die.

Possibilities

If we reorient our thinking about who is old, many possibilities arise. Certain prejudices against the elderly will disappear and intergenerational relationships will improve. Society will become less age-segregated. Schools will offer more continuing education and retraining programs to prepare people for second or third careers. The young-old will eschew welfare and become productive members of society again.

Many people can expect to experience three stages of marriage, each meeting a specific need: trial marriage or individual marriage during which people test their relationship and decide whether or not to make it permanent; parental marriage after children are born; and couple marriage after the children leave home. Couples who do not survive all three stages could be encouraged to marry again. Women, half of whom are separated from their husbands or widowed by age sixty, could be expected to marry again, many to younger men because of the scarcity of men of their own age. Grandparents could play an increasingly important role in the family if they desired. With adults of all ages remaining healthy, productive family members, the aged could retain at least part of their status in extended family networks.

Housing will continue to be a problem, especially the increasing cost of single-family houses. Many elderly who can afford the cost are completely happy in retirement communities, but they object if they are too far from their families. Helping the active elderly keep their own homes as long as possible through home subsidies, rather than senior citizen housing subsidies, would meet a real need. But society will be limited in the help it can give.

Segregating the elderly in retirement and nursing homes is not a completely satisfactory solution. Some elders prefer to mix with younger people. Planners need to think in terms of intergenerational neighborhoods, condominiums, apartments, and houses. Part of the responsibility for the elderly will inevitably fall on families, many of whom should consider multigenerational living quarters, with different generations having their own apartments within the housing complex. Certainly, neither the elderly nor their children want to live together totally, but they can share expenses if their individual living spaces are grouped together.

PSYCHOLOGY OF ADULTHOOD

The Need

What is the role of a psychology of adulthood? The purpose of psychology is to help people understand human thought, emotions, and behavior; the ultimate goal is to enrich and improve human life. As the population becomes older, a psychology of adulthood becomes more important. The present need is to place more emphasis on understanding the seasons of life, throughout life, and to help people prepare for and adjust to the changes as life progresses. Adult psychology should play an increasingly important role in preparing people for life, not simply help them to pick up the pieces when things go wrong.

Research Emphases

Research in the psychology of aging has progressed at a rapid pace. Naïve, sometimes misleading cross-sectional analyses have been partially replaced by highly sophisticated, longitudinal and cross-sequential analyses that reveal the positive capabilities of adults throughout the life cycle. These efforts will continue to expand our knowledge of aging. However, more research has been conducted on physiological and cognitive changes than on emotional, social, and psychological factors. The latter are harder to measure and pinpoint but are equally important in understanding the total person.

There is, however, a paucity of research on early and middle adulthood, except perhaps for the college-age group. The war boom babies, now young adults, were the subject of much investigation during their activist college days. But they have been largely forgotten since then, in spite of their intense struggles and the enormous problems they face. We need a much broader, deeper, and longer research base to understand this generation as they move from their current tenuous place in society toward an uncertain future as senior citizens. There is a definite need for longitudinal studies, beginning with the early adulthood generation. Hopefully, psychologists and researchers who belong to this age group will undertake the study of themselves.

Although not as sparse as the research on early adulthood, the studies on middle age are scarce. Researchers continue to focus on old age, skipping over those important middle years that lead to and prepare for old age. Much more has to be done to understand the psychological, social, familial, and vocational crises of middle age that are real to many people.

Also, much past research has focused on white, middle-class Americans. Blacks and other minority groups who bear the brunt of America's prejudices need to be understood better. The Hispanic populations are growing rapidly and will outnumber blacks in the future. As America's largest minority, they will need to become the focus of more attention from social scientists and politicians.

Hopefully, the aging of society will be accompanied by a shift in emphasis in college and university psychology departments, so that offerings in the psychology of adulthood will expand to meet the changing needs.

Bibliography

Abel, M. "The Visual Trace in Relation to Aging." Ph.D. dissertation, Washington University, 1972.

Abraham, S.; Lowestein, F. W.; and Johnson, C. L. "Preliminary Findings of the First Health and Nutrition Examination Survey, United States, 1971–1972: Dietary Intake and Biochemical Findings." DHEW Publication no. (HRA) 74–1219–1 (1974).

Abramson, L.; Seligman, M. E. P.; and Teasdale, J. D. "Learned Helplessness in Humans: Critique and Reformulation." *Journal of Abnormal Psychology* 87 (1978): 49–74.

Achenbaum, W. A., and Stearns, P. N. "Essay: Old Age and Modernization." *The Gerontologist* 18 (June 1978): 307–312.

Adamowicz, J. K. "Visual Short-Term Memory and Aging." *Journal of Gerontology* 31 (January 1976): 39–46.

Adams, B. N., and Cromwell, R. E. "Morning and Night People in the Family: A Preliminary Statement." *The Family Coordinator* 27 (January 1978): 5–13.

Adams, G. M., and deVries, H. A. "Physiological Effects of an Exercise Training Program Upon Women Aged 52 to 79." *Journal of Gerontology* 28 (1973): 20–55.

Adams, V. "Sex Therapies in Perspective." *Psychology Today* 14 (August 1980): 35, 36.

Almquist, E. M., and Angrist, S. S. "Women's Career Aspirations and Achievements: College and Seven Years After." Paper presented at the American Sociological Association Meeting, Chicago, September 1977.

Althof, S. E. "Women's Sexual Recovery Following Coronary Bypass." *Medical Aspects of Human Sexuality* 18 (January 1984): 153.

American Heart Association. *The American Heart Association Cookbook.* 3d ed. New York: David McKay, 1979.

American Psychiatric Association. *Diagnostic and Statistical Manual of Mental Disorders.* 3d ed. Washington, D.C.: APA, 1980.

Amster, L. E., and Krauss, H. H. "Life Crises and Mental Deterioration." *International Journal of Aging and Human Development* 5 (1974): 51–55.

Arenberg, D. "The Effects of Input Condition on Free Recall in Young and Old Adults." *Journal of Gerontology* 31 (September 1976): 551–555.

Arenberg, D. "Estimates of Age Changes on the Benton Visual Retention Test." *Journal of Gerontology* 37 (January 1982): 87–90.

Arenberg, D., and Robertson-Tshabo, E. A. "Learning and Aging." In *Handbook of the Psychology of Aging,* edited by J. A. Birren and K. W. Schaie, 421–449. New York: Van Nostrand Reinhold, 1977.

Arlin, P. K. "Cognitive Development in Adulthood: A Fifth Stage?" *Developmental Psychology* 11 (1975): 602–606.

Arlin, P. K. "Piagetian Operations in Problem Finding." *Developmental Psychology* 13 (1977): 297–298.

Arling, G. "The Elderly Widow and Her Family, Neighbors, and Friends." *Journal of Marriage and the Family* 38 (November 1976): 757–768.

Arvidson, K. "Location and Variation in Number of Taste Buds in Human Fungiform Papillae." *Scandinavian Journal of Dental Research* 87 (1979): 435–442.

Bach, G. R., and Deutsch, R. M. "Intimacy." In *Love, Marriage, Family: A Developmental Approach,* 157–161. Glenview, Ill.: Scott, Foresman and Co., 1973.

Bader, J. E. "Attitudes toward Aging, Old Age, and Old People." *Aged Care and Services Review* 2 (1980): 2, 3–14.

Bagramian, R. A., and Heller, R. P. "Dental Health Assessment of a Population of Nursing Home

Residents." *Journal of Gerontology* 32 (March 1977): 168–174.

Bahrick, H. P.; Bahrick, P. O.; and Wittlinger, R. P. "Fifty Years of Memory for Names and Faces: A Cross-Sectional Approach." *Journal of Experimental Psychology: General* 104 (1975): 54–75.

Balkwell, C., and Balswick, J. "Subsistence Economy, Family Structure and the Status of the Elderly." *Journal of Marriage and the Family* 43 (May 1981): 423–429.

Balkwell, C., and Halverson, C. F., Jr. "The Hyperactive Child as a Source of Stress in the Family: Consequences of Suggestions for Intervention." *Family Relations* 29 (October 1980): 550–557.

Baltes, P. B., and Schaie, K. W. "On the Plasticity of Intelligence in Adulthood and Old Age: Where Horn and Donaldson Fail." *American Psychologist* 31 (1976): 720–725.

Barclay, D. "Growing Number of Women Leave Home to Live Alone." *Portland Press Herald,* May 5, 1976, 6.

Barfield, R. E., and Morgan, J. N. "Trends in Planned Early Retirement." *The Gerontologist* 18 (February 1978): 13–18.

Barwick, J. "Middle Age and a Sense of Future." Paper presented at the 70th annual meeting of the American Sociological Association, San Francisco, August 26, 1975.

Barnes, R. F., and Raskind, M. A. "DSM–III Criteria and the Clinical Diagnosis of Dementia: A Nursing Home Study." *Journal of Gerontology* 36 (January 1981): 20–27.

Barrett, T. R., and Wright, M. "Age-Related Facilitation in Recall Following Semantic Processing." *Journal of Gerontology* 36 (March 1981): 194–199.

Bartley, D. L. "Through 'Caring' and Job Restructuring Older Employees Obtain Excellent Record in Attendance, Safety, and Health." *Long Term Care and Health Services Administration* 3 (Fall 1977): 236–242.

Basen, M. M. "The Elderly and Drugs—Problem Overview and Program Strategy." *Public Health Reports* 92 (1977): 43–48.

Bayley, N. "Behavioral Correlates of Mental Growth: Birth to Thirty-Six Years." *American Psychologist* 23 (1968): 1–17.

Beck, J. D.; Ettinger, R. L.; Glenn, R. E.; Paule, C. L.; and Holtzman, J. M. "Oral Health Status: Impact on Dental Students' Attitudes Toward the Aged." *The Gerontologist* 19 (December 1979): 580–585.

Bell, B.; Rose, C. L.; and Danon, A. "The Normative Aging Study: An Interdisciplinary and Longitudinal Study of Health and Aging." *Aging and Human Development* 3 (1972): 5–18.

Bell, C. S.; Johnson, J. E.; McGillicuddy-DeLisi, A. V.; and Sigel, I. E. "Normative Stress and Young Families: An Adaption and Development." *Family Relations* 29 (October 1980): 453–458.

Belmore, S. M. "Age-Related Changes in Processing Explicit and Implicit Language." *Journal of Gerontology* 36 (May 1981): 316–322.

Bengtson, V. L.; Cuellar, J. B.; and Ragan, P. K. "Stratum Contrasts and Similarities in Attitudes toward Death." *Journal of Gerontology* 32 (January 1977): 76–88.

Beres, C. A., and Baron, A. "Improved Digit Symbol Substitution by Older Women as a Result of Extended Practice." *Journal of Gerontology* 36 (September 1981): 591–597.

Bergman, M. "Changes in Hearing with Age." *The Gerontologist* 11 (1971): 148–151.

Bergman, M.; Blumenfeld, V. G.; Cascardo, D.; Dash, B.; Levitt, H.; and Margulies, M. K. "Age-Related Decrement in Hearing for Speech." *Journal of Gerontology* 31 (September 1976): 533–538.

Berman, P. W.; O'Nan, B. A.; and Floyd, W. "The Double Standard of Aging and the Social Situation: Judgments of Attractiveness of the Middle-Aged Woman." *Sex Roles* 7 (February 1981): 87–96.

Bernard, S. "Fatherless Families: Their Economic and Social Adjustment." *Paper in Social Welfare No. 7.* Waltham, Mass.: Florence G. Heller Graduate School for Advanced Studies in Social Welfare, Brandeis University, 1971.

Bischof, L. J. *Adult Psychology.* 2d ed. New York: Harper and Row, 1976.

Blanding, F. H. *Pulse Point Plan.* New York: Random House, 1982.

Block, J. "Easing the Tax Pinch." *Dynamic Years* 19 (March-April 1984): 30–35.

Blumental, L. "Upsurge in Violence, Stress, Blamed on Eruptions." *Seattle Times,* July 25, 1980, A1.

Boeckman, C. "Your Health As You Get Older." *Dynamic Years* 14 (May-June 1979): 24–27.

Bolen, J. S. "Meditation and Psychotherapy in the Treatment of Cancer." *Psychic* (July/August 1973): 19–22.

Booth, A. "Sex and Social Participation." *American Sociological Review* 37 (1972): 183–192.

Borges, M. A., and Dutton, L. J. "Attitudes toward Aging." *The Gerontologist* 16 (June 1976): 220–224.

Borkan, G. A., and Norris, A. H. "Assessment of Biological Age Using a Profile of Physical Parameters." *Journal of Gerontology* 35 (March 1980): 177–184.

Borland, D. C. "Research on Middle Age: An Assessment." *The Gerontologist* 18 (August 1978): 379–386.

Boss, P. G. "Normative Family Stress: Family Boundary Changes across the Life Span." *Family Relations* 29 (October 1980): 445–450.

Botwinick, J. *Cognitive Processes in Maturity and Old Age.* 1st, 2d, 3d eds. New York: Springer-Verlag, 1967, 1978, 1984.

Botwinick, J., and Storandt, M. *Memory Related Functions and Age.* Springfield, Ill.: Charles C. Thomas, 1974.

Botwinick, J., and Storandt, M. "Recall and Recognition of Old Information in Relation to Age and Sex." *Journal of Gerontology* 35 (January 1980): 70–76.

Brackenridge, C. J. "Daily Variation and Other Factors Affecting the Occurrence of Cerebrovascular Accidents." *Journal of Gerontology* 36 (March 1981): 176–179.

Branconnier, R. J., and Cole, J. O. "The Impairment Index as a Symptom—Independent Parameter of Drug Efficacy in Geriatric Psychopharmacology." *Journal of Gerontology* 33 (March 1978): 217–223.

Brandwein, R. A.; Brown, C. A.; and Fox, E. M. "Women and Children Last: The Social Situation of Divorced Mothers and Their Families." *Journal of Marriage and the Family* 36 (August 1974): 498–514.

Bray, G. P. "Sexual Function Poststroke." *Medical Aspects of Human Sexuality* 18 (March 1984): 115–123.

Brickfield, C. F. "Can Age Discrimination Laws Be Enforced?" *Dynamic Years* 15 (September-October 1980a): 48.

Bridge, T. P.; Cannon, H. E.; and Wyatt, R. J. "Burned Out Schizophrenia: Evidence for Age Effects on Schizophrenic Symptomatology." *Journal of Gerontology* 33 (November 1978): 835–839.

Briley, M. "Estrogen Therapy—What's New." *Dynamic Years* 15 (May-June 1980a): 24–27.

Briley, M. "Burnout." *Dynamic Years* 15 (July-August 1980b): 36–39.

Brim, O. G., Jr., and Kagan, J., eds. *Constancy and Change in Human Development.* Cambridge, Mass.: Harvard University Press, 1980.

Bromley, D. B. *The Psychology of Human Ageing.* New York: Penguin Books, 1974.

Brown, A. S. "Satisfying Relationships for the Elderly and Their Patterns of Disengagement." *The Gerontologist* 14 (June 1974): 258–262.

Bryson, J. B., and Bryson, R. A. "Dual-Career Couples." *Psychology of Women Quarterly* 3 (1978): entire issue.

Buhler, C. "The Curve of Life as Studied in Biographies." *Journal of Applied Psychology* 19 (1935): 405–409.

Buhler, C. "Meaningfulness of the Biographical Approach." In *Readings in Adult Psychology: Contemporary Perspectives,* edited by L. R. Allman and D. T. Jaffe, 20–27. New York: Harper and Row, 1977.

Buhler, C., and Massarik, F. *The Course of Human Life: A Study of Goals in the Humanistic Perspective.* New York: Springer, 1968.

Bultena, G., and Marshall, D. G. "Family Patterns of Migrant and Nonmigrant Retirees." *Journal of Marriage and the Family* 32 (February 1970): 89–93.

Bultena, G. L., and Powers, E. A. "Denial of Aging: Age Identification and Reference Group Orientations." *Journal of Gerontology* 33 (September 1978): 748–754.

Burger, P. C., and Vogel, F. S. "The Development of the Pathologic Changes of Alzheimer's Disease and the Senile Dementia in Patients with Down's Syndrome." *American Journal of Pathology* 73 (1973): 457–468.

Burke, D. M.; DeMicco, F. J.; Taper, L. J.; and Ritchey, S. J. "Copper and Zinc Utilization in Elderly Adults." *Journal of Gerontology* 36 (September 1981): 558–563.

Burkhauser, R. V., and Tolley, G. S. "Older

Americans and Market Work." *The Gerontologist* 18 (October 1978): 449–453.

Butler, R. N. "How to Live a Longer Life and Enjoy It More." *U.S. News and World Report* (July 12, 1976): 29.

Butler, R. N. "The Alliance of Advocacy with Science, Kent Lecture—1979." *The Gerontologist* 20 (April 1980): 154–162.

Cain, L. D. "Evaluative Research and Nutrition Programs for the Elderly." In *Evaluative Research on Social Programs for the Elderly.* DHEW Publication no. (OHD) 77–20120, 137–150. Washington, D.C.: U.S. Government Printing Office, 1977.

Cameron, P. "Stereotypes about Generational Fun and Happiness versus Self-Appraised Fun and Happiness." *The Gerontologist* 12 (1972): 120–123.

Cameron, P. "Mood as an Indicant of Happiness: Age, Sex, Social Class and Situational Differences." *Journal of Gerontology* 30 (1975): 216–224.

Cameron, P., and Biber, H. "Sex and the Older Years: Sexual Thought throughout the Life-Span." *The Gerontologist* 13 (1973): 144–147.

Campbell, A.; Converse, P.; and Rogers, W. *The Quality of American Life.* New York: Russell Sage, 1976.

Campbell, S. "Delayed Mandatory Retirement and the Working Woman." *The Gerontologist* 19 (June 1979): 257–263.

"Cancer: Who Gets It? Risk Groups Reported." *Science News* 109 (January 1976): 69.

Cantor, D. J. "A Matter of Right." *The Humanist* (May/June 1970).

Carey, R. G., and Posavac, E. J. "Attitudes of Physicians on Disclosing Information to and Maintaining Life for Terminal Patients." *Omega: Journal of Death and Dying* 9 (1978–79): 67–77.

Cargan, L., and Melko, M. *Singles. Myths and Realities.* Beverly Hills, Calif.: Sage Publications, 1982.

Carlson, E. "Family Background, School, and Early Marriage." *Journal of Marriage and the Family* 41 (May 1979): 341–343.

Carlson, E. "The Troubled Waters of Pension Reform." *Dynamic Years* 15 (September-October 1980): 20–23.

Carter, H., and Glick, P. C. *Marriage and Divorce: A Social and Economic Study.* Cambridge, Mass.: Harvard University Press, 1970.

Cattell, R. B. "Theory of Fluid and Crystallized Intelligence: A Critical Experiment." *Journal of Educational Psychology* 54 (1963): 1–22.

Cavan, R. S. "Roles of the Old in Personal and Impersonal Societies." *The Family Coordinator* 27 (October 1978): 315–319.

Cawley, M. A. "Euthanasia: Should It Be Choice?" *American Journal of Nursing* 77 (May 1977): 859–861.

Chance, J.; Overcast, T.; and Dollinger, S. J. "Aging and Cognitive Regression: Contrary Findings." *The Journal of Psychology* 98 (March 1978): 177–183.

Charness, N. "Visual Short-term Memory and Aging in Chess Players." *Journal of Gerontology* 36 (September 1981): 615–619.

Cherlin, A. "Postponing Marriage: The Influence of Young Women's Work Expectations." *Journal of Marriage and the Family* 42 (May 1980): 355–365.

Cherlin, R. S. "Male Hypogonadism" *Medical Aspects of Human Sexuality* 18 (March 1984): 195–199.

Chilton, R. J., and Markle, G. E. "Family Disruption, Delinquent Conduct and the Effect of Subclassification." *American Sociological Review* 37 (February 1972): 93–99.

Chiriboga, D. A. "Evaluated Time: A Life Course Perspective." *Journal of Gerontology* 33 (May 1978): 388–393.

Circirelli, V. G. "Categorization Behavior in Aging Subjects." *Journal of Gerontology* 31 (November 1976): 676–680.

Citizen's Advisory Council on the Status of Women. *Memorandum: The Equal Rights Amendment and Alimony and Child Support Laws.* Washington, D.C.: U.S. Government Printing Office, January 1972.

Clark, M. "The Poetry of Aging: Views of Old Age in Contemporary American Poetry." *The Gerontologist* 20 (April 1980): 188–191.

Clausen, J. A. "Glimpses Into the Social World of Middle Age." *International Journal of Aging and Human Development* 7 (1976): 99–106.

Cohen, D. "The Twin and Twin-Family Approach to Cross-Cultural Aging Research." *The Gerontologist* 16 (February 1976): 77–81.

Cohn, R. M. "Age and the Satisfactions from Work." *Journal of Gerontology* 34 (March 1979): 264–272.

Commons, M. L.; Richards, F. A.; and Kuhn, D. "Systematic and Metasystematic Reasoning: A Case for Levels of Reasoning beyond Piaget's Stage of Formal Operations." *Child Development* 53 (1982): 1058–1069.

Connor, C. L. et al., "Evaluation of Job Applicants: The Effects of Age Versus Success." *Journal of Gerontology* 33 (March 1978): 246–252.

Consumer and Food Economics Institute. *Composition of Foods, Dairy and Egg Products—Raw, Processed, Prepared.* Agriculture Handbook no. 8–1. Washington, D.C.: U.S. Department of Agriculture, 1977a.

Consumer and Food Economics Institute. *Composition of Foods, Fats and Oils—Raw, Processed, Prepared.* Agriculture Handbook no. 8–4. Washington, D.C.: U.S. Department of Agriculture, 1978.

Consumer and Food Economics Institute. *Nutritive Value of Foods.* Rev. ed. Home and Garden Bulletin no. 72. Washington, D.C.: U.S. Department of Agriculture, 1977b.

Consumer and Food Economics Institute. *Fats in Food and Diet.* Rev. ed. Agriculture Information Bulletin no. 361. Washington, D.C.: U.S. Department of Agriculture, August 1976.

Consumers Union Report on Family Planning. Mt. Vernon, N.Y.: Consumers Union of United States, 1966.

Conway, J. *Men in Mid-Life Crisis.* Elgin, Ill.: David C. Cook, 1978.

Cornell, E. B. "Postmenopausal Libido." *Medical Aspects of Human Sexuality* 18 (June 1984): 265–270.

Cowgill, D. O. "Aging and Modernization: A Revision of the Theory." In *Dimensions of Aging. Readings,* edited by J. Hendricks and C. D. Hendricks, 54–68. Cambridge, Mass.: Winthrop Publishers, 1979.

Craik, F. I. M., and Lockhart, R. S. "Levels of Processing: A Framework for Memory Research." *Journal of Verbal Learning Behavior* 11 (1972): 671–684.

Crawford, M. P., and Hooper, D. "Menopause, Aging and Family." *Social Science and Medicine* 7 (1973): 469–482.

Cuber, J. F., and Harroff, P. B. *The Significant Americans.* New York: Appleton-Century, 1965.

Cumming, E., and Henry, W. *Growing Old: The Process of Disengagement.* New York: Basic Books, 1961.

Cunningham, W. R.; Clayton, V.; and Overton, W. "Fluid and Crystallized Intelligence in Young Adulthood and Old Age." *Journal of Gerontology* 30 (1975): 53–55.

Cutler, R. G. "Evaluation of Human Longevity and the Genetic Complexity Governing Aging Rate." *Proceedings of the National Academy of Sciences USA* 72 (1975): 4664–4668.

Darling, J. "An Interactionist Interpretation of Bachelorhood and Late Marriage: The Process of Entering into, Remaining in, and Leaving Careers of Singleness." Ph.D. dissertation, University of Connecticut, 1976.

Darnley, F. "A Response to 'Morning and Night People in the Family: A Preliminary Statement.'" *The Family Coordinator* 27 (January 1978): 14, 15.

Davies, M. E.; Lanzel, L. H.; and Cox, A. B. In *Osteoporosis,* edited by U. S. Barzel, 140–149. New York: Grune and Stratton, 1970.

Davitz, J., and Davitz, L. *Making It: Forty and Beyond, Surviving The Mid-Life Crisis.* Minneapolis, Minn.: Winston Press, 1979.

Deakin, D. "The Surgical Pursuit of Youth." *Dynamic Maturity* 12 (January 1977a): 28–31.

Deakin, D. "the Surgical Pursuit of Youth." *Dynamic Years* 12 (November-December 1977b): 34–36.

Demos, V., and Jache, A. "When You Care Enough: An Analysis of Attitudes toward Aging in Humorous Birthday Cards." *The Gerontologist* 21 (April 1981): 209–215.

Denney, N. W. "Classification Abilities in the Elderly." *Journal of Gerontology* 29 (1974): 309–314.

Denney, N. W. "Task Demands and Problem-Solving Strategies in Middle-Aged and Older Adults." *Journal of Gerontology* 35 (July 1980): 559–564.

Denney, N. W., and Palmer, A. M. "Adult Age Differences on Traditional and Practical Problem-Solving Measures." *Journal of Gerontology* 36 (May 1981): 323–328.

Dennis, W. "Creative Productivity between the Ages of 20 and 80 Years." *Journal of Gerontology* 21 (January 1966).

DeVries, H. A., and Adams, G. M. "Comparison of Exercise Responses in Old and Young Men: I. The Cardiac Effort Total Body Effort Relationship." *Journal of Gerontology* 27 (1972): 344–348.

Dietz, P. E. "Long-Term Effects of Rape." *Medical Aspects of Human Sexuality* 18 (March 1984): 251.

Douglas, K., and Arenberg, D. "Age Changes, Cohort Differences, and Cultural Change on the Guilford-Zimmerman Temperament Survey." *Journal of Gerontology* 33 (September 1978): 737–747.

Dowd, J. J. "Aging As Exchange: A Preface to Theory." *Journal of Gerontology* 30 (September 1975): 584–594.

Dowd, J. J., and Bengtson, V. L. "Aging in Minority Populations. An Examination of the Double Jeopardy Hypothesis." *Journal of Gerontology* 33 (May 1978): 427–436.

Downey, C. "Displaced Homemaker: Out of Work, No Prospects." *Dynamic Years* 16 (May-June 1981): 43–46.

Duberman, L. "Step-Kin Relationships." *Journal of Marriage and the Family* 35 (May 1973): 283–292.

Dullea, G. "Salk Divorce Case Different." *Maine Sunday Telegram,* November 9, 1975, 12B.

DuPont, R. L. "Antilibidinal Effects of Heroin." *Medical Aspects of Human Sexuality* 18 (March 1984): 251.

Duvall, E. M. *Marriage and Family Development.* 5th ed. Philadelphia: J. B. Lippincott, 1977.

Einzig, J. E. "The Child Within: A Study of Expectant Fatherhood." *Smith College Studies in Social Work* 50 (March 1980): 117–164.

Eisdorfer, C.; Nowling, J.; and Wilkie, F. "Improvement of Learning in the Aged by Modification of Autonomic Nervous System Activity." *Science* 170 (1970): 1327–1329.

Eisdorfer, C., and Wilkie, F. "Intellectual Changes with Advancing Age." In *Intellectual Functioning in Adults,* edited by L. F. Jarvik, C. Eisdorfer, and J. E. Blum, 21–29. New York: Springer, 1973.

Ekerdt, D. J.; Bosse, R.; and Mogey, J. M. "Concurrent Change in Planned and Preferred Age for Retirement." *Journal of Gerontology* 35 (March 1980): 232–240.

Elsayed, M.; Ismail, A. H.; and Young, R. J. "Intellectual Differences of Adult Men Related to Age and Physical Fitness before and after an Exercise Program." *Journal of Gerontology* 35 (May 1980): 383–387.

Elwell, C. C. "The Image of Cancer." *Human Behavior* 4 (August 1985): 41–43.

England, J. L., and Kuntz, R. P. "The Application of Age-Specific Rates to Divorce." *Journal of Marriage and the Family* 37 (February 1975): 40–46.

Erber, J. T.; Botwinick, J.; and Storandt, M. "The Impact of Memory on Age Differences in Digit Symbol Performance." *Journal of Gerontology* 36 (September 1981): 586–590.

Erikson, E. H. *Identity and the Life Cycle.* New York: International Universities, 1959.

Erikson, E. H. *Childhood and Society.* 2d rev. ed. New York: W. W. Norton and Co., 1963.

Erikson, E. H. *Identity: Youth and Crisis.* New York: W. W. Norton and Co., 1968.

Erikson, E. H. "Reflections on Dr. Borg's Life Cycle." *Daedalus* 105 (1976): 1–28.

Eskin, B. A. "Loss of Libido in a Young Woman Following Delivery." *Medical Aspects of Human Sexuality* 18 (January 1984): 160.

"Executive Stress: Keep It At Bay." *Dynamic Years* 14 (May-June 1979): 14.

Eysenck, M. W. "Age Differences in Incidental Learning." *Developmental Psychology* 10 (1974): 936–941.

Feier, C. D., and Gerstman, L. J. "Sentence Comprehension Abilities throughout the Adult Life Span." *Journal of Gerontology* 35 (September 1980): 722–728.

Feinberg, I. "Changes in Sleep Patterns with Age." *Journal of Psychiatric Research* 10 (1974): 283–306.

Feldman, H., and Feldman, M. "The Family Life Cycle: Some Suggestions for Recycling." *Journal of Marriage and the Family* 37 (May 1975): 277–284.

Fink, P. J. "Sexually Unresponsive Husbands." *Medical Aspects of Human Sexuality* 18 (July 1984): 157.

Fishburne, P. M.; Abelson, H. I.; and Cisen, I. "National Survey on Drug Abuse: Main Finding: 1979." DHHS Publication no. (ADM) 80–976. Rockville, Md.: National Institute on Drug Abuse, 1980.

Fishman, N. H., and Roe, B. B. "Cardiac Valve Replacement in Patients over 65 during a 10-Year Period." *Journal of Gerontology* 33 (September 1978): 676–680.

Fletcher, E. C. "Sexual Dysfunction in Men with Chronic Obstructive Pulmonary Disease."

Medical Aspects of Human Sexuality 18 (March 1984): 151–157.

Fox, J. H.; Topel, J. L.; and Huckman, M. S. "Use of Computerized Tomography in Senile Dementia." *Journal of Neurology, Neurosurgery, and Psychiatry* 38 (1975): 948–953.

Fozard, J. L.; Nuttal, R. L.; and Waugh, N. C. "Age-Related Differences in Mental Performance." *Aging and Human Development* 3 (1972): 19–43.

Fozard, J. L., and Popkin, S. J. "Optimizing Adult Development." *American Psychologist* 33 (November 1978): 975–989.

Freed, D. J., and Foster, H. H., Jr. "Divorce American Style." In *Encounter, Love, Marriage, and Family,* edited by R. E. Albrecht and E. Wilbur Bock, 180–205. Boston: Holbrook, 1972.

Freeman, F. *Sleep Research: A Critical Review.* Springfield, Ill.: Charles C Thomas, 1972.

Freese, A. S. "Adjustments in Later Life." *Dynamic Years* 12 (November-December 1977a): 37–39.

Freese, A. S. "When Jobs Cause Stress." *Dynamic Years* 12 (September-October 1977b): 16–17.

Frenkel-Brunswick, E. "Adjustments and Reorientation in the Course of the Life Span." In *Psychological Studies of Human Development.* Rev. ed., edited by R. G. Kuhlen and G. G. Thompson, 161–171. New York: Appleton-Century-Crofts, 1963.

Freud, S. *Collected Papers.* Vol. 5. New York: Basic Books, 1959.

Friedman, H. "Interrelation of Two Types of Immediate Memory in the Aged." *Journal of Psychology* 87 (1974): 177–181.

Friedman, N. "What's New in The Composing Room: The Printer's Response to Automation." *Aging and Work* 1 (Spring 1978): 85–91.

Fries, J. F., and Crapo, L. M. *Vitality and Aging: Implications of the Rectangular Curve.* New York: W. H. Freeman and Co., Publishers, 1981.

Fritz, D. "Decision Makers and the Changing Retirement Scene." *Aging and Work* (Fall 1978): 221–230.

Funk, V. "Growing More Beautiful Year after Year." *Dynamic Years* 15 (July-August 1980): 18–23.

Gadow, S. "Medicine, Ethics, and the Elderly."

The Gerontologist 20 (Dec. 1980): 680–685.

Gallup, G. H. *The Gallup Poll: Public Opinion 1978.* Wilmington, Del.: Scholarly Resources, 1979.

Garn, S. M. "Bone Loss and Aging." *Nutrition* 27 (1973): 107.

Garn, S. M. "Bone Loss and Aging." In *The Physiology and Pathology of Human Aging,* edited by R. Goldman and M. Rockstein, 39–57. New York: The Academic Press, 1975.

Garn, S. M. *The Earlier in Nutritional Perspective: Gain and Later Loss of Cortical Bone.* Springfield, Ill.: Charles C Thomas, 1970.

Geiger, D. L. "Note: How Future Professionals View the Elderly: A Comparative Analysis of Social Work, Law, and Medical Students' Perceptions." *The Gerontologist* 18 (December 1978): 591–594.

Gendzel, I. B. "Dependence, Independence, Interdependence." In *Choice and Challenge,* edited by C. E. Williams and J. F. Crosby, 97–103. Dubuque, Iowa: William C. Brown, 1974.

Gerber, I., et al. "Anticipatory Grief and Aged Widows and Widowers." *Journal of Gerontology* 30 (1975): 225–229.

Getzels, J. W., and Csikzentmihalyi, M. "Concern for Discovery: An Attitudinal Component of Creative Production." *Journal of Personality* 38 (1970): 91–105.

Gilbert, L. A.; Holahan, C. K.; and Manning, L. "Coping with Conflict between Professional and Maternal Roles." *Family Relations* 30 (July 1981): 419–426.

Gilliland, N. C. "The Problem of Geographic Mobility for Dual Career Families." *Journal of Comparative Family Studies* 10 (Autumn 1979): 345–358.

Ginsburg, S. D., and Orlofsky, J. L. "Ego Identity Status, Ego Development, and Loss of Control in College Women." *Journal of Youth and Adolescence* 10 (August 1981): 297–307.

Glenn, N. D. "Psychological Well-Being in the Postparental Stage: Some Evidence from National Surveys." *Journal of Marriage and the Family* 37 (1975): 105–110.

Glenn, N.. D., and Weaver, C. N. "A Note on Family Situation and Global Happiness." *Social Forces* 57 (March 1979): 960–967.

Gleser, G. C.; Green, B. L.; and Winget, N. C. "Quantifying Interview Data on Psychic Impairment of Disaster Survivors." *Journal of*

Nervous and Mental Disease 166 (1978): 209–216.

Glick, I. O.; Weiss, R. S.; and Parkes, C. M. *The First Year of Bereavement.* New York: John Wiley and Sons, 1974.

Glick, P. C. "A Demographer Looks at American Families." *Journal of Marriage and the Family* 37 (February 1975): 15–26.

Glick, P. C. "Updating the Life Cycle of the Family." *Journal of Marriage and the Family* 39 (February 1977): 5–13.

Glick, P. C., and Norton, A. J. "Frequency, Duration, and Probability of Marriage and Divorce." *Journal of Marriage and the Family* 33 (May 1971): 307–317.

Goddard, H. L., and Leviton, D. "Intimacy—Sexuality Needs of the Bereaved: An Exploratory Study." *Death Education* 34 (Winter 1980): 347–358.

Golant, S. M. "Residential Concentrations of the Future Elderly." *Gerontologist* 15 (1975): 16–23.

Goldstine, D. et al. *The Dance-Away Lover.* New York: Morrow, 1977.

Goodman, M. J.; Stewart, C. J.; and Gilbert, F., Jr. "Patterns of Menopause, A Study of Certain Medical and Physiological Variables among Caucasian and Japanese Women Living in Hawaii." *Journal of Gerontology* 32 (1977) 291–298.

Gordon, D. M. "Eye Problems of the Aged." *Journal of the American Geriatric Society* 13 (1965): 398–417.

Gould, R. L. "The Phases of Adult Life: A Study in Developmental Psychology." *American Journal of Psychiatry* 129 (November 1972): 521–531.

Gould, R. L. "Adult Life Stages: Growth toward Self-tolerance." *Psychology Today* 8 (1975): 74–78.

Gould, R. L. *Transformations: Growth and Change in Adult Life.* New York: Simon and Schuster, 1978.

Gould, R. L. "Transformations in Mid-Life." *New York University Education Quarterly* 10 (Winter 1979): 2–10.

Graber, E. A., and Barber, H. R. K. "The Case for and against Estrogen Therapy." *American Journal of Nursing* 75 (1975): 1766–1771.

Graff, T. O., and Wiseman, R. F. "Changing Concentrations of Older Americans." *Geographical Review* 68 (1978): 379–393.

Graney, M. J., and Cottam, D. M. "Labor Force Nonparticipation of Older People: United States, 1890–1970." *The Gerontologist* 21 (April 1981): 138–141.

Granick, S.; Kleban, M. H.; and Weiss, A. D. "Relationships between Hearing Loss and Cognition in Normally Hearing Aged Persons." *Journal of Gerontology* 31 (1976): 434–440.

Grant, E. A.; Storandt, M.; and Botwinick, J. "Incentive and Practice in the Psychomotor Performance of the Elderly." *Journal of Gerontology* 33 (May 1978): 413–415.

Green, B. "The Politics of Psychoactive Drug Use in Old Age." *The Gerontologist* 18 (December 1978): 525–530.

Green, M. "Aspects of Old Age." *British Journal of Social Work* 7 (Autumn 1977): 301–320.

Greenberg, A. "Effects of Opiates on Male Orgasm." *Medical Aspects of Human Sexuality* 18 (May 1984): 207.

Greene, L. M. "Only the Beginning on Freeing Job Opportunities for Older Workers." *The Journal of the Institute for Socioeconomic Studies* 3 (Summer 1978): 39–47.

Greger, J. L. "Dietary Intake and Nutritional Status in Regard to Zinc of Institutionalized Aged." *Journal of Gerontology* 32 (September 1977): 549–553.

Gruber, H. E., and Barrett, P. H. *Darwin on Man: A Psychological Study of Creativity.* New York: E. P. Dutton, 1973.

Gruman, G. J. "A History of Ideas about the Prolongation of Life. The Evolution of Prolongevity Hypothesis to 1800." *Transactions of the American Philosophical Society 56* (1966): Part 9.

Grzegorczyk, P. B.; Jones, S. W.; and Mistretta, C. M. "Age-Related Differences in Salt Taste Acuity." *Journal of Gerontology* 34 (November 1979): 834–840.

Gubrium, J. F. "Being Single in Old Age." In *Time, Roles, and Self in Old Age,* edited by J. F. Gubrium. New York: Human Sciences Press, 1976.

Gutmann, E., and Hanzlikova, V. "Fast and Slow Motor Units in Aging." *Gerontology* 22 (1976): 280–300.

Guttmacher, A. F. *Pregnancy, Birth, and Family Planning.* New York: NAL, 1973.

Guttman, D. V. "A Study of Legal Drug Use by Older Americans." *NDA Services Research Report.* Washington, D.C.: U.S. Government Printing Office, 1977.

Hammond, D. C., and Middleton, R. G. "Penile Prosthesis." *Medical Aspects of Human Sexuality* 18 (July 1984): 204–208.

Harkins, E. B. "Effects of Empty Nest Transition on Self-Report of Psychological and Physical Well-Being." *Journal of Marriage and the Family* 40 (August 1978): 549–556.

Harkins, S. W., and Chapman, C. R. "Detection and Decision Factors in Pain Perception in Young and Elderly Men." *Pain* 2 (1976): 253–264.

Harkins, S. W.; Chapman, C. R.; and Eisdorfer, C. "Memory Loss and Response Bias in Senescence." *Journal of Gerontology* 34 (January 1979): 66–72.

Hartley, A. A. "Adult Age Differences in Deductive Reasoning Processes." *Journal of Gerontology* 36 (November 1981): 700–706.

Hartley, J. T., and Walsh, D. A. "The Effect of Monetary Incentive on Amount and Rate of Free Recall in Older and Younger Adults." *Journal of Gerontology* 35 (November 1980): 899–905.

Hartung, G. H., and Farge, E. J. "Personality and Physiological Traits in Middle-Aged Runners and Joggers." *Journal of Gerontology* 32 (September 1977): 541–548.

Haug, M. "Aging and the Right to Terminate Medical Treatment." *Journal of Gerontology* 33 (July 1978): 586–591.

Havighurst, R. J. *Developmental Tasks and Education.* 3rd ed. New York: David McKay, 1972.

Hayflick, L. "Aging under Glass." *Experimental Gerontology* 5 (1970): 291–303.

Haynes, S. G.; McMichael, A. J.; and Tyroler, H. A. "Survival after Early and Normal Retirement." *Journal of Gerontology* 33 (March 1978): 269–278.

Hayslip, B., and Sterns, H. L. "Age Differences in Relationships between Crystallized and Fluid Intelligence and Problem Solving." *Journal of Gerontology* 34 (1979): 404–414.

Hellebrandt, F. A. "Aging among the Advan-

taged: A New Look at the Stereotype of the Elderly." *The Gerontologist* 20 (August 1980): 404–417.

Henker, F. O. "Sudden Disappearance of Libido." *Medical Aspects of Human Sexuality* 18 (January 1984): 167–172.

Heymont, G. "A Star Is Reborn." *Dynamic Years* 15 (July-August 1980): 61–64.

Hiltz, S. R. "Widowhood: A Roleless Role." *Marriage and the Family Review* 1 (November/December 1978): 1–10.

Hite, S. *The Hite Report: A Nationwide Study on Female Sexuality.* New York: Dell Publishing Co., 1977.

Hite, S. *The Hite Report on Male Sexuality.* New York: Ballantine, 1982.

Hobbs, D. F., and Wimbish, J. M. "Transition to Parenthood by Black Couples." *Journal of Marriage and the Family* 39 (November 1977): 677–689.

Holahan, C. K., and Gilbert, L. A. "Conflict between Major Life Roles: The Women and Men in Dual-Career Couples." *Human Relations* 32 (1979): 451–467.

Hollowell, E. E. "The Right to Die: How Legislation Is Defining the Right." *The Journal of Practical Nursing* 27 (October 1977): 20–21, 36.

Holmstrom, L. L. *The Two-Career Family.* Cambridge, Mass.: Schenkman Publishing Co., 1973.

Honig, M. "AFDC Income, Recipient Rates, and Family Dissolution." *The Journal of Human Resources* 9 (1974): 303–322.

Horn, J. L. "Organization of Abilities and the Development of Intelligence." *Psychological Review* 75 (1968): 242–259.

Horn, J. L., and Cattel, R. B. "Age Differences in Fluid and Crystallized Intelligence." *Acta Psychologica* 26 (1967): 107–129.

House, J. S. et al. "Occupational Stress and Health among Factory Workers." *Journal of Health and Social Behavior* 20 (1979): 139–160.

"How Much Does He Do around the House?" *Changing Times* 25 (April 1971): 41.

"How People Will Live to Be 100 or More." *U.S. News and World Report,* July 4, 1983, 73, 74.

Howard, D. V.; Lasaga, M. I.; and McAndrews, M. P. "Semantic Activation during Memory

Encoding across the Life Span." *Journal of Gerontology* 35 (November 1980): 884–890.

Hoyer, W. J.; Rebok, G. W.; and Sved, S. M. "Effects of Varying Irrelevant Information on Adult Age Differences in Problem Solving." *Journal of Gerontology* 34 (July 1979): 553–560.

Hultsch, D. F. "Adult Age Differences in Free Classification and Free Recall." *Developmental Psychology* 4 (1971): 338–342.

Hunziker, O.; Abdel'Al, S.; and Schulz, U. "The Aging Human Cerebral Cortex: A Stereological Characterization of Changes in the Capillary Net." *Journal of Gerontology* 34 (May 1979): 345–350.

Ingman, S. R.; Lawson, I. R.; Pierpaoli, P. G.; and Blake, P. "A Survey of the Prescribing and Administration of Drugs in a Long-Term Care Institution for the Elderly." *Journal of the American Geriatrics Society* 23 (1975): 309–316.

Inhelder, B., and Piaget, J. *The Growth of Logical Thinking*. New York: Basic Books, 1958.

Institute for Social Research. "Boring Jobs Are Hardest on Health, A Study of 23 Occupations Reveals." *Newsletter* (Spring 1975): 3, 4.

Iversen, L. I. "The Chemistry of the Brain." *Scientific American* (September 1979).

Ivester, C., and King, K. "Attitudes of Adolescents toward the Aged." *The Gerontologist* 17 (February 1977): 85–89.

Jackson, D. W. "Advanced Aged Adults' Reflections of Middle Age." *Gerontologist* 14 (1974): 255–257.

Jacobs, R., and Krohn, D. L. "Variations in Fluorescence Characteristics of Intact Human Crystalline Lens Segments as a Function of Age." *Journal of Gerontology* 31 (November 1976): 641–647.

Jacoby, A. P. "Transition to Parenthood: A Reassessment." *Journal of Marriage and the Family* 31 (November 1969): 720–727.

James, I. "Prescribing for the Elderly: Check the Interaction and Cut Down Your Calls." *Modern Geriatrics* 6 (1976): 7–14.

Jantz, R. K. et al. "Children's Attitudes toward the Elderly." *Social Education* 41 (October 1977): 518–523.

Johnson, F. A., and Johnson, C. L. "Role Strain in High-Commitment Career Women." *Journal of the American Academy of Psychoanalysis* 4 (1976): 13–36.

Johnson, R., and Strehler, B. L. "Loss of Genes Coding for Ribosomal RNA in Ageing Brain Cells." *Nature* 240 (1972): 412–414.

Johnson, V. E. *I'll Quit Tomorrow*. New York: Harper and Row, 1973.

Jorgensen, S. R. "Socioeconomic Rewards and Perceived Marital Quality: A Re-Examination." *Journal of Marriage and the Family* 41 (November 1979): 825–835.

Kalchthaler, T.; Coccaro, E.; and Lichtiger, S. "Incidence of Polypharmacy in a Long-Term Care Facility." *Journal of American Geriatrics Society* 25 (July 1977): 308–313.

Kangas, J., and Bradway, K. "Intelligence at Middle Age: A Thirty-Eight Year Follow-Up." *Developmental Psychology* 5 (1971): 333–337.

Karasawa, A.; Kawashima, K.; and Kasahara, H. "Mental Aging and the Medico-Psycho-Social Background in the Very Old Japanese." *Journal of Gerontology* 34 (September 1979): 680–686.

Kargman, M. W. "The Revolution in Divorce Law." *The Family Coordinator* 22 (April 1973): 245–248.

Kastenbaum, R.; Derbin, V.; Sabatini, P.; and Artt, S. "The Ages of Me: Toward Personal and Interpersonal Definitions of Functional Aging." *Aging and Human Development* 3 (1972): 197–211.

Kaufman, S. A. "Loss of Interest in Intercourse Following Ectopic Pregnancy." *Medical Aspects of Human Sexuality* 18 (January 1984): 15.

Kausler, D. H., and Puckett, J. M. "Adult Age Differences in Memory of Sex of Voice." *Journal of Gerontology* 36 (January 1981): 44–50.

Keith, P. M. "Life Changes and Perceptions of Life and Death among Older Men and Women." *Journal of Gerontology* 34 (November 1979): 870–878.

Keith, P. M., and Schafer, R. B. "Role Strain and Depression in Two-Job Families." *Family Relations* 29 (October 1980): 483–488.

Kell, D., and Patton, C. V. "Reaction to Induced Retirement." *The Gerontologist* 18 (April 1978): 173–179.

Kennedy, E. C. *The New Sexuality: Myths, Fables, and Hang-Ups*. Garden City, N.Y.: Doubleday and Co., 1972.

Kety, S. S. "Disorders of the Human Brain." *Scientific American* (September 1979).

Kinsey, A. C.; Pomeroy, W. B; and Martin, C. E. *Sexual Behavior in the Human Male*. Philadelphia: W. B. Saunders, 1948.

Kinsey, A. C.; Pomeroy, W. B.; Martin, C. E.; and Gebhard, P. H. *Sexual Behavior in the Human Female*. Philadelphia: W. B. Saunders, 1953.

Kivett, V. R. "Loneliness and the Rural Widow." *The Family Coordinator* 27 (October 1978): 389–394.

Kleban, M. H.; Lawton, M. P.; Brody, E. M.; and Moss, M. "Behavioral Observations of Mentally Impaired Aged: Those Who Decline and Those Who Do Not." *Journal of Gerontology* 31 (May 1976): 333–339.

Kogan, N. "Categorization and Conceptualizing Styles in Younger and Older Adults." *Human Development* 17 (1974): 218–230.

Krantzler, M. *Creative Divorce*. New York: New American Library, 1974.

Krasnegor, N. A., ed. *The Behavioral Aspects of Smoking*. Rockville, Md.: National Institute on Drug Abuse, 1979.

Kriesberg, L. *Mothers in Poverty*. Chicago: Aldine, 1970.

Kronenberg, R. S., and Drage, C. W. "Attenuation of the Ventilatory and Heart Rate Responses to Hypoxia and Hypercapnia with Aging in Normal Men." *Journal of Clinical Investigation* 52 (1973): 1812–1819.

Krupka, L. R., and Vener, A. M. "Hazards of Drug Use among the Elderly." *The Gerontologist* 19 (February 1979): 90–95.

Kubler-Ross, E. *On Death and Dying*. New York: Macmillan, 1969.

Kubler-Ross, E. *Questions and Answers on Death and Dying*. New York: Macmillan, 1974.

Kuypers, J. A., and Bengtson, V. L. "Social Breakdown and Competence: A Model of Normal Aging." *Human Development* 16 (1973): 181–201.

Labouvie-Vief, G., and Gonda, J. N. "Cognitive Strategy Training and Intellectual Performance in the Elderly." *Journal of Gerontology* 31 (May 1976): 327–332.

Lair, C., and Moon, W. H. "The Effects of Praise and Reproof on the Performance of Middle-Aged and Older Subjects." *Aging and Human Development* (1972): 279–284.

LaRiviere, J. E., and Simonson, E. "The Effect of Age and Occupation on Speed of Writing." *Journal of Gerontology* 20 (1965): 415, 416.

Laslett, P. "Societal Development and Aging." In *Handbook of Aging and the Social Sciences*, edited by R. H. Binstock and E. Shanas, 87–116. New York: Van Nostrand Reinhold, 1976.

Lauersen, N. H., and Graves, Z. R. "Pretended Orgasm." *Medical Aspects of Human Sexuality* 18 (March 1984): 74–81.

Lawrence, B. S. "The Myth of the Midlife Crisis." *Sloan Management Review* 21 (Summer 1980): 35–49.

Lawson, J. S.; Rodenburg, M.; and Dykes, J. A. "A Dementia Rating Scale for Use with Psychogeriatric Patients." *Journal of Gerontology* 32 (March 1977): 153–159.

Lear, M. W. "Loneliness: More Common Than the Common Cold." *Redbook* (November 1980): 33.

Lehman, H. C. "The Creative Production Rates of Present Versus Past Generations of Scientists." *Journal of Gerontology* 17 (1962): 409–417.

Lehman, H. C. "The Psychologists Most Creative Years." *American Psychologist* 21 (1966): 363–369.

Leon, A. S., and Blackburn, H. "Exercise Rehabilitation of the Coronary Heart Disease Patient." *Geriatrics* 32 (December 1977): 66–76.

LeRoux, R. S. "Communicating with the Dying Person." *Nursing Forum* 16 (1977): 145–155.

LeShan, E. *The Wonderful Crisis of Middle Age*. New York: David McKay, 1973.

Levendusky, P. G. "Effects of Social Incentives on Task Performance in the Elderly." *Journal of Gerontology* 33 (July 1978): 562–566.

Levinson, D. J. "The Midlife Transition: A Period in Adult Psychosocial Development." *Psychiatry* 40 (1977): 99–112.

Levinson, D. J.; Darrow, C. N.; Klein, E. B.; Levinson, M. H.; and McKee, B. "Periods in the Adult Development of Men: Ages 18 to 45." *Counseling Psychologist* 6 (1976): 21–25.

Levinson, D. J.; with Darrow, C. N.; Klein, E. B.;

Levinson, M. H.; and McKee, B. *The Seasons of a Man's Life.* New York: Alfred A. Knopf, 1978.

Lewinsohn, P. M., and Talkington, J. "Studies on the Measurement of Unpleasant Events and Relations with Depression." *Applied Psychological Measurement* 3 (1979): 83–101.

Lewis, R. A.; Freneau, P. J.; and Robert, C. L. "Fathers and the Postparental Transition." *The Family Coordinator* 28 (October 1979): 514–520.

Lichter, D. T.; Fuguitt, G. V.; Heaton, T. B.; and Clifford, W. B. "Components of Change in the Residential Concentration of the Elderly Population: 1950–1975." *Journal of Gerontology* 36 (July 1981): 480–489.

Lindeman, R. D. "Age Changes in Renal Function." In *The Physiology and Pathology of Human Aging,* edited by R. Goldman and M. Rockstein, 19–38. New York: Academic Press, 1975.

Lobsenz, N. M. "Sex and the Senior Citizen." *New York Times Magazine,* January 29, 1974, 28–31.

Locke-Connor, C., and Walsh, R. P. "Attitudes toward the Older Job Applicant: Just As Competent and More Likely to Fail." *Journal of Gerontology* 35 (November 1980): 920–927.

Longino, C. F., and Kitson, G. C. "Parish Clergy and the Aged: Examining Stereotypes." *Journal of Gerontology* 31 (May 1976): 340–345.

Lopata, H. Z. "Contributions of Extended Families to the Support Systems of Metropolitan Area Widows: Limitations of the Modified Kin Network." *Journal of Marriage and the Family* 40 (May 1978): 355–365.

Loranger, A. W., and Levine, P. M. "Age at Onset of Bipolar Affective Illness." *Archives of General Psychiatry* 35 (1978): 1345–1348.

Loria, A.; Hershko, C.; and Konijn, A. M. "Serum Ferritin in an Elderly Population." *Journal of Gerontology* 34 (July 1979): 521–524.

Lowe, J. "Could You, Should You, Would You Retire Early?" *Dynamic Years* 13 (May-June 1978): 36–38.

Lundin, D. V. "Medication Taking Behavior of the Elderly: A Pilot Study." *Drug Intelligence and Clinical Pharmacy* 12 (1978): 518–522.

Lynd, R., and Lynd, H. *Middletown.* New York: Harcourt, 1929.

Maas, H. and Kuypers, J. *From Thirty to Seventy.* San Francisco: Jossey-Bass, 1974.

Maddox, G. L. "Themes and Issues in Sociological Theories of Human Aging." *Human Development* 13 (1970): 17–27.

Marcia, J. E., and Friedman, M. L. "Ego Identity Status in College Women." *Journal of Personality* 38 (1970): 249–263.

Marshall, J. R. "Changes in Aged White Male Suicide: 1948–1972." *Journal of Gerontology* 33 (September 1978): 763–768.

Marshall, S. "Urinary Infections after Coitus." *Medical Aspects of Human Sexuality* 18 (April (1984): 235.

Martin, J. D. "Power, Dependence, and the Complaints of the Elderly: A Social Exchange Perspective." *Aging and Human Development* 2 (May 1971): 108–112.

Maslow, A. H. *Toward a Psychology of Being.* Princeton, N.J.: Van Nostrand, 1962.

Masters, W. H., and Johnson, V. E. *Human Sexual Response.* Boston: Little, Brown, 1966.

Masters, W. H., and Johnson, V. E. *Human Sexual Inadequacy.* Boston: Little, Brown, 1970.

Maultsby, M. C. "Why a Man Fakes Orgasm." *Medical Aspects of Human Sexuality* 18 (March 1984): 233.

Maynard, F. "Understanding the Crises in Men's Lives." In *Choice and Challenge,* edited by C. E. Williams and J. F. Crosby, 135–144. Dubuque, Iowa: William C. Brown, 1974.

McPherson, J. R.; Lancaster, D. R.; and Carroll, J. C. "Stature Change with Aging in Black Americans." *Journal of Gerontology* 33 (January 1978): 20–25.

Mecke, G., and Mecke, V. "The Development of Formal Thought As Shown by Explanation of the Oscillations of a Pendulum: A Replication Study." *Adolescence* 6 (1971): 219–228.

Mednick, S. A., and Schulsinger, F. "Some Premorbid Characteristics Related to Breakdown in Children with Schizophrenic Mothers." *Journal of Psychiatric Research* 6 (1968): 267–291.

Meichenbaum, D. "Cognitive Modification of Test Anxious College Students." *Journal of Consulting and Clinical Psychology* 39 (1972): 370–380.

Michalewski, H. J.; Thompson, L. W.; Smith, D. B. D.; Patterson, J. V.; Bowman, T. E.; Litzelman, D.; and Brent, G. "Age Differences in the Contingent Negative Variation (CNV): Reduced Frontal Activity in the Elderly." *Journal of Gerontology* 35 (July 1980): 542–549.

"Middle Age. The Best of Times." *U.S. News and World Report,* October 25, 1982, 67, 68.

Miller, B. C., and Sollie, D. L. "Normal Stress during the Transition to Parenthood." *Family Relations* 29 (October 1980): 459–465.

Miller, H. "Why We Oppose Mandatory Retirement." *Dynamic Years* 12 (September-October 1977): 18.

Miller, J. D. et al. *National Survey on Drug Abuse: Main Findings 1982.* DHHS Publication no. (ADM) 83–1263. Rockville, Md.: National Institute on Drug Abuse, 1983.

Miller, M. "Geriatric Suicide: The Arizona Study." *The Gerontologist* 18 (October 1978): 488–495.

Miller, P. Y., and Simon, W. "Do Youth Really Want to Work: A Comparison of the Work Values and Job Perceptions of Younger and Older Men." *Youth and Society* 10 (1979): 379–404.

Misler-Lachman, J. L. "Spontaneous Shift in Encoding Dimensions among Elderly Subjects." *Journal of Gerontology* 32 (January 1977): 68–72.

Mock, M. B. "Rehabilitation of the Elderly Cardiac Patient Hampered by Bias." *Geriatrics* 32 (December 1977): 22–23.

Modell, J.; Furstenberg, F. F.; and Hershberg, T. "Social Change and Transitions to Adulthood in Historical Perspective." *Journal of Family History* 1 (Autumn 1976): 7–32.

Moenster, P. A. "Learning and Memory in Relation to Age." *Journal of Gerontology* 27 (1972): 361–363.

Monahan, T. P. "National Divorce Legislation: The Problem and Some Suggestions." *The Family Coordinator* 22 (July 1973): 353–357.

Monge, R. H., and Gardner, E. F. *A Program of Research in Adult Differences in Cognitive Performance and Learning: Backgrounds for Adult Education and Vocational Training.* Final Report, Project no. 6–1963, Grant no. OEG 1–706193–0149, 1972.

Monk, A., and Donovan, R. "Pre-Retirement Preparation Programs." *Aged Care and Services Review* 1 (1978–79): 1–7.

Moore, L. M.; Nielsen, C. R.; and Mistretta, C. M. "Sucrose Taste Thresholds: Age-Related Differences." *Journal of Gerontology* 37 (January 1982): 64–69.

"More Age Bias?" *Dynamic Years* 17 (January-February 1982): 6.

Morehouse, L. E., and Gross, L. *Total Fitness in 30 Minutes a Week.* New York: Simon and Schuster, 1975.

Morgan, R. E. "The Adult Growth Examination: Preliminary Comparisons of Physical Aging in Adults by Sex and Race." *Perceptual and Motor Skills* 27 (1968): 595–599.

Morimatsu, M.; Hirai, S.; Muramatsu, A.; and Yoshikawa, M. "Senile Degenerative Brain Lesions and Dementia." *Journal of American Geriatrics Society* 23 (1975): 390–406.

Moritani, T., and deVries, H. A. "Potential for Gross Muscle Hypertrophy in Older Men." *Journal of Gerontology* 35 (September 1980): 672–682.

Morrison, M. H. "Planning for Income Adequacy in Retirement." *The Gerontologist* 16 (December 1976): 538–543.

Morselli, P. L.; Garattini, S.; and Cohen, S. N., eds. *Drug Interactions.* New York: Raven Press, 1974.

Mortimer, J. T., and Simmons, R. G. "Adult Socialization." *Annual Review of Sociology* 4 (1978): 421–454.

Muchinsky, P. M. "Age and Job Facet Satisfaction: A Conceptual Reconsideration." *Aging and Work* 1 (Summer 1978): 175–179.

Mueller, J. H.; Rankin, J. L.; and Carlomusto, M. "Adult Age Differences in Free Recall as a Function of Basis of Organization and Method of Presentation." *Journal of Gerontology* 34 (May 1979): 375–380.

Muiesan, G.; Sorbini, C. A.; and Grassi, V. "Respiratory Function in the Aged." *Bulletin of Physio-Pathological Respiration* 7 (1971): 973–1007.

Muller, H. F., and Schwartz, G. "Electroencephalogram and Autopsy Findings in Geropsychiatry." *Journal of Gerontology* 33 (July 1978): 504–513.

Murdock, B. B., Jr. *Human Memory: Theory and Data.* Potomac, Md.: Lawrence Erlbaum Associates, 1974.

Murphy, D. P. "Maternal Age and Malformation." *Annals of the New York Academy of Science* 57 (1954): 505.

Murrell, F. H. "The Effect of Extensive Practice on Age Differences in Reaction Time." *Journal of Gerontology* 25 (1970): 268–274.

Muson, H. "The Lessons of the Grant Study." *Psychology Today* 11 (September 1977): 42, 48, 49.

Myers, G. C. "Cross-National Trends in Mortality Rates among the Elderly." *The Gerontologist* 18 (October 1978), Part I: 441–448.

Myska, M. J., and Pasewark, R. A. "Death Attitudes of Residential and Non-Residential Rural Aged Persons." *Psychological Reports* 43 (December 1978), Part II: 1235–1238.

Nagi, M.; Pugh, M.; and Lazerine, N. "Attitudes of Catholic and Protestant Clergy toward Euthanasia." *Omega* 8 (1977): 153–164.

Nam, C. B., and Okay, K. A. "Factors Contributing to the Mortality Crossover Pattern." *XVIII General Conference of the International Union for the Scientific Study of Population.* Mexico City, 1977.

National Council on Aging. *Triple Jeopardy: Myth or Reality.* Washington, D.C.: National Council on Aging, 1972.

National Council on Aging. *The Myth and Reality of Aging in America.* Washington, D.C.: National Council on Aging, 1975.

National Foundation—March of Dimes. *Birth Defects: Tragedy and Hope,* 1977.

National Opinion Research Center. *General Social Survey,* 1973.

National Research Council, Food and Nutrition Board. *Recommended Dietary Allowances.* 8th rev. Washington, D.C.: National Academy of Sciences, 1974.

Nebes, R. D. "Verbal-Pictoral Recoding in the Elderly." *Journal of Gerontology* 31 (July 1976): 421–427.

Nelson, F. L., and Farberow, N. L. "Indirect Self-Destructive Behavior in the Elderly Nursing Home Patient." *Journal of Gerontology* 35 (November 1980): 949–957.

Nelson, H. "Doctors of Elderly Patients Concerned over 'Spaced-Out Grandma' Syndrome." *Los Angeles Times* 11, March 8, 1976, 1, 3.

Neubeck, G. "In Praise of Marriage." *The Family Coordinator* 28 (January 1979): 115–117.

Neugarten, B. L., ed. *Middle Age and Aging. A Reader in Social Psychology.* Chicago: The University of Chicago Press, 1968.

Neugarten, B. L. "Adaptation and the Life Cycle." *Counseling Psychologist* 6 (1976): 16–20.

Newman, B. M., and Newman, P. R. *Development Through Life: A Psychosocial Approach.* 2d ed. Homewood, Ill.: Dorsey Press, 1984.

Niinimaa, V., and Shephard, R. J. "Training and Oxygen Conductance in the Elderly." *Journal of Gerontology* 33 (May 1978): 354–361.

Nock, S. L. "The Family Life Cycle: Empirical or Conceptual Tool?" *Journal of Marriage and the Family* 41 (February 1979): 15–26.

Norborn, M. A. "Are You Working Too Hard?" *Dynamic Years* 14 (September-October 1979): 35–36.

Norris, A.; Mittman, C.; and Shock, N. W. "Lung Function in Relation to Age: Changes in Ventilation with Age." In *Aging of the Lung,* edited by L. Cander and J. H. Moyer. New York: Grune and Stratton, 1964.

Norton, A. J. "The Influence of Divorce on Traditional Life-Cycle Measures." *Journal of Marriage and the Family* 42 (February 1980): 63–69.

Nowak, C. "The Appearance Signal in Adult Development." Ph.D. dissertation, Wayne State University, 1975.

Nuttal, R. L.; Fozard, J. L.; Rose, C. L.; and Spencer, B. "The Ages of Man: Ability Age, Personality Age, and Blood Chemistry Age." *Proceedings of the 79th Annual Convention of the American Psychological Association* 6 (1971): 605–606.

Nye, F. I., and Berardo, F. M. *The Family: Its Structure and Interaction.* New York: Macmillan, 1973.

O'Brien, P. *The Woman Alone.* New York: Quadrangle, 1973.

Obrist, W. D.; Busse, E. W.; Eisdorfer, C.; and Kleemeier, R. W. "Relation of Electroencephalogram to Intellectual Function in Senescence." *Journal of Gerontology* 17 (1962): 197–206.

O'Connell, A. N., and Rotter, N. G. "The Influence of Stimulus Age and Sex on Person Perception." *Journal of Gerontology* 34 (March 1979): 220–228.

O'Connor, J. F., and Stern, L. O. "Results of

Treatment in Functional Sexual Disorders." *New York State Journal of Medicine* 72 (1972): 1927–1934.

Ovesey, L., and Meyers, H. "Retarded Ejaculation." *Medical Aspects of Human Sexuality* (November 1970): 98–119.

Owens, W. A., Jr. "Age and Mental Abilities: A Second Adult Follow-Up." *Journal of Educational Psychology* 51 (1966): 311–325.

Palmore, E. "The Effects of Aging on Activities and Attitudes." *Gerontologist* 8 (1968): 259–263.

Palmore, E. "Advantages of Aging." *The Gerontologist* 19 (April 1979): 220–223.

Palmore, E., and Cleveland, W. "Aging, Terminal Decline, and Terminal Drop." *Journal of Gerontology* 31 (January 1976): 76–81.

Palmore, E.; Cleveland, W.; Nowlin, J. B.; Ramm, D.; and Siegler, I. C. "Stress and Adaptation in Later Life." *Journal of Gerontology* 34 (November 1974): 841–851.

Palmore, E., and Kivett, V. "Change in Life Satisfaction: A Longitudinal Study of Persons Ages 46–70." *Journal of Gerontology* 32 (May 1977): 311–316.

Palmore, E., and Luikart, C. "Health and Social Factors Related to Life Satisfaction." *Journal of Health and Social Behavior* 13 (1972): 68–80.

Papalia, D. E., and DelVento Bielby, D. "Cognitive Functioning in Middle and Old Age Adults." *Human Development* 17 (1974): 424–443.

Parkes, C. M. *Bereavement.* New York: International Universities Press, 1972.

Parkinson, S. R.; Lindholm, J. M.; and Urell, T. "Aging, Dichotic Memory and Digit Span." *Journal of Gerontology* 35 (January 1980): 87–95.

Parlee, M. B. "The Rhythms in Men's Lives." *Psychology Today* 11 (April 1978): 82.

Passin, H. "The Single Past Imperfect." *Single* 1 (August 1973).

Pattison, E. M. *The Experience of Dying.* Englewood Cliffs, N.J.: Prentice-Hall, 1977.

Patton, C. V. "Early Retirement in Academia." *The Gerontologist* 17 (August 1977): 347–354.

Pearlman, C. K. "Frequency of Intercourse in Males at Different Ages." *Medical Aspects of Human Sexuality* (November 1972): 92–113.

Penrose, L. S., and Smith, G. F. *Down Anomaly.* Boston: Little, Brown, 1966.

Perlmutter, M. "Age Differences in Adults' Free Recall, Cued Recall, and Recognition." *Journal of Gerontology* 34 (July 1979): 533–539.

Perry, J. S., and Varney, T. L. "College Students' Attitudes toward Workers' Competence and Age." *Psychological Reports* 42 (1978): 1319–1322.

Peters, G. R. "Self-Conceptions of the Aged, Age Identification, and Aging." *Gerontologist* 11 (1971): 69–73.

Peterson, D. A.; Powell, C.; and Robertson, L. "Aging in America. Toward the Year 2000." *The Gerontologist* 16 (June 1976): 264–270.

Pfeiffer, E., and Davis, G. C. "The Use of Leisure Time in Middle Life." *Gerontologist* 11 (1971): 187–195.

Pfeiffer, E., and Davis, G. C. "Determinants of Sexual Behavior in Middle and Old Age." *Journal of the American Geriatrics Society* 20 (1972): 151–158.

Pfeiffer, E.; Verwoerdt, A.; and Davis, G. C. "Sexual Behavior in Middle Life." *American Journal of Psychiatry* 128 (1972): 1262–1267.

Phillips, J. S.; Barrett, G. V.; and Rush, M. C. "Job Structure and Age Satisfaction." *Aging and Work* (Spring 1978): 109–119.

Piaget, J. "Intellectual Evolution from Adolescence to Adulthood." *Human Development* 15 (1972): 1012.

Piaget, J., and Inhelder, B. *The Psychology of the Child.* New York: Basic Books, 1969.

Plemons, J. K.; Willis, S. L.; and Baltes, P. "Modifiability of Fluid Intelligence in Aging: A Short-Term Longitudinal Training Approach." *Journal of Gerontology* 33 (March 1978): 224–231.

Plonk, M. A., and Pulley, M. A. "Financial Management of Retired Couples." *The Gerontologist* 17 (June 1977): 256–261.

Poon, L. W., and Fozard, J. L. "Speed of Retrieval from Long-Term Memory in Relation to Age, Familiarity, and Datedness of Information." *Journal of Gerontology* 33 (September 1978): 711–717.

Poon, L. W., and Fozard, J. L. "Age and Word Frequency Effects in Continuous Recognition Memory." *Journal of Gerontology* 35 (January 1980): 77–86.

Porter, S. *Sylvia Porter's Money Book.* Garden City, N. Y.: Doubleday and Co., 1975.

Posner, J. "Old and Female: The Double Whammy." *Essence: Issues in the Study of Ageing, Dying, and Death* 2 (1977): 41–48.

Potash, M., and Jones, B. "Aging and Decision Criteria for the Detection of Tones in Noise." *Journal of Gerontology* 32 (July 1977): 436–440.

Powell, D. A.; Milligan, W. L.; and Furchtgott, E. "Peripheral Autonomic Changes Accompanying Learning and Reaction Time Performance in Older People." *Journal of Gerontology* 35 (January 1980): 57–65.

Powers, W. G., and Hutchinson, K. "The Measurement of Communication Apprehension in the Marriage Relationship." *Journal of Marriage and the Family* 41 (February 1979): 89–95.

Prinz, P. A. "Sleep Patterns in the Healthy Aged: Relationship with Intellectual Function." *Journal of Gerontology* 32 (1977): 179–186.

Proper, R., and Wall, F. "Left Ventricular Stroke Volume Measurements Not Affected by Aging." *American Heart Journal* 83 (1972): 843–845.

"Prosperity Looks 50-Plus." *Dynamic Years* 14 (September-October 1979): 58.

Puglisi, J. T. "Semantic Encoding in Older Adults as Evidenced by Release from Proactive Inhibition." *Journal of Gerontology* 35 (September 1980): 743–745.

Quinn, R. P.; Graham, L. S.; and McCullough, M. R. "Job Satisfaction: Is There a Trend?" *Manpower Research Monograph No. 30.* U.S. Department of Labor. Washington, D.C.: U. S. Government Printing Office, 1974.

Raffoul, P. R.; Cooper, J. K.; and Love, D. W. "Drug Misuse in Older People." *The Gerontologist* 21 (April 1981): 146–150.

Randall, O. A. "Aging In America Today—New Aspects in Aging." *The Gerontologist* 17 (February 1977): 6–11.

Rankin, J. L., and Kausler, D. H. "Adult Age Differences in False Recognitions." *Journal of Gerontology* 34 (January 1979): 58–65.

Rawson, I. G.; Weinberg, G. I.; Herold, J.; and Holtz, J. "Nutrition of Rural Elderly in Southwestern Pennsylvania." *The Gerontologist* 18 (February 1978): 24–29.

"Recreation for All Is Latest Goal in Cities." *U.S. News and World Report,* May 23, 1977, 72, 73.

Rice, F. P. *The Change of Life.* Bulletin 541. Orono, Maine: University of Maine, Cooperative Extension Service, 1967.

Rice, F. P. *Sexual Problems in Marriage.* Philadelphia: Westminster Press, 1978a.

Rice, F. P. *Stepparenting.* New York: Condor, 1978b.

Rice, F. P. *Contemporary Marriage.* Boston: Allyn and Bacon, 1983.

Rice, F. P. *The Adolescent: Development, Relationships, and Culture.* 4th ed. Boston: Allyn and Bacon, 1984.

Richman, J. "The Foolishness and Wisdom of Age: Attitudes toward the Elderly as Reflected in Jokes." *The Gerontologist* 17 (June 1977): 210–219.

Ridley, J. C.; Bachrach, C. A..; and Dawson, D. A. "Recall and Reliability of Interview Data from Older Women." *Journal of Gerontology* 34 (January 1979): 99–105.

Riege, W. H., and Inman, V. "Age Differences in Nonverbal Memory Tasks." *Journal of Gerontology* 36 (January 1981): 51–58.

Riley, L. E., and Spreitzer, E. A. "A Model for the Analysis of Lifetime Marriage Patterns." *Journal of Marriage and the Family* 36 (February 1974): 64–70.

Rives, N. W. "The Effect of Census on Life Table Estimates of Black Mortality." *American Journal of Public Health* 67 (1977): 867–868.

Roberts, F. B., and Miller, B. C. "Infant Behavior Effects on the Transition to Parenthood: A Mini-theory." Paper presented at a Workshop of the National Council on Family Relations, October 1978.

Robertson, J. F. "Women in Midlife: Crises, Reverberations, and Support Networks." *The Family Coordinator* 27 (October 1978): 375–382.

Robinson, P. "Five Models for Dying." *Psychology Today* 15 (March 1981): 85–91.

Rockstein, M., and Sussman, M. *Biology of Aging.* Belmont, Calif.: Wadsworth, 1979.

Rogers, C. J., and Gallion, T. E. "Characteristics of Elderly Pueblo Indians in New Mexico." *The Gerontologist* 18 (October 1978): 482–487.

Rollin, B. C. "The American Way of Marriage, Remarriage." In *Love, Marriage, Family,* edited by M. E. Lasswell and T. E. Lasswell, 489–495. Glenview, Ill.: Scott, Foresman and Co., 1973.

Rollin, B. C., and Cannon, K. L. "Marital Satisfaction over the Family Life Cycle: A Reevaluation." *Journal of Marriage and the Family* 36 (May 1974): 271–282.

Rose, C. L., and Mogey, J. M. "Aging and Preference for Later Retirement." *Aging and Human Development* 3 (1972): 45–62.

Rosel, N. "Toward a Social Theory of Dying." *Omega: Journal of Death and Dying* 9 (1978–79): 49–55.

Rosen, L. "The Broken Home and Male Delinquency." In *Sociology of Crime and Delinquency,* edited by M. Wolfgang, N. Johnson, and L. Savitz, 489–495. New York: John Wiley and Sons, 1970.

Rosenberg, M. *Society and the Adolescent Self-Image.* Princeton, N.J.: Princeton University Press, 1965.

Rosenberg, S. D., and Farrell, M. P. "Changes in Life Course at Mid-Life: A Pattern of Psychosocial Decline." Paper presented at the 70th annual meeting of the American Sociological Association, San Francisco, August 26, 1975.

Rosenblatt, P. C. "Behavior in Public Places: Comparison of Couples Accompanied and Unaccompanied by Children." *Journal of Marriage and the Family* 36 (November 1974): 750–755.

Rubenstein, C. "Money and Self-Esteem, Relationships, Secrecy, Envy, and Satisfaction." *Psychology Today* 15 (May 1981): 29–44.

Rubin, K. H. "Extinction of Conservation: A Life Span Investigation." *Developmental Psychology* 12 (1976): 51–56.

Rubin, L. B. *Women of a Certain Age: The Midlife Search for Self.* New York: Harper and Row, 1979.

Russell, C. S. "Transition to Parenthood: Problems and Gratifications." *Journal of Marriage and the Family* 36 (May 1974): 294–302.

Russell, M. A. H. "Cigarette Smoking: Natural History of a Dependence Disorder." *British Journal of Medical Psychology* 44 (1971): 9.

Sabbahi, M. A., and Sedgwick, E. M. "Age-Related Changes in Monosynoptic Reflex Excitability." *Journal of Gerontology* 37 (January 1982): 24–32.

Sacher, G. A. "Longevity, Aging, and Death: An Evolutionary Perspective." *The Gerontologist* 18 (April 1978): 112–119.

Sanders, R. E.; Murphy, M. D.; Schmitt, F. A.; and Walsh, K. K. "Age Differences in Free Recall Strategies." *Journal of Gerontology* 35 (July 1980): 550–558.

Sanders, R. E., and Sanders, J. C. "Long-term Durability and Transfer of Enhanced Conceptual Performance in the Elderly." *Journal of Gerontology* 33 (May 1978): 408–412.

Sarason, I. G. "The Revised Life Experiences Survey." Unpublished manuscript, University of Washington, 1981.

Sarason, I. G.; Johnson, J. H.; and Siegel, J. M. "Assessing the Impact of Life Stress: Development of Life Experiences Survey." *Journal of Consulting and Clinical Psychology* 46 (1978): 932–946.

Sass, T. "Demographic and Economic Characteristics of Nonbeneficiary Widows: An Overview." *Social Security Bulletin* 42 (November 1979): 3–14.

Sataloff, J., and Vassallo, L. "Hard-of-Hearing Senior Citizens and the Physician." *Geriatrics* 21 (1966): 182–186.

Sato, I.; Hasegawa, Y.; Takahashi, N.; Hirata, Y.; Shimomura, K.; and Hotta, K. "Age-Related Changes of Cardiac Control Function in Man." *Journal of Gerontology* 36 (September 1981): 564–572.

Saunders, E. "Precoital Therapy for Hypertensives." *Medical Aspects of Human Sexuality* 18 (January 1984): 247–255.

Schaie, K. W. "External Validity in the Assessment of Intellectual Development in Adulthood." *Journal of Gerontology* 33 (September 1978): 695–701.

Schaie, K. W., and Baltes, P. B. "On Sequential Strategies and Developmental Research." *Human Development* 18 (1975): 384–390.

Schaie, K. W., and Labouvie-Vief, G. "Generational Versus Ontogenetic Components of Change in Adult Cognitive Behavior: A Fourteen-Year Cross-Sequential Study." *Developmental Psychology* 10 (1974): 305–320.

Schaie, K. W.; Labouvie, G. V..; and Buech, B. U. "Generational and Cohort-Specific Differences in Adult Cognitive Functioning: A Fourteen-

Year Study of Independent Samples." *Developmental Psychology* 9 (1973): 151–166.

Scher, J., and Rogers, D. "Sexual Adjustment in the Presence of Various Gynecologic Conditions." *Medical Aspects of Human Sexuality* 18 (June 1984): 145–153.

Schmitt, J. F., and McCroskey, R. L. "Sentence Comprehension in Elderly Listeners: The Factor of Rate." *Journal of Gerontology* 36 (July 1981): 441–445.

Schonfield, D. "Memory Changes with Age." *Nature* 28 (1965): 918.

Schram, R. W. "Marital Satisfaction Over the Family Life Cycle: A Critique and Proposal." *Journal of Marriage and the Family* 41 (February 1979): 7–12.

Schuckman, T. *Aging Is Not for Sissies.* Philadelphia: Westminster Press, 1975.

Schultz, N. R.; Dinnen, J. T.; Elias, M. F.; Pentz, C. A.; and Wood, W. G. "WAIS Performance for Different Age Groups of Hypertensive and Control Subjects during the Administration of a Diuretic." *Journal of Gerontology* 34 (March 1979): 246–253.

Scott, J. P., and Kivett, V. R. "The Widowed, Black, Older Adult in the Rural South: Implications for Policy." *Family Relations* 29 (January 1980): 83–90.

"See No Evil." *Dynamic Years* 17 (January-February 1982): 6, 8.

Seefeldt, C.; Jantz, R. K.; Galper, A.; and Serock, K. "Using Pictures to Explore Children's Attitudes toward the Elderly." *The Gerontologist* 17 (December 1977): 506–512.

Sekuler, R., and Hutman, L. P. "Spatial Vision and Aging. I: Contrast Sensitivity." *Journal of Gerontology* 35 (September 1980): 692–699.

Selye, H. *The Stress of Life.* Rev. ed. New York: McGraw-Hill, 1976.

Semmens, J. P., and Tsai, C. C. "Some Gynecologic Causes of Sexual Problems." *Medical Aspects of Human Sexuality* 18 (January 1984): 174–181.

Shanas, E. "Family Help Patterns and Social Class in Three Countries." *Journal of Marriage and the Family* 29 (May 1967): 257–266.

Shapiro, H. D. "Do Not Go Gently." *The New York Times Magazine,* February 6, 1977, 36–40.

Shapiro, M. "Legal Rights of the Terminally Ill."

Aging, No. 289–290 (November/December 1978): 22–27.

Shaver, P., and Freidman, J. "Your Pursuit of Happiness." *Psychology Today* (August 1976): 26ff.

Sheehy, G. *Passages. Predictable Crises of Adult Life.* New York: E. P. Dutton, 1976.

Sheppard, A. "Response to Cartoons and Attitudes toward Aging." *Journal of Gerontology* 36 (January 1981): 122–126.

Sherman, B. M.; Wallace, R. B.; Bean, J. A.; Chang, Y.; and Schlabaugh, L. "The Relationships of Menopausal Hot Flushes to Medical and Reproductive Experience." *Journal of Gerontology* 36 (May 1981): 306–309.

Shideler, M. M. "An Amicable Divorce." *Christian Century* (May 5, 1971).

Shimonaka, Y., and Nakazato, K. "Psychological Characteristics of Japanese Aged: A Comparison of Sentence Completion Test Responses of Older and Younger Adults." *Journal of Gerontology* 35 (November 1980): 891–898.

Shin, K. E., and Putnam, R. H., Jr. "Age and Academic-Professional Honors." *Journal of Gerontology* 37 (March 1982): 120–129.

Shock, N. W. "Systems Integration." In *Handbook of the Biology of Aging,* edited by C. E. Finch and L. Hayflick, 639–665. New York: Van Nostrand Reinhold, 1977.

Shore, H. "Designing a Training Program for Understanding Sensory Losses in Aging." *The Gerontologist* 16 (April 1976): 157–165.

Shuman, E. "The Midlife Career Change—Is It for You?" *Dynamic Years* 14 (March-April 1979): 11–13.

Shuman, E. "Arthritis and the Middle Years." *Dynamic Years* 15 (March-April 1980): 39–42.

Sidney, K. H., and Shephard, R. J. "Maximum Testing of Men and Women in the Seventh, Eighth and Ninth Decade of Life." *Journal of Applied Physiology* 43 (1977): 280–287.

Siegel, J. S. "Prospective Trends in the Size and Structure of the Elderly Population, Impact of Mortality Trends, and Some Implications." *Current Population Reports.* Series P–23. No. 78. Washington, D.C.: U.S. Department of Commerce, Bureau of the Census, January 1979.

Siegler, I.; Roseman, J.; and Harkins, S. "Complexities in the Terminal Drop Hypothesis." Paper presented at the International Congress of Gerontology, Jerusalem, June 1975.

Sigusch, V. et al. "Psychosexual Stimulation: Sex Differences." *Journal of Sex Research* 6 (February 1970): 10–24.

Silberfarb, P. M. "Psychosexual Impact of Gynecologic Cancer." *Medical Aspects of Human Sexuality* 18 (May 1984): 212–226.

"65 and Over—Where They Are." *U.S. News and World Report,* July 5, 1982, 66.

Skinner, J. S. "Age and Performance." In *Limiting Factors of Skeletal Performance,* edited by J. Keul. Stuttgart: G. Thieme, 1973.

Slesinger, D. P.; McDivitt, M.; and O'Donnell, F. M. "Food Patterns in an Urban Population: Age and Sociodemographic Correlates." *Journal of Gerontology* 35 (May 1980): 432–441.

Smith, M. C. "Portrayal of the Elderly in Prescription Drug Advertising." *The Gerontologist* 16 (August 1975): 329–334.

Sohngen, M. "The Experience of Old Age as Depicted in Contemporary Novels." *The Gerontologist* 17 (February 1977): 70–78.

Sohngen, M., and Smith, R. J. "Images of Old Age in Poetry." *The Gerontologist* 18 (April 1978): 181–186.

Spanier, G. B., and Glick, P. C. "The Life Cycle of American Families: An Expanded Analysis." *Journal of Family History* 8 (Spring 1980): 97–111.

Spanier, G. B.; Lewis, R. A.; and Cole, C. L. "Marital Adjustment over the Family Life Cycle: The Issue of Curvilinearity." *Journal of Marriage and the Family* 37 (May 1975): 263–275.

Spence, D., and Lonner, T. "The 'Empty Nest,' a Transition within Motherhood." *The Family Coordinator* 20 (1971): 369–375.

Spicer, J. W., and Hampe, G. D. "Kinship Interaction after Divorce." *Journal of Marriage and the Family* 37 (February 1975): 113–119.

Spingarn, N. D. "Coping with the Midlife Crisis." *Dynamic Maturity* 12 (March 1977): 11–14.

Spreitzer, E., and Riley, L. E. "Factors Associated with Singlehood." *Journal of Marriage and the Family* 36 (August 1974): 533–542.

Starr, J. R., and Carns, D. E. "Singles in the City," *Society* 9 (1972): 43–48.

Stehouwer, J. "The Household and Family Relations of Old People." In *Old People in Three Industrial Societies,* edited by E. Shanas et al., 177–226. New York: Atherton, 1968.

Stein, J., ed. *The Random House Dictionary of the English Language.* New York: Random House, 1973.

Stein, P. J. "The Lifestyles and Life Chances of the Never-Married." *Marriage and Family Review* 1 (July/August 1978): 1, 3–11.

Stein, S. L., and Weston, L. C. "College Women's Attitudes toward Women and Identity Achievement." *Adolescence* 17 (Winter 1982): 895–899.

Stein, S. P.; Holzman, S.; Karasu, T. B.; and Charles, E. S. "Mid-Adult Development and Psychopathology." *American Journal of Psychiatry* 135 (June 1978): 676–681.

Sternberg, R. J. "The Nature of Intelligence." *New York University Education Quarterly* 12 (Spring 1981): 10–17.

Steuer, J.; Bank, L.; Olsen, E. J.; and Jarvik, L. F. "Depression, Physical Health, and Somatic Complaints in the Elderly: A Study of the Zung Self-Rating Depression Scale." *Journal of Gerontology* 35 (September 1980): 683–688.

Stevenson, J. S. *Issues and Crises During Middlescence.* New York: Appleton-Century-Crofts, 1977.

Super, D. E. et al. *Career Development: Self-Concept Theory.* Princeton, N.J.: College Entrance Examination Board, 1963.

Talbert, G. B. "Aging of the Reproductive System." In *Handbook of the Biology of Aging,* edited by C. E. Finch and L. Hayflick, 318–356. New York: Van Nostrand Reinhold, 1977.

Targ, D. B. "Toward a Reassessment of Women's Experience at Middle Age." *The Family Coordinator* 28 (July 1979): 377–382.

Taylor, W. "Federal Supplemental Benefits Study." *Industrial Gerontology* 4 (Summer 1977): 211–217.

Tennebaum, F. *Over Fifty-Five Is Not Illegal: A Resource Book for Active Older People.* Boston: Houghton Mifflin, 1979.

Tentler, T. N. "Death and Dying in Many Disciplines: A Review Article." *Comparative Studies in Society and History* 19 (October 1977): 511–522.

Thomae, H. "Theory of Aging and Cognitive Theory of Personality." *Human Development* 13 (1970): 1–16.

Thomas, J. C.; Waugh, N. C; and Fozard, J. L. "Age and Familiarity in Memory Scanning." *Journal of Gerontology* 33 (July 1978): 528–533.

Thompson, L. W.; Nichols, C R.; and Obrist, W. D. "Relation of Serum Cholesterol to Age, Sex, and Race." *Journal of Gerontology* 20 (1965): 160–164.

Thompson, L. W., and Wilson, S. "Electrocortical Reactivity and Learning in the Elderly." *Journal of Gerontology* 21 (1966): 45–51.

Thornburg, J. M., and Mistretta, C. M. "Tactile Sensitivity as a Function of Age." *Journal of Gerontology* 36 (January 1981): 34–39.

Thurstone, L. L., and Thurstone, T. G. *SRA Primary Mental Abilities*. Chicago: Science Research Associates, 1949.

Tissue, T. "Low-Income Widows and Other Aged Singles." *Social Security Bulletin* 42 (December 1979): 3–10.

"To Your Health." *Dynamic Years* 14 (July-August 1979): 50.

Tomlinson-Keasey, C. "Formal Operations in Females from Eleven to Fifty-Four Years of Age." *Developmental Psychology* 6 (1972): 364.

Treas, J. "The Great American Fertility Debate: Generational Balance and Support of the Aged." *The Gerontologist* 21 (February 1981): 98–103.

Tupper, C. J. "Health Factors in Aging." In *The Later Years. Social Applications of Gerontology*, edited by R. A. Kalish, 159–166. Monterey, Calif.: Brooks/Cole Publishing Co., 1977.

Turner, J. S., and Helms, D. B. *Contemporary Adulthood*. Philadelphia: W. B. Saunders, 1979.

Turner, N. W. "Sex Problems in Middle-Aged Patients." *Medical Aspects of Human Sexuality* 18 (May 1984): 76–82.

Udry, J. R., and Morris, N. M. "Relative Contribution of Male and Female Age to the Frequency of Marital Intercourse." *Social Biology* 25 (Summer 1978): 128–134.

Uhlenberg, P. "Cohort Variations in Family Life Cycle Experiences of U.S. Females." *Journal of Marriage and the Family* 36 (May 1974): 284–292.

U.S. Department of Commerce, Bureau of the Census. "Marriage, Divorce, Widowhood, and Remarriage by Family Characteristics: June 1975." *Current Population Reports,* ser. P–20, no. 312, 1977.

U.S. Department of Commerce, Bureau of the Census. "Population Profile of the United States: 1978." *Current Population Reports,* ser. P–20, no. 336, April 1979a.

U.S. Department of Commerce, Bureau of the Census. *Statistical Abstract of the United States: 1979.* 100th ed. Washington, D.C.: U.S. Government Printing Office, 1979b.

U.S. Department of Commerce, Bureau of the Census. "Social and Economic Characteristics of the Older Population: 1978." *Current Population Reports,* ser. P–23, no. 85, 1979c.

U.S. Department of Commerce, Bureau of the Census. "American Family and Living Arrangements." *Current Population Reports,* ser. P–23, no. 104, May 1980.

U.S. Department of Commerce, Bureau of the Census. *Statistical Abstract of the United States: 1980.* 101st ed. Washington, D.C.: U.S. Government Printing Office, 1980a.

U.S. Department of Commerce, Bureau of the Census. "A Statistical Portrait of Women in the United States: 1978." *Current Population Reports,* ser. P–23, no. 100, February 1980b.

U.S. Department of Commerce, Bureau of the Census. *Statistical Abstract of the United States: 1982–83.* 103d ed. Washington, D.C.: U.S. Government Printing Office, 1983.

U.S. Department of Commerce, Bureau of the Census. *Statistical Abstract of the United States: 1984.* 104th ed. Washington, D.C.: U.S. Government Printing Office, 1984.

U.S. Department of HEW. *The Surgeon General's Report: The Health Consequences of Smoking.* Public Health Service Publication no. 1696, 1967.

U.S. Department of HEW. *Remarriages: United States.* Publication no. (HRA) 74–1903. Washington, D.C.: U.S. Government Printing Office, 1973.

U.S. Department of HEW, Public Health Service. *The Health Consequences of Smoking 1974.* Washington, D.C.: U.S. Government Printing Office, January 1974.

U.S. Department of HEW, Public Health Service. *The Alcohol, Drug Abuse, and Mental Health*

National Data Book. Rockville, Md.: Alcohol, Drug Abuse, and Mental Health Administration, 1980a.

U.S. Department of HEW, Public Health Service. *National Institute on Alcohol Abuse and Alcoholism*. 7th Annual Report. Rockville, Md.: 1980b.

U.S. Department of HHS. "Births, Marriages, Divorces, and Deaths for June 1983." *Monthly Vital Statistics Report,* Vol. 32, no. 6, September 21, 1983.

United States National Health Survey. *Monocular-Binocular Visual Acuity of Adults*. Public Health Service Publication no. 100, ser. 11, no. 30, 1960–62. Washington, D.C.: U.S. Department of HEW, 1968.

U.S. Pharmacopoeial Convention. *The Physicians' and Pharmacists' Guide to Your Medicines*. New York: Ballantine Books, 1981.

Vaillant, G. E. *Adaptation to Life*. Boston: Little, Brown, 1977a.

Vaillant, G. E. "The Climb to Maturity: How the Best and the Brightest Came of Age." *Psychology Today* 11 (September 1977b): 34, 37, 38, 41, 107, 108, 110.

Verbrugge, L. M. "Multiplicity in Adult Friendships." *Social Forces* 57 (June 1979): 1286–1309.

Vermeulen, A.; Rubens, R.; and Verdonck, L. "Testosterone Secretion and Metabolism in Male Senescence." *Journal of Clinical Endocrinology and Metabolism* 34 (1972): 730.

Vinokur, A., and Selzer, M. L. "Desirable Versus Undesirable Life Events: Their Relationship to Stress and Mental Distress." *Journal of Personality and Social Psychology* 32 (1975): 329–337.

Voydanoff, P. "Work Roles as Stressors in Corporate Families." *Family Relations* 29 (October 1980): 489–494.

Wallis, C. "Hold the Eggs and Butter." *Time* 123 (March 26, 1984): 56–63.

Wang, H. S.; Obrist, W. D.; and Busse, E. W. "Neurophysiological Correlates of the Intellectual Function." *American Journal of Psychiatry* 126 (1970): 1205–1212.

Ward, R. A. "Age and Acceptance of Euthanasia." *Journal of Gerontology* 35 (May 1980): 421–431.

Warren, L. R.; Wagener, J. W.; and Herman, G. E. "Binaural Analysis in the Aging Auditory System." *Journal of Gerontology* 33 (September 1978): 731–736.

Warrington, E. K., and Silberstein, M. "A Questionnaire Technique for Investigating Very Long Term Memory." *Quarterly Journal of Experimental Psychology* 22 (1970): 508–512.

Waterman, A. S., and Whitbourne, S. K. "Androgeny and Psychosocial Development among College Students and Adults." *Journal of Personality* 50 (June 1982): 121–133.

Watson, W. H., and Maxwell, R. J. *Human Aging and Dying. A Study in Sociocultural Gerontology*. New York: St. Martin's Press, 1977.

Waugh, N. C., and Norman, D. A. "Primary Memory." *Psychological Review* 72 (1965): 89–104.

"A Way to Reduce the Estrogen Risk?" *Dynamic Years* 13 (July-August 1978): 35.

"The Ways 'Singles' are Changing U.S." *U.S. News and World Report,* January 31, 1977, 59, 60.

Webster, I. W., and Logie, H. R. "A Relationship between Functional Age and Health Status in Female Subjects." *Journal of Gerontology* 31 (September 1976): 546–550.

Wechsler, D. *Manual for the Wechsler Adult Intelligence Scale*. New York: Psychological Corporation, 1955.

Weg, R. "More Than Wrinkles." In *Looking Ahead. A Woman's Guide to the Problems and Joys of Growing Older,* edited by L. E. Troll, J. Israel, and K. Israel, 22–42. Englewood Cliffs, N.J.: Prentice-Hall 1977.

Weinberger, L. E., and Millham, J. "A Multi-dimensional Multiple Method Analysis of Attitudes toward the Elderly." *Journal of Gerontology* 30 (1970): 343–348.

Weinstock, C., and Bennett, R. "Social Environmental Effects on Cognitive Functioning." *Aging and Human Development* 2 (1971): 46–58.

Weisman, and Psykel, E. "Moving and Depression in Women." *Society* 9 (July-August 1972): 24–28.

Weitzman, L. J.; Kay, H. H.; and Dixon, R. B. "No-Fault Divorce in California: The View of the Legal Community." Paper presented at the annual meeting of the American Sociological Association in Montreal, Canada, August 25–29, 1974.

Westman, J. C., and Cline, D. W. "Divorce Is a Family Affair." In *Love, Marriage, Family,* edited by M. E. Lasswell and T. E. Lasswell, 465–470. Glenview, Ill.: Scott, Foresman and Co., 1973.

"Who Gets Fired and Why." *Dynamic Years* 15 (May/June 1980): 8.

Wigdor, B.T., and Morris, G. "A Comparison of Twenty-Year Medical Histories of Individuals with Depressive and Paranoid States." *Journal of Gerontology* 32 (March 1977): 160–163.

Wilkie, F., and Eisdorfer, C. "Terminal Changes in Intelligence." Paper presented at the 25th annual meeting of the Gerontological Society, December 22, 1972.

Williams, C. E. "Conflict: Modeling or Taking Flight." In *Choice and Challenge,* edited by C. E. Williams and J. F. Crosby, 218–223. Dubuque, Iowa: William C. Brown, 1974.

Williams, S. A.; Denney, N. W.; and Schadler, M. "Elderly Adults' Perception of Their Own Cognitive Development during the Adult Years." *International Journal of Aging and Human Development,* 1980.

Wilson, G. T., and Lawson, D. M. "Expectancies, Alcohol, and Sexual Arousal in Women." *Journal of Abnormal Psychology* 87 (June 1978): 358–367.

Wisoff, B. G.; Hartstein, M. L.; Aintalian, A.; and Hamby, R. I. "Results of Open Heart Surgery in the Septuagenarian." *Journal of Gerontology* 31 (May 1976): 275–277.

"Women at Work." *Dynamic Years* 16 (November-December 1981): 9.

Wood, V., and Robertson, J. F. "Friendship and Kinship Interaction: Differential Effect on the Morales of the Elderly." *Journal of Marriage and the Family* 40 (1978): 367–375.

Wright, J. D., and Hamilton, R. F. "Work Satisfaction and Age: Some Evidence for the Job Change Hypothesis." *Social Forces* 56 (June 1978): 1140–1158.

Wright, R. E. "Adult Age Similarities in Free Recall Output Order and Strategies." *Journal of Gerontology* 37 (January 1982): 76–79.

Wylie, E. M. "The Disgrace of Our Divorce Laws." In *Current Issues in Marriage and the Family,* edited by J. G. Wells. New York: Macmillan, 1975.

Wylie, F. M. "Attitudes toward Aging and the Aged among Black Americans: Some Historical Perspectives." *Journal of Aging and Human Development* 2 (1971): 66–70.

Wyly, M. V., and Hulicka, I. M. "Problems and Compensations of Widowhood." In *Empirical Studies in the Psychology and Sociology of Aging,* abstracted by I. M. Julicka. New York: Thomas Y. Crowell, 1977.

Wyshak, G. "Hip Fracture in Elderly Women and Reproductive History." *Journal of Gerontology* 36 (July 1981): 424–427.

Yamaura, H.; Ito, M.; Kubota, K.; and Matsuzawa, T. "Brain Atrophy during Aging: A Quantitative Study with Computed Tomography." *Journal of Gerontology* 35 (July 1980): 492–498.

Yankelovich, D. "New Rules in American Life: Searching for Self-Fulfillment in a World Turned upside Down." *Psychology Today* 15 (April 1981): 35–69.

Yearick, E. S.; Wang, M. L.; and Pisias, S. J. "Nutritional Status of the Elderly: Dietary and Biochemical Findings." *Journal of Gerontology* 35 (September 1980): 663–671.

Zalusky, J. "Shorter Work Years—Early Retirement." *The AFL-CIO American Federationist* 84 (August 1977): 4–8.

Zarit, S. H.; Cole, K. D.; and Guider, R. L. "Memory Training Strategies and Subjective Complaints of Memory in the Aged." *The Gerontologist* 21 (April 1981): 158–165.

Zawadski, R. T.; Glazer, G. B.; and Lurie, E. "Psychotropic Drug Use among Institutionalized and Noninstitutionalized Medicaid Aged in California." *Journal of Gerontology* 33 (November 1978): 825–834.

Zepelin, H.; Wolfe, C. S.; and Kleinplatz, F. "Evaluation of a Year-long Reality Orientation Program." *Journal of Gerontology* 36 (January 1981): 70–77.

Zusman, J. "Some Explanation of the Changing Appearance of Psychotic Patients: Antecedents of the Social Breakdown Syndrome Concept." *The Milbank Memorial Fund Quarterly* 64 (January 1966).

Zusne, L. "Age and Achievement in Psychology." *American Psychologist* 31 (1976): 805–807.

Glossary

Abnormal and clinical psychology: emphasize emotional growth, personality development and adjustment, and factors that contribute to healthy or unhealthy mental hygiene.

Abstract: exists only as an idea or thought.

Accommodation: the power of the eye's lens to focus.

Acquisition deficits: decline in abilities to record, encode, and store information.

Activity calories: energy expended through physical activities.

Activity theory: a theory of aging suggesting that continuance of an active life cycle has a positive effect on the sense of well-being and satisfaction of older people.

Adaptation: ability of the eye to adjust to different intensities of light.

Adjustment disorder: a maladaptive reaction to stress that may impair social or occupational functioning.

Adult life span: the years of life from early adulthood to old age.

Adversary approach: an approach to divorce in which one party must bring charges against and prove the other party guilty of some fault.

Affective disorders: disorders that disrupt the emotions or feelings, such as depression or mania.

Age grading or stratification: the division and social segregation of people according to age.

Ageism: prejudice and discrimination against the elderly.

Alarm reaction: secretion of adrenaline in the bloodstream to prepare the body for action when frightened.

Alveoli: air cells of the lungs.

Alzheimer's disease: a presenile dementia characterized by rapid deterioration and atrophy of the cerebral cortex.

Amnesia: a loss of memory.

Androgen: hormones with masculinizing influence.

Angina pectoris: pain caused by constriction of blood vessels leading to the heart, causing an insufficient blood supply.

Anovulatory: without ovulation (during menstruation).

Antacid: drugs used to prevent, neutralize, or counteract the acidity of the stomach.

Antibiotic: a large group of drugs, such as penicillin, having the capacity to destroy or inhibit the growth of bacteria and other microorganisms.

Anticholinergics: nerve medications that prevent the action of acetylcholine.

Antihistamines: drugs that neutralize or inhibit the effects of histamine in the body; used to treat allergic disorders and colds.

Anxiety disorders: mental illnesses that include phobias, anxiety states, obsessive-compulsive behavior, or posttraumatic stresses without psychotic symptoms.

Aorta: largest artery of the heart.

Applied psychology: applies psychological principles to everyday living.

Arrhythmia: irregular heartbeat.

Arteries: vessels that carry the blood from the heart to the body.

Arteriosclerosis: hardening of the arteries by a buildup of calcium in the middle muscle layer of arterial tissue; results in decreased elasticity.

Associational cortex: areas of the cortex involved in cognitive functions.

Associative strength: degree of association, as between two words.

Atherosclerosis: a buildup of fatty deposits between the middle muscular layer and lining layer of arterial tissue.

Atrophic vaginitis: vaginal inflammation from estrogen deficiency.

Auditory nerve: carries the sound images to the brain.

Autoimmunity theory: a biological theory of aging that describes the process by which the immune system of the body rejects its own tissues through the production of autoimmune antibodies, thus causing the body to die gradually.

Autonomic arousal: stimulation of the autonomic nervous system resulting in an increase in adrenalin in the blood stream, in heart rate, blood pressure, skin conductance, and other physiological changes.

Autonomy: independence, freedom, self-government.

Baby boom generation: large population born in the years following World War II (1945 to 1960).

Basal calories: the energy metabolized by the body to carry on physiological functions and to maintain normal body temperature.

Beta blockers: a group of drugs that decrease the demands of the heart for oxygen.

Biological time clock: the timetable of physical and physiological changes in the life of the adult.

Bipolar disorders: psychoses characterized by alternation between periods of mania and depression.

Blackout: a chemically induced loss of memory due to excessive drinking.

Bromides: drugs that are salts of hydrobromic acid.

Body transcendence: learning to adjust to and overlook physical handicaps and discomforts and to find happiness, not in physical prowess, but in social and mental activities.

Burnout: a phrase used to describe the situation of a person who becomes emotionally and physically exhausted from too much job pressure.

Calcium blockers: a group of drugs that prevent the buildup of calcium in the arteries (arteriosclerosis).

Capillaries: the tiniest blood vessels carrying blood to bodily tissues.

Cardiovascular system: the heart and blood vessels.

Cataracts: an abnormality of the eye in which the lens becomes cloudy and opaque.

Catatonia: a type of schizophrenia characterized by disturbance of motor ability (either immobile or agitated, purposeless activity).

Caval vein: the largest vein entering the chest.

Cellular aging theory: a biological theory of aging that says that aging occurs when the replicative potential of cells is exhausted and they fail to replace themselves.

Central nervous system: the brain and spinal cord.

Central processing: analysis of information reaching the brain.

Cerebrovascular disease: vascular disease in the brain.

Cerebrum: the anterior, largest part of the brain consisting of two hemispheres that control voluntary movements and coordinate mental activities.

Cholesterol: a chemical occurring in all animal fats that is a major contributing cause of atherosclerosis.

Chronic brain syndrome: an organic brain syndrome irreversible because of permanent brain damage.

Chronological age: number of years one has lived since birth.

Cirrhosis: a disease of the liver in which the connective tissue becomes dead, lumpy, and shriveled.

Click fusion studies: measure the ability to determine when clicks in rapid succession are perceived as one.

Clinical death: the cessation of all brain activity.

Clitoris: sensitive external sexual organ of the female, equivalent to the male penis.

Cognitive psychology: focuses on the thought process: the development of memory, thinking, and the ability to solve problems.

Cohort: a group of people born during the same time period.

Cohort-sequential study: a minimum of two age groups and two cohort groups are measured three different times. This research design comes closest to sorting out differences due to age versus cohort effects, if the time of testing is assumed to have no effect.

Coitus: sexual intercourse.

Collagen: protein in connective tissues and bones.

Collusion: when couples work out an agreement in relation to their divorce; formerly used as grounds for denying their divorce.

Community property: marital property belonging equally to the husband and wife.

Concrete: something actual or real.

Concrete operational stage: Piaget's stage of cognitive development during which the child learns to solve problems involving concrete objects or experiences and to understand the principles of seriation, classification, symmetry, associativity, negation, and conservation.

Condonation: possessing knowledge of an offense of one's spouse and forgiving by an act of reconciliation or by continued cohabitation; used by the defense as a basis for denying a divorce.

Congestive heart failure: diminutive cardiac output accompanied by increased blood pressure, which results in a buildup of fluids in the body.

Connivance: one party gives assent to or encourages certain conduct of the other party in order to have grounds for a divorce.

Cornea: the clear tissue covering the iris and pupil of the eyeball.

Coronary occlusion: obstruction of a coronary artery.

Cortex: the outer layer of the cerebrum.

Craniocerebral Index (CCI): an index of the volume of the cranial cavity.

Creativity: originality of thought and expression, or the ability to produce new products or services.

Cross-sectional study: one age group or cohort is compared with another at one time of testing.

Cross-sequential study: a combination of cross-sectional and longitudinal designs that tests different age-cohort groups at different times.

Crystallized intelligence: a person's ability to learn or profit from experience; includes knowledge and skills as measured by tests of vocabulary, general information, and reading comprehension.

Cyclothymic disorder: alternation between brief periods of depression and hypomania.

Defense mechanisms: according to Freud, the unrealistic strategies used by the ego to discharge tension.

Demographics: social statistics, such as births, ages, deaths, and marriages, in relation to populations.

Developmental tasks: the skills, knowledge, functions, and attitudes individuals have to acquire at different points in their lives.

Dexterity: skill, adroitness, or agility in using the hands or body.

Diabetes: a disease characterized by excess sugar in the system due to insufficient insulin production in the pancreas.

Diastolic blood pressure: the pressure produced when the chambers of the heart dilate and fill with blood.

Dichotic listening studies: measure echoic memory when information is presented simultaneously to each ear.

Dilators: a group of drugs that expand the blood vessels and increase blood flow.

Disengagement theory: a theory of aging saying that aging people have a natural tendency to withdraw socially and psychologically from the environment, social activities, and other people.

Disorders of impulse control: failure to resist such impulses as pathological gambling, kleptomania, pyromania, or intermittent explosive behavior.

Disorganized type of schizophrenia: incoherent, silly, inappropriate emotional responses.

Displaced homemaker: a woman whose last child has left home and who now needs to fill her life with something besides home and family.

Dissociative disorders: sudden, temporary loss of memory or identity; existence of distinct multiple personalities; or episodes of depersonalization.

Diuretics: drugs used to decrease body fluids by increasing the volume of urine secreted.

Doctrine of comparative rectitude: a law recognizing that a court can grant a divorce to the party least at fault.

Dopamine: a chemical involved in the transmission of nerve impulses.

Dowager's hump: osteoporosis of the upper spine, which causes the vertebrae to collapse and the upper spine to bend forward.

DSM-III. Diagnostic and Statistical Manual of Mental Disorders, published by the American Psychiatric Association.

Dual-career marriage: a marriage in which both the husband and wife pursue careers, usually on a full-time basis.

Dyspareunia: painful intercourse.

Dysthymic disorder: periodic depression or depressive neurosis.

Early adulthood: defined here as the twenties and thirties.

Echoic memory: the auditory sensory store.

Edema: retention of excess fluids in body tissues and cavities.

EEG: electroencephalogram; used to measure brain wave activity.

Egalitarian: in marital terms, the husband and wife equally share roles, responsibilities, and privileges in the family.

Ego integrity: according to Erikson, the ability to evaluate and accept one's life without regret; the development of this ability is the chief psychosocial task of late adulthood.

Ejaculatory incompetence: the inability of the male to ejaculate while his penis is in the vagina.

Embolism: blockage from a blood clot.

Emotional stability: the capacity to tolerate tensions and frustrations without undue upset or anxiety.

Empathy: the ability to identify with the feelings, thoughts, and attitudes of another person.

Emphysema: a degenerative disorder of the walls separating the air sacs in the lungs so they become distended, inelastic, and incapable of expelling stale air.

Empty nest period: that period in life after the last child is launched.

Encoding: linking information to concepts and categories already learned in order to store it in long-term memory.

Endometrial cancer: cancer of the inner lining of the uterus.

Erection: enlargement of a sexual organ as it becomes swollen and engorged with blood.

Erogenous zones: areas of the body that are sexually sensitive to stimulation.

Error theory: a biological theory of aging describing the cumulative effects of a variety of mistakes the body makes that impair cell functioning.

Estrogen: hormone with feminizing influence.

Euthanasia: allowing a terminally ill patient to die naturally without mechanized life support; putting to death a person who suffers from an incurable disease (mercy killing); or killing a person who is no longer considered socially useful (death selection).

Exchange theory: a theory, which has been applied to relationships among aged and their families, that maintains that persons with the greatest needs lose the most power and those supplying needs gain power.

Excitement phase: the first stage of sexual response from the beginning of sexual stimulation until a high degree of sexual excitation is reached.

Experimental psychology: emphasizes research methods for the study of human behavior.

Extended family: a family group consisting of a nucleus of husband, wife, and children, plus various relatives.

Extremely long-term memory: ability to remember over a period of years.

Extrinsic work satisfaction: derived from economic and material rewards given for work.

Factitious disorders: the production of physical or psychological symptoms voluntarily in order to play the patient role.

Fault divorce: divorce obtained in which legally recognized faults are claimed and proven in relation to one's spouse.

Female orgasm dysfunction: inability of the woman to reach a sexual climax.

Fluid intelligence: a person's ability to think and reason abstractly as measured by reasoning tests.

Formal operation stage: Piaget's final stage of cognitive development, during which the person learns to think abstractly, symbolically, and logically, and to use hypothetic-deductive reasoning.

Frustration tolerance: the ability to accept frustration without undue upset.

Functional age: age as measured by the ability to perform physical or mental functions.

Gastritis: inflammation of the stomach lining.

Gastrointestinal system: mouth, esophagus, stomach, small and large intestines, liver, pancreas, and gall bladder.

Generalized anxiety disorder: overanxiety with

symptoms of motor tension, or autonomic hyperactivity or hyperattentiveness.

Generational effect: changes in behavior as a result of different sociocultural influences on different generations.

Generativity: according to Erikson, this chief psychosocial task of middle adulthood means becoming productive in one's life and guiding the next generation.

Geriatrics: the branch of medicine dealing with the diseases, debilities, and care of aged persons.

Gerontology: the branch of science that studies aging.

Glabrous skin: smooth, bald skin, for example, of the palm or sole.

Glaucoma: a disease of the eye in which the fluid pressure within the eyeball increases causing progressive vision loss.

Global rigidity: inflexibility in all aspects of one's personality or life.

Gout: a disease characterized by an excess of uric acid in the blood.

Hallucinogens: psychedelic drugs such as LSD, peyote, mescaline, PCP, STP, DMT, and MDA.

HDL: high-density lipoprotein, a beneficial cholesterol that helps lower the level of low-density lipoprotein in the blood.

Hemoglobin: the red pigment of the blood.

Heredity theory: a biological theory of aging that says that the theoretical length of life is inherited.

Homeostasis: the tendency of the organism to sense biological imbalances and to stimulate actions to restore equilibrium.

Homeostatic imbalance theory: a biological theory of aging that emphasizes the gradual inability of the body to maintain vital physiological balances.

Human life cycle: consists of recurring periods of time; a series of repeated occurrences as one passes through the various phases or stages of life.

Hydrocephalus: a birth defect characterized by water on the brain.

Hypertension: elevated blood pressure.

Hypertensives: drugs used to control high blood pressure.

Hysterectomy: the surgical removal of the uterus.

Iconic memory: the visual sensory store.

Identification: the process by which one person adopts and internalizes the characteristics, attitudes, values, and traits of another or of a group.

Identity: who a person is; individual characteristics that make a person unique, the development of which is the chief psychosocial task of adolescence, according to Erikson.

Impotence: inability to produce an erection so that coital connection can take place.

Incontinence: inability to control excretory functions.

Industrial psychology: focuses on vocational choice, guidance, and growth, and on worker satisfaction, adjustments, and productivity.

Insulin: a hormone secreted in the pancreas that regulates the blood sugar level.

Interlocutory period: a period of time between the divorce decree of dissolution and the final granting of it.

Intimacy: a close, loving relationship with another person, the achievement of which is the chief psychosocial task of young adulthood, according to Erikson.

Intrinsic work satisfaction: derived from intangible, emotional, ego-building components of work.

IQ: a measure of intellectual ability: $\frac{\text{Mental age}}{\text{Chronological age}} \times 100 = \text{IQ}.$

IRA: individual retirement account.

Ischemic heart diseases: diseases that impede blood flow to the heart resulting in inadequate oxygen supply.

Jaundice: an abnormal increase in bile pigments in the blood that causes a yellowing of the skin and whites of the eyes.

Joint custody: both parents are given legal responsibility for the care of children and decisions related to them.

KEOGH plan: a retirement program for self-employed persons.

Late adulthood: defined here as the period from age sixty on.

LDL: low-density lipoprotein, a harmful cholesterol that contributes to the buildup of fatty deposits in the arteries.

Longevity: a long duration of life.

Longitudinal study: the same group of people studied repeatedly over a period of years.

Long-term memory: also called long-term storage or secondary memory (SM); the period of time during which information is perceived and processed deeply so it passes into the layers of memory below the conscious level.

Macular diseases: diseases of the macula, the part of the retina that possesses maximum visual acuity.

Male climacteric: syndrome experienced by about 5 percent of men over age sixty; marked by irritability, decreased sexual drive and potency, impaired ability to concentrate, weakness, fatigue, and poor appetite.

Mania: elevated, expansive, irritable mood.

Marijuana: an intoxicant derived from the dried leaves of the wild hemp plant.

Marital adjustment tasks: adjustments married couples have to make to live together harmoniously and achieve maximum satisfaction in the relationship.

Maturational effect: changes in behavior as a result of biological development.

Medullary cavity: tubular cavity inside the bone.

Menopause: the permanent cessation of menstruation at mid-life.

Metabolic waste or clinker theory: a biological theory of aging that says that aging is caused by the accumulation of deleterious substances within various body cells.

Microcephaly: a birth defect characterized by an abnormally small head.

Middle age: defined here as the forties and fifties.

Middlescence: according to LeShan, an identity crisis of middle age.

Mid-life crisis: the reevaluation of one's life during middle age.

Mongolism: Down's syndrome, an inherited chromosome disorder that causes mental retardation.

Mons pubis: pubic mound, or mound of Venus of the female, consisting of fatty tissue covered by skin and pubic hair.

Motor ability: the ability to move fingers, hands, arms, legs, and other parts of the body in a useful, coordinated way.

Motor cortex: the portion of the cortex that coordinates voluntary body movements.

Mutation theory: a biological theory of aging that emphasizes that as body cells develop harmful mutations, they become inefficient and senescent.

Myocardial infarction: a necrosis (dying) of a localized area (an infarct) of heart muscle caused by blood deprivation.

Myotonia: involuntary contraction of muscle during sexual excitement and orgasm.

Narcotics: drugs derived from opium, such as heroine and morphine, that blunt the senses.

Nervous system: consists of the central nervous system and peripheral nervous system.

Neurochemical transmitters: chemical substances produced by axons that transmit messages across the synapses.

Neuron: nerve cell.

No-fault divorce: divorce in which one party does not have to prove fault in the other in order to obtain the divorce.

Nuclear family: a social unit composed of father, mother, and their children.

Nutrient density: percentage of essential nutrients in food in relation to calories.

Obsessive compulsive disorder: irresistible desire to perform repetitive, often senseless acts.

Oophorectomy: surgical removal of the ovaries.

Orgasm: the sudden discharge of accumulated sexual tension.

Orgasmic phase: third phase of sexual response, during which a climax is reached and accumulated sexual tension is suddenly discharged.

Organic brain syndrome: mental disorder caused by impairment of brain tissue function.

Organic mental disorder: temporary or permanent brain dysfunction caused by specific organic factors or abuse of substances affecting the brain.

Osteoarthritis: a degenerative joint disease.

Osteoporosis: decalcification and loss of bone mass.

Ovulation: the maturation and discharge of a mature ovum from the female ovary.

Pacing: time intervals between stimuli.

Paired-associate learning: learning to make associations between pairs of items.

Panic disorder: an anxiety disorder in which one develops a feeling of panic.

Paranoid disorder: a psychosis characterized by delusions of persecution and delusional jealousy.

Paranoid type of schizophrenia: characterized by persecution delusions, grandiose delusions, delusional jealousy, or hallucinations with persecutory or grandiose content.

Passages: according to Sheehy, the routes or stages through which a person passes, including both stable periods and critical turning points in life.

Perception: the process of evaluating and giving meaning to information gathered by the senses.

Periodontal disease: a disease of the gums in which they become infected, swell, and shrink away from the teeth.

Peripheral nervous system: the nerves that branch off from the brain and spinal cord to all parts of the body.

Peripheral processing: transmission of information to the brain.

Peripheral vision: ability to see objects to either side of the line of sight in front of one's face.

Pernicious anemia: a severe anemia with a great reduction in red blood cells, an increase in their size, and the presence of large, primitive cells containing no hemoglobin.

Personality and life-style theory: a theory of aging that shows the relationship between personality type and patterns of aging.

Personality disorders: a wide range of disorders that cannot be labeled psychoses, such as schizoid, histrionic, narcissistic, antisocial, and dependent disorders.

Phobias: persistent, irrational fears that may restrict particular activities.

Physiological death: all the vital organs, such as the lungs and heart, cease to function.

Physiological psychology: concerned with biological growth, adaptation, and change, and with the physiological functioning of the human organism.

Pick's disease: severe atrophy and cell loss in the outer layer of the frontal and temporal regions of the cortex.

Plateau phase: second phase of sexual response (following excitement) during which sexual tensions level off.

Posttraumatic stress disorder: reliving, or reexperiencing, a traumatic event after it is over, which causes repeated stress.

Premature ejaculation: the inability to delay ejaculation long enough for the woman to have orgasm 50 percent of the time.

Presbycuses: hearing impairment associated with advancing age.

Presbyopia: farsightedness characterized by lack of clear focus at close distances.

Primary Mental Abilities Test (PMA): mental ability as measured by five subtests.

Problem-finding stage: a hypothetical fifth stage of cognitive ability in which the individual can discover and formulate problems not yet delineated.

Processing information: the series of actions involved in storing information in long-term memory.

Progesterone: female hormone secreted by the corpus luteum of the ovary, which prepares the uterus for a fertilized ovum and maintains pregnancy.

Prolongevity: deliberate efforts to extend the length of life.

Psychic death: acceptance of death and regression into self, often long before physiological death.

Psychological gerontology: studies the aging process and the behavior of older adults.

Psychomotor ability: skill in tasks requiring physical and mental coordination.

Psychosexual disorders: deviant sexual thought and behavior.

Psychosis associated with cerebral arteriosclerosis: chronic brain syndrome caused by hardening and narrowing of the blood vessels to the brain.

Psychosocial tasks: see *Developmental tasks.*

Psychosomatic illnesses: physical illnesses that have emotional causes or origins.

Psychotherapeutic drugs: drugs of four classes: stimulants, sedatives, tranquilizers, and analgesics (pain killers).

Psychotropics: mood-altering drugs.

Pulmonary embolism: blockage of blood vessels to the lungs by a blood clot.

Pulmonary infections: lung infections.

Pulmonary thrombosis: blockage of blood vessels to the lungs.

Pulse rate: the number of heart beats per minute.

Racism: prejudice and discrimination against racial minorities.

Random sample: subjects from a group to be studied are chosen at random.

Rationalize: to make excuses for one's behavior.

Reaction time: the interval between stimulation and response.

Reality shock: realization that idealized image does not match reality.

Recall: remembering information without verbal cues.

Recognition: remembering information for which verbal cues have been given.

Recording information: exposure to and storage of information.

Relaxation training: learning to relax in order to combat stress.

REM sleep: a period of sleep during which rapid eye movements and dreaming occur; important in getting adequate sleep.

Representative sample: a select population that includes the same percentages of people from different elements in that population as exist in the larger group.

Repress: to reject disagreeable ideas, memories, and feelings from the conscious mind.

Resolution phase: last stage of sexual response (following orgasm) during which sexual excitement subsides and the body returns to its unstimulated state.

Retina: the innermost layer of the posterior part of the eyeball, which receives the image produced through the lens; it contains light-sensitive rods and cones.

Reversible brain syndrome or acute brain syndrome: an organic brain syndrome that can be treated and cured.

Rheumatoid arthritis: a chronic disease marked by inflammation and swelling of the joints and often accompanied by deformities.

Rites of passage: initiation ceremonies through which children become adults.

Role strain: stress from too many demands to perform a variety of functions.

Sandwich generation: that generation between aging parents and young adult offspring.

Saturated fats: animal fats.

Schizophrenic disorder: a psychosis characterized by chronic and bizarre behavior, delusions, hallucinations, illusions, incoherence, and social isolation.

Search and retrieval: finding information that has been in memory stores and remembering it.

Self-actualization: the result of the inner drives of human beings to grow, improve, and use their potential to the fullest.

Self-concepts: our perceptions of who we are and what we are like.

Self-esteem: respect for or a favorable impression of oneself.

Senescence: biological aging.

Senile psychosis: a decline in mental functioning caused by the atrophy and degeneration of brain cells.

Senility: a disease of aging characterized by physiological deterioration of brain functioning.

Sensory cortex: that portion of the cortex that interprets changes in the environment received through the senses of vision, hearing, smell, taste, touch, and pain.

Sensory memory: also called sensory storage; period of time during which information is received and transduced by the senses, usually a fraction of a second.

Serial learning: learning items in a list in the exact order of presentation.

Sex flush: temporary, blotchy reddening of the skin during sexual excitement.

Sexism: prejudice and discrimination against women.

Sex ratio: the proportion of males to females, or females to males, in the population.

Sex roles: masculine-feminine, male-female roles as defined by one's culture.

Sexual dysfunction: a malfunctioning of the human sexual response system.

Short-term memory: also called short-term storage or primary memory (PM); period of time during which information is still in one's conscious mind being rehearsed and focused on.

Social age clock: the timetable by which the sequence of important events in life take place.

Socialization: learning and adopting the norms, values, expectations, and social roles of a particular group.

Socially accelerated dying: permitting any societal

condition or action that shortens life and hastens death.

Social phobia: an irrational fear of social situations.

Social psychology: focuses on interpersonal relationships, social interaction, and the social behavior of individuals in groups in relation to social stimuli.

Social reconstruction theory: a theory of aging describing how society brings about negative changes in the self-concept of the aged.

Sociological death: withdrawal and separation from other people as though dead, often long before physiological death.

Somatoform disorders: physical symptoms caused by psychological factors.

Spina bifida: a birth defect characterized by an incomplete closure of the lower spinal canal.

Stage theory: divides life into periods or phases and seeks to describe the qualitative differences of each phase and the changes required in passing from one phase to the other.

Stress: physical, mental, or emotional strain.

Stroke: paralysis that occurs when the blood supply to part of the brain is cut off and affected brain cells die.

Stroke volume: the volume of blood the heart pumps with each beat.

Sublimate: to divert energy from one goal to another.

Substance use disorder: impairment of social or occupational functions due to drug abuse.

Synapse: the space between the axon of one neuron and the dendrite of another.

Systolic blood pressure: pressure produced by the heart pumping blood out to the body.

Tactual memory: memory of touch.

Target pulse rate: the optimum rate one's pulse should achieve while exercising.

Terminal decline: marked decline in human functions before death, during a period ranging from a few weeks to a few years.

Terminal drop: decline in performance before death.

Testosterone: the most important hormone in sexual function, present in both sexes; often called the male sex hormone.

Test-retest interval: the time period between initial testing and repeated testing.

Thermoregulation: maintenance of correct body temperature during exposure to heat or cold.

Three-factor description of intelligence: verbal ability, problem-solving ability, and practical intelligence.

Thrombophlebitis: blood clot in a vein.

Thrombosis: blockage from any kind of undissolved material in the blood.

Time lag study: a lag in the time of measurement during which people of the same age but of different cohorts are examined.

Time-sequential study: a time lag analysis in which people of the same age and different cohorts are examined at different times and compared during these times with people of another age and different cohorts.

Tuberculosis: an infectious disease of the lungs.

Undifferentiated schizophrenia: characterized by prominent delusions, hallucinations, and incoherence; the illness does not meet the criteria for other types of schizophrenia.

Urinary system: includes the kidneys, the bladder, the ureters, and the urethra.

Vaginismus: powerful and painful involuntary contraction of the muscles surrounding the vaginal tract.

Vasocongestion: an increased amount of blood in the genitals and female breasts during sexual excitement.

Veins: the blood vessels that carry the blood to the heart.

Vested: to be given a permanent right under a pension plan, regardless of whether one changes companies.

Visual acuity: the ability to see small details.

Vital capacity: volume of air inhaled by the lungs with each breath.

Vitreous humor: fluid in the inner portion of the eye.

WASP: white, Anglo-Saxon, Protestant.

Wear and tear theory: a biological theory of aging that says that the organism wears out.

Wechsler Adult Intelligence Scale (WAIS): six subtests comprise verbal scores, five subtests comprise performance scores.

Workaholic: a person driven to overwork.

Author Index

Lawson, I. R., 376
Lawson, J. S., 198, 377
Lawton, M. P., 377
Lawrence, B. S., 47, 377
Lazerine, N., 380
Lear, M. W., 273, 377
Lehman, H. C., 256, 257, 377
Leon, A. S., 91, 377
LeRoux, R. S., 175, 377
LeShan, E., 46, 47, 50, 377
Levendusky, P. G., 344, 377
Levine, P. M., 195, 378
Levinson, D. J., 4, 5, 11, 14, 15,
    18, 19, 20, 21, 30, 39, 43,
    52, 300, 317, 377, 378
Levinson, M. H., 11, 15, 19, 43,
    52, 317, 377, 378
Leviton, D., 296
Levitt, H., 368
Lewinsohn, P. M., 195, 378
Lewis, R. A., 39, 284, 293, 378
Lichter, D. T., 57, 378
Lichtiger, S., 376
Lindeman, R. D., 95, 378
Lindholm, J. M., 381
Litzelman, D., 378
Lobsenz, N. M., 143, 145, 378
Locke-Connor, C., 344, 378
Lockhart, R. S., 232, 371
Logie, H. R., 85, 387
Longino, C. F., 58, 378
Lonner, T., 385
Lopata, H. Z., 296, 378
Loranger, A. W., 195, 378
Loria, A., 144, 378
Love, D. W., 382
Lowe, J., 348, 378
Lowestein, F. W., 367
Luikart, C., 45, 381
Lundin, D. V., 154, 378
Lurie, E., 388
Lynd, H., 65, 378
Lynd, R., 65, 378

Maas, H., 74, 75, 378
McAndrews, M. P., 375
McCroskey, R. L., 237, 255, 384
McCullough, M. R., 382
McDivitt, M., 385
McGillicuddy-Delisi, A. V., 368
McKee, B., 377, 378
McMichael, A. J., 375
McPherson, J. R., 95, 378
Maddox, G. L., 72, 378
Manning, L., 373

Marcia, J. E., 317, 320, 378
Margunes, M. K., 368
Markle, G. E., 306, 370
Marshall, D. G., 293, 369
Marshall, J. R., 202, 378
Marshall, S., 378
Martin, C. E., 377
Martin, J. D., 75, 378
Maslow, A. H., 8, 378
Massarik, F., 8, 369
Masters, W. H., 125, 127, 131,
    135, 144, 145, 309, 378
Matsuzawa, T., 388
Maultsby, M. C., 132, 378
Maynard, F., 288, 290, 291, 378
Maxwell, R. J., 175, 387
Mecke, G., 248, 378
Mecke, V., 248, 378
Mednick, S. A., 196, 378
Meichenbaum, D., 189, 378
Melko, M., 184, 266, 269, 271,
    272, 273, 309, 370
Meyers, H., 381
Michalewski, H. J., 217, 378
Middleton, R. G., 131, 135, 375
Miller, B. C., 290, 379
Miller, H., 351, 379
Miller, J. D., 149, 150, 155, 159,
    160, 379
Miller, M., 200, 201, 202, 379
Miller, P. Y., 323, 379
Millham, J., 61, 387
Milligan, W. L., 382
Misler-Lachman, J. L., 236, 379
Mistretta, C. M., 101, 374, 379,
    386
Mittman, C., 93, 380
Mock, M. B., 91, 379
Modell, J., 34, 38, 379
Moenster, P. A., 236, 379
Mogey, J. M., 349, 372, 383
Monahan, T. P., 302, 379
Monge, R. H., 254, 379
Monk, A., 346, 379
Moon, W. H., 344, 377
Moore, L. M., 101, 379
Morehouse, L. E., 110, 111, 379
Morgan, J. N., 348, 350, 368
Morgan, R. E., 105, 379
Morimatsu, M., 89, 378
Moritani, T., 121, 122
Morris, G., 195, 388
Morris, N. M., 129, 386
Morrison, M. H., 352, 379
Morselli, P. L., 153, 379

Mortimer, J. T., 321, 379
Moss, M., 377
Moyer, J. H., 93, 380
Muchinsky, P. M., 345, 379
Mueller, J. H., 235, 379
Muiesan, B., 93, 379
Muller, H. F., 200, 379
Muramatsu, A., 379
Murdock, B. B., Jr., 231, 379
Murphy, D. P., 137, 379
Murphy, M. D., 383
Murrell, F. H., 380
Muson, H., 16, 380
Myers, G. C., 166, 380
Myska, M. J., 169, 170, 380

Nagi, M., 176, 380
Nakazato, K., 37, 384
Nam, C. B., 165, 380
Nebes, R. D., 236, 380
Nelson, F. L., 380
Nelson, H., 152, 380
Neubeck, G., 280, 380
Neugarten, B. L., 73, 74, 380
Newman, B. M., 38, 380
Newman, P. R., 38, 380
Nichols, C. R., 386
Nielsen, C. R., 379
Niinimaa, V., 93, 380
Nock, S. L., 284, 380
Norborn, M. A., 339, 380
Norman, D. A., 233, 387
Norris, A. H., 85, 93, 369, 380
Norton, A. J., 284, 301, 311, 374,
    380
Nowlin, J. B., 381
Nowling, J., 372
Nowak, C., 108, 380
Nuttal, R. L., 105, 373, 380
Nye, F. I., 306, 380

O'Brien, P., 274, 380
Obrist, W., 217, 368, 380, 387
O'Connell, A. N., 61, 380
O'Connor, J. F., 136, 380
O'Donnell, F., 385
Okay, K. A., 165, 380
Olsen, E. J., 385
O'Nan, B. A., 368
Orlofsky, J. L., 317, 373
Overcast, T., 370
Overton, W., 371
Ovesey, L., 381
Owens, W. A., Jr., 209, 381

Subject Index

socioenvironmental effects on, 222
specific factors in, 207
three-factor description of, 208
and terminal decline, 226
tests and testing, 208
two-factor theories of, 207
Intimacy, 9, 18, 38
and love, 280, 281
and marriage, 287
need for, 280
Late adulthood:
attitude toward aging and the aged, 57
demographics, 53
developmental tasks of, 77
growing old in America, 64
as happiest years, 31
housing and living conditions, 294
and marriage, 293, 294
the older worker, 343
and relationships with grown children, 293, 294
social-psychological theories of aging, 71
Legal dimensions of adulthood, 33

Marriage:
adjustment tasks of, 11, 38, 286, 287
adults view of, 281, 282
age at, 18
and careers, 282, 288
and companionship, 273, 287
communication in, 289
conflict, 287
and decision making, 289
delay of, 263
and divorce, 39, 299–310
early years of, 284–290
and extrafamily relationships, 287
and the family life-cycle, 283
ideology, 287, 288
later years of, 293
and leisure time, 271, 272
and mate selection, 11, 38
motives for, 268, 279–281
never married, 263–277
the postparental years, 284, 292
pushes and pulls to marry, 267, 268
rates, 283

reflection, 40, 41
remarriage, 39, 310–312
revitalizing, 50
roles, 288
satisfaction, 12, 39, 284–286
and sex, 130, 135
sharing and cooperation in, 289, 290
and social life, 287, 289
trends, 263–266, 283, 363
and widowhood, 295
Memory:
and acquisition, recording, encoding, and processing, 236
echoic, 232, 233
extremely long-term, 235
iconic, 232, 233
and learning, 238
long-term or secondary, 234
recall, 237
recognition, 237
and search and retrieval, 236
sensory, 232
short-term or primary, 233
three-stage model of, 231
training, 237
what it involves, 231
Menopause, 138–141
age at, 139, 140
artificial or operative, 139
definition of, 138
hormonal replacement therapy, 141
physical changes in, 138, 139
signs and symptoms of, 140, 141
Mental health:
and cognitive abilities, 221
mental illness, 191
positive, 183
and relaxation training, 189
and stress, 184
and suicide, 200
and thought patterns, 184
Mental illness:
Alzheimer's disease, 199
anxiety disorders, 197
bipolar disorders, 195
classification of, DSM–III, 192
depression, 193
incidence of, 190, 191
organic brain syndromes, 198
Pick's disease, 199
psychosomatic, 183
schizophrenia, 196
Metabolism, 94, 113, 167

Middle adulthood:
body image during, 106
and career achievement, 324
crisis during, 18, 20
demographics, 43
developmental phases during, 8–10, 12–19
developmental tasks of, 47
as happiest years, 31
and income, 324
male climacteric, 141
and memory, 232
menopause, 138–141
paradox of middle age, 44
who is middle aged?, 43
Mid-life crisis, 18, 20, 46
Minority aged, 69
Money:
and affluence of never-married adults, 274
conscious, 325
and divorce, 304, 309
financial planning and management, 77, 78, 352–354
and job satisfaction, 323
income during middle years, 334, 335
and life satisfaction, 318
and life styles, 327
and marriage, 274, 279, 287
and retirement, 346–354
and unemployment, 335, 345
and widowhood, 296
Muscles, 106

Nervous system:
auditory nerve, 101
brain, 88
central, 88
cerebrum, 88
conduction, velocities, 89
cortex, 89
neurochemical transmitters, 89
neurons, 88
peripheral, 88
spinal cord, 88
synapses, 89
Nutrition:
and calories, 113
and cholesterol, 109, 116–118
deficiencies, 114–116
diet and weight, 112, 113
and fats, 116–119
glycogen, 94
and heart attacks, 91, 117